Situated Fathering

Situated Fathering

A Focus on Physical and Social Spaces

Edited by
William Marsiglio, Kevin Roy,
and Greer Litton Fox

ROWMAN & LITTLEFIELD PUBLISHERS, INC.
Lanham • *Boulder* • *New York* • *Toronto* • *Oxford*

ROWMAN & LITTLEFIELD PUBLISHERS, INC.

Published in the United States of America
by Rowman & Littlefield Publishers, Inc.
A wholly owned subsidiary of The Rowman & Littlefield Publishing Group, Inc.
4501 Forbes Boulevard, Suite 200, Lanham, Maryland 20706
www.rowmanlittlefield.com

PO Box 317
Oxford
OX2 9RU, UK

British Library Cataloguing in Publication Information Available

Library of Congress Cataloging-in-Publication Data

Situated fathering : a focus on physical and social spaces / edited by William
Marsiglio, Kevin Roy, and Greer Litton Fox.
    p. cm.
  Includes bibliographical references and index.
  ISBN 0-7425-4568-7 (cloth : alk. paper)—ISBN 0-7425-4569-5 (pbk. : alk. paper)
1. Fatherhood. 2. Fatherhood—Psychological aspects. 3. Spatial behavior. I.
Marsiglio, William. II. Roy, Kevin, 1966– III. Fox, Greer Litton. HQ756.S5453 2005
  306.874'2—dc22
                                          2005001529

Printed in the United States of America

♾™ The paper used in this publication meets the minimum requirements of American
National Standard for Information Sciences—Permanence of Paper for Printed Library
Materials, ANSI/NISO Z39.48-1992.

Contents

Part III: Fathering in Community Space

Foreword

Thirty years ago, the study of father–child relationships enjoyed a renaissance with the publication of the first edition of Michael E. Lamb's *The Role of the Father in Child Development*. Lamb's edited volume (and subsequent editions) highlighted the significant and multiple ways fathers from diverse backgrounds are involved with their young and adolescent children while clarifying how fathers contribute to children's emotional, psychological, and cognitive development.

Similarly, Marsiglio, Roy, and Fox's *Situated Fathering* represents a landmark advancement in understanding fatherhood, for it situates fathering in everyday settings. It considers a diversity of fathering contexts and involvement patterns in a way that enriches our empirical and theoretical foundations. By focusing on the fathering relationships of diverse groups of men— long distance truckers, inmates, and dads in their backyards tossing baseballs— the everyday contexts and events of fathering are brought to a new level of analysis, understanding, and scholarship.

To "study" a father without having the ability to view and appreciate the other multiple facets of his life and experience is to strip fathering of all of the meaning, history, constraints, hopes, dreams, prescriptions, proscriptions, and prohibitions that define it. To look at men within the diverse and multiple contexts of fathering is to situate them where they live and breathe. Understanding fathering as an outgrowth of the various contexts and constraints is a different and richer enterprise than describing it void of contextualization. This is the premise of *Situated Fathering*.

Fathers are firmly situated in relationships and those relationships unfold within spatial environments defined by practical contingencies and colored by social/symbolic meanings. Although technically men are fathers only in relationship to a child, fathers frequently do fathering while relating to mothers and others as well. The father–child relationship (and fathers' interactions with others who have vested interests in the child) changes and is shaped over time by the contexts, settings, meanings, and events within which it is located, by which it is shaped, and which, in turn, it shapes. Clearly, fathering is situated in contexts of time, culture, space, work, and ongoing events. Fathers are situated in neighborhoods, careers, subcultures, policies, legal systems, and ethics. They are situated in cultural prescriptions of masculinity, provision, protection, nurturance, the best interest of the child, and paternity. And they deal with policies, practices, and issues such as garnishment of wages, welfare, incarceration, substance use, anger management, and countless other contexts.

Because individual men engaged in fathering have unique characteristics, as do their children, relationships represent a diversity of types, styles, and textures that defy description and cataloguing. By presenting theoretical literature along with empirical evidence and rich accounts of the lived experiences of fathers and children in diverse situations, the contributors to this volume have expanded our lenses. Not just our interpretive lenses, but practical lenses for designing interventions for real dads in real situations, men in need of situationally sensitive support.

Situated Fathering represents a new and needed advancement in fathering scholarship because it makes bold inroads toward conceptualizing the often-overlooked physical, social, and symbolic attributes of fathering contexts. In the pages that follow, a diverse array of chapters integrate theory and data from multiple disciplinary approaches and across a wide expanse of fathering contexts to sharpen our understanding of and appreciation for fathering. The collection expands the literature on fathering by setting forth different ways father involvement and fathers' experiences are nuanced by the specifics of their situations. It brings vivid understanding to the effects of nonresidential living, incarceration, and work that takes fathers from their homes for extended periods of time. It also elucidates the common elements of fathering across these varied contexts and challenges. This is the stuff in which fathering is immersed, by which it is circumscribed, molded, honed, constrained, shaped, restricted; and in which it must be supported. In reading the various accounts of men's lived experiences, numerous factors associated with physical and social spaces come to life, enabling us to see how men's fathering is affected in subtle ways. These factors affect fathers' decisions about how they spend their time, negotiate familial boundaries, respond to challenges to their "rights" and responsibilities, and guide their relationship building. In short, research presented here identifies fertile new ground for the growth of scholarship on fathering.

The study of fathering as a field is now coming of age. This volume's innovative and nuanced understandings of the interplay between fathering and specific situations is exactly the forward thinking that will give meaning to the growing volume of data on fathers. It is time that we situate data concerning father involvement and fathering styles directly in the context of men's lives. It is time that we situate fathering as part of something greater than a narrow range of behaviors conducted by a person during his child's infancy or early childhood. It is time that we give serious consideration to the meanings and the motives, as well as the motions, of fathering. It is time to begin to consider the variations in patterns of fathering that are associated with varying contexts, and it is time to begin situating the theory and empirical findings regarding fathering in the physical and social spaces in which they occur.

Rob Palkovitz

Preface

In November 2002, I asked Kevin Roy to help organize a research symposium on fatherhood, Situated Fatherhood: Negotiating Involvement in Physical and Social Contexts, for the 2003 National Council on Family Relations meeting in Vancouver. The impetus for the symposium theme emerged from the muddled thoughts I was processing at the time about the challenges stepfathers and nonresident fathers sometimes face when navigating the daily routines of their nontraditional families. My interviews with these men revealed their diverse reactions to spatial concerns. Some felt uncomfortable, whereas others felt surprisingly at ease, in my view, about how physical space issues were related to their experiences either in stepfamilies or as nonresident fathers. I was most interested in the men who were affected; they talked about matters such as property ownership, house size, movement in and out of residences, and perceptions of public and private space. The interviews led me to ponder more rigorously how the tangible and symbolic aspects of physical and social contexts could affect the myriad and diverse situations in which men do fathering.

Aware of Roy's research on poor inner-city fathers and fathers participating in a prison work-release program, I assumed his work could highlight quite effectively the relationship between spatial issues and fathering. After accepting my invitation, Kevin and I invited my longtime friend and colleague Greer Litton Fox to join us on the symposium panel, in part because she and her students had researched fathers who were either long-haul truck drivers or participants in support groups for male batterers. This research offered unique opportunities to consider how particular contexts influence the way men "do fathering" and construct their father identities. The three of us were delighted that Kerry Daly agreed to serve as the discussant for our session. His theorizing on family time pushed us to refine our thinking, incorporate elements of time into our model more explicitly, and consider more closely the relations between time and physical space.

We were eager to theorize fathering in a way that emphasized how it occurs and is represented in varied sites that had a physical, spatial dimension. In our view, the most practical way to showcase our perspective was to recruit a cadre of scholars who could apply a spatially sensitive lens to their respective substantive area. Thus, during the months leading up to and immediately following the symposium, we began to recruit a multidisciplinary group of researchers who could examine one of the various fathering sites we deemed significant. Our goal was to develop a thematically focused volume covering a wide range of topics. Although we were unable to secure chapters on all sites of interest to us (e.g., hospitals, family therapy sessions, resort communities, nonfarming businesses fostering father–child apprenticeships), we were able to address the sites we viewed most crucial.

Eventually we circulated to the contributing authors the initial draft of a document outlining our thoughts about fathers and physical and social spaces that we have since developed into chapter 1 — our theoretical framework for situated fathering. By exposing authors early on to our vision of situated fathering, we sought to reinforce the unifying theme connecting the diverse chapters. Notably, the uniqueness of our approach became more apparent to us during this process. We struggled sometimes to convey our perspective clearly to the prospective authors who had rarely considered a spatially sensitive view of fathering. Throughout, we encouraged them to be mindful of this perspective so they could expand how they both framed their analysis and proposed directions for future research.

The book, in its final version, reveals that authors vary in how explicitly they address either the central theme of our framework or the specific properties we delineate. However, they all consider to some degree how fathering is affected by circumstances and perceptions of physical and social spaces. We are grateful to our colleagues for conscientiously responding to our detailed, sometimes multiple requests for chapter revisions that were often designed to ensure chapters were in line with the thematically driven volume.

Because we envisaged this volume as being a valuable resource for graduate students, we asked all contributors to conclude their respective chapters with a series of future research questions. These questions provide students and other scholars with fascinating avenues for research on fathering, while foregrounding the importance of physical settings and the symbolic/social aspects associated with them.

Like a richly detailed grounded theory, the framework has continued to emerge, evolving as we journeyed through the project's writing and editing phases. In the years ahead, we anticipate continuing to search for insights to sharpen our theoretical model through our own work and in dialogue with others. We welcome the opportunity to learn how others evaluate, apply, refine, and expand the version of our model we present here.

As this project unfolded we individually and collectively became more comfortable applying our framework to our own experiences with either fathering or the process of being fathered. Thus one qualitative avenue for considering our model's utility is to turn inward. To complement our abstract theorizing, we reflected on the meaning physical space and its attendant symbolism had for the fathering we personally either received or expressed. We share illustrations of this self-reflective exercise here as a means of sensitizing readers to the types of core issues that give this volume its unique character.

Recalling my youth, I have vivid memories of playing with my dad along the narrow strip of yard next to our modest red brick home situated in a working-class neighborhood. In the spring and summer, I practiced my baseball pitching and fielding; in the fall and winter, I perfected my football quarterback/receiver skills. The positioning of the pine trees was such that the open area was just long enough for me to practice pitching and fielding ground balls. And even though the yard was cramped to run pass routes, my dad and I improvised to execute our plays. My childhood experiences are consistent with Ralph LaRossa's observations in chapter 7. Easy access to a yard can foster memorable games of catch between father (and mother) and child. The modest yard, that to this day still elicits nostalgic memories, provided my dad and me numerous chances for bonding through sport, often nonverbally and at a physical distance. The nonverbal play in the yard was consistent with my dad's reserved, quiet style. Moreover, the yard's convenience meant that my dad, who worked long and labor-intensive hours at a local factory, had a difficult time saying no to my simple requests for a game of catch.

Although my yard's proximity prompted a form of one-on-one father involvement, characteristics of my father's factory work site precluded opportunities to mix work and family. When my father went to work, he was essentially beyond my reach. I knew my mother could phone him in an emergency, but I recall this happening only once. Dad was not just out of my reach while working; my visions of my father at work were murky because the physical and cultural aspects of his workplace environment were a mystery to me. Unlike the kids who were free to visit their father's workplace, my first and only visit to the factory came when I was eighteen years old during a public relations day.

Because my father had always worked at the factory, I had grown so accustomed to the arrangement that I was largely oblivious to it. My childhood stands in stark contrast to the overlap between family and work life experienced by the Iowa farm fathers and their children described by Greg Peter and his colleagues in chapter 11. I became more aware of how my father's job and work place policies curtailed my relationship with my dad when I forged a teenage friendship with Greg. I recognized the "oddity" of how much time he spent with his dad working side by side remodeling homes. Even though I did not at the time possess the conceptual tools to make sense of the entire set of circumstances, I recognized that Greg had a different sort of familial arrangement with his dad than I did with mine. While working, they shared physical space and father–son time; for them, family and work were interwoven.

Later in life, spatial issues first became a prominent feature of my experiences as a new nonresident father when my son turned four. From then on, he lived in another state far away. In addition to the challenges posed by the geographic distance separating us, I was not in a position to duplicate the kind of personalized physical space he had at his mother's house. We improvised and made do, but the physical limitations of my different apartments and homes over the years, as well as the minimal presence of symbolic representations of us sharing a home, meant that we both largely viewed his time with me as "visiting" time rather than "home" time. Some of the struggles I faced were similar to those Beth Catlett and her colleagues describe for the nonresident fathers in chapter 5. Though I resigned myself to manage the discomfort, I was frustrated trying to sustain a fatherly presence in my son's life from a distance, and in a physical setting that did not carry the force of year-round, daily routines laced with family memories attached to physical space.

William Marsiglio

In contrast, daily family routines have been a vital part of my fathering. I first became a father while working at a fatherhood program similar to the one described by Anderson and Letiecq in chapter 9. As I rode the El train back to an apartment with my weeks-old son, I remember weighing the advice and stories offered to me by low-income fathers in the hallways of a community college on Chicago's south side. I noted the relative ease of my travels across the city's spatial and racial boundaries in comparison to the difficulty those fathers had in gaining access to, and even spending a few hours with, their children. They were monitored and supervised by courts and welfare systems that forced them to "answer to someone" for their parenting on a regular basis.

I have been more fortunate because I have been perceived as a "new father" who is seldom expected to publicly account for his parenting behavior. My two preschool sons' sense of their father's profession is related somehow to the time they spend in my office, playing on the computer or getting into the mix of highlighters, cassette tapes, and paper clips at my desk. They also enjoy entering the classroom to say hello to students or even attend class lectures (usually full of interruptions to get my attention about the pictures they are drawing). Although we enjoy raking leaves and playing in the piles—and running around with the soccer ball on the side of the house—we spend most of our time in the basement, drawing superheroes or wrestling with dress-up clothes splayed around us. To me, though, the most important space for my fathering is the family bed where I read countless library books or spin stories right before they fall asleep each night. "Doing" fathering in these physical and social spaces has shaped my views about what is underdeveloped in research on men in families. My own fathering experiences are only a few among many parenting experiences with men of different race/ethnicity, social status, income, and age. Across many "family spaces," there are unspoken legacies of privilege and discrimination, of high expectations and bitter disappointments.

I return to my relationship with my own father to attend to spaces where stories are, and where they should be, but are not. My father is a funeral director, and his participation in the "business" of death is physical and immediate to me. From my earliest memories, I recall spending countless hours with him in the mortuary. When I was young I watched through the door of the embalming room, and when I was older I debated politics with him as he prepared bodies. I remember how he would get up and leave the house at all hours of the night to respond to coroner calls from hospitals across Los Angeles. He directed funerals while I served as an altar boy, managing the incense for priests. During my first summer home from college, I hauled flowers to cemeteries, I hand-pressed mass cards on the block-type printer, and I listened in as he supported grieving family members through the funeral rituals.

At home, however, my father often detached himself from family life. The one place where we found each other, and where I learned the most from him, was during many silent hours under the palm trees in our backyard. Although I was not too interested as an adolescent, I look back fondly on setting bricks to build a patio, breaking glass and crushing aluminum cans for recycling, and tending the large garden: blackberry bushes, zucchini, and trees loaded with plums, lemons, and avocados. My parents separated a few years before I left home for college, and since that time I have had difficulty "situating" my father even in my memories of physical places. He has remarried, becoming a fatherly figure for another set of children. As many authors in this volume suggest, our new dance of involvement, with me as the child of a nonresident father, is shaped by subtle understanding of who visits and who hosts, who attends holiday celebrations, or who picks up the phone when we talk across thousands of miles.

Kevin Roy

When I joined this project, Bill and Kevin were already well into the conceptualization of space as a factor in men's fathering. Thinking about fathering in a new (or, for those of us old enough to recall Lewinian field theory, a renewed) light has been rewarding. One of the delights of academic life is engaging in "mindfulness" with good colleagues—the experience of thinking aloud, reasoning with friends, taking delight in the exercise of intellect. Putting together this book has been such an experience. Late in the project Bill invited Kevin and me to contribute to the preface by remembering our own experiences as fathers, or in my case, with fathers.

Thinking about my father is bittersweet because of his sudden departure from life, taking with it my shattered expectations for the role he would play in my daughters' lives as a wise, playful, and cherished grandfather—a role he never got to play. So my spatially sensitized thoughts of his fathering are framed by the memory distance of the twenty years since I last spoke with him. When challenged to think of the spatial components of my father's fathering, I immediately thought of his chair in the living room. To set the context, it is important to realize that the square footage of middle-class homes when I was young was much less generous than today's mega-homes. There were no libraries, sunrooms, studies, or workshops; my brothers shared a bedroom, as did my sister and I. Privacy may be a central family value in the United States, but privacy certainly was not a characteristic of internal family space during the middle decades of the twentieth century. In our house, the bathroom door was the only door with a lock; the bathroom the only place one could find privacy. Our living room was truly public space, that is, a public-to-the-family space. When my father was not physically present, his chair was; and his large chair, positioned next to my mother's more diminutive one, easily became a powerful symbol of his dominance of our family space. It was around that chair that my brothers, sister, and I used to play on rainy mornings. It was in that chair that my father tried to help me with my high school physics and calculus. A brilliant man, my father couldn't grasp why I failed to understand what was so clear to him, so he merely repeated more loudly his explanations until my tears and his frustration with my incomprehension would end our homework sessions, no doubt each of us silently despairing at my dull wittedness. It was in that chair that I sat one evening after a date when I was home from college, long after my parents had quit waiting up for us, to sit and feel the presence of my parents—in truth, the presence of their values—as I thought about the events of the evening. So where *was* my father during my childhood? He was so often in that chair—every evening after work, on Saturday afternoons during baseball season, and on Sundays after church reading the newspapers—that the chair on its own became a proxy father.

Like Bill, I was prohibited from my father's workplace—an oil refinery—because of its inherent danger. I never was in his workplace until I was in graduate school and my dad was engineering vice president of a small oil company. When I visited his workplace, I learned that his office was not in the refinery itself—it was a small office in a rather drab concrete-block building—and it was not during the workday but after hours that he took me there. Although I never saw my dad at work, somehow I knew that work was the most important thing in his life—except for us, his family, the time he was at home, in his chair. Whether he was seated there, or whether it is only in my mind's eye, I can't say for sure now. One thing I do know is that the fathering patterns of my husband Bruce, a self-employed businessman who works out of our home, are starkly different from the patterns of father presence that I knew. My daughters have experienced the actual physical presence of their father in our home during the entirety of their lives. Their experience of fathering is thus quite distinct from the fathering experiences I recall. Whether and how it matters remains to be explored, but I will say this: a few years ago Bruce was called during a workday morning to come to the high school parking lot to rescue a kitten inadvertently left in the car of one of our daughter's school friends. I can't imagine approaching my father with such a request: the audacity—and his inaccessibility—would make such a request unimaginable.

Greer Litton Fox

With our anecdotal stories as a backdrop, we have set the stage for a more scholarly exploration of situated fathering. The personal stories, combined with the research reported in this volume, should convince others that it is worthwhile to consider how fathering is influenced by the distinctive physical and social/symbolic elements of diverse settings. In our introductory theoretical chapter, we bring the key elements more squarely to the foreground, then rely on empirically based studies to show how our perspective sheds new light on the ways men act fatherly and construct their identities as fathers. A few of these studies accentuate conceptual issues, so we group them with our initial chapter under the section labeled "Theoretical Approaches to Fathering and Space." We loosely group the next seven chapters under the heading "fathering and institutional space" because they examine fathering in relation to social institutions: family, prison, work, and the military. Although the final four chapters are also closely associated with institutions (e.g., family, work, and religion), they emphasize how fathering is situated within a larger community domain in which spatial dimensions, local resources and conditions, and a cultural ethos influence how fathering is perceived and practiced. The chapters in this volume showcase new ways of conceptualizing how men negotiate and do fathering and identity work in intimate spaces, public places, and in locations physically removed from their children.

We dedicate this volume to the unsung professionals who strive to enhance fathers' positive contributions to their children's lives, while implicitly or explicitly recognizing how fathering is affected by aspects of physical and social spaces. A sampling of these individuals include those who: advocate for on-site day care and paternal leave policies in workplaces, diversify options for deployed military fathers to remain in touch with their children, organize community-based resources that strengthen men's commitments to good fathering, develop programs to offer men in correctional facilities a "second chance" to redeem their lives through meaningful relationships with their children, and create on-site programs and incentives for fathers to become more involved in their children's educational experience at school.

I

THEORETICAL APPROACHES
TO FATHERING AND SPACE

1

Situated Fathering: A Spatially Sensitive and Social Approach

William Marsiglio, Kevin Roy, and Greer Litton Fox

$\mathbf{F}$amily life, inherently social, is played out within a spatial context. Most family activities involving shared time, for example, confrontations about family rules and responsibilities, decision making, rituals, playful episodes, familial identity constructions, and so on, are framed by realities linked to physical sites and social settings. Though some activities may be more sensitive than others to the physical and spatial elements of a particular site, individuals "do family" in specific places and structured settings.

Scholars who study family interaction have seldom given serious thought to how physical and spatial issues, as well as the social/symbolic processes associated with them, matter (Daly 2003). The invisibility of the physical/spatial dimension in family scholarship is consistent with sociologists' and psychologists' failure to make problematic the effects of physical/spatial factors on social organization and interaction (Gieryn 2000). Although ethnographers of urban life (Anderson 1990; Stack 1974) and selected others (e.g., Goffman 1959; Urry 1985) have seriously considered physical context and spatial issues, sociologists and psychologists have been far less interested in understanding the spatial aspects of social life than have students of anthropology, geography, urban planning, and architecture (Hillier and Hanson 1984; Pellow 1996; Spain 1992).

We address this shortcoming in family scholarship by identifying elements of a general framework that conceptualizes fathering in its varied, situated forms. The framework underscores the value of accounting for how features of physical sites and social settings, along with the related subjective processes of social life, are interwoven and affect fathering and fatherhood. Thus our conceptual analysis takes seriously Spain's (1992, 5) observation that "spatial and social aspects of a phenomenon are inseparable." Although we focus our spatially sensitive perspective on fathering, our comments in many respects may be relevant to mothering as well.

As fathers, men construct their identities and are involved with their children in diverse settings that have distinct, and often interrelated, physical, social, and symbolic dimensions. Much has been written in recent years about the varied ways fathers are involved with their children and the consequences of that involvement (Marsiglio, Amato, Day, and Lamb 2000). Increasingly, scholars are also drawing attention to the diverse social demography of fatherhood (Marsiglio, Day, and Lamb 2000; Tamis-LeMonda and Cabrera 2002). However, we know little about the physical and organizational contexts of fathering (Marsiglio and Cohan 2000). Further examination of the practical realities, social dimensions, and symbolic meanings associated with diverse physical sites (e.g., households: own and others, homeless shelters, workplaces, schools, communities, prisons, athletic/recreational venues, churches) illuminate how men perceive, negotiate, and spontaneously engage in or refrain from fathering in these settings. Such an analysis also reveals how the fathering ideologies generated in specific contexts influence men's approach to fathering.

A focus on the interplay of the attributes of physical space and social/symbolic processes fosters a novel and nuanced understanding of the fluid, negotiated nature of men's experiences as fathers. Because definitions of physical space are often directly or indirectly linked to notions of power, the negotiation of situated fathering as related to social stratification by gender, class, and race/ethnicity is also relevant.

Our main objective in this introductory essay is to articulate the rudimentary elements of a conceptual framework identifying the multidimensional, interrelated aspects of fathering sites—the diverse places where men "do fathering" and/or learn about fathering. A deep theoretical treatment of fathers' situated experiences accentuates the varied properties associated with fathering sites, some of which individual fathers and others may take for granted and not fully recognize. We discuss how five primary and interrelated properties associated with fathering sites (*physical conditions*, *temporal dynamics*, *symbolic/perceptual*, *social structural*, and *public/private*), and an assortment of related but more secondary properties (*institutional and cultural conditions*, *transitional elements*, *personal power and control*, *gender attributes*, and *fatherhood discourses*), provide a basis for constructing a spatially sensitive perspective on fathering in diverse settings.

Our analysis highlights that social relationships, such as parent–child relations, are contained and shaped by spatial environments, although men can also act on physical space in ways that influence their fathering experiences. Although much of what fathers do in physical sites involves perfunctory, routine choices, fathers can act deliberatively to orchestrate their involvement and identity work as fathers. In some instances, fathers may take or invite children into certain places (hunting/fishing in the wilderness); at other times fathers can reconfigure a physical space itself to accommodate their desire to interact with their children in particular ways (e.g., paving a driveway and placing a basketball goal on it). Social and spatial contexts, in these ways, are confounded and difficult to discern from each other.

THE PROBLEMATIC

The theoretical problematic—the problem or focus our framework is designed to inform—is twofold. Although the number of possible foci for an analysis of fathering is very large, the first focus we take as problematic is men's behavior as fathers, often during interactions with their children, sometimes in interactions with others, and occasionally alone. The second focus is the meaning of fatherhood—and the values; norms; and social, emotional, and cultural materials out of which men construct a fathering identity for themselves. Thus men's identity work as fathers is the second problematic for the framework we propose.

Our conceptual analysis is largely deductive, though we draw selectively on our own empirical work and the studies we incorporate in this edited volume. Researchers can employ the concepts we discuss in a manner similar to how sensitizing concepts are typically used in qualitative research (van den Hoonard 1997). These concepts can frame aspects of a study dealing with fathering in a particular setting, providing an entry point into data and a lens for interpreting findings.

The conceptual map of situated fathering assumes broad definitions of fathering and father involvement that involve primarily interactive behaviors, but we also comment on purely cognitive expressions. We address situations where fathers and their children are both present, as well as circumstances where the child is not physically present or interacting directly with the father. Though less central for our purposes, some relevant fathering sites will not be prime settings for father–child interaction, rather they represent places where fathers are acting on their children's behalf, sometimes building social capital (e.g., schools, neighborhoods). Others will represent places where a distinct discourse and ideology about fathering may be displayed, developed, negotiated, and learned (e.g., fathers' rights meetings). In a few instances, the physical site in which the presentation and use of a fathering discourse takes place may coincide with a setting for episodic hands-on fathering (e.g., Promise Keepers stadium rally).

How we conceptualize fathering and physical sites is indirectly related to the history of research on father absence and recent critiques of the literatures using the muddled "father absence," "fatherlessness," and "being there" concepts (Marsiglio and Pleck 2005). Recent efforts to describe what "presence" could mean and what "being there" entails are relevant to understanding how fathering is expressed within a physical/social framework. Although "being there" has become a fatherhood mantra, what it means may vary, and it may have no relationship to actual behavior. Studying some men's efforts to act as fathers who must do so without the luxury of being physically present with their children provides important opportunities for insight. We can learn how these men define, negotiate, and manage the absence of shared physical space for fathering. Not having access to shared physical space, or private physical space more specifically, may be as consequential or more so than having it, for fathers and children alike.

Interaction Form

Scholars have debated the virtues of defining father involvement in various ways (Lamb, Pleck, Charnov, and Levine 1987; Marsiglio et al. 2000; Palkovitz 1997; Pleck and Masciadrelli 2004; Pleck and Stueve 2001). Much of what is viewed as father involvement includes an interaction component that is either behavioral or cognitive, though the former is more relevant to our purposes. In other words, fathers can be engaged in an activity that directly or indirectly involves their child, or they can think about how they might contribute to the child's welfare by addressing his or her numerous needs.

Whether fathers are cooperating, competing, comforting, berating, being playful, giving serious advice, providing spiritual guidance, or building social capital, they are engaged in interaction relevant to their child. *Interaction* can also take place at fathering sites when the child is only indirectly implicated. Here, fathers will be talking about their children with school teachers, coaches, neighbors, counselors, and others.

When situated fathering includes experiences that are exclusively cognitive, social interaction related to a child is not occurring. Though fathers' interactive experiences are tied in more obvious ways to the notion of "situated fathering," the mental imaging required to make plans for a child or to contemplate how to intervene on the child's behalf could be influenced by circumstances linked to particular fathering sites. For instance, fathers confined to a prison cell or those who spend much of their time driving a truck across the country may have little opportunity to interact with their children directly, but they have plenty of free time to contemplate how they would like to be involved with their children and help raise them.

Identity Work

As applied to fathering, identity work involves men's activities that are designed to create, present, and sustain personal identities as certain types of fathers. Sometimes men are fully conscious of what they are attempting to accomplish in terms of their father identities; on other occasions they are largely unaware. Men can do identity work to sustain the symbolic image of being a full-fledged father rather than an adoptive, step-, or foster father. Some, however, may feel no need to negotiate the legitimacy of their father status. Fathers may feel compelled to convince their children, themselves, and others that they are a particular type of father (e.g., good provider, spiritual leader of the family, caregiver). Various types of situated circumstances can affect men's desire to engage in identity work, the impression management strategies they use, and their ultimate success in achieving their goals. Living apart from children, whether because of being in jail, on military assignment, or being a nonresident father, can lead fathers to engage in various forms of identity work. Similarly, living and interacting with children in particular types of impoverished/affluent, dangerous/safe, religious/nonreligious surroundings may affect how men attempt to shape others' image of them as fathers.

PROPERTIES OF SITUATED FATHERHOOD

Having described the key issues our framework is designed to address, we now turn our attention to a number of properties that characterize physical sites where fathering in a broad sense takes place or is constructed. We propose that five primary properties and an assortment of secondary ones are essential for developing an analytic lens suitable for addressing the wide scope of situated fathering. To capture its complexity, we first briefly highlight the five main properties, then discuss how other closely related considerations sharpen a perspective underscoring how characteristics of physical/social settings can affect fathering.

Primary Properties

Physical Conditions

As noted above, fathering experiences are connected to a wide range of physical locations, including those based on natural or human-made boundaries — housing units and other buildings being the most obvious example of the latter. Physical settings are defined by a variety of characteristics relevant to how fathers are involved with their children. As alluded to above, a physical setting may be linked to boundaries associated with a natural or human-made structure, or perhaps both. We can speak of a particular setting as being open (neighborhood park) or closed (sheltered domain of a house or office space) to varying degrees. Similarly, the site may be small, thereby limiting personal space and privacy (e.g., car), or more expansive, with private spaces (large house with separate rooms). Having a spacious yard or field immediately outside one's home can offer fathers unique opportunities to play spontaneously with their child in specific ways, some cooperative (e.g., catching a baseball). Even variations related to weather (warm/cold, rain/sunshine, light/darkness) might create physical conditions that influence how fathers perceive and respond to their children in specific instances. A snowy northern weekend may offer fathers an ideal situation to bond with their children while sled riding, and a warm spring day may inspire fathers to go for a walk or play catch with their children outside. Thus the climatic conditions of locations can influence the degree and form of father involvement. Although it is impossible to say how meaningful physical conditions may be because researchers have not explored this question, it is reasonable to assume that these conditions may be consequential at times; hence studies seeking to explore the connection are warranted.

Temporal Dynamics

The social construction of father identities depends not only on "where" men act as fathers but on "when" they act as fathers, as time always unfolds in a particular context. Temporal dynamics reflect the orientations of fathers involved in a particular setting and help to define the "pace, duration, value, and cadence" of an event (Daly 1996, 46). In this way, attention to time in context acknowledges changing fathering relationships, as well as changes in the physical locations of father activities themselves. When fathers move through or within a spatial context during common, everyday routines, they experience how movement in space is bounded by time. For example, a father's decision to have lunch with his school-age child may require him to leave his office to interact with the child at his or her school. The father's work location may make it exceedingly costly in terms of time expenditure to trek across the city. Thus, spatial concerns during the daily round are also temporal concerns. Intersecting space/time concerns may be of particular importance during transitional moments when fathers are moving from one fathering site to another.

By giving meaning to time in particular spaces, social institutions and groups surface new social expectations for men's parenting (Bengston and Allen 1993). For example, face-to-face talks between fathers and children may become "displaced" due to new technologically defined spaces, such as cyberspace communication over e-mail and cell phones. Physical spaces may change over time, requiring different roles and interactions between fathers and children ("I remember when my dad used to take me fishing here—but now it's a mall"). Physical spaces may also remain unchanged, yet what is expected fathering behavior has changed ("I remember when my parents always ate dinner with us at the dining room table—but I never sit down for a meal with my kids"). Recognition of the temporal dynamics of physical locations may highlight differences and shifting roles between generations within families, or they may reference dramatic social changes, which can be traced to changing fatherhood roles across birth cohorts.

Symbolic/Perceptual

When individuals experience a setting, they are likely to come equipped with ready-made definitions of it, or they will form judgments while there. A setting may be viewed on a series of continuums associated with such matters as being safe/dangerous, work/leisure oriented, child-centered/adult-centered, poor/affluent, informal/formal, emotionally warm/cold, and so on. In some instances, these continuums may be measured with objective indicators but we are interested in individuals' perceptions. Obviously how fathers, children, and others perceive situations can influence how fathers and children perceive and treat each other. For example, when fathers define their neighborhoods as unsafe, they may assert their protective paternal roles more forcefully, thereby limiting their children's independence while educating them about safety issues (Letiecq and Koblinsky 2004). Or consider how fathers who farm the land may perceive the purpose of the land and their children's responsibilities to work on it. When fathers view their land as their workspace, they may expect children to spend more time helping with chores than playing in the fields. This type of socially constructed perspective, based on symbolic interpretations of aspects of the physical setting, is likely to influence how fathers interact with their children. Of course, individuals' perceptions of the social aspects defining a setting are likely to be consequential as well.

A potentially important aspect of this property involves fathers' type and level of familiarity with a particular setting. Fathers may base their perceptions of a setting on their firsthand experience, or they may rely on reports from family, friends, or the media. For example, a man who has lived all of his life on a farm and is now raising his children in this setting is situated differently than the father who was raised in the city, lived as an adult family man in the suburbs, and is now embarking on an "alternative" lifestyle raising his children on an Iowa farm. Although he will develop firsthand experience of farm fathering once he's on the farm, his initial perspective will be shaped by other sources. This scenario also captures the dimension of how much experience a father has in a particular setting. A father's perceptions of prison are likely to be affected by whether he has recently been imprisoned for the first time or has been locked up for years. Familiarity with a setting influences everyday life routines as well. For instance, the father who plays with his children regularly at the local pool may have a different perspective and comfort level than the man who goes there only on rare occasions with or without his children.

Social Structural

Each setting has some type of negotiated normative order associated with it that helps individuals determine how they are expected to relate to each other. Consequently a setting has a compositional feature defined by the presence and relative status of individuals. This property highlights that individuals in a setting may have different or similar levels of power, privilege, knowledge, and access to valued resources. In some instances, individuals' status in a formal setting is determined by their organizational affiliation, or lack of it, as well as their access to various types of capital. Fathers interacting with their children in a hospital setting, for instance, must interact with health care professionals who have certain rights and responsibilities vis-à-vis the children that are connected to the professionals' affiliation with the hospital and their profession. Biological fathers have more rights than stepfathers who have not legally adopted the children. On the home front, parents and stepparents may be viewed as having varying levels of power relative to their children. Although there are preestablished patterns associated with particular normative orders, individuals may modify them.

Private/Public

Men can act as fathers in settings viewed to varying degrees as either private or public space. Although most fathering is enacted in private contexts, a great deal of fathering occurs in settings that can be considered public. The most private context is one where the father and child are entirely on their own, not being supervised or watched by others. Privacy might also be conceptualized to include situations that take place within the home and among individuals defined as immediate family members. A clearly public venue for fathering would include instances where the father and child are in the presence of strangers at places like a shopping mall, athletic event, or religious outing.

The private/public distinction can be thought of as being rooted in a physical location as well as having a social/symbolic dimension. Although the house/home may be viewed as private physical space, the "private" connections between family members may transcend that physical site. Family members may experience their private familial bond while away driving in a car, in a hotel, or hiking through a national park. Similarly, public faces of fathering may creep into the confines of the house when outsiders venture into it. The distinction can be seen vividly in how some stepfathers negotiate their experiences within various settings (Marsiglio, chapter 4). Notably, ownership and control issues associated with private settings become more problematic in public contexts as other actors and definitions of situations enter the equation. In short, the intersection between physical and social aspects helps to define unique "situated" contexts for men to "do fathering."

Secondary Properties

Although the primary properties noted previously direct our attention to important issues related to men's situated experiences as fathers, they do so in a rather general way. We turn now to a collection of related considerations, though more limited in scope, shaping how men act as fathers in specific settings. These properties, overlapping in some instances with the previous five, offer additional insights about situated fathering.

Institutional and Cultural Conditions

The conditions associated with some sites for fathering may be affected by explicit or informal organizational policies about how space is to be used and how fathers can navigate within it. Several examples include policies affecting involvement in terms of visitation to prison facilities, court-ordered visitation by divorced fathers, guidelines for therapy sessions, and policies at medical facilities. In addition, cultural norms associated with institutions such as family, religion, or education, as well as those prominently featured in particular communities, may influence the perception and use of the physical and social settings in which fathers and children interact.

The process of "doing fathering" acknowledges that physical spaces and situated social interaction are inherently gendered. Structural inequalities embedded in race/ethnicity, class, and sexual orientation distinctions also prominently shape the contexts of fatherhood experiences. Through personal interaction (such as hearing and responding to discriminatory remarks in public settings) and institutionalized racism or classism (such as in encounters with law enforcement or public officials), some fathers are marginalized in sites where stratified systems promote inequality and bias. Their public behavior and creation of private meaning in response to inequality are at the very heart of their parenting roles. Men struggle to protect their children in such settings and to socialize them about inequality through stories, language, and modeled behavior. However, certain physical settings may also provide opportunities for fathers to construct solidarity and alternative cultural norms around their racial/ethnic identities or class identifications. For example, men's participation at Native American sacred sites and ceremonies, at Kwanzaa celebrations, or at visits to family graveyards for Dia de Los Muertos can signal a contextualized fatherhood that challenges, or at least complicates, stereotypes of "machismo," "absent fathers," and other images of low-income and/or minority fathers.

Transitional Elements

Although we can think of particular sites as being discrete settings, fathers may experience transitional moments when they negotiate the terrain of moving from one site to another (e.g., home to community recreation space, military base to civilian space, prison to residential neighborhood/home). Many transitions of this sort occur frequently, though some occur perhaps only once in a lifetime. Transitions that occur frequently often involve fathers moving back and forth from private to public spaces. Sometimes their children accompany them on this journey, other times fathers meet children at a designated location. Fathers dealing with certain types of familial circumstances may be influenced most dramatically by these transitions. Stepfathers, abusive fathers, nonresident fathers, and fathers with children with special needs or other stigmas exemplify those who may face frequent challenges in navigating the reciprocal transitions between private and public venues. Significant challenges may face fathers whether they are moving from private to public physical and social settings or vice versa.

Fathers sometimes adjust to changes within a particular site that alter the context within which they interact with their children. A single father who invites his romantic partner and her children into his home may alter the degree of privacy to which the father and his child were accustomed. Expanding a house by adding a room or two could also produce more privacy for family members, including a father and child. Another significant household change could occur if a self-employed father fundamentally shifts his work life by creating a home office, resulting in his spending forty or more hours at home during the work week. Though this shift is likely to have the biggest impact on families with preschool children, family dynamics in families with school-age children can be altered as well. Finally, fathers sometimes purposively alter their separate spaces so they can interact with children who are not present. For example, they may equip a trucker's cab with Internet service or redesign the cab to allow the child to join them on the road (Sayers and Fox, chapter 6). Relying on communication technology, in this example, allows fathers to manage relationships across distances and to craft a remote identity as an involved parent.

Personal Power and Control

In any given situation, fathers may experience varying levels of power and control, consistent with our earlier comments regarding social structure. Although fathers' perceptions regarding these matters may transcend any particular situation, they may also be linked to circumstances related to a given site. Fathers in prison are likely to feel frustrated by their inability to control when and where they see their children and how they can interact with them. Some inner city fathers may be reluctant to play with their children in the streets or take them for walks through specific neighborhoods because they fear that harm may come to them (Roy 2004). And some stepfathers, especially those new to their roles, may feel inhibited asserting themselves as fathers in the confined space of their in-laws' home. These same men may at varying points in the evolution of their stepfamily develop paternal tendencies related to their understanding of who owns the house where their stepchildren reside. Is the house/apartment their partner's, their own, or is it jointly owned/rented?

Issues of power may arise, too, when some kind of spatial intrusion or exclusion occurs. Fathers may resist efforts to abide by organizational norms regarding their interaction with children. For instance, divorced fathers under court order not to have contact with their children may assert their personal power by defying the order and attending their child's athletic event or seeing them in some other place.

Gendered Attributes

Men's and others' perceptions of particular fathering sites may be influenced by the way and extent to which they view them as being gendered. Prisons, farms, military bases, and the distant highways that consume a long-haul truck driver's time are likely to be viewed as having masculine elements associated with them, whereas dance recitals, church, and home may be viewed in less masculine, perhaps even feminine, terms. Such images may in subtle ways affect how fathers respond to their children in particular settings. Although more masculine environments may predispose fathers to accentuate a masculine style of interaction, some fathers may make a concerted effort to balance this site-based masculinity with a more expressive, nurturing paternal style. Looked at differently, the masculine climate, say, of the athletic field, may enable some fathers to express a nurturing style selectively because they sense that the masculine atmosphere offers them a secure buffer to express their feelings. In general, sites that exude a softer image may encourage fathers to perceive and treat their children in a gentler way. However, some men may be inclined to compensate for a feminine image by resorting to more masculine fathering displays.

Fatherhood Discourses

Depending on the site, formal or informal activities may take place that contribute to men's understanding of and perceptions about fatherhood. These activities can provide an accessible language, user-friendly symbols, and basic conceptual frameworks that attach values and beliefs to fatherhood and that promote or discourage certain fathering practices. Discourses that emerge from site-based activities draw from local constructions of fatherhood, as well as public and popular notions of fatherhood (Lupton and Barclay 1997). Some sites, such as workplaces, churches, talk shows, correctional facilities, and family reunions, are not explicitly related to men's roles as fathers. Other sites, such as child support court, fathers' rights meetings, or foster care caseworkers' offices, are in part designed around men's participation with their children. For example, the variety of fatherhood programs through the United States (ranging from teen fathers groups, Promise Keepers, New Warriors, and groups for low-income or nonresidential fathers) are designed to increase men's awareness of their children's needs and improve their ability to nurture and economically provide for them. Fathers involved with these all-male programs are likely to be exposed to an ideology emphasizing fatherhood responsibility. In some of these settings, programmatic discourse can provide men the means to do identity work in order to foster, regain, or preserve their father identities.

DISTINCT CONTRIBUTIONS OF THIS VOLUME

Before suggesting what needs to be done, we comment briefly on how the scholars contributing to this volume have provided groundbreaking work for future researchers to build on. Collectively they have generated new theoretical and methodological insights about how spatial issues and related social/symbolic processes affect aspects of fathers' interactions with their children and men's identity work as fathers. While continuing to draw on theoretical traditions such as symbolic interactionism, social constructionism, social ecological models, phenomenology, and life course perspectives, their efforts have opened the door to explore how men socially construct their identities and negotiate the borders of fatherhood within a variety of diverse settings. Research in this volume has showcased to varying degrees the five primary properties of our framework for situated fatherhood (physical conditions, temporal dynamics, symbolic/perceptual, social structural, and public/private), as well as the five secondary properties (institutional and cultural conditions, transitional elements, personal power and control, gender attributes, and fatherhood discourses). Although most of the scholarly work in this volume focuses on fathers' involvement with their children (interaction form) rather than fathers' identity work, the authors advance our knowledge considerably in both areas. Because authors present their own detailed suggestions for future research related to the fathering site of interest to them, we only summarize several key issues here, emphasizing the interrelationship between properties while considering the interrelated mix of community- and institutional-oriented sites for doing fathering.

Taking a broad view, Hamer's (chapter 12) ethnography of East St. Louis offers powerful images of how dangerous and unhealthy physical conditions associated with a largely abandoned, impoverished community can shape men's perceptions of themselves as fathers and the gendered strategies they adapt to protect their sons and daughters. Her work provides a timely example of how a variety of our primary (physical conditions and the symbolic/perceptual) and secondary (institutional/cultural conditions, personal power and control, and gender attributes) properties are interrelated. Faced with daily reminders of the pervasive environmental risks and hazards in their poor neighborhood, some fathers are inspired to take protective measures on behalf of their children. Unfortunately, their limited resources for controlling the adverse conditions threatening their children often frustrate them. This case study poignantly illustrates how fathering/parenting styles can be changed in the situated context of a community due to larger social processes of disinvestment tied to corporate interests and public relations.

Whereas the men in Hamer's study appear to do much of their protective fathering in an environment in which they perceive danger and little social support, Coltrane and colleagues' (chapter 13) analysis of Mexican American men's fathering accentuates the role that community solidarity may play in poor communities. The social bonds Mexican American men perceive between neighbors in a particular region of California appear to influence fathers' ability to minimize hardships for their children and protect them from neighborhood threats. The authors paint a rather complex picture of these fathers as "restrictive, protective, and loving at the same time" (chapter 13, p. 294). Importantly, this study underscores the value of considering how men's approach to fathering is influenced by aspects of neighborhood and ethnic climates.

Religious institutions may represent a distinctively important resource for men living in disadvantaged inner-city areas like East St. Louis, Illinois. As Wilcox and Bartkowski (chapter 14) conclude, based on their multimethod analysis of the relationship between religiosity, social class, and father involvement, religious institutions offer "crucial moral, social, and spiritual support for decent dads striving to do right by their children in low-income communities" (chapter 14, p. 315). Their qualitative portrait of the faith-based fatherhood program in Mississippi hints at the significance of theorizing about and studying how the physical and spatial characteristics of religiously oriented sites and programs, including those that target men separately, affect poor men's fathering. They provide a viable option for disadvantaged men to develop skills and a sense of moral worth and dignity that can affect their fathering.

Like Hamer, Goodsell (chapter 2) uses a St. Louis sample, but his sample is restricted to suburban middle-class parents. He provides a conceptual lens for interpreting how people frame their orientation toward places while explaining their perceptions and performance of good fathering. Put differently, Goodsell considers how individuals use alternative conceptions of place as a linguistic resource to articulate their sense of what good fathering entails. As was often evident in the East St. Louis low-income fathers' stories, those living in this city's suburbs connected their community images to their understanding of fathering. Using the methods of grounded theory, Goodsell identifies three levels of "vertical space" (*immediate, intermediate,* and *imagined*), which can be loosely characterized as the commonly experienced home, the intermittently visited and idealized places like vacation spots, and the abstract domain—like the world—that can never be experienced directly. He showcases the value of studying how fathers (and others) use different "levels of spatial aggregation as resources from which they can draw cultural symbols and justification of meanings and action" (chapter 2, p. 44). Thus these conceptual devices allow individuals to articulate their perception of good fatherhood while providing men conceptual tools for explaining their own fathering.

Goodsell's discussion of "immediate" space overlaps Allen and Daly's (chapter 3) and LaRossa's (chapter 7) work, which focuses attention on home life and how activities therein are socially constructed. Allen and Daly integrate data from two qualitative studies of Canadian families to reveal how fathers' and mothers' perceptions of space and time are related to the "symbolic and ideological meanings of home and family, the organization of family activities, identities and responsibilities, and the dynamics of power and control in gender relationships" (chapter 3, p. 53). They argue, consistent with our model's *personal power and control* property, that time and space are "*contested* dimensions of experience" (chapter 3, p. 64). LaRossa's unique analysis of the historical roots and interpersonal symbolism of fathers playing catch with their children reveals in several ways how time and space issues are merged with respect to a specific activity. For example, he suggests that the availability of an adjacent yard at home may influence children's expectations for how their fathers should spend time playing with them. Given the accessibility of space for playing, fathers' and children's feelings may be affected more noticeably if fathers do not play. Thus, having a yard or field next door has implications for perceptions about time and father involvement. In short, fathers' decisions occur within a familial context in which spatial and temporal considerations matter.

The home context is also central to Marsiglio's (chapter 4) conceptual model that considers how forty different types of scenarios—implicitly linked to Goodsell's notions of immediate and intermediate places—are relevant to the multilayered process of stepfathering. The model delineates how key physical and social dimensions distinguish the various scenarios. An important feature of the model is its emphasis on how individuals define situations as either private or public, and how those perceptions may affect how men experience themselves as stepfathers. At times, private and public merge when family outsiders visit stepfathers' homes, potentially placing the stepfathers' negotiated paternal status and fatherly involvement on display.

For some, "home" means more than the space or place wherein family life unfolds. As Peter and his colleagues (chapter 11) reveal in their ethnographic study of farm fathering in Iowa, the symbolic meaning of place can become quite complicated when home and work are intertwined. Here, again, time and space come together as fathers socially construct the legacy of their private land and their options for sharing their land-based heritage with their children. Although much remains to be learned about how farm fathers interact with their children, their approach to fathering is likely to be filtered through their firm attachment to geography, rural culture, and a form of land-based intergenerational family life.

In their analysis of fathers returning from recent military duty in Iraq, Mac-Dermid and colleagues (chapter 10) also highlight how contingencies related to dangerous, remote physical conditions influence fathering. But, unlike on the streets of East St. Louis, men's limited fathering opportunities occur at a distance from their families. American soldiers with children are spared the tension and frustration of protecting their children directly from the bombs, bullets, and wreckage of war; however, they face the unique challenge of harnessing their father identity so that paternal sentiments do not jeopardize their ability to remain alert to war zone threats.

Concerns about the physical conditions of war affected fathers before and after their deployment. Anticipating that they would be stationed far away for an indefinite period of time, and knowing they would have limited chances to communicate with their families, some fathers took creative steps to guarantee that their "presence" with their children would be ensured even though they were far away (e.g., father being videotaped reading bedtime stories). Once deployed, soldiers, like incarcerated fathers, were not at liberty to contact their children at their discretion. Higher-ranking officers often determined whether soldiers had the time and resources to express themselves as fathers through letter writing, e-mails, or phone calls. Soldier fathers also faced significant challenges when they reentered their children's lives once they returned home. The challenges were reinforced or created by their time away and isolation from their family. When at home, returning soldiers, far more so than incarcerated fathers, had autonomy over how they chose to interact with their children and more appealing chances for doing identity work.

Fathers deployed in times of war vividly highlight how fathering occurs in a situated context that in many ways is beyond fathers' control. Furthermore, social structural arrangements, institutional conditions, physical conditions, temporal dynamics, personal power and control, symbolic and gender attributes, fatherhood discourses, and transitional elements related to a specific fathering context are often enmeshed. Incarcerated fathers, like those in work release programs described by Roy (chapter 8), also cope with institutionally regulated space that shapes family relationships. Sentenced to up to eighteen months of incarceration for a variety of alcohol- or substance-related charges, these fathers are required to work on a full-time basis in the local community, but they can only have limited interaction with their families. They must apply for sporadic visitation passes or nightly phone calls. Fathers also cover large distances quickly during release time in order to spend time with their children. The process of incarceration unravels normative expectations for father roles, and men and their families are often unsure how to resolve their relations. Faced with this sense of "liminality" (neither in nor out of local community life), many fathers resist and reclaim previous roles by stretching facility rules to visit with their children outside of the facility. They also conduct identity work to promote positive changes in their lives, including desistance from alcohol or substance use and enhanced commitment to their children upon release.

Many of these same properties are in play with the long-haul truck drivers described by Sayers and Fox (chapter 6). To varying degrees, these fathers prepare their children for their departure, manage their father identities while away, and then employ strategies to reunite with their children. Unlike the military fathers, over-the-road truckers do not have to deal with hostile physical surroundings. Nonetheless, the distance and sometimes time differentials between the road and home require men to go out of their way to remain active fathers for their children. In some ways, these men are also like nonresident fathers who see their children only every third or fourth weekend (Catlett, Toews, and McKenry, chapter 5). Fathers who are physically absent from their children's home are faced with the challenge of sustaining the father–child bond without regularly taking part in the child's daily routine. Nonresident fathers and those fathers away on the road sometimes acclimate, and may actually prefer, their limited involvement with their children. Others resign themselves to their situation, feeling as though they are victims of circumstance. In either case, these men's experiences illustrate how the contingencies of space and time affect fathers' options for treating their children in particular ways. As shown elsewhere, nonresident fathers with superior financial resources are better positioned to minimize the negative consequences of fathering children who live elsewhere (Catlett and McKenry 2004).

Whereas the message for fathers in the war zone is that they are soldiers first, family men second, fatherhood programs are designed to encourage men to privilege fathering. Anderson and Letiecq (chapter 9) and Wilcox and Bartkowski (chapter 14) provide two diverse examples of how specific fathering programs can expose men to fathering discourses that encourage them to engage in more positive father involvement. Neither the former, an inner-city program targeting disadvantaged fathers, nor the latter, a faith-based program, currently provides a physical location for father–child interaction. However, they each reveal how aspects of a contextualized fatherhood are meaningful.

FUTURE RESEARCH

Although this volume incorporates research on fathers in a wide variety of sites, some promising areas are not addressed. First, examination of more varied characteristics of fathers themselves will expand our understanding of how men's experiences are shaped by spatial contexts. For example, an expanded focus on cultural contexts would move beyond this volume's analyses of low-income African American and Mexican American fathers. Localized cultural enclaves associated with Native American, Asian, or "new American" fathers in recently immigrated families would be intriguing sites

for future research. How do the physical circumstances and associated so-
cial/symbolic meanings influence father involvement? To what extent and
how do fathers in these settings try to instill their children with a sense of
pride in their heritage by emphasizing traditions that are tied to the land or
embedded community? Does the economic infrastructure of these areas, such
as the poor agricultural quality of most reservation land for Native American
communities, shape how fathers see themselves and treat their children?

These various cultural contexts include segregated communities (such as
Asian families in San Francisco, New York, and Los Angeles) that are likely
to face a unique set of conditions that are affected by the high ethnic/racial
density of their physical and social surroundings. Alternatively, other cultural
communities are more dispersed in urban or rural areas (such as multiethnic
or multiracial families), and this dispersal may affect how fathers socialize
their children to the importance of cultural context. More needs to be learned
about the conditions affecting whether fathers encourage their children to develop certain forms of human capital (e.g., speaking English) or create social
capital either within or outside their ethnic/racial enclave.

Children can also be socialized in cultural contexts by multiple biological
parents, social parents, and other adults without children. Some chapters in
this volume suggest that men can be encouraged to view "collective fathering" in what Bould (2003) describes as the "caring neighborhood." Here men
serve as nonbiological social fathers, as well as biological fathers, to an assortment of children in their communities. How can different physical spaces
facilitate, or inhibit, collective socialization and monitoring of children?
Which aspects of physical and social spaces allow fathers and father figures
to draw on ethnic identities to shield children from discrimination, disadvantage, and harm?

Close attention to life course issues may lead researchers to compare and
contrast the situated fathering of diverse birth cohorts of fathers. Do younger fathers spend more time parenting actively outside the home than older fathers?
Do older fathers receive different sets of social expectations for their fathering,
and in which settings are these expectations apparent? Cross-cohort alliances
between senior and junior fathers, and the intergenerational transmission of lessons learned between fathers and sons who have become parents as well, are
fertile areas for study, particularly when we can investigate where and how
these interactions unfold. At the other end of the life course, family researchers
interested in aging issues might consider how living in a nursing/retirement
home affects the way older fathers attempt to interact with their adult children.
Obviously, men's lives as fathers do not end when their children turn eighteen
or leave home, but researchers have seldom considered how older men continue
to express themselves as fathers throughout the later years of life. Thus study-

ing fathers in nursing/retirement homes provides a unique opportunity to consider a form of situated fatherhood among older fathers.

The impact of social expectations for gay fathers is also an understudied aspect of parenting. How and where have gay fathers crafted supportive communities that encourage their involvement with children? Are there patterns of geographic or regional support for gay fatherhood, and how are these spaces related to state policies or local laws that affect gay relationships? Ultimately, closer attention to the ways that space can influence an entire range of negotiations about gender and parenting is important. Are there physical spaces in which fathering is more contested, and what are the processes by which contestation unfolds and is resolved? Such frameworks would be useful in research with stay-at-home fathers, single custodial fathers, or nonbiological social fathers.

Second, this volume challenges researchers to continue to explore unique physical and social spaces for men's fathering. For example, a novel and promising site for studying fathers includes places where "leisure" defines the generic setting and money is a prerequisite for participation. These would include resort communities, luxury cruises, wilderness expeditions, ski lodges, country clubs, and so on. Here, participation is predicated on a father's having the financial means to provide his children with an exclusive form of entertainment. For some men, the mere provision of such leisure may be tantamount to discharging their parental obligations, while other men may seek such experiences to express themselves as fathers exclusively, having constructed a "temporal space" unimpinged on by other concerns.

More traditional recreation sites (e.g., baseball and soccer fields, beaches, playgrounds) can provide researchers with significant opportunities to study fathers' interactions with their children. Many fathers, for example, coach their young children's athletic teams. To our knowledge, no one has explored how fathers who are coaches interact with their children in this unique context. These men manage a dual father–coach relationship with their own children while negotiating relationships with the other young participants and their parents. Questions about transitional issues may come into play when father–coaches relate to their children at home in ways that draw on their coaching responsibilities. Likewise, men's fathering styles at home may infuse how men relate to their own children while coaching them. Another intriguing recreational context involves the rare sites where fathers and their children take lessons together in a leisure activity (e.g., martial arts). Fathers find themselves in the unusual position of being both pupil and father (perhaps quasi-teacher) in the same setting. The masculine attributes associated with the physical and social/symbolic meanings attached to the dojo (training school for self-defense) provide an interesting backdrop to examine father–child interaction.

As authors in this volume note, situated fathering is often mediated by spe-cific institutional systems. Health-related institutions, for instance, offer a window to view the dynamics of institutional mediation of men's parenting. Most hospitals have children's wards, and some stand-alone clinics house children with serious illnesses such as cancer. Unfortunately, researchers have paid scant attention to fathers' level and type of participation in managing ei-ther their children's routine or more serious health care concerns. Likewise, we can examine the reciprocity of parent/child relationships through closer attention to how adult children care for fathers with illnesses, in hospice care or under the care of other family members. Situational aspects of fathering can be illuminated by taking into account the relevance of policies, practices, and physical design features associated with hospitals and treatment centers. What types of factors facilitate or inhibit certain types of father involvement?

An obvious extension of the study of situated fathering is the significance of workplace site and its culture and how it shapes men's parenting. Al-though recent theoretical frameworks have more fully articulated men's par-enting to include care work, work as providers remains a core component of men's conceptions of themselves as responsible fathers. Workplace policies concerning paternal leave and flexible hours for sick care or transportation of children are each vital aspects in our understanding of the structure of workplaces for fathers. Examining workplace cultures draws attention to re-lated issues, such as informal discourse of parenting behavior and the acces-sibility of a workplace to children. Is the site "child-friendly" and able to ac-commodate children's presence, perhaps through on-site child care—or is it a toxic or dangerous site that could threaten safety and health of family members?

Researchers have opportunities to study how a small family business envi-ronment produces a context for father involvement. Similar types of research could be done with self-employed fathers whose relationship with their chil-dren includes an informal, work-related apprenticeship (e.g., plumbers, elec-tricians, carpenters, real estate brokers). For example, large numbers of Asian immigrants historically have established a foothold in the American economy as small business owners and shopkeepers. In high-density cultural enclaves, they have recruited their children to assist in family business. How does the work-related apprenticeship aspect of a father–child relationship affect fa-thers' interactions with their children more generally?

Related to sites of work and providing, fathers also participate as consumers with their children. The sentimentalized stereotype of children asking fathers for money for their latest coveted purchase can inform studies of father–child interaction around shopping and consumption. In particular, how and where do these interactions occur? How are they shaped by Internet sites that encourage purchase of "dad gear" or by local shopping mall cultures? Shopping can take place in explicitly gendered spaces (e.g., certain clothing stores, sporting good stores), and we know little about how fathers manage their interactions with their sons and daughters in these sites.

Men's parenting is often monitored and regulated through the legal system. Over the course of the dissolution of marital relationships, the space of court-room negotiations plays a significant role in how men's roles are constructed. As a site of potential conflict or consensus, a focus on the situated mechanisms—judges and other legal personnel—and interaction concerning fathering could be extremely useful in understanding men's experiences as divorced fathers. Family therapy sessions are also potent sites in which to examine family negotiation over fathering roles. Both the courtroom and the therapy room are mediated spaces, and researchers could do the important work of delineating how father-ing is encouraged or discouraged by systems of authority or the involvement of clinical staff in contentious family issues.

As many chapters in this volume suggest, communication technologies are a relevant but understudied conduit that connect individuals in different phys-ical and social spaces while mediating men's fathering. Fathers interact with their children regularly over e-mail, cell phones, instant messaging, phone lines, and even Internet sites. Virtual monitoring of children's activities or regular contact between fathers and children who live thousands of miles apart are understudied family phenomena. Obviously access to technology becomes an issue for this aspect of situated fathering. However, technology may provide a bridge to involvement for fathers who are "desituated," or dis-tanced, from their children. For example, attention to men's jobs that require travel would also lead researchers to examine the central role of technology that secures continued father involvement.

Homeless shelters or supportive housing are also desituated or temporary spaces for fathering. Although it is difficult to estimate the number of home-less fathers who have children under their care, a sizable number of men spend at least a portion of each year facing the unenviable challenge of being a father figure while living on the streets or in shelters. For many, their expe-rience of fathering is tied to a transient lifestyle where they are unable to pro-vide their family the stability of living in one place where they have any sense of control over their affairs and property. How does the lack of privacy or property ownership affect fathers' self-perceptions and the way they treat their children in homeless shelters? How does the public evidence of a fa-ther's failure to protect and provide affect his expectations and the expecta-tions of others for his involvement with his children?

Finally, these chapters suggest intriguing new directions in explicit theoriz-ing about space and family life (Daly 2003). As family researchers, we need to become more attuned to the aspects of spaces in which family is created (Gubrium, Holstein, and Buckholdt 1994). Many studies of father involvement are acontextual and atemporal. We do not often account for the process of "meaning shifts" of fatherhood—especially as fathers and children move in time across physical and social spaces. A focus on fathering may offer family researchers the opportunity to articulate fully how physical and social space are confounded, how they shape each other, and why. For example, situated studies can directly inform the debate over differences between fathering and mothering roles. Is men's parenting dependent on context in different ways than women's parenting? If so, how?

A more explicit attempt to create theory with a focus on process and context can capture the diversity of men's parenting across spaces, across cultural contexts, and over time. In particular, researchers can explore how time changes the spaces for fathering. Research presented in this volume offers a few examples of how space for situated fathering is altered over historical and biographic time. Future studies in the tradition of family history may benefit from stronger emphasis on situated fathering.

Perhaps even more promising are continued efforts to situate social structures and systems of power in our understanding of family life. The authors provide models to think about how institutions and individuals can take control over local spaces in which parents and children interact. They also suggest that families act to resist such control. Future studies may use spatial frameworks to distinguish material and symbolic consequences of social policies regarding families, including social security, military deployment, welfare reform, foster care, and even the emergence of a homeland security system that seeks to secure "safe" space for family life in the United States.

Men, as illustrated above, do not express themselves as fathers in a spatial vacuum. By identifying a number of key properties that define our spatially sensitive perspective, we offer researchers new insights for conducting research exploring fathers' involvement and identity work in a broader, more nuanced context. We expect future research to expand, refine, and integrate the properties we discuss. As this work proceeds, researchers should consider how this model helps researchers identify promising avenues for promoting positive father involvement.

REFERENCES

Anderson, E. (1990). *Streetwise: Race, class, and change in an urban community.* Chicago: University of Chicago Press.

Bengston, V., and Allen, K. (1993). The life course perspective applied to families over time. In P. Boss, W. Doherty, R. LaRossa, W. Schumm, and S. Steinmetz (Eds.), *Sourcebook of family theories and methods: A contextual approach* (pp. 469–98). New York: Plenum.

Bould, S. (2003). Caring neighborhoods: Bringing up the kids together. *Journal of Family Issues, 24,* 427–47.

Catlett, B. S., and McKenry, P. C. (2004). Class-based masculinities: Divorce, fatherhood, and the hegemonic ideal. *Fathering, 2,* 165–90.

Daly, K. (1996). *Families and time.* Thousand Oaks, CA: Sage.

Daly, K. (2003). Family theory versus the theories families live by. *Journal of Marriage and Family, 65,* 771–84.

Gieryn, T. (2000). A space for place in sociology. *Annual Review of Sociology, 26,* 463–96.

Goffman, Erving (1959). *The presentation of self in everyday life.* Garden City, NY: Doubleday.

Gubrium, J., Holstein, J., and Buckholdt, D. (1994). *Constructing the life course.* Dix Hills, NY: General Hall.

Hillier, B., and Hanson, J. (1984). *The social logic of space.* Cambridge: Cambridge University Press.

Lamb, M. E., Pleck, J. H., Charnov, E. L., and Levine, J. A. (1987). A biosocial perspective on paternal behavior and involvement. In J. B. Lancaster, J. Altmann, A. S. Rossi, and L. R. Sherrod (Eds.), *Parenting across the lifespan: Biosocial dimensions* (pp. 111–42). Hawthorne, NY: Aldine de Gruyter.

Letiecq, B. L., and Koblinsky, S. A. (2004). Parenting in violent neighborhoods: African American fathers share strategies for keeping children safe. *Journal of Family Issues, 25,* 715–34.

Lupton, D., and Barclay, L. (1997). *Constructing fatherhood: Discourses and experiences.* Thousand Oaks, CA: Sage.

Marsiglio, W., and Cohan, M. (2000). Contextualizing father involvement and paternal influence: Sociological and qualitative themes. *Marriage and Family Review, 29,* 75–95.

Marsiglio, W., Amato, P., Day, R. D., and Lamb, M. E. (2000). Scholarship on fatherhood in the 1990s and beyond. *Journal of Marriage and the Family, 62,* 1173–91.

Marsiglio, W., Day, R. D., and Lamb, M. E. (2000). Exploring fatherhood diversity: Implications for conceptualizing father involvement. *Marriage and Family Review, 29,* 269–93.

Marsiglio, W., and Pleck, J. H. (2005). Fatherhood and masculinities. In M. S. Kimmel, J. Hearn, and R. W. Connell (Eds.), *The handbook of studies on men and masculinities* (pp. 249–69). Thousand Oaks, CA: Sage.

Palkovitz, R. (1997). Reconstructing "involvement": Expanding conceptualizations of men's caring in contemporary families. In A. J. Hawkins and D. C. Dollahite (Eds.), *Generative fathering: Beyond deficit perspectives* (pp. 200–216). Thousand Oaks, CA: Sage.

Pellow, D. (1996). *Setting boundaries: The anthropology of spatial and social organization*. Westport, CT: Bergin & Garvey.

Pleck, J. H., and Masciadrelli, B. P. (2004). Paternal involvement by U.S. residential fathers: Level, sources, and consequences. In M. E. Lamb (Ed.), *The role of the father in child development* (4th ed., pp. 222–71). New York: Wiley.

Pleck, J. H., and Stueve, J. L. (2001). Time and paternal involvement. In K. Daly (Ed.), *Minding the time in family experience: Emerging perspectives and issues* (pp. 205–26). Oxford: Elsevier Science.

Roy, K. (2004). Three-block fathers: Spatial perceptions and kin-work in low-income neighborhoods. *Social Problems, 51,* 528–48.

Spain, D. (1992). *Gendered spaces*. Chapel Hill: University of North Carolina Press.

Stack, C. (1974). *All our kin: Strategies for survival in a black community*. New York: Random House.

Tamis-LeMonda, C. S., and Cabrera, N. (2002). *Handbook of father involvement: Multidisciplinary perspectives*. Mahwah, NJ: Erlbaum.

Urry, J. (1985). Social relations, space and time. In D. Gregory and J. Urry (Eds.), *Social relations and spatial structures* (pp. 20–48). New York: St. Martin's.

van den Hoonard, W. C. (1997). *Working with sensitizing concepts: Analytical field research*. Thousand Oaks, CA: Sage.

2

Fatherhood and the Social Organization of Space: An Essay in Subjective Geography

Todd L. Goodsell

When men and women talk about fatherhood, they situate the concept in a spatial framework that has a subjective and moral structure. The spatial organization of fatherhood entails both horizontal and vertical axes. The former is probably the more familiar mode of thought about spatial organization: when one walks across a room or moves from one city to another, that movement is across the horizontal axis of social space. Vertical organization—as I speak of it—is also familiar to everyday perception, but we are less prone to think of it explicitly. It is based on the assumption that any given place is simultaneously part of an infinite number of larger spatial aggregates of various sizes. Thus a given living room may be simultaneously part of a home, a historic neighborhood, a lower-middle-class suburb, and a metropolitan area—each being of a progressively larger spatial magnitude.

I will speak of three levels of vertical spatial organization. Those levels I call "immediate" (places commonly experienced directly, such as the home), "intermediate" (places intermittently experienced directly, such as vacation spots), and "imagined" (places never experienced directly, such as "the world"). All space—however intimate—is imagined, and my distinction between these three levels is somewhat arbitrary. The number of levels of aggregate spatial organization is limited only by the imaginations of members of a cultural community. However, I propose them as analytic tools that are relevant in the present effort to understand the relationship between space and fatherhood, based on the subjective accounts of research participants.

Of course, one does not typically think of any given place in the sense of its horizontal and vertical organization and situation all the time. Rather, it is more common to think of a "place" as simply a unitary (a word I take from Lefebvre [1991, 20]) entity—a given or a field in which relevant social action occurs

(Lefebvre 1991, 94). A city can be a place just as well as a backyard garden can be. However, we must inquire into the constellation of meaning that surrounds the use of the concept of "place" itself. In so doing, I argue, we will find that everyday understandings of place reveal it as a cultural artifact. In a given community, place structures the experiences of community members, but also provides images, which community members are able to reinterpret and manipulate.

While "place" and "space" are often used interchangeably in the vernacular, and each at least implies the other, in my analysis I will use the word "place" when I choose to speak of a site of whatever size as a single entity, and "space" when I choose to emphasize the internal, spatial structure of a place, the relationship between different places, or the contingency of geographic referents on human subjectivity. I recognize that this distinction is primarily analytic since the selection criteria called for explicit reference to "place" by the research participants. However, since one of my goals is to show the reader that "place" is problematic—neither simple nor always equivalent—I suggest a soft distinction in emphasis between the two terms.

I will illustrate the reinterpretation and manipulation of space through the concept of "moral leverage." I use the word "leverage" to mean the rhetorical advantage gained by pulling in or appealing to an external referent to justify social action or a social situation. In the present study, it is a significant mechanism by which individuals exercise social agency. Sometimes people take actions or make decisions that create an uncomfortable or ironic juxtaposition of social conditions linked to space. This might include the decision to leave one's home, family, and friends, and move to another part of the country (a horizontal movement). The physical separation combined with the empirical differences of everyday life in the two places can be experienced as painful. Moral leverage to justify this action may be gained by appealing to a larger or smaller spatial referent, such as by suggesting that the move reflects the cultural image of upward progress toward the "American Dream"—a movement up the vertical axis that synthesizes two smaller, disparate experiences (life there and life here) into a common social narrative.

I proceed through this chapter in the following manner: I begin by observing that conceptions of fatherhood and of place are linked to each other—first in interpretive data gathered from research participants and then insufficiently in the fatherhood literature. I explain briefly the components of my St. Louis fatherhood study. Then I present findings, beginning with the meaning of vertical spatial organization and three levels at which it is meaningful to the research participants (immediate, intermediate, and imagined). I discuss the meaning of horizontal spatial organization, and it is in this section that I focus my argument that moral leverage is one mechanism by which individuals express human agency by acting on their subjectively perceived social world. They often do this by appealing up or down the vertical axis vis-à-vis a given horizontally situated place, in an effort to maintain or justify a given social reality. Finally, I will suggest ways in which this understanding of the relationship between place and fatherhood might inform future research.

FATHERHOOD AND SUBJECTIVE PLACE

Joseph—soon to become a father for the first time—recognized that fatherhood is practiced in empirical places, and those places have implications for understandings of fatherhood. I interviewed him in the living room of his home in suburban St. Louis—the same home in which he himself was raised. When his mother passed away a few years previous to my visit, he moved in. He said that he and his wife loved the home and the neighborhood and had no plans to leave. Joseph's impending transition to fatherhood continued to evoke memories of his own childhood. From his old teddy bear that he found in the basement, to the spot in the backyard where his father helped him pitch a tent, the physical environment gave him prompts, constraints, and opportunities for his own fatherhood. Joseph told me, "I'm going to do these same things with my kids in the same place, and I'm really excited to get the perspective, *not just as a father but a father in the exact same physical surroundings*" (emphasis added).

Place is one resource from which people in their everyday lives draw meanings relevant to their own identities and actions. (For culture as a resource, see Swidler 2001.) However, place is not a unitary social fact. Place itself is structured. For that reason, one goal of this chapter is to unsettle the meaning of place itself, in the context of a discussion of the cultural construct of fatherhood. From the position of Schutzian phenomenology and using grounded theory techniques (an inductive process that aims at generating theory from social data), I will suggest that one everyday construction of space is structured vertically and horizontally. This structuring provides a rich variety of sources for individuals' ideas about what it means to be a good father, and they use these ideas—subjectively located in places—to construct, maintain, and justify a sense of good fatherhood.

To date, little work has explicitly dealt with the connection between fatherhood and place. Some of the work on fatherhood has sought to explain the culture of fatherhood in America generally and outline the major problems related to it, giving little if any attention to local variation or to spatial theories (e.g., Blankenhorn 1995; Griswold 1993). Other fatherhood studies have used place as background to the central (often decontextualized) presentation of findings, or have used place as a methodological side note, in terms of where the study was done or the characteristics of the research participants (e.g., Coltrane 1996; Dienhart 1998; Gerson 1993; Townsend 2002).

Two categories of work deserve special note for trying to connect place and fatherhood. One is the ethnographic tradition, which has focused narrowly on the experience of inner-city fatherhood (e.g., Furstenburg 1995; Liebow 1967). In these studies, the meaning of fatherhood is tightly connected to the places in which the men reside, and to understand fatherhood for them requires an intimate understanding of the context that frames it. Since these fathers are typically disenfranchised, their agency as fathers is often subsumed under the larger narrative of structural disadvantage. The other category is historical approaches to fatherhood (e.g., Johansen 2001; Lombard 2003). The authors of these sources frequently foreground the importance of space and place. For example, the characteristics of fathering Lombard (2003) presents in her description of colonial New England are clearly linked to the legal, economic, and familial climate of that area. And even though Johansen (2001) tries to describe fatherhood in one social class in nineteenth-century America generally, he still points out how cross-country moves, business trips, and local economies all facilitated and constrained different types of fatherly behaviors. Again, there is not in these works a theory of place which is then linked to fatherhood, but they remind us that fatherhood is simply not a uniform construct across all places and spatial relationships.

METHOD

Knowledge resides in places (Lefebvre 1991, 57, 404), but places themselves are not uniform entities (Lefebvre 1991, 86–88). Consequently it is important to understand the relationship between knowledge and the places in which that knowledge is produced, changed, and applied.

Theoretically, this discussion of the relationship between fatherhood and space is based on the premise that we must come to understand the social world as it is perceived by the people who inhabit it. It is not inherently meaningful. The lived world is incoherent, inconsistent, and only partially clear (Schutz 1970, 75–76), but social agents retrospectively fit their social worlds with meaning (Schutz 1967, 75). The goal of this kind of cultural inquiry is to access and articulate "the spontaneous, unintentional, basic impulse of a culture" (Mannheim 1952, 39), rather than deductively imposing theoretical boundaries around social data. Space itself is a social construction (Lefebvre 1991)—something that is experienced in various ways at the same time, and a product of historical processes, perceptions, and often competing interests.

Space is not a scientific object removed from ideology or politics; it has always been political and strategic. If space has an air of neutrality and indifference with regard to its contents and thus seems to be "purely" formal, it is precisely because it has already been occupied and used, and has already been the focus of past processes whose traces are not always evident in the landscape. (Lefebvre 1976, 31)

To inquire into the meaning of space and a cultural concept such as fatherhood, one must keep one's mind open to various meanings of space. Thus the analysis followed principles of grounded theory (Glaser and Strauss 1999) in order to obtain, as much as possible, a view of fatherhood and place as they are experienced and understood by the men and women who participated in the study.

Seventy-nine men and women in the St. Louis area (forty-two men and, for thirty-seven of them, their partners also)—nearly all of whom are middle class and most of whom are white—were interviewed for this study. Their assumptions about daily life are grounded in the experience of middle-class, suburban America. No single place can represent all of America, and St. Louis has been noted for its tightly connected economic networks that seem to have produced enduring cultural templates (Marquis 2003; Ratcliff 1980; Ratcliff, Gallagher, and Ratcliff 1979). These researchers have suggested that St. Louis has maintained a more traditional model of political economy, and this may have been reflected in comments I often heard in the field that local residents perceive the St. Louis area as one in which it is easier to perform normative (often traditional) middle-class standards of family life. The field period lasted twelve months, from August 2001 to August 2002. Most participants were obtained through the cooperation of a major medical center that allowed me to announce the project during prenatal education classes. Others were obtained through contacts in the community, geared toward obtaining diversity in the pool of research participants.

Participants lived across the St. Louis area, with a relative spatial concentration in the western suburbs along the I-270 corridor. Fewer than 20 percent lived in St. Louis City. They ranged in age from eighteen to thirty-seven and were, on the whole, well-educated. Of the seventy-nine, seventy-two had at least some college experience, fifty-six had at least a bachelor's degree, and twenty-one had an advanced degree (M.S.W., M.B.A., Ph.D., M.D., etc.). Since several were in school, this measure probably underestimates the predominance of the upper middle class among this group. Thirteen participants initially identified their race or ethnicity as some racial or ethnic minority (Puerto Rican, [Asian] Indian, African American, etc.), but this may be underestimated also, since during the interviews a few spoke of their mixed heritage. One man initially reported that he was white, but in the interview spoke of his relationship with his father being affected by his father being Filipino. Fifty-three of the seventy-nine reported affiliation with Christianity or a Christian denomination, while the rest reported an affiliation with another faith group or none at all. However, oral histories revealed religiosity as being quite fluid. Finally, of the forty-two couples represented, only two were cohabitating rather than married.

All were in heterosexual couples pregnant with their first child when they consented to join the study. They were informed that the purpose of the study is to investigate what it means to be a good father, and that this would be done by gathering stories. (See MacIntyre 1984 for the importance of narrative in defining the self.) All interviews were recorded and transcribed with the intent of preserving the integrity and flow of the stories told. When possible — such as when narrators mentioned places in the St. Louis area that were publicly accessible — I would visit the places mentioned in the stories to obtain for myself an approximate, visual image of what they described.

I selected out the narrative contexts (seventy-three cases) of every instance in which the narrators used the term "place" or "places," referring to something physical or geographic. I recognize that this implies setting aside particular places from analysis when they are not expressly designated as a "place." However, the purpose of this chapter is to tackle the prior task of what "place" is to begin with in relation to fatherhood, after which given places may be considered. These cases were then coded and analyzed for the narrator's intuitive understanding of the relationship between fatherhood and place. Open coding was used to discover the intuitive spatial structures of fatherhood (vertical and horizontal), while axial coding identified the levels and characteristics of each spatial axis, along with the mechanisms by which narrators appeal to space (Strauss and Corbin 1998). (For more information on this project's epistemology and method, see Goodsell 2004.)

FINDINGS

The narrators constructed space pertaining to fatherhood as multiple and embedded; that is, space is organized horizontally and vertically (terms I have chosen to describe the perspective). To illustrate the embeddedness (vertical organization) of space, let me take the example of the home of Kyle and Kaitlyn, a couple I interviewed. We spoke in their living room, which was decorated with items harking back to nineteenth-century St. Louis. Instead of a coffee table, a crate sat on the floor in front of the sofa. On it was some literature and an antique barn lantern. On the wall was a print of a map made during the 1830s of the Mississippi riverbed in front of the port of St. Louis. The original map was made in preparation for an Army Corps of Engineers project to keep the main flow of the river from shifting to the Illinois side—thereby retaining St. Louis as a key river port. In spite of the antique décor of the living room, the house as a whole was functional with the amenities of a twentieth-century middle-class home.

As we talked, I learned that Kyle and Kaitlyn's home is unique among homes in the neighborhood. It was the first home built in the neighborhood (the original part dating from the late nineteenth century), and was constructed as a farmhouse from which a family worked on the land that is now occupied by a modest residential neighborhood. The neighborhood, in turn, was located in a middle-suburban position in the St. Louis metropolitan area—neither experiencing the wealth and growth of the more outlying suburbs nor suffering the crime and decay of the inner city. Its single-family homes were well spaced but also small and boxy, contributing to the sense that this is a suburban location that is middle-class but timeworn.

Meanwhile, at the time of this research (2001–2002), the metropolitan area as a whole was reflecting on its histories and heritage. In many historical commemorations and anniversaries, there was much discussion of St. Louis's place in history. And when a young couple anticipating their own impending parenthood decorate their home with symbols of the regional past, they are drawing from rich and multiple meanings of place that are found in several levels of spatial aggregation. The place in which we met was their living room, their home, their neighborhood, their suburb, and their metropolitan area—all at once.

I am not the first to propose the significance of embedded communities to everyday social life. The idea draws on Aristotle's (2001) description of the *polis* and on embedded community models proposed by members of the first Chicago School (e.g., Park, Burgess, and McKenzie 1967; Shaw 1966; Zorbaugh 1976), and is used in some more recent studies, such as Erikson's (1976) analysis of Appalachian culture. Likewise, Redfield (1955) argues that we need to think of space not merely in terms of "community" but in terms of "levels" and "interpenetration." Like Lefebvre's (1991) later argument, Redfield was observing that it is too common to treat space as a neutral abstraction—a background—as neither having a structure nor being a social fact that interacts with human consciousness. Often the embeddedness of space is left implicit, as places are assumed uncritically as uniform entities—at least within the boundaries of the project—and either analyzed as a simple context or contrasted across two or more different but comparable contexts (horizontal spatial organization). Thus to study fatherhood in one home in contrast to fatherhood in another home in the neighborhood or to study fatherhood in one city in contrast to fatherhood in another city (horizontal comparisons) is to further our understanding of the importance of *place* in fatherhood. However, to understand the ways that space is also organized vertically adds a critical dimension to our discussion, as the structure of space in which places are found likewise provides cultural resources with which agents may construct, perform, or challenge received meanings.

To move through a social world is to move, horizontally and vertically, through a world of embedded communities. To construct meaning in a social world is to draw on knowledge that resides in various spatial components of these socially constructed communities. Communities in contemporary America are becoming increasingly fragmented (Bauman 1992; Delanty 2003), but in the course of so doing, they are providing more sites of cultural resources from which individuals may construct meaning.

Vertical Spatial Organization

Narrators not only recognized that their social worlds are composed of larger and smaller spatial aggregates, but they connected those aggregates with a moral hierarchy. (By "moral" I simply mean that which refers to an understanding of what "ought" to be done and not to any absolute standard of good and bad.) This would be important for how they used the vertical organization of space in their discussions of fatherhood. However, the moral hierarchy of space does not mean that any one spatial referent was better than another. True, assumptions about what "the world" is like can hardly be questioned, but involvement in the small and mundane "everyday" is also unquestionably valuable. Instead, by "moral hierarchy" I mean that each spatial level provides leverage for the understanding of other levels and for action in other levels.

For example, the belief that "the world" is threatening or at least in need of improvement is a motif that can be maintained in part because it is sustained at such a large spatial referent. Women sometimes spoke of the world as being generally dangerous (sometimes with specific reference to the events of September 11, 2001), and added that they have reservations about bringing a child into this kind of world. Men were likely to be more specific, saying that the world is anti-Muslim or anti-Semitic, for example. In either case, it was common for men and women to speak of their hope that having a child would contribute to the betterment of the world. Their belief in the nature of the world did not have to be validated in everyday interaction; a few striking cases (like the events of 9/11) were sufficient to build the impression in these men and women.

Further, change at one spatial level can be justified by an appeal to another spatial level. As an example of this, Robert and Chloe's move from California to Missouri could be interpreted as a radical break with their past in search of some different lifestyle, or one could appeal—as they did—to moral authority of larger American culture, one element of which indicates that parents should scale back their own material success, if necessary, in the interests of their children. Robert explained that once his son is born, he wanted either him or his wife to be home when their child was home, and neither could see that happening in the context of California's high cost of living.

Moral justification can also be done by moving down the vertical spatial hierarchy. This is commonly done by narrators who speak of the home as a place of safety, privacy, or control. Alexander said that he and his wife belonged to rival gangs when they lived in New York. "We seen a lot of bad things. We've done a lot of bad things," he told me. "We just don't want our kid in that place." Then he admitted that he would not be able to control a lot of what his son does ("I can't say nothing"), unless he tries smoking or taking drugs at home:

> I mean, if it gets to the point where he's smoking in the house, and we're not doing it, then I'll have some problems. I'll be right there. If we start, then he can smoke in the house, but until then, back yard, front yard, friend's house. And if he starts taking drugs, I'm going to flush it down the toilet.

For Alexander and several others, home was a place he had the right to defend against unwanted encroachments. If he does not want smoking in the house, then his child will have to smoke elsewhere, such as someone else's house. And if the child takes drugs, Alexander will put them "down the toilet"—a disdainful way of removing them from his house.

I have argued that narrators speaking about fatherhood organize their social worlds in vertical spatial hierarchies. This vertical spatial organization carries moral ramifications. Narrators were able to use this recognition of the various meanings of place to justify decisions and evaluations relevant to their notions of what it means to be a good father. I will next consider what fatherhood means at three levels of spatial aggregation. I call these three levels immediate place, intermediate place, and imagined place. These are fundamental, spatial categories that men and women use when talking about the meaning of fatherhood.

Immediate Place

Immediate places are the places of the everyday, and discussion about the multiple meanings of place frequently occurs here. As I have been arguing, however, the meaning of place relevant to fatherhood has to do with much more than with just what is immediate. Other levels of place are also important, and different

levels of place interact with each other in the subjectivity of the people who occupy those places. Nevertheless, discussion of immediate place and fatherhood
is still warranted. Immediate places tend to carry a certain set of meanings that
correspond to certain understandings of fatherhood. Those meanings tend to center on the safety, security, and confidence that should be found there, and hence
we see negative fatherly evaluations when they are not.

Of course, there is a certain irony in calling them places of the everyday. A
ballpark can be an everyday place in which to produce various types of fatherhoods (see Connell 1995 on multiple meanings of masculinity), or it can
be more distant—a place to which one goes to perform a more narrow definition of fatherhood. Some narrators spoke of ballparks as immediate places,
while others spoke of them as intermediate places. Place and fatherhood can
interact not just across levels but also within a given level; the more multi-
purpose and the more common a particular place is, the greater the diversity
of fatherhoods that can be constructed inside it. Thus the nature of a place can
facilitate or constrain the performance of different types of fatherhoods. The
ordinary perspectives of the people who occupy it determines what type of
place a given place is.

The preeminent immediate place to which narrators appealed in the context
of fatherhood is the home. Cities or neighborhoods can also be spoken of as
immediate places, but there are a variety of places in which everyday life is
lived that are not fully intermediate in the sense of vacation places or business trips, but still involve some "going out." These places include schools,
stores, and offices. Located at the border between immediate and intermediate, they become places in which the performance of fatherhood is at risk in
the eyes of the children; when fathers assert control and security in these
places, narrators spoke of those fathers particularly well.

The first way in which narrators spoke of place and fatherhood was specifically in terms of the home, the common expression being "a place." A few
narrators did not yet have homes, and spoke of the home as a key place for
raising children. One example comes from Sarah, a teenage mother-to-be
with an unemployed husband, who went back and forth between saying that
the most important thing is that a father is involved, and saying that a father
needs to earn money. When I asked her to clarify, she said,

> You can't have a nice place for kids to grow up in if you can't afford it. You
> can't watch your kids grow up in somebody else's apartment. The kid's not go-
> ing to have a home. You keep moving around because you can't afford the
> rent. That's no way to raise kids—the way I was raised. You can't just keep
> hopping the kid around. They don't get friends. They move from school to
> school. Basically that's not healthy for kids. You have to be able to financially
> support a child.

Having a home, an adequate home, provides a place in which and out of which other fatherly activities can occur. Providing a home, an immediate place, is itself an element of good parenthood. Thus when Sarah said, "I'm living with my aunt because I can't afford to get a place right now and buy all the stuff for the baby," or when William told of how he and a friend "always talked about moving out and getting a place together and just becoming independent," or when Isabella spoke of how her father protected her in the bad neighborhood in which was located "the first place [she] had rented out of college," all of them were referring to the strong sense that obtaining a home, a place of one's own, is a basic step toward adulthood and a prerequisite for good parenthood.

The home as a place is imbued with meanings of security, safety, and control. Ryan illustrated this when he spoke of the type of home his parents had created while he was a teenager, a home that he hoped to replicate when he became a father. His parents' "place" was a place where they exercised control to assure the safety of the kids who came there:

> As my brother and I got older, my friends tended to congregate more at our house than at other people's houses. . . . My folks didn't care if people spent the night. Even as we started, after high school, going into college—we were drinking age. My mom would stand at the door and people would drop their keys in a little bucket and they would go upstairs and go to sleep and everybody would just have to spend the night at our place. . . . That's kind of how my parents raised me. They laid down the guidelines loosely, and also showed us the possible consequences of our actions, and allowed us to make our own choices for the most part, socially and I guess academically and athletically.

In a similar vein, Samuel told me that Christians have to raise their children "in a void," and that his goal as a father would be to make home into a place of safety and goodness.

The narrators recognized that home as a place has several meanings. We have already seen the example of Robert and Chloe, who moved from California to Missouri to obtain what they perceived to be a more family-friendly lifestyle. Looking back on what it was like to raise children in wealthy suburban neighborhoods, Robert said,

> I think parents get their kids way too involved in extracurricular activities. They're overwhelmed. Like I said, the endless summer schools, but also multiple sports. Some of my nieces and nephews are in more than one sport at a time, plus Brownies and Cub Scouts and all the other stuff. Home is more like a hotel than it was a home base. It's a place you go to to sleep for most families and it's not a place that you hang out all day on Saturday. You always have this soccer game or that dance recital. Which is good, but I think it can rule your life if you have too many things going on.

For Robert, pressures from outside the home greatly changed the nature of the home itself: a hotel, not a home base; a place to sleep, not a place to spend time. The only way that he believed that he could make his home the type of place he wanted it to be, was by locating his home in an environment where a certain constellation of meanings would be attached to home life. For Robert and his wife, St. Louis represented that type of environment.

Narrators spoke of many other types of everyday places, and in those cases, the interpretation of place and fatherhood becomes more varied. In some cases, narrators spoke positively of living in the "same place" (city, neighborhood, or house) for a period of time (usually one's entire life is suggested). Matthew and Alexis (who are not spouses) each spoke of their respective hometowns—among other larger-scale aggregates—in this fashion, and in each case they were emphasizing a key element of continuity in their respective upbringings. Everyday activities happened in the same physical context year after year. Interestingly, both Matthew and Alexis each experienced familial disruption, too—Matthew's father passing away when he was seventeen, and Alexis's parents getting divorced. In cases such as these, place at a larger scale than the home is appealed to in the situation of life inside the home becoming unstable—an example of the leverage obtained by the vertical organization of space. As an example, Matthew could accept his father's death without losing faith in the importance of family as an institution. His own family may have suffered disruption, but good families are still needed in "the world"—the ultimate appeal up the vertical axis. He said,

> I think that's what the world lacks, is good families. That causes a lot of social problems, and a lot of social problems can also be overcome with good families.

Such strategies allowed narrators to be more optimistic about family in general and fatherhood in particular than might otherwise have been the case.

Many other sites are also spoken of as places, though they are not in the same category as fully intermediate places—going to them is not a "special" experience, requires no particular planning, happens frequently, and occupies much less time than vacations or business trips do. Still, they often contain much of the same ambivalence of places more easily categorized as intermediate. Ryan said that the private Midwestern university where he chose to go to school is "not a cheap place," but that his father sensed how much he wanted to go there and helped him find a way to attend. Jason got to spend more time with his father when his father was laid off during the 1970s. While he said the time spent with his father was nice, it was also frustrating for his father. He recalled going with his father to "the unemployment place." As a child, he thought it was "strange" to see everyone standing in lines and could

feel that "something wasn't right." In these and other cases, fathers were going with their children to a variety of places on trips of short duration. These
places came to be associated with the father exhibiting his skill or lack thereof
in navigating public settings. To the extent that the father's performance and
the general outcome were successful, as in Ryan's case, the result is holding
the father in greater esteem. In other cases, such as Jason's, the father's very
involvement in the place was problematic, and Jason could only acknowledge
the benefit of simply spending more time with his father. Thus as immediate
places blend into intermediate places, we see greater risk on the part of the fathers and others who cross the boundaries between them. The meaning of immediate space for good fatherhood is security.

Intermediate Place

Some places important to fatherhood are not places of the everyday. They are
partially places of direct (immediate) experience and partially places of pure
imagination. Narrators told of episodic excursions into these intermediate
places and connect them with good fatherhood, but in a way that is as problematic and contradictory as is the hybrid nature of the places themselves. Intermediate places are idealized, and often as good. They are an escape, a contrast, to the drudgery of the everyday. They are fun and relaxing, but they are
only places that you go to and not places that you live in. On the other hand,
by their very nature as intermediate places, they are not easily accessible.
When one's father lives at some distance, for example, visiting him may be a
treat, but it is in part the rarity of it that makes it a treat. Moreover, to load intermediate places with images of enjoyment, cooperation, and emotional
closeness potentially risks—or at least suggests—lack of the same in the immediate places in which narrators spend the great majority of their time. I will
discuss vacations as a key example of intermediate places, but other examples
could also be used, such as the relation between parental visits or business
trips and fatherhood.

Vacations are perhaps the most common example narrators gave of these
intermediate places of fatherhood. They commonly used the word "fun" to describe their memories of "going places" with their own fathers. Kevin, for example, spoke of one former boss in a typically blunt way: "There couldn't
have been a worse boss, but he was a really great person." What made that
boss so great as a person—at least in Kevin's eyes—was how he treated his
children. He continued,

> He had a lot of fun with his kids. He would do things like, he would take them
> camping by himself. They would go out someplace and get a hotel. He would
> go out with dinner with his kids. . . . He had a lot of fun with his kids. So I think

that's something I want to experience. . . . That's something I want with our son. . . . I want to have fun with our kids. I want the responsibility and security thing, but I want to have a lot of fun with my kids.

Distant places like rural campgrounds and entertainment centers in Florida become constructed as places where the traditional norms structuring parent–child relationships are loosened, where fathers and children can speak as equals and enjoy the same activities. Victoria told of when her family went on vacation to Florida and were waiting in a parking lot of a movie theater when she was practicing her cheers but "just couldn't seem to get the toe touch":

> And he was like, "What's a toe touch? You mean this?" And he just jumps up so high with his legs in the air. . . . I've never seen a man do that. It looked like he was like ten feet off the ground. . . . He looked like a little stuffed teddy bear doing the toe touch. . . . Me and my mom thought that was the funniest thing in the whole world.

Trips such as these provide episodic verification that different norms and structures do exist. Because they are episodic, they are easy to idealize; since one's experience in them is only short term, it is easy to maintain a certain façade while there. Still, for many narrators, their memories of these places were the primary repositories of positive memories of their fathers.

Sometimes these memories of intermediate places provide such a contrast with the everyday that a comparison of them with immediate places ends in a bittersweet tone. Daniel said that his father, a skilled blue-collar auto worker, worked evening shifts: "He was a nonfactor during the week." Since Daniel and his father would not see each other for days at a time, his father communicated with him by leaving Daniel a note each day pointing out something Daniel had done wrong that day. Daniel resignedly called that "a tough part of growing up . . . when I did get communication from him, they were negative." And yet, almost in the same breath, Daniel told of how important it was to his father for the family "to go places and have a good time." He went right in to talking about one day when they caught a bunch of blue gills in a pond at his grandparents' farm in central Michigan (a long day's drive from their home in St. Louis) and "later had them for dinner. I'll always remember that," he concluded. Likewise, Daniel spoke enthusiastically about the "quality time" he had with his father when the family rented a camper and enjoyed Upper Peninsula's sand dunes. "We just had a blast together. Just being together." These distant places were a reprieve from the drudgery and disappointments of the everyday, but in being such a reprieve, they betray a painful ambivalence about the father. In Daniel's narrative, the places with all of their accoutrements correlate with two radically different images he had of his father.

Perhaps it is the irony contained in this everyday understanding of the relationship between fatherhood and place that occasionally led a narrator to suggest that places should not be so rigidly correlated with particular meanings of fatherhood. As Alyssa said of her father,

> He's fun in the sense that he's goofy. He kind of tries to crack jokes to make you smile. It's not like he goes really far out of his way to take you someplace that's a lot of fun, like taking you to Six Flags [amusement park] or something. He just makes little things enjoyable.

Of course, that one must argue in favor of reducing the difference between everyday and special places, suggests that there are problems with fatherhood in one of those places. In Alyssa's case, the problem is that home (immediate place) should be just as "fun" as a vacation spot (intermediate place)—but often is not.

Imagined Place

One of the basic spatial categories of place that defines fatherhood is place that only exists on such a scale that it can only be imagined. I call it an imagined place because it is understood not to be experienced directly. (I acknowledge, though, that any interpretation of the social world requires at least some imagination.) For the men and women who participated in this study, the expression they typically used to apply to imagined place is "the world." The planet Earth is not typically intended as the referent, although it comes closest to the social significance of the term. It is asserted to be universal of human experience. No matter where one goes, certain characteristics will apply.

Narrators generally saw the world in which men are fathers as something threatening, and sometimes expressed the hope that either by their having a child or by what the child will do, the world will be made better. Sometimes the characterization of the world as a dangerous place was explicit, as when Brandon spoke of what he expects to do as a father as in direct response to the nature of the world:

> I still think the world is a very anti-Semitic place. . . . And I think it's important to arm my child with that knowledge rather than with a gun—arm my child with the knowledge of how to speak the native tongue if he or she wants to go over there and participate in a meaningful way in the living history of the Jewish people.

Dylan likewise asserted that when he and his wife had children and raised them well, they would be contributing to the improvement of the world by

sending into it "good people," which he later defined as including the quali-
ties of being educated and self-disciplined.

> I see a lot of people that I don't think are qualified to have kids, but maybe are
> going to have kids and maybe just ignore them. Those kids don't have a very
> good chance to become good people. . . . We do see a lot of kids that aren't be-
> ing raised correctly or what we don't think is correctly—what we think is going
> to make the world not a better place. And we want to do something.

Imagined places tend to provide the justification for the entire fatherly enterprise. The nature of the world is an assumption from which narrators discuss the meaning of fatherhood. To be a good father is to be aware of current
problems and trends in society, and to act appropriately in response.

Horizontal Spatial Organization

Moving horizontally within a single level of spatial organization is a common
experience. It includes going from one room to another within the same
house, going from one house to another within the same city, or moving from
one part of the country to another. One can justify such a change by appealing to a reality residing at a higher or lower spatial level. We have seen one
example of that in Robert and Chloe's move from California to Missouri to
attain what they believed was an ideal, American, middle-class family life.

To go through everyday life is to move through a social world that is organized both horizontally and vertically. However, movement is not the only
way in which having horizontal spatial organization is relevant. The meaning
of immediate place varies according to the higher spatial levels in which it is
embedded. That can be seen in Robert's realization that regardless of what he
does as a father in his own home, the neighborhood, school district, and local
economy are going to place constraints on his behavior as a father that make
his chosen model of fatherhood inadvisable in California. Thus Robert and
Chloe believed that while a particular lifestyle—spending long hours at work,
driving long commutes, and keeping their children in day care and summer
camps—would be normal and expected in one neighborhood or regional context (if only in a resigned fashion by some parents), the same behavior on the
micro scale would carry very different meaning if exhibited in a different region.

The justification of horizontal movement is not always decided so consciously as in the case of Robert and Chloe. Take, for example, William. He
was raised partially in the home of his father and his stepmother, and partially
in the home of his mother and his stepfather. His movement between them
was rather haphazard and fraught with tension, as he spoke of himself as hav-

ing been a troubled youth. In retrospect, though, he said that in his mother and stepfather's home he learned about religion, and in his father and step-mother's home he learned about hard work and freedom. William concluded that he would try to provide both for his own child. In the end William could construct a narrative of how his horizontal movement between the two homes of his families of origin helped him appreciate different aspects of the larger society—aspects that can constitute an integrated whole. And that is what he wanted to present once he becomes a father himself. This story was remark-able in that narrators almost always evaluated horizontal moves because of family breakup as negative experiences. William's optimism may have re-sulted from his social connections that helped him integrate his assessment of his life history.

Many stories center on a family moving from place to place because of a father's employment. This is typically taken as a stressor, contrasting with the father's duty to contribute stability to his family. In this context, the changing place constitutes a challenge to fatherly roles. This challenge can be answered in several ways. For example, Joshua's family moved to California when he was twelve so that his father, a physician, could take a position at the medical school at which he had earned his degree. His father was absent from home fifteen hours a day, which his family concluded was unacceptable. Conse-quently Joshua's father found a new job in Arizona that placed fewer de-mands on his time and allowed him to be with his family more. Joshua's fam-ily felt the interstate moves were justified in the context of an ongoing search to find the best way for his father to both provide for his family and be in-volved in the home. As long as each move was an improvement in one of those areas, and the long-term result was considered an acceptable balance, the movements from place to place could, in the end, be justified.

In military families such horizontal movement is sometimes dispassion-ately cataloged rather than considered and justified. It is taken for granted that families move, and they move often. Nicholas's father was in the air force, and he quickly listed their moves from place to place and around the world—as near as Nebraska and as far away as Japan—as if there were not much to say about them. However, he went on to comment on the contrasting stabil-ity inside of his family.

> I did a lot of things I'm sure that hurt him, and stuff like that. He never kicked me out of the house or anything. I believe he still loved me enough to keep me around. And eventually I straightened up on my own, kind of. I did hear that people were telling him that he should kick me out, but he didn't. And I'm glad for that 'cause if he did, I might not've straightened up because I'd've probably moved out with somebody that would've still been a bad influence on me. So that worked out. That worked out good.

Nicholas's narrative may present an argument against the tyranny of place, or it may affirm the centrality of place. On the one hand, Nicholas presented his father as single-minded and consistent. Perhaps that has something to do with pressure in military communities to maintain cohesive families even under circumstances of high stress. If the spatial context changes so frequently, there is little time for any one place to leave a social impact or fatherhood develops into a unique style—fatherhood under conditions of constantly changing place. On the other hand, Nicholas's family's moves from place to place were an essential introduction to the rest of his oral history. One can respect his father's parenting even more when one realizes how much—to Nicholas—his social context seemed confusing and fluid.

CONCLUSION

In this chapter I have argued that space is a meaningful problematic in relation to fatherhood. The place in which a man is a father is a resource for his fatherhood, but places have relevant structures of their own. Men and women who are just becoming parents recognize various levels of spatial aggregation as resources from which they can draw cultural symbols and justification of meanings and actions. I showed how three spatial levels, which I called immediate place, intermediate place, and imagined place, each carry implications for the concept of fatherhood. Each of them influences a notion of fatherhood that implies security, confidence, control, and stability. These levels interact with each other, such that the existence of multiple levels gives narrators "moral leverage" to advocate or justify a particular concept of good fatherhood even in the face of change in a given spatial unit.

FUTURE RESEARCH

Researchers have not explained well the relationship between spatial structure and specific social phenomena such as fatherhood. Much of this volume addresses fatherhood in various, specific places. My purpose was to problematize space itself, in relationship to fatherhood. The way that I did that was by considering how men and women meaningfully structure place when they talk about what it means to be a good father. Since I attempted to open up the discussion of "levels" and the "interpenetration" of space with regard to fatherhood, there is still much that could be done to address this aspect of space. I suggest four major areas for further investigation. First, future research might consider the class basis of hierarchical perceptions of space and fatherhood. Most of the men and women I interviewed were middle-class, and it is possible that their perception of the relationship between place and fatherhood is connected to the fact that in the contemporary United States, members of the middle class overwhelmingly tend to live in particularly embedded community contexts. It is unclear whether embedded relationships figure so prominently in the minds of men and women otherwise located geographically or socioeconomically.

Second, it is unclear whether the meaning of embedded spatiality changes over an individual's life course. All of the men and women whom I interviewed were just making the transition into parenthood, and it is certainly possible that concerns over security, control, and justification were heightened in this unsettled period of their lives. The meaning of different spatial layers, along with the mechanisms by which the layers interact with each other, may differ under circumstances of different cultural imperatives driven by the concerns of other stages of the life course.

Third, we may ask whether different orientations toward gender are linked to different orientations toward space. Such analyses would be relevant both across gender (for men versus for women) and within gender—in the latter case asking whether men who have different orientations toward gender construct space and fatherhood differently as a result of their stances toward masculinity.

Finally, I have raised the question of whether a "tyranny of place" can ever be overcome. That is an important question, because when researchers have spoken in terms of a universal concept of fathering, fathers, or fatherhood, they typically were not arguing against the importance of place, but only that for the sake of their respective studies, place was not *a priori* considered a relevant factor. This and the other chapters in this volume suggest that such is not the case. However, neither approach directly handles the question of whether place can be made to be irrelevant.

REFERENCES

Aristotle. (2001). *Politica* (B. Jowett, Trans.). In R. McKeon (Ed.), *The basic works of Aritotle* (pp. 1113–316). Introduction by C. D. C. Reeve. New York: Modern Library.

Bauman, Z. (1992). *Intimations of postmodernity*. London: Routledge.

Blankenhorn, D. (1995). *Fatherless America: Confronting our most urgent social problem*. New York: HarperPerennial.

Coltrane, S. (1996). *Family man: Fatherhood, housework, and gender equity*. New York: Oxford University Press.

Connell, R. W. (1995). *Masculinities*. Berkeley: University of California Press.

Delanty, G. (2003). *Community*. London: Routledge.

Dienhart, A. (1998). *Reshaping fatherhood: The social construction of shared parenting*. Thousand Oaks, CA: Sage.

Erikson, K. T. (1976). *Everything in its path: Destruction of community in the Buffalo Creek flood*. New York: Simon & Schuster.

Furstenburg, F. F., Jr. (1995). Fathering in the inner city: Paternal participation and public policy. In W. Marsiglio (Ed.), *Fatherhood: Contemporary theory, research, and social policy* (pp. 119–47). Thousand Oaks, CA: Sage.

Gerson, K. (1993). *No man's land: Men's changing commitments to family and work*. New York: Basic.

Glaser, B. G., and Strauss, A. L. (1999). *The discovery of grounded theory: Strategies for qualitative research*. New York: Aldine de Gruyter.

Goodsell, T. L. (2004). "My job will be . . .": New fathers and mothers reflect on fatherhood. Ph.D. diss. University of Michigan, Ann Arbor.

Griswold, R. L. (1993). *Fatherhood in America: A history*. New York: Basic.

Johansen, S. (2001). *Family men: Middle-class fatherhood in early industrializing America*. New York: Routledge.

Lefebvre, H. (1976). Reflections on the Politics of Space (M. J. Enders, Trans.). *Antipode: A Radical Journal of Geography, 8* (2), 30–37.

Lefebvre, H. (1991). *The production of space* (D. Nicholson-Smith, Trans.). Malden, MA: Blackwell.

Liebow, E. (1967). *Tally's corner: A study of Negro streetcorner men*. Foreword by Hylan Lewis. Boston: Little, Brown.

Lombard, A. S. (2003). *Making manhood: Growing up male in colonial New England*. Cambridge, MA: Harvard University Press.

MacIntyre, A. (1984). *After virtue: A study in moral theory* (2nd ed.). Notre Dame, IN: University of Notre Dame Press.

Mannheim, K. (1952). On the interpretation of *Weltanschauung*. In *Essays on the sociology of knowledge* (pp. 33–83). London: Routledge & Kegan Paul.

Marquis, C. (2003). The pressure of the past: network imprinting in intercorporate communities. *Administrative Science Quarterly, 48,* 655–89.

Park, R. E., Burgess, E. W., and McKenzie, R. D. (1967). *The city*. Introduction by M. Janowitz. The Heritage of Sociology. Series edited by M. Janowitz. Chicago: University of Chicago Press.

Ratcliff, R. E. (1980). Banks and corporate lending: An analysis of the impact of the internal structure of the capitalist class on the lending behavior of banks. *American Sociological Review, 45* (4), 553–70.

Ratcliff, R. E., Gallagher, M. E., and Ratcliff, K. S. (1979). The civic involvement of bankers: An analysis of the influence of economic power and social prominence in the command of civic policy positions. *Social Problems, 26* (3), 298–313.

Redfield, R. (1955). A community within communities. In *The little community: Viewpoints for the study of a human whole* (chapter 8, pp. 113–31). Chicago: University of Chicago Press.

Schutz, A. (1967). *The phenomenology of the social world* (G. Walsh and F. Lehnert, Trans.). Introduction by G. Walsh. Evanston, IL: Northwestern University Press.

Schutz, A. (1970). *On phenomenology and social relations: Selected writings*. Edited and with an introduction by H. R. Wagner. The Heritage of Sociology. Series edited by M. Janowitz. Chicago: University of Chicago Press.

Shaw, C. R. (1966). *The jack-roller: A delinquent boy's own story*. New introduction by H. S. Becker. Chicago: University of Chicago Press.

Strauss, A., and Corbin, J. (1998). *Basics of qualitative research: Techniques and procedures for developing grounded theory* (2nd ed.). Thousand Oaks, CA: Sage.

Swidler, A. (2001). *Talk of love: How culture matters*. Chicago: University of Chicago Press.

Townsend, N. W. (2002). *The package deal: Marriage, work, and fatherhood in men's lives*. Philadelphia: Temple University Press.

Zorbaugh, H. W. (1976). *The Gold Coast and the slum: A sociological study of Chicago's Near North Side*. Introduction by H. P. Chudacoff. Chicago: University of Chicago Press.

3

Fathers and the Navigation of Family Space and Time

Sarah M. Allen and Kerry Daly

Space and time serve as primary dimensions for delineating everyday family experience. "Home" serves as a spatial construct for understanding the way family members organize, manage, and negotiate the key coordinates of their place-based reality. "Schedules" and "family time" serve as the primary temporal constructs for examining the way family members navigate the demands of the clock for both individual and shared activities. Everyday participation in home and family schedules is part of identity work whereby individuals in families exhibit "territories of self" that show how they use time and space to manage existential boundaries in everyday life (Nippert-Eng 1996).

Although space is the organizing theme of this volume, our goal is to demonstrate the strong interconnections between space and time. As authors, we each started by looking at these dimensions separately (Daly on time, Allen on space). When we examined the patterns in our work, we realized that there were remarkable parallels in the way that women and men talk about their familial experience of space and time. As we explored these parallels, it became abundantly clear that time and space are fully confounded. As a result, we focus attention on how fathers navigate family space while attending to the way that time affects place-based activities and movements.

Even though women and men are joint participants in the construction and negotiation of the meaning of home and schedules, these are not gender neutral activities. Rooted in their different experiences and traditions as "mother" and "father," women and men have different definitions, exert different levels of control, and must contend with gendered cultural constraints in the way they construct their everyday experience of home and schedules. In this chapter, we focus on the experience of fathers, but we take this from data sets that examine the way that mothers and fathers actively construct time and space in their everyday lives.

To this end, we report on the combined results of two parallel ethnographic studies: a study by Allen that examined the way that highly mobile couples socially construct the meaning and experience of home (N = 24 couples); and a study by Daly that examined the social construction of time in dual-earner families (N = 17 couples). Both studies are based on semistructured, in-depth interviews that were carried out separately with primarily Caucasian mothers and fathers living in two-parent families with young children living at home. For both studies, the collection and analysis of data were based on the principles of grounded theory and constant comparative method (Glaser and Strauss 1967). The open-ended, discovery-oriented design provided the basis for analyzing how women and men subjectively experience space and time negotiations in the household. Focusing on the experience of fathers (with reference to how their experience was similar or different to that of mothers), we demonstrate the ways that fathers create and negotiate the meanings of space and time.

LITERATURE REVIEW

Time and space are fundamental to the very structure and possibility of the human experience. We are spatial beings grounded in a temporal order. Our lives are "place oriented" and "place saturated" (Casey 1993). "Where" we are not only provides the objective structure to our daily experience by directing, constraining, or enhancing our choices in activity, but also is fundamental to our subjective experience. Geographers have long pointed to the reciprocal relationship between the social and the spatial. Dear and Wolch (1989, 3–4) argue that "it is impossible to understand human society without accounting for its geographical underpinnings . . . [and] the way social life structures territory, and the way territory shapes social life." For example, space influences how the self will be presented, how the situation will be defined, and what aspects of the self will be made visible in different situations. One's identity is also shaped by the spaces one chooses to enact the self in, particularly one's choice of residence, work, and leisure. These spaces, in somewhat reciprocal fashion, also shape and are shaped by a developing sense of identity (Cuba and Hummon 1993; Feldman 1990; Korpela 1995; Lovell 1998; Proshansky, Fabian, and Kaminoff 1995; Rapoport 1985; Schutz 1967; Stone 1970).

Time, like space, has an absolute, objective, and structural form but is also deeply embedded in our subjectively situated experience. As such, time has been argued to be the "central organizing feature of family activities" (Presser 1989, 536), shaping the "pace, duration, value, and cadence" of family life (Daly 1996, 46). Because the meaning and experience of time and space are found in the interplay between the structural and the social components of everyday life, they are best understood when examined as a shared social construction process. For example, the creation of a home place is a meaningful process that emerges from everyday, habitual time-space routines, its meaning being shared, negotiated, and sustained in an intricate network of social relations (Bollonow 1967; Groat 1995; Hay 1998; Smith, Light, and Roberts 1998; Tuan 1977). Likewise, the meaning of time is shaped by the interplay between the subjective definition of the self and the objectively available cues that are present in the situation (Daly 1996). Thus the meaning and definitions of time and space are situated in a context (Stone 1981) and are shaped by key social demographic factors of the individual, such as age, gender, personality, and socioeconomic status (Allen 2003; Daly 1996). Accordingly, the doing of family life and the management of family identities involves the interplay between "pace" and "place" (Shaw 2001).

Because the social relations in which the meaning of time and space arise are full of subjective meaning and power, time and space have multiple and variegated meanings that are not gender neutral. Research findings highlight gender differences in men and women's feelings of entitlement to personal time, differences in the value they attach to public and private spaces, varying levels of commitment to work and family times and spaces, and competing spatial and temporal responsibilities (Allen 2003; Daly 1996). Words like power, privilege, expertise, disparity, control, entitlement, coordination, inequality, conflict, and management are ubiquitous in these literatures and suggest that gender is deeply implicated in the shaping of the experience of time and space.

SPACE STUDY: SAMPLE AND DESIGN ISSUES

The primary focus of my (Allen) study on family space was threefold: (1) to explore participants' ideas, definitions, and meanings for home; (2) to identify the place-making processes participants engaged in when creating new home spaces; and (3) to compare men and women's responsibilities in managing, negotiating, controlling, and creating home spaces. Interviews with participants were semistructured and consisted of open-ended questions designed to explore these three areas of inquiry. I began each interview by gathering some general demographic information and then invited participants to tell me about the different places they had lived in over their life, why they had moved, how long they had stayed in each place, and which family members accompanied each move. I then began asking questions that were related more specifically to the three research foci. Some examples of pertinent questions include: "How would you define home?" "What were some of the things you did when you first moved here to make this place feel more like home to you?" and "Do you think that you and your partner have different priorities or responsibilities when it comes to creating a new place called home?"

Participants were recruited for the study in four ways: through a community service that visits, welcomes, and provides community information to families who have recently moved to the area; through a nonprofit child care facility; through press and media advertising; and through snowballing. Only heterosexual couples who had moved to the area in the past five years from another place in Canada, were married, remarried, or cohabiting, and had at least one child under the age of five were included in the study.

Twenty-four couples (forty-eight individuals) participated in the study, with forty-four participants being white. On average, participants were thirty-seven years old and had two children (average age four and a half years); thirty-eight had completed a bachelor's degree, and they had a family income ranging between Can$75,000 and 90,000. Couples had been married (twenty-three couples) or cohabiting (one couple) for an average of nine years and had made, on average, three and a half moves during that period, meaning they had been moving approximately every two and a half years. The average amount of time in their new area was two years and the average distance of the most recent move was 916 kilometers. All of the men in the sample were employed full time and the majority of them, seventeen, were commuting to another city for work. In contrast, only twelve of the women were employed, and of that subset, only three commuted outside the city limits to work and eight were employed part-time.

TIME STUDY: SAMPLE AND DESIGN ISSUES

All interviews consisted of open-ended questions that were directed at the general topic of time as experienced in families. We began with loosely structured questions based on key themes such as the meaning of family time, differences between men and women with regard to experiences of time, negotiation over time, and pace of life. Each interview addressed the range of themes but was flexible and open, to permit the participants to raise and focus on the issues that were of central importance to them.

We recruited seventeen heterosexual dual-earner couples with at least one child through a nonprofit child care facility. Although this was located at the university, it also served the community. Eight of the dual-earner families in this sample were two-child families, six had one child and the remaining three couples had three children. The average length of marriage for this sample was 11.8 years, with a span of 5 to 24 years. The average age of the participating males was 37.3 years and for females, 35.8 years. Nine of the females and eight of the males had graduate degrees. One participant was a full-time graduate student. The women worked an average of forty-two hours a week, while men reported an average of fifty-one hours a week. Eleven couples reported combined incomes ranging between Can$50,000 and 100,000, four fell into the higher range of Can$100,000 to 150,000, and two reported a lower range, which was less than Can$50,000.

FINDINGS

In this analysis, we report on the ways that perceptions of space and time by fathers provide insight into the symbolic and ideological meanings of home and family, the organization of family activities, identities and responsibilities, and the dynamics of power and control in gender relationships. We also explore the ways that the separate concepts of space and time operate at an experiential level in interconnected ways. For example, one's experience and expectations for family spaces are carried through time (bringing past experiences of home forward)—and over space (accompanying moves from one location to another), thus continually acting to shape and inform the day to day ways individuals evaluate the adequacy of their current space in meeting the social, psychological, emotional, and physical needs of self and family.

Idealizations of Family through the Lens of Space and Time

The temporal and spatial dimensions of family experience are laden with social, psychological, and ideological meanings. One of the most central dialectical tensions embedded in family time and space is the pull between the real and the ideal. The symbolic ideology of home, as shaped by values, norms, and expectations, is carried through time and space in continual struggle with the mundane, place-based, temporal reality of day-to-day family living. Although both mothers and fathers straddled this tension, fathers offered a unique perspective on the meaning of home and family through their discussions of family space and time.

Men defined home as a place that was "safe," "comfortable," "predictable," "familiar," and "stable," a place where family members could feel "happy," "relaxed," "accepted," and "grounded." These expectations for family spaces influenced the strategies men chose when trying to create a place called home. For example, Jared observed, "If you grew up in a stable, loving home and you were happy to go home then I think when you get older you say, oh I would like to try and do that, so you copy it." It wasn't until Jared was "older" that trying to replicate the "stable, loving home" he grew up in became a concern. This later recognition of an increased importance in the spatial environment was not unusual for men. Deeper psychological investments in family spaces often coincided with a corollary shift in roles and identity when men became fathers. For example, Scott, a thirty-eight-year-old high school teacher with two young children said,

> I don't think I really had ideas of home until we developed a family; that's kind of selfish in a sense, but basically you are selfish throughout your teens and your twenties for the most part . . . you're just trying to develop your identity. . . . So when you get older and develop and you are at that point in your life where you are changing who you are and what you are becoming and you are developing closer relationships with your partner and you develop children and so on, then the whole mind set changes and then you start to consider these ideas of home more so I think.

Thus family spaces become, as Ryan said, "more important when you have kids, you become more aware of it." As such, men expressed an increased investment in their immediate spatial environment when they became fathers. For example, Tom, a thirty-three-year-old client director with one young child, said, "I think that as soon as you have kids it probably hits you right in between the eyes as to what the implications of the home are, or not. . . . As family comes then there is more implications to creating a better home environment type of thing."

In the same way that fathers were investing themselves in the creation of a home space for their children, they were also responding to the unspoken imperative that they invest themselves in the creation of family time for their children. For some fathers this investment in family time was fuelled by fears of being seen like their own fathers who they perceived as not being devoted to family time, while for others, it was pushed along by the strong desire to provide their children with "a nice happy childhood . . . and good memories." For many of these fathers, family time was expressed as an idealization that was foundational to their cohesiveness as a family. When I (Daly) asked Alex what he valued most about family time, he responded by emphasizing the importance of both temporal and spatial cohesion:

> I think that keeping things glued together, keeping us together as a family. You know, it's easy to kind of get off doing your own thing and so what I value is,

it's a chance to regroup, get everybody together, have fun together, stick together; it sort of keeps you together.

Approaching Ideals: Fathers Taking Responsibility for Their Spatial and Temporal Environment

Not only did the presence of children bring the importance of "creating a better home environment" and the "importance of family time" to the fore of men's *awareness,* but it also increased men's feelings of *responsibility* to create an ideal spatial and temporal environment for their family. For example, Matt, a thirty-five-year-old data network analyst with two young children, talked about how he had changed developmentally and increasingly felt the "importance of building a place":

> When you are growing as a child, probably you have some responsibilities but not as much so really you don't take care of that home, but then as we grow and mature, now you are more responsible for building that house. You are building it, somebody else is not building it for you . . . you are building a place. Your home becomes a place that is more, a sacred place and that comes with a responsibility as well.

This sense of increased responsibility for home spaces was central to their father identity. Taking responsibility for the creation of a secure space was of utmost importance to their children and therefore a critical dimension of their fathering work. Austin, a forty-four-year-old health care professional with three children, articulated this well when he said,

> I feel a responsibility to the kids to have somewhere they look forward to coming and they are comfortable and what not and that they feel safe. . . . I really think that it's when they drive in the driveway and there is that sigh of relief that they can come in and put their feet up and be themselves. . . . I would like to create an environment here . . . that it just feels like it's a good familiar place to be and they feel welcome and there is good memories.

Fathers were acutely aware of their sense of responsibility to create optimal family times and spaces for their children. This striving for the ideal drove men's spatial and temporal choices. For example, continuity of family space and time were highly valued by many of these fathers. The presence of children was a strong influence on mobility decisions and often guided fathers' choices to stay in a place for a longer period of time. For example, Alan, a thirty-seven-year-old systems analyst with two children, said, "We're planning on staying here for a long time; . . . the primary reason is because we have kids and we want them to have a stable environment. . . . The kids have a school, they have friends here. This is where they want to stay." Other fathers talked about the "need to stay put" to "be fair to the kids" or not wanting to "uproot them" because "it's harder for [them] to adapt."

When families decided that it was in their best interests to move, men spent significant time looking for an optimal level of fit between their sense of responsibility to provide a "safe," "secure," and "stable" environment for their children and many of the structural components of their new space that would either enhance or mitigate their ability and opportunity to do so. When Will was looking for a new house, he was searching for an environment that would be "best for his family." He continued,

> Well, when you are choosing a place you've got to think about the security of your family, you've got to think about the quality of the schooling system and that sort of thing; those are important to me. . . . You don't want a bad school system where your kids come home bullied and everything like that. We also wanted a university close by; university towns are good towns by my estimation and also my little girl will be going there, you know, down the road; you've got to think that far ahead when you're . . . um . . . nine years from now. . . . I checked the crime rates, called the urban planning department, checked the land zoning and stuff . . . so you really have got to do your homework, what's best for your family.

This quotation suggests that many of the less visible dimensions of father involvement, such as worrying about your son being bullied at school or planning for your daughter's future education had a spatial component to them that men were interested in controlling. By choosing to invest in certain kinds of spaces, fathers were also hoping to enable certain types of social processes and experiences for their children. Therefore, matters like proximity to schools, quality of neighborhood, presence of other children, a big lot for the kids to play on, and the safety of the streets, were some of the important things men told me they were looking for in a new space before they chose to financially, socially, and psychologically invest in that space as a home place to raise their children. Aaron, a thirty-nine-year-old marketer and father of one young child, elaborated, "Number one importance, as far as I am concerned, is moving into a place that the family can be comfortable with; I will put high priority on that over anything else."

As these analyses indicate, fathers in both studies were acutely aware of the importance of creating secure home spaces and engaged family time for the well being of their families. They were also acutely aware of their paternal responsibilities to manage time and space in order to create, as Ryan said, "a good stable, healthy, happy environment" for their kids. These were important ideals that drove men's spatial and temporal choices. Against the backdrop of these underlying beliefs and values, fathers engaged in a number of practices that at times brought them closer to the realization of these ideals and at other times kept them distant from them.

The Provision of Paternal Care: Temporal and Spatial Practices

The fathers in these studies undertook a number of activities that involved adjusting or modifying time and space in order to meet the needs of their children. Underlying these activities was a recognition that children's needs often controlled the decisions and activities that they made around the household. For example, when I (Daly) asked a general question about how they think about time and control in their family, Jamie indicated that "where kids are involved, they usually come first." Similarly, Fred responded that his daughter "is our control now." He went on to explain how the presence of his daughter shaped his movements in both time and space:

> It's no matter what you do, it's always in the back of your mind that, you know, she has to be taken care of. I mean, she's only a little girl, you know; you have to be home here for her when she gets off the bus she's in, you know. I don't want her to be a latch key kid or anything like that. I don't want her to come home and find there's nobody there, you know. Heaven forbid that should happen, whether it should happen to Cheryl or myself. She has to be picked up from day care. We know when she has to be picked up from day care and we know she has to be taken care of.

Fathers talked about the ways they sought to modify time and space at home by increasing safety for children and making changes that would enhance interactions with their children.

Increasing Safety for Children: Fathers as Protectors

Fathers invested copious amounts of time modifying the home environment to increase its health and safety. For example, Ken built a fence to keep his kids off of a busy street; Greg removed an old aluminium shed in his backyard because its sharp edges were becoming dangerous for his active toddler; Will installed a security system; and Liam had plans to "redo the back porch because it's all uneven and dangerous." Sam cared for his wife and children by building a home that was allergy free. Ironically, fathers often carried out the work of creating safety for their children by compromising their own safety. Many of the ways men modified and maintained their family spaces required using things like power tools, hammers, nails, chain saws, and other "high-risk" materials such as paint, paint strippers, and various adhesive glues. Whenever a risk of harm to spouse or child was perceived in the place modification process, men often asked them to leave the space until the task was complete. These were spatial modifications that required considerable time and effort and highlight some of the generative work fathers did in order to provide a safe environment for their children.

Although many of the ways that men modified their space to increase its safety were done in highly visible ways, some men also talked about creating a psychological space that was also safe for their children. Adam, a forty-one-year-old government employee and father of one child, told me (Allen) of the significance of turning off the lights and locking the doors each night in creating a safe place. He said,

I really like one of the last things I do in the evening is turning off the lights, . . . and there is a picture in the kitchen of our wedding symbol and that is the last light that I click off at night and the light at my dad's desk. . . . And those are all part of the rituals that is part of me and the house, and it's just usually me on my own in the house making those close down things and I feel safe with all those things and I go over and lock up the door to my "castle." We are safe, we are safe and we have felt from day one safe in our house.

In addition to the ways that fathers invested time in order to create safe spaces for their children, they spoke about their responsibilities to manage their work time and orchestrate their schedules so that they could ensure safe transitions for their children from day care and school. Fathers also talked about creating family time that was safe for children: strategies such as staying home, unplugging telephones, or staying in pajamas on a Saturday morning were identified as ways to put a protective fence around their family time and space. For working fathers, it was a way to strip away obligation and responsibility from the everyday routines of work schedules and spatial departures. Overall, this section illustrates the various ways men were assigned to, and took on, the protector role in their families. By utilizing various strategies to modify time and space, fathers were able to protect their children and secure the safety of their families.

Enable Father–Child Interaction

There were a number of examples of the way that time and space interfered with fathers' interactions with their children. For example, in both studies, fathers talked about how commuting stood out as both a spatial and temporal barrier to having more time with their children. Similarly, discussions of home renovations, while at one level perceived to be in the service of children, sometimes also took away direct interaction time with children.

Nevertheless, fathers demonstrated care for their children when they modified, or had plans to modify, either their time or their living space in order to increase father–child interactions. With respect to time, Kevin talked about how he might have worked until eight when things got busy, "but not anymore; . . . since we've had kids . . . home takes over."

Other fathers talked about ways of modifying space to enhance their time with their children. For example, Jacob had plans to build a skating rink behind the house the following winter so he could play hockey with his kids, and Brad had plans to "add a patio and a swing set for the kids [in the backyard] . . . making it with a sandbox . . . or a pool." Many fathers had already completed various projects. They told me (Allen) how they had built a tree house in their backyard, added a tire swing, built an outdoor climbing gym, or built a deck so they could have the spaces to spend more time outside with their kids and family. Likewise, Scott told me how he had intentionally left a large section of his backyard as grass, despite the fact that he was "not a big grass fan" just so that his kids would have plenty of room to "run around." Often the process of modifying the space was just as important as the finished product because it gave men opportunities to connect with their children as they worked along side them modifying the space. Although fathers often talked about including their children in activities that they as fathers were involved in, they also talked about being able to enter into their child's world. In the same way that Scott talked about not imposing anything on the yard space so that children could move freely in the large grassy spaces, Bob talked about how important it was for him as a father to not put too many encumbrances on time: "It's fun to kind of let time go lightly with children. So it's fun to have a bit of a second childhood and just goof around and chase each other down the hall and stuff like that."

In addition to modifying the space to improve its safety and health and to enable increased father–child interactions, men also demonstrated generativity when they modified their space in order to improve family functioning and maintain the rhythms of day-to-day family living. For example, men would talk about the process of setting up TVs, stereos, VCRs, washers, and their child's room when they moved into their new house so that their spatial environment could facilitate the daily routine to which they were accustomed.

Fathers also modified their spaces in order to provide a functional shelter for their family's day-to-day living. For example, men would talk about maintaining their home by fixing a leaking faucet, cleaning the eaves and gutters, replacing the shingles, fixing the air conditioner, installing a new roof, hooking up a new water softener, fixing the driveway, or replacing broken patio stones. Perhaps most fundamentally, maintaining the spatial environment was a way of caring for home and family because it provided a safe and functional shelter for them. There were times when men talked about this as involving a trade-off between spending time with their children and "doing stuff' around the house. When I asked Adrian whether he and his wife were different in their approach to the organization of time, he said, "She tends to be a little bit more focused on the kids than I am, and I tend to be doing stuff around the house a little more, or trying to. . . . She would be more willing to, um, to leave that stuff until after the kids are in bed."

Overall, the presence of children guided men's decisions about time and space. The concern about being flexible about their time and a sense of responsibility to provide optimal home spaces for their children guided men's decision-making processes when selecting or modifying the physical environments in which they enacted fathering. Men were neither passive occupants of home spaces nor passive recipients of mother-only homemaking. They were actively modifying family time and space in order to create a home place where they could enjoy family time with their children.

Identity Work in Space and Time

Although men and women were joint participants in socially constructing a place called home, it was not a gender-neutral activity. Many of the roles and responsibilities taken on in the creation of a home place or the orchestration of family time were situated in men and women's different experiences as mothers and fathers. One way this was done was by selecting different kinds of home and community spaces to enact their mothering and fathering roles. For example, as I (Allen) interviewed men about some of the strategies they employed to make a place feel more like home, I noticed a significant difference in spatial priorities between men and women. When I compared men's responses with the ones I received from women, I noticed that instead of women's lengthy descriptions as to what they had done to learn and engage with their new community, men's responses were often more descriptive of why they hadn't been able to do so as extensively as their wives. Men often told me that they didn't have the time to, didn't want to, or didn't feel the need to branch out in the community as extensively as their wives had. Consistent with these ideas, I (Daly) found that men tended to attribute these differences to the dominance of work in their lives and the limitations it presented for them in being more actively engaged both spatially and temporally in their community. David talked about his awareness of the difference:

> I guess what's right for us right now would be for me to have more time to spend at home to participate in things that my daughter does and try to even the balancing time in household responsibilities that my wife and I share and that, you know, currently she keeps a lot [more] of the household responsibilities afloat

than I do. And so she really covers for me on that end and accommodates the work demands that I have. . . . You know, my wife does a lot of the chauffeuring around of my daughter to, you know, swim lessons, dance lessons, gymnastics and, you know, well that can be kind of a duty and it's something that she's doing and sort of a family responsibility thing that I should be helping out more. And it's also sort of a sharing in my daughter's growing up that I'm missing out on and sort of participating in fun things and development things that she's growing up in and I'm not probably participating enough in.

As these analyses suggest, not only were men and women using community spaces in different ways and for different purposes, but they also had different spatial priorities and values regarding community spaces. For example, women were more likely than men to be actively engaged in seeking, finding, and occupying spaces that provided child related services, food, or health services for their families. A large majority of the women said that when they moved into their new community, they were primarily responsible for finding child care, a doctor or dentist, school programs, play groups, parks, libraries, recreation centers, drop-in programs, or piano lessons for their children. Men, on the other hand, were more likely to seek out and occupy spaces in the community that were more congruent with a personal interest. For example, they were more likely than women to seek out running groups, join a gym, join a sports league, or join a political party. The difference between men and women in spaces sought out and occupied at the community level is reflected in Ryan's statement:

I think we are probably both at a point where this feels like home; we have approached it [in] different ways, Nicole with the kid-centered activities. . . . I guess the major difference is probably a practical one more than anything in terms of interacting with the community is being more centered around kids' activities; she is at home with the kids and for me it has been centered more around recreational activities, like things like [mountain biking] or I joined a gym around the corner and getting to know some people in there and I started teaching a spin class in there.

These differences in the use of time and space meant that women were more likely than men to be accompanied by their children as they moved through and engaged with public community spaces. The visibility of these mothering tasks suggests that what it means to be a "good mother"—to nurture the growth and development of their children—was often worked out in a very public sphere when compared to men. It was, therefore, very important for women to be seen by other men and women doing things like attending play groups, volunteering at their child's school, taking their kids to the park, or signing up for library programs, simply because it confirmed to themselves and to other women that they were a "good mom."

Although these things were sometimes done by men, their under representation (when compared to women) in these types of community spaces with their children suggests that perhaps the bulk of men's identity work as "good" fathers was worked out either at work or in the more private spaces of the home. For example, in both studies men told us that because they spent "too much time at work," when they came home, they "just wanted to spend time with their family." This suggests that the criteria for being a good dad had a lot to do with "being there"—in both space and time. It meant coming home from work and staying home. For example, Bruce said,

> In my work I fairly intimately talk with thirty or forty people every day. I am social by profession, and when I come home I don't necessarily need to hang out with the neighbors every night or go to the Lion's club, invite people over for my free time. I like spending time with my family and I like them to know that, the kids, that I am here for them and interested in their school and interested in my marriage, so I look more in than out.

Therefore the identity work done to sustain the symbolic image of being an involved father was not typically worked out on in a public space because the public spaces men tended to occupy in the community were closely tied to their work or leisure behaviors—both activities that were typically done without their children. It could be argued, however, that the work spaces men occupied during the day were a critical space in which men enacted what it meant to be a "good father" because they were being "good providers." The link between being a "good father" and a "good provider" has been well documented in the fathering research. For example, status production work on behalf of the family via men's employment has been found to be an important component of men's community-centered identity work (Snarey 1993). However, this link was either implicitly understood or so taken for granted that men didn't talk about their workspaces in that manner. Clearly what it meant to be a good father for these men was more intimately tied to direct fathering pathways such as face-to-face interactions with their children at home. Home, therefore, was clearly the most important space in which "good fathering" was enacted.

Parenthetically, a plausible influence on men's choices to enact good fathering in private rather than public spaces could be that many of the spaces in the community were "feminized"—built to provide services for and by primarily women with children. For example, for the first six months after Alan moved into a new city, he was on parental leave and often took his kids to a nearby drop-in center. He didn't find this to be effective in building friendships or becoming integrated in his new community space, however, because almost all the other participants in the program were women.

Negotiating Time and Space: Issues of Power and Control

As these women and men enacted their parenting roles in time and space, issues regarding power and control were evident. For example, women appeared to be the "space managers" of the family in that they were primarily responsible for finding, organizing, managing, coordinating, delegating, and screening the community spaces that their spouse and children moved through. This distribution of spatial responsibilities is highlighted in Krista's observation:

> I pretty much do most of that. I found the swimming lessons for the kids, and it's just something that is part in parcel of—I think we fall into our roles fairly well and what needs to be done. . . . Generally I do that part, the kids, the school, the projects, field trips—that's all really important for me to get a handle on all those things—where they are going for the field trip, like which grocery store is best, the post office, with the business I am involved with a lot of other services too. So for the most part, as far as my activity compared to Brad's with the community, I am probably 80 to 90 percent involved, whereas he has probably got 20 percent involvement.

In the same way that women were the primary architects of space in the family, they were typically identified as the primary time managers in the family. Mothers were identified as the organizers and were usually the keepers of the family calendar. Not only did they have their eye on the careful orchestration of appointments and deadlines in the routine on any given day, but they were always scanning the temporal horizon and making sure that upcoming plans and activities were planned, recorded, and prepared for.

Because women spent more time finding and engaging with new spaces in the community, they were often thought to have more spatial expertise. This spatial expertise put them in a position to delegate or suggest community spaces or navigation pathways to other family members. For example, women would enter their new community, explore and learn what was available for their family by sifting through the spaces, services, facilities, and people that they found, and then return home with ones that seemed worthwhile for them to engage their spouse or children in. They would then often coordinate and orchestrate how their family moved through that space. For example, Nicole told me she was primarily responsible for finding a bank, grocery store, doctor, dentist, school, and child care when they moved to a new city and managed how her family moved through those spaces on a daily basis. She said, "I had to say, 'This is where you go.' I feel like a secretary; I have booked an appointment for this time and this place." Men tended to defer to their wives on these matters because they were perceived as controlling both temporal and spatial movements. When fathers acknowledged women's authority, they complied when it came time to execute plans.

Because women were screening spaces, husbands tended to experience the community and acquire social contacts through the spatial patterns established by their wives. Of course, there were many examples of men who were involved with their children in community spaces, but they were usually either also with their wife (attending a community summer festival as a family) or were taking their son to T-ball games for which the woman researched, found out about, and signed up the child.

As this discussion suggests, both space and time were subject to the dynamics of control. Although many of the comments provided by parents in both studies were in keeping with our cultural discourse about the importance of equal or shared contributions between fathers and mothers, it was evident that mothers exerted greater control over the orchestration of both time and space in the family. For fathers, not only did they acknowledge and respect this control, but it meant that they were more likely to take direction, execute tasks, and move through family space and time in ways that were determined by their wives.

FUTURE RESEARCH

This analysis of fathers, as they navigate time and space in their everyday lives, suggests a number of theoretical directions for thinking about the complex interplay of temporal and spatial dimensions of experience. There are three key theoretical ideas that have emerged from this analysis. First, we see time and space as inseparable dimensions of experience. Second, in contrast with the notions of time and space as value neutral containers of experience, we see them as deeply imbued with values, meanings, and idealizations. As such, we treat time and space as *socially constructed and mediated*. As part of this, the ongoing construction and management of identity is rooted in and shaped by the contingencies of time and space. Third, space and time are subject to the dynamics of possession, control, and conflict in relationships. Accordingly, we see time and space as *contested* dimensions of experience.

Time and Space as Inseparable Dimensions of Experience

Although we both came to this analysis with a focus on either time or space, it quickly became apparent in carrying out this work that it was difficult to sustain the analysis of one without attending to the other. Like the paparazzi who captures a secret relationship on film, once seen together and recorded in the public eye, it is difficult to erase the image of them being together. This is in contrast with a traditional, dualistic perspective which viewed time as the domain of dynamism and space as the realm of stasis (May and Thrift 2001).

More recent theoretical efforts have identified the limitations of this approach and have argued that we need to look at the dynamic, temporal aspects of space as they play out in a dialectical tension. To think about time and space as a dialectic is to consider the dynamic interplay, tension, and unity of these forces (Baxter and Montgomery 1996). For example, movement into different places is often motivated by the desire to shift temporal pace (Shaw 2001). Hence we argue there is a reciprocal contingency between time and space: the organization of spatial networks is accompanied by the situational requirement to schedule activities in a certain way; the way that schedules are constructed in organizations presents the situational requirement that spatial pathways be organized in a certain way.

In our analysis there are many illustrations of this dialectical interplay between time and space. As men move through time, their spatial work, awareness, responsibilities, and priorities change. For example, with mobility choices, deciding when to move and where to move are equally important. Additionally, deciding to modify one's space not only evolves through and takes time (the process creates family memories as they work on a project), but also creates the space in which family time together can happen (the product).

Furthermore, "when" men became fathers, the "where" of their lives became more important. They became more concerned about creating an optimal home space for their children and finding optimal spaces that could structurally enable the types of opportunities they wanted available to their children. As these men struggled with the management of time in their lives, they also struggled with creating and managing spatial environments for their children that were safe, secure, and stimulating. Fathers in particular place a great deal of importance on the modification of family space as a way to optimize their experience of family time. Future research could examine the dynamic interplay between space and time by addressing the way that fathers deliberately orchestrate temporal and spatial concerns in their everyday life. For example, decisions about where to work in relation to home (e.g., distance to workplace, whether commuting is involved, able to work at home) have very significant implications for being available for family activities and responsibilities (e.g., eating lunch at home, picking up children after school). Whereas our research focused on families with young children, it would be valuable to explore the ways that time and space concerns change for fathers as they move through the family life course.

Time and Space as Socially Constructed

Although it is tempting to think of both time and space as external, objectified containers in which we enact our lives, it is impossible to think of any course of action that is not mediated in some way by the vagaries of time and space. In this regard, we are fully enmeshed in time space (Davies 2001). According to Bakhtin (1981), all meaning-making activity is enacted through temporal-spatial definitions which both enable and constrain human dialogue. Consistent with social constructionist principles, there is a reciprocal relationship between the way that people construct their temporal and spatial landscapes and, in turn, the way that the shared understandings of time and space influence the meanings and dialogues that can be sustained in relationships. Specifically, there is a strong sense of agency associated with the activities of making the conditions of space and time fit with one's goals, values, and family activities, and, in return, there are strong collective understandings of what constitutes meaningful family time or secure family space that influence how those activities are constructed.

In this analysis, conceptualizations of "home" and "family time" were powerful spatial and temporal constructions that couples created and sustained, but which also acted on them as they endeavoured to live up to this standard. For fathers, there was an ongoing interplay between their desire to create for their children idealized family time and space and the competing demands of their everyday reality. These fathers worked hard to find the right spaces and to mold them into a place that would feel like home. They worked hard to attain a very high standard of family time that involved a vigilance not only to work hours, but a vigilance to making the home space optimally conducive to the experience of family time. Future research might fruitfully examine the degree to which social class has an effect on these constructions of family time and space.

It was also apparent in this analysis that fathers differed from mothers in the spatial and temporal staging of their father identity. Mothers were more likely to be doing mother work in the context of the broader community. Mothers took more responsibility for, and expressed a greater comfort with, moving in and through the essential community spaces that provide for the health, education, and social needs of the family. Fathers, by contrast, seemed to be more preoccupied with work and the movement from work to family. In this way, they sought to optimize their time for what they valued most highly—provisioning and time to be with their children. Although there has been considerable emphasis placed on the interchangeability of mothers and fathers in the tasks that they carry out, future research could deepen our understanding of the unique ways that men and women create and sustain family space and time.

Time and Space as Contested Dimensions of Experience

In families, the responsibility to provide care involves a responsiveness to the needs of others. Care involves commitments of time and space in the context of family needs and demands. At the center of family relationships is a dynamic of giving and taking as needs are not only expressed, but also responded to and negotiated. Furthermore, as families are increasingly mobile and time schedules increasingly complex, the negotiation of time and space has become more problematic.

Time and space are contested aspects of experience because they are part of the dynamics of possession and control that exist in any family relationship. To speak of time or space as subject to possession is to acknowledge the agency that individuals bring to the acts of claiming authority, expressing entitlements, or imposing conditions on the way that time and space are used in the relationship. In our analyses of these fathers, there were two main axes on which the dynamics of temporal and spatial control were experienced. First, as fathers, their decisions and actions about parenting were made with mothers in mind. Davies (2001) argues that time and space are "inextricably gendered" (135). The structural positioning of women and men in public and private spheres profoundly shapes their mundane, everyday choices about time and space including how, when, and where they provide care for children, how they schedule their day based on spatial location of work, and how they negotiate shopping and service tasks based on hours of operation and physical proximity. One of the manifestations of this different structural positioning was found in the character of the activity. Whereas men's experience of modifying time and space seemed to have a more permanent, fixed, visible nature (renovations, completing a project), women's strategies to modify schedules and move through the space were less tangible and predictable and were continually evolving (meeting everyday needs). Second, many of the decisions these fathers made about the organization of time and space were made in relation to needs and expectations presented to them by their children. As a result, there was a sense in which fathers were controlled by the routine requirements of providing care to children as opposed to the more common expectation that they controlled their children (Thorpe and Daly 1999).

In this analysis of fathers, spatial and temporal power, responsibility, and control seemed to belong primarily to women. In the same way that women were in charge of schedules (temporal concerns) in the family, they were also in charge of how the home was organized, used, and positioned (spatial concerns). Fathers were active participants in many of the discussions about time and space, but, in the end, women made many of the decisions about the where's and when's of their everyday lives. Although these fathers did talk about making choices about space and time in the home, it was usually because they had been delegated the authority to do so. Thus, in contrast with arguments that women exert relatively little power in the home, our data would suggest that by controlling the temporal and spatial organization of the household, they seem to control much of what fathers do at home and arguably much of family life itself. There are many aspects of this power dynamic that merit further investigation. For example, one could argue that by positioning themselves to be compliant, husbands may not have to take on the time-consuming tasks of managing, coordinating, orchestrating, and monitoring how their families move through time and space—thereby gaining time and reducing their spatial responsibilities. Questions also arise about the degree to which either women or men wish to maintain or change these dynamics of control and responsibility. Although there is a long-standing feminist call for men to take more of these responsibilities for the orchestration of time and space, it is apparent that there are significant forces of resistance encountered by both women and men that need to be more clearly identified.

To say that fathers were controlled by the temporal and spatial needs of their children would be to overlook and diminish the importance of their fathering intentions as they carried out renovations and created play spaces for their children. Although it was children's needs that created projects on dad's list at home, his motivation to carry out these projects was rooted in a desire to be a good father, to ensure safety, and to create opportunities for play with their children. This was expressed through feelings of attentiveness and responsibility that helped them to focus their activities on "what was best for the children." On this axis of control, we observed fathers routinely responding to the needs of their children for time or some kind of spatial modification or accommodation. It is in this regard that time and space are not so much abstract concepts as they are a central part of the father–child relationship and are shaped by the needs, demands, and opportunities of the relationship. Hence, while control was an important dimension of the relationship between fathers and their children, temporal and spatial needs of children were not so much contested as they were acquiesced in the name of generativity. Future research could better address the ways that fathers build relationships with their children by creating and modifying meaningful spaces that can be used for their mutual benefit.

REFERENCES

Allen, S. (2003). Voluntary intra-national migration and the process of creating a place called home. (Doctoral dissertation, University of Guelph 2003). *Dissertation Abstracts International*.
Bakhtin, M. M. (1981). *The dialogic imagination: Four essays* (C. Emerson and M. Holquist, Trans.) Edited by M. Holquist. Austin: University of Texas Press.

Baxter, L. A., and Montgomery, B. M. (1996). *Relating: Dialogues and dialectics.* New York: Guilford.

Bollonow, O. F. (1967). Lived-space. In N. Lawrence and D. O'Connor (Eds.), *Readings in existential phenomenology* (pp. 178–86). Toronto: Prentice-Hall of Canada.

Casey, E. (1993). *Getting back into place: Toward a renewed understanding of the place world.* Indianapolis: Indiana University Press.

Cuba, L., and Hummon, D. M. (1993). A place to call home: Identification with dwelling, community and region. *Sociological Quarterly, 34* (1), 111–31.

Daly, K. J. (1996). *Families and time: Keeping pace in a hurried culture.* Thousand Oaks, CA: Sage.

Davies, K. (2001). Responsibility and daily life: Reflections over timespace. In J. May and N. Thrift (Eds.), *Timespace: Geographies of temporality* (pp. 133–48). London: Routledge.

Dear, M., and Wolch, J. (1989). How territory shapes social life. In J. Wolch and M. Dear (Eds.), *The power of geography: How territory shapes social life* (pp. 3–18). Boston: Unwin Hyman.

Feldman, R. M. (1990). Settlement-identity: Psychological bonds with home places in a mobile society. *Environment and Behavior, 22* (2), 183–229.

Glaser, B., and Strauss, A. L. (1967). *The discovery of grounded theory: Strategies for qualitative research.* New York: Aldine.

Groat, L. (1995). Introduction: Place, aesthetic evaluation and home. In L. Groat (Ed.), *Giving places meaning* (pp. 1–25). New York: Academic.

Hay, R. (1998). A rooted sense of place in cross-cultural perspective. *Canadian Geographer, 42* (3), 245–66.

Korpela, K. M. (1995). Place identity as a product of environmental self-regulation. In L. Groat (Ed.), *Giving places meaning* (pp. 115–30). New York: Academic.

Lovell, N. (1998). Introduction: Belonging in need of emplacement? In N. Lovell (Ed.), *Locality and belonging* (pp. 1–23). New York: Routledge.

May, J., and Thrift, N. (2001). *Timespace: Geographies of temporality.* London: Routledge.

Nippert-Eng, C. E. (1996). *Home and work: Negotiating boundaries through everyday life.* Chicago: University of Chicago Press.

Presser, H. B. (1989). Can we make time for children? The economy, work schedules, and child care. *Demography, 26,* 523–43.

Proshansky, H. M., Fabian, A. K., and Kaminoff, R. (1995). Place-identity: Physical world socialization of the self. In L. Groat (Ed.), *Giving places meaning* (pp. 87–113). New York: Academic.

Rapoport, A. (1985). Thinking about home environments: A conceptual framework. In I. Altman and C. M. Werner (Eds.), *Home environments* (pp. 255–86). New York: Plenum.

Schutz, A. (1967). *The phenomenology of the social world.* Evanston, IL: Northwestern University Press.

Shaw, J. (2001). "Winning Territory": Changing place to change pace. In J. May and N. Thrift (Eds.), *Timespace: Geographies of temporality* (pp. 120–32). London: Routledge.

Smith, J. M., Light, A., and Roberts, D. (1998). Introduction: Philosophies and geographies of place. In A. Light and J. M. Smith (Eds.), *Philosophy and geography III: Philosophies of place* (pp. 1–19). Lanham, MD: Rowman & Littlefield.

Snarey, J. (1993). *How fathers care for the next generation: A four-decade study.* Cambridge, MA: Harvard University Press.

Stone, G. P. (1970). Appearance and the self: A slightly revised version. In G. P. Stone and H. A. Farberman (Eds.), *Social psychology through symbolic interaction* (pp. 187–202). New York: Wiley.

Stone, G. P. (1981). Appearance and the self: A slightly revised version. In G. P. Stone and H. A. Farberman (Eds.), *Social psychology through symbolic interactionism,* (pp. 187–202). New York: Wiley.

Thorpe, K., and Daly, K. J. (1999). Children, parents, and time: The dialectics of control. In *Through the eyes of the child: Revisioning children as active agents of family life* (pp. 199–223). Stamford, CT: JAI Press.

Tuan, Y. (1977). *Space and place: The perspective of experience.* Minneapolis: University of Minnesota Press.

II

FATHERING AND INSTITUTIONAL SPACE

4

Contextual Scenarios for Stepfathers' Identity Construction, Boundary Work, and "Fatherly" Involvement

William Marsiglio

When men construct their identities as stepfathers and negotiate their involvement in stepchildren's lives, they do so in various contexts. Although scholars increasingly have refined the conceptualization of what father involvement entails (Marsiglio, Day, and Lamb 2000; Palkovitz 1997, 2002; Pleck 1997; Pleck and Masciadrelli 2004), remarkably little has been done to map out and explore the varied types of scenarios wherein this involvement occurs (Marsiglio and Cohan 2000). From a theoretical perspective, this shortcoming is particularly noteworthy for stepfathers who find themselves managing their lives in an "incomplete institution" where ambiguous and often dynamic family norms prevail (Cherlin 1978).

Social demographers have focused considerable attention on how aspects of family structure or "situational constraints" (e.g., physical distance from children's home or current family responsibilities associated with stepchildren, new biological children, and partners) affect father involvement in diverse settings (Cooksey and Craig 1998). The type, amount, quality, and consequences of stepfathers' involvement is often interpreted by either comparing it to resident and nonresidential biological fathering (Cooksey and Fondell 1996; Cooksey and Craig 1998; Hofferth, Pleck, Stueve, Bianchi, and Sayer 2002), or it is assessed while controlling for the biological father's involvement (White and Gilbreth 2001). Although stepfathers, compared to biological fathers, appear to be involved less (or invest less) in (step)children overall (Cooksey and Fondell 1996; Thomson, Hanson, and McLanahan 1994; Thomson, McLanahan, and Curtin 1992), these differences may be attributable largely to selection factors rather than the absence or presence of a genetic tie (Hofferth and Anderson 2003). Highlighting the social psychological aspects of men's situated experiences as stepfathers can augment this complex demographic portrait of stepfathers' involvement.

The scenarios for stepfathers' identity construction, boundary work, and involvement with stepchildren include significant physical and social dimensions. Generally speaking, most stepfather–stepchild interaction occurs within physical settings replete with symbolic meaning: the birth mother's home, the man's home, living space shared with a birth mother, the personal living space of someone whom the stepfather knows, or some type of public site, such as a business establishment, school, or neighborhood. If stepfathers' sense of being in control, or perception of having some authority in specific settings is important, it is reasonable to assume that characteristics of the physical setting may influence their comfort level and self-perceptions as stepfathers. A social or interpersonal dimension can also influence stepfathers' sense of control and authority during interaction episodes. For example, are stepfathers interacting with stepchildren alone or in the presence of one or more persons capable of judging their behavior? Who are these others? And how do stepfathers perceive others' views of and reactions to them?

The first step toward a better understanding of how various scenarios might shape stepfathers' opportunities for developing and expressing their identities is to sharpen the conceptual lens for considering how men define and navigate their physical and social surroundings related to stepfathering. My approach, informed by a symbolic interactionist perspective and augmented selectively with qualitative data obtained through in-depth interviews with a diverse sample of formal and informal stepfathers, proposes that variations of two contextual factors (physical and social) can affect stepfathers' experiences.

THEORETICAL INSIGHTS

A basic premise of symbolic interactionism is that the meanings assigned to social life emerge out of social interaction (Blumer 1969; Mead 1934; Stryker 1980). People socially construct meanings for physical sites, interaction scenarios, and individuals. These processes are alive in stepfamilies as individuals struggle to make sense of the shifting contours of their ill-defined familial environments, including the people in them. Stepfathers, for example, are challenged as they confront an evolving set of circumstances that require them to define their roles relative to stepchildren in numerous circumstances. In conscious and unconscious ways, these men seek to establish, manage, and display relationship and familial identities for others and themselves.

In practical terms, stepfathers are likely to be more aware of their stepfather or adult male identity and do boundary work (Nippert-Eng 1996) when facing situations where the borders defining their relationship to a stepchild come into focus. They may be particularly attuned to their situation when their identity is contested. When the border of a stepfather–stepchild relationship is accentuated, the parties grow more aware that their relationship is socially constructed in different ways than the typical biological child relationship. In this instance, stepfathers' "situated self," by definition, is activated by cultural and physical contingencies external to their subjectively experienced stepfather identity. Thus stepfathers' self-perceptions and presentation of self may be responsive to particular conditions of a setting. In turn, how stepfathers subjectively process and respond to situational factors reflects their claim to and expression of human agency, their ability to mold their own identities and behavior. One interpretation of men's more enduring biographical self as stepfathers is that it represents a working compromise built up over time as men experience their situated self in various settings with physical and social attributes. Admittedly, some settings, and the symbolic events that transpire within them, are likely to play a much more prominent role in shaping stepfathers' identities and experiences. Furthermore, individual stepfathers are likely to be affected to varying degrees by particular settings and events.

Conventional meanings associated with parenting are closely tied to the formal rights and responsibilities typically accorded persons involved with minor children for whom they have a legal stake. Informal expectations for how parents are to treat their children also define the boundaries that represent the parent–child relationship. These borders offer parents a socially sanctioned license to treat a child in certain ways: showing affection, giving praise, consoling, protecting, disciplining, and teaching. For biological parents, this message comes with the territory, generally dissolving into a taken-for-granted reality. Rebellious children and custody disputes may force parents to deal with challenges to their "license" to treat children in particular ways, but for the most part the legitimacy of their rights is assumed.

From a stepfather's perspective, however, especially during the early phases of his involvement with a stepchild, he seldom possesses the taken-for-granted privileges of parenting. Of course, privileges may be earned to varying degrees over time, but they can still be relinquished, challenged, or usurped in certain types of settings, especially those where a biological parent(s) is implicated. Although families of all types continuously construct their symbolic and interpersonal worlds, those involving stepfathers (or stepmothers) have an added layer of complexity.

How men achieve, sustain, and mange their stepfather identity, including perceptions about their roles in a stepchild's life, is part of a poorly understood, socially constructed process central to stepfamilies' labors to build a sense of "family." Efforts to claim and assign symbolic value to being recognized as a stepfather surface repeatedly for many as they negotiate their feelings about their rights and responsibilities vis-à-vis a stepchild. Many of these negotiated moments occur in the company of the stepchild and others, including the birth mother, biological father, and other adults and children. Their reactions and the stepfather's interpretation of them can figure significantly into the stepfather's desire and ability to express himself in a fatherly way.

DATA

To illustrate aspects of the contextual framework I outline below, I selectively use data from forty-two audiotaped, in-depth interviews with a racially and economically diverse sample of men residing in north central Florida. Thirty-six men were interviewed in 2001; six others were recruited in 2003–2004 as part of a theoretical sampling effort (Strauss and Corbin 1998) to identify men who had circumstances relevant to the contextual scenarios described below. A more extensive discussion of the methodology and sample is provided elsewhere (Marsiglio 2004).

The data I present are taken from a larger project in which my interviewing and analytic strategy focused on stepfathers' experiences with an eye toward the chronology of how men met their current partner, got romantically involved, met the stepchild, and then became increasingly involved (and sometimes subsequently disengaged) in both their partner's and her child's life. My principal objective in using these data is to highlight my framework using empirical data that underscores the complexity of stepfathers' experiences while revealing future avenues for research that are sensitive to the contextual issues I raise. Consistent with the practice of theoretical sampling (Strauss and Corbin 1998), I am currently recruiting additional stepfathers with distinct features so that I may conduct more focused interviews to flesh out aspects of the various contextual scenarios I describe here.

I used a variety of recruitment strategies to secure participants, including flyers, announcements in selected community outlets, and word of mouth. My purposive sampling strategy identified men with the kinds of diverse experiences that are likely to affect their relationships with children who are not their offspring. To be included, the men had to describe themselves as being actively involved in the lives of their romantic partner's children who were nineteen years of age or younger and living with the mother. In addition, I made a concerted effort to recruit a sample that took into account stepfathers' age, social class, race, marriage and residence status, duration and level of relationship commitment with partner, and previous/current experience with own biological children and the target child's gender and age. The youngest man I interviewed was twenty, the oldest fifty-four; the average age was thirty-six. Thirty-one were currently married and living with their partner, seven cohabited with their partner but were not married, and four lived in a residence separate from their partner. Nineteen of the men had completed college, fifteen had completed high school and had some college experience, and eight had either completed high school and not attended college or had not obtained a high school degree. Thirty-one self-identified white and ten were African American with two white and one black man claiming some Hispanic ancestry. Five men had legally adopted the target stepchild and several were thinking about doing so. Twenty-two had fathered their own biological child and eleven were living with at least one of their biological children at the time of the interview. Of those living with biological children, three men had children with their current partner. I spoke with stepfathers of sons and daughters who were infants, toddlers, young children, and adolescents of all ages. Two men had partners who were currently pregnant with their first child. Excluding these pregnancies, the average age of the oldest child living with the stepfather's partner was ten. These children were roughly five and a half years old on average when stepfathers began their relationships with the children's mothers.

Interviews, lasting ninety minutes on average, were loosely organized according to a semistructured interview guide. I sought to uncover the meanings men associate with their evolving identities and life circumstances as stepfathers. In general, the direction of the interviews provided men an opportunity to describe their experience with their partner and stepchild(ren) chronologically, but participants were free to move back and forth as they focused on particular issues and told their stories. The direction of the interviews varied somewhat, depending on the participants' initial answers and the flow of the exchanges. After the first several interviews, I began to make a more concerted effort to ask the stepfathers questions that at least indirectly addressed issues associated with the different contexts they found themselves in with their stepchildren. I encouraged the men to discuss issues related to the way they navigated the terrain of stepfathering and managed their identities as men who present themselves in a fatherly way or as an adult authority figure. However, my interviewing strategy was not based explicitly on the contextual framework presented here. I developed this framework after completing the interviews. Thus, it blends deductive and inductive theorizing.

Although the interviews focused men's attention on the oldest target stepchild living with the mother, I asked participants numerous questions about all of their children (biological and step). The men often commented on children other than the oldest stepchild without being prompted.

A CONTEXTUAL FRAMEWORK

By presenting the expansive set of forty scenarios in table 4.1, I illustrate the wide range of contexts relevant to men's subjective experiences as stepfathers. Although some of these scenarios are much more prevalent than others, and some probably more consequential for stepfathers, I present the full range for heuristic purposes. Their practical relevance and degree of symbolic significance for stepfathers and other stepfamily members await empirical grounding.

Physical Setting

In table 4.1, I delineate five permutations of physical settings based loosely on a combination of an occupancy/ownership principle involving property as well as a distinction between a private versus public setting. A man's home represents a common physical site for much of what a man does as a stepfather (or father). Similarly, the time a man spends with a stepchild in places like the man's office, car, and fishing boat can be thought of as time spent in the context of a man's private property. In places such as these a stepfather, especially one who is married to the birth mother, is most likely to spend time with his stepchild and negotiate the terms of his day-to-day living and participation in family rituals. During the course of his daily activities, a stepfather will also act on and immerse himself in his personal physical surroundings that include furniture, tools, clothes, food, telephone, cars, computer, garden/yard, and so forth, that may be implicated in the stepfather–stepchild interaction.

Unlike how a biological father constructs his relationship with his child, as a stepfather gradually assumes a position in which others view him, and he sees himself, as having more of a fatherly presence to a stepchild, he is likely to negotiate his roles within the birth mother's home and other forms of personal space (e.g., car). In addition to spending time in the birth mother's home, stepchildren sometimes spend time in the home of the prospective stepfather while the stepfather and birth mother are dating but living apart. Ultimately, if the partners decide to live together, the bulk of a stepfather's domestic time spent with a stepchild will occur either in his home, the birth mother's home, or their jointly owned/rented home. During the course of a stepfather–stepchild relationship, the ownership/rental arrangement may shift as the stepfather and birth mother make residential moves. Space issues can influence the stepfather's feelings in various ways. For example, Dean, thirty-seven, moved in with this partner and her eighteen-month-old boy, Michael. In his words, "[I felt] pretty uncomfortable in the apartment. . . . I was kinda cramped, and I still had a lot of mixed emotions about moving in with a

Table 4.1. Selective Contextual Scenarios for Stepfathers' Identity Construction, Border Work, and "Fatherly" Involvement

Physical Setting	Social Setting for Stepfather–Stepchild Involvement							
	No Other Adult Present			Selective Other Adult(s) Present				
	Alone with Stepchild	Bio Child Present	Non-family Kids Present[1]	Birth Mother[1]	Bio Father[1]	Birth Mother and Bio Father[1]	Non-parent(s)[2]	Mixed Adults and Other Kids[2]
Birth mother's home or other personal space	1	6	11	16	21	26	31	36
Stepfather's own home or other personal space	2	7	12	17	22	27	32	37
Stepfather's and birth mother's shared home or other shared space	3	8	13	18	23	28	33	38
Personal space of stepfather's or birth mother's friends or extended family	4	9	14	19	24	29	34	39
Public site (e.g., playground, sporting venue, shopping mall, restaurant, school, neighborhood)	5	10	15	20	25	30	35	40

[1]Scenarios 11–15, 16–20, 21–25, and 26–30 can be differentiated further depending on whether the stepfather's biological child is present.
[2]Scenarios 31–35 and 36–40 can be differentiated further depending on whether the stepfather's biological child, or one or both biological parents of the stepchild, is present.

woman and [one] who already had a baby. . . . [It] took me a while to feel at home." After finding a house together three months later, Dean grew more comfortable with "home," but he continued to struggle with space issues, pondering whether these issues affected his relationship with Michael. He laments not having his own private space, saying "Sometimes I find myself a little jealous, like Michael gets his own room."

In addition to physical settings tied to the stepfather's and birth mother's ownership/rental arrangement, a stepfather may find himself with his stepchildren in other people's homes, most notably those occupied by his own or his partner's friends and family. Depending on individual circumstances, the amount of time a stepfather finds himself in these types of settings may vary widely. How a man perceives his stepfather identity in these settings is likely to be influenced by the way the occupants respond to him.

Although a high percentage of time stepfathers spend with stepchildren is likely to occur within a physical domestic setting, many activities occur in public physical space, such as shopping malls, grocery stores, soccer fields, schools, playgrounds, day care facilities, and other locations that are not perceived to be a person's own physical space. These public venues may be further differentiated by characteristics that shape their symbolic significance to the stepfather and stepchild, for example, spaces perceived to be oriented toward children (playground, child care, video arcades) or adults (office, church). Dean mentions that unlike his early struggles with managing space issues at home with his new stepfamily, he "felt more at ease when we [partner, child, and him] were doing stuff . . . things that were entertaining" away from the home.

Social Setting

In addition to the physical criteria mentioned above, each interaction scenario involving a stepfather and stepchild can be defined by the interpersonal circumstances of who is present. Eight potentially significant variations of the social configuration of a stepfather–stepchild scenario are displayed in table 4.1. Being alone with a stepchild (or perhaps several stepchildren) represents the most private, personal type of scenario for a stepfather. This type of scenario is represented by the first set of scenarios (1–5) where the stepfather is the sole adult figure in the interaction setting. In scenarios 1–5, a stepfather can focus most directly on his stepchild without help or interference from others. The same holds true for the stepchild who can, in theory, direct his or her undivided attention toward the stepfather. Of course, the physical absence of others in a particular setting does not mean that the stepfather or the stepchild will not, in their mind's eye, be thinking about what others might feel or do if they were actually there in person. In some instances, the mental images a stepfather and stepchild have of others will make a difference and influence their decisions even though they are alone with each other. Despite their significance, such thoughts are ultimately only mental images. Consequently they usually do not carry the same weight as the other people being there in person. Nathan, a stepfather of a ten-year-old girl, fondly recalls picking her up by himself from her father's house on one occasion because their private time in the car produced a memorable chat. "She confided in me and told me I couldn't tell her mom, though, but she had her first kiss this weekend, and I kinda kidded her and stuff with that."

Being the only adult figure present, especially when the stepchildren are young, may represent a temporary asset for the stepfather. It may buttress his sense of authority in the child's eyes as well as his own. Alternatively, the experience may reveal in vivid fashion, especially with adolescent stepchildren, the borders defining the stepfather's outsider role.

All of the settings where a stepfather is alone with his stepchild can be altered abruptly when others are introduced into the setting. In the case of the public scenario (5), stepfathers may interact with others intermittently and often in the course of the shared "alone time" they spend with their stepchild. For instance, during the course of an afternoon, a stepfather and his stepchild may interact alone in the car for extended periods of time as they drive from one store to another, interspersed with joint interactions with numerous store clerks at different stops. Those involved in these interactions may explicitly or implicitly acknowledge or inquire about the stepfather's relationship to his stepchild. Thus the fluidity of moving from an "alone" context to one that includes others in public (or other) sites presents stepfathers and stepchildren opportunities to manage the borders of their relationship (e.g., making introductions or clarifying their respective roles in each other's lives in terms of rights and obligations).

Clearly, the solo stepfather–stepchild scenario becomes less private and intimate when others enter the interaction frame (Goffman 1974). The dynamics of intimacy and a stepfather's perception of being in charge or having a particular sense of his fatherly identity in this type of setting may depend on who these others are. For example, having other stepchildren present may change the dynamics very little for a stepfather. Meanwhile, having his own biological child physically present, as is the case in scenarios 6–10, may accentuate a stepfather's tendency to think and feel as though he's acting in a fatherly way. This pattern may surface most often when the stepfather is committed in thought and practice to treating his stepchildren and biological children the same. Under certain conditions, the biological child's physical presence in the immediate interaction setting may become less important if there is an understanding that the child has an established presence in that space.

For example, the biological child may live part- or full-time in the house, perhaps even sharing a room with the stepchild, but not always be physically present when the stepfather is interacting with the stepchild.

The stepfather's sense of privacy and his having a fatherly presence may be drastically reduced if the mother or another authority figure is present (scenarios 16–40). In some instances, especially early on in his involvement with a stepchild, he may feel less secure about his "fatherly" roles. In short, he may sense that his claim to authority is undermined when the mother, biological father, or grandparent is present and consequently feel less fatherlike. Nathan, referring to his stepdaughter, offers, "She actually responds much better when it's just her and I. Sometimes when her mom's around she'll test it and see what her mom says."

Viewed from a different perspective, a stepfather's and stepchild's perception of their interaction taking place in a private venue may remain largely intact so long as only immediate (step)family members are present. Even though they may not all share a similar bloodline, those involved may feel that they are part of a family unit, enjoying their own family dance. When this occurs, a stepfather may feel relaxed and not perceive that his claim to a fatherly status is being challenged. He may feel connected to his stepchild and feel as though his private stepfathering scenario includes the entire stepfamily.

To the extent persons outside the man's stepfamily or his own biological children are introduced into or are already present in a particular setting, it is likely that the stepfathering experience will become increasingly less private. If, for example, children other than the stepchildren are present in the situation (scenarios 11–15, 36–40), the stepfather may consider how others perceive and respond to him. Whereas in the scenarios 11–15 the stepfather will be the only adult, in scenarios 36–40 other adults will be present. Being the only adult present, especially when the children are young, may shape how the stepfather is viewed, as well as how he perceives himself compared to situations where other adult authority figures are involved. Sometimes, though, stepfathers make a concerted effort to remain constant irrespective of who is present. Ryan's description illustrates how his interactions are similar with his twelve-year-old stepdaughter, whether they are alone or her friends are present. "She's less likely to be, act stupid. So, when her friend's there, she knows I'm gonna act the same way. So, that's a way, I don't have to worry about her disrespecting me."

Perhaps more significantly, if the biological father is factored into a (step)child's setting in which the stepfather is present (scenarios 21–25), or the birth mother and biological father are both present (scenarios 26–30), the stepfather is likely to face unique challenges requiring him to manage any thoughts and feelings he might have about being a fatherly figure to his stepchild. One stepfather, Eddie, has a friendly relationship with his eight-year-old stepdaughter's father who is a coworker. Eddie describes how his wife, the child's father, and he get along. "I mean, it's just—we all have that chemistry. It looks like everybody is looking out for the best interests of her [Rhendy]; it's just to make the kid happy. I think that's how it should be." Asked about times where the adults and Rhendy are all present, Eddie admits he feels a bit awkward when Rhendy is affectionate toward him in front of her father. "She'll even come sit on my lap while he's there. She'll just play with me." [Interviewer: How does that make you feel?] "Well, sometimes I'm saying like—I wonder what it's going to do to his mind? He knows that I wouldn't hurt her." Eddie's reaction is seemingly mild, but other stepfathers who do not have as friendly of a relationship with the biological father may feel even more awkward if their stepchild displays affection in similar circumstances.

In reality, stepfathers seldom confront scenarios where they are alone with stepchildren and the biological father, but these situations do occur and could theoretically increase if concerted efforts were made to improve relations between stepfathers and biological fathers (see Oxhorn-Ringwood, Oxhorn, and Krausz 2002 for related discussion of CoMammas organization to enhance relationships between birth mothers and stepmothers). The more likely circumstance is that both the biological father and birth mother will be present. Here, then, the stepfather is potentially faced with feeling as though he is an outsider to the coparental alliance of the birth mother and biological father. Each situation may take on its own flavor depending on its peculiarities. Is it the first time for everyone to be together in this way or are the circumstances similar to many others where all the parties have been present? How the parental figures choose to interact, or physically position themselves during an event that requires attendance, may influence how attentive a man is to his stepfather identity and how he manages it. Furthermore, how a stepfather perceives and presents himself may be affected by situations where the biological parental figures provide advice or discipline for a child, thereby accentuating the parents' and child's legal and biological relatedness.

The distinguishing characteristic of the final set of scenarios (31–35) where only adults are present (not counting the stepchild) is that at least one adult other than either of the biological parents will be present. In scenarios 36–40, the stepfather will find himself among a mix of adults and children (in addition to his stepchild). The specific composition of scenarios 31–40 will vary widely, differentiated by combinations that may include the stepchild's friends; family, coworkers, or friends of the stepfather or birth mother; school teachers or administrators; religious leaders; athletic coaches; day care workers; health care providers; employees in a wide range of stores and restaurants; neighbors; strangers; as well as others. These settings are the most public and could be differentiated further if consideration is given to whether one or both of the biological parents are also present. Although they are the most public scenarios, thereby denying stepfathers the immediate opportunity to sustain a private exchange with their stepchild, these settings can provide stepfathers with numerous chances to assert their fatherly presence in a stepchild's life by advocating for or assisting the child (e.g., signing a child up for a recreational activity, helping a child buy a bike at a store) or managing the child's exchanges with persons other than the child's biological parents (e.g., mediating a dispute between a child and his friend).

Intersection of the Physical and Social Dimensions

A combination of physical and social dimensions define stepfathering scenarios, offering men diverse arrangements for constructing their stepfather identities and making decisions about whether and how to express themselves in fatherly ways. Men's experiences with these private and public scenarios are often part of a dynamic process in which they either physically move from one type of scenario to another, or a key feature(s) of the scenario changes while the men remain in place.

In many instances, the first set of scenarios (1–5) may afford the stepfather ideal opportunities to build affinity with his stepchild because he is alone with him or her in the confines of his own home or elsewhere. When the stepfather is in his own home (or a place that he shares with the birth mother), the stepfather may be most likely to feel in control and capable of seeing himself as a legitimate authority figure. So, too, he may develop a sense of having a fatherlike presence in this type of scenario. Those scenarios where the stepfather has a clear ownership stake in the housing may matter most during the earlier phases of a stepfamily's evolution. Over time, the significance may wane as to whether it is the stepfather's place, the birth mother's home, or the home becomes a joint legal responsibility of the birth mother and stepfather.

Though private in many respects, the home can clearly take on characteristics of a public place where a stepfather is on display to those who may or may not view him as a father figure to the stepchild in question. Grandparents, aunts, uncles, friends of the mother or stepchildren, neighbors, and even the biological father himself may, under certain conditions, give a stepfather reason to pause and consider, perhaps publicly defend, the nature of his relationship to his stepchild. Persons outside the stepfather's stepfamily can come inside the home and see for themselves how the stepfather interacts with his stepchild. While there, they are free to comment on, judge, challenge, support, or be indifferent to any signs or symbols of parenting. After these people leave, the stepfather can reassert his private stepfathering face in the privacy of his own home—assuming he is now alone with the stepchild.

Sometime later, the same stepfather may take his stepchild out to a more public setting, say, a playground. If other kids are playing there, especially if they are interacting with or clearly observing the stepfather with his stepchild, the stepfather will now find himself wearing the public face of stepfathering in both a physical and social sense. He will be away from the security of his home and he will be in the presence of others who can observe him interact with his stepchild. Of course, some may have no idea that he is a stepfather. In addition, some stepfathers may be oblivious to their circumstances and spend little if any time consciously thinking about being a stepfather in public spaces.

A man's concerns about the legitimacy or nature of his stepfather identity may affect the extent to which he is concerned about others' perceptions of him. If he wonders about what others might think, then he will alter his behavior accordingly. Herman, for example, talks about how he has been reluctant to hug his fourteen-year-old stepdaughter in public for fear that others might wonder about his sexual motives and see him as a "pervert." Although Herman does not have his own teenage daughter to make a comparison, I suspect that if he did he would feel less inhibited to be affectionate toward her in public. He would be less self-conscious of his fathering identity.

If the physical surroundings of the hypothetical playground were the same but no one else were around, then the stepfather could present his public stepfather face in a physical setting while experiencing the privacy of stepfathering in a social sense. Of course, a man may not be mindful of these types of differences unless he is confronted with an event that draws his attention to this private/public distinction in his stepfathering experience. Because a man's initial encounter with his stepchild in public is likely to occur prior to him developing a firm sense of having a fatherly identity, his experience will vary over time as he becomes more involved with his stepchild.

Settings and Circumstances for Negotiating Stepfather Identities

Focusing on the physical and social dimensions related to stepfathering sites highlights why and how a man works at managing his identity as a stepfather. A stepfather may be fortunate and never find himself in situations where he or others question his relationship with his stepchild. In this instance, the overriding perception is that the man assumes a fatherly role in all settings. His fatherly ways and stepfather identity are never seriously challenged or negotiated. He is a father or at least a stepfather, pure and simple.

But not all stepfathers are so lucky. Many go to great lengths to try and secure their position and roles as stepfather. They negotiate, debate, plead, and
generally struggle to have others see them in a particular light, as a father figure of some sort. Men's status as stepfathers or authority figures is often contested on some level, sometimes on a regular basis.

The biggest category of men probably fall somewhere between these two
extremes. These men are typically seen as stepfathers, but in novel situations
with people they don't know, they may be forced to manage their identities to
help others understand who they are in relation to the stepchild. For many
men, these situations are no big deal, but for some the process of negotiating
their identity and roles may provide them with anxious moments. Although
some men may have to adjust repeatedly to a range of situations throughout
their time as a stepfather, perhaps spanning a stepchild's childhood and adolescent years, others may need only to deal with particular issues for an ab-
breviated period.

Monty is one of those stepfathers who never fully established his identity
as a stepfather because his twelve-year-old stepdaughter, Beverly, repeatedly
refused to acknowledge him in that way.

> We basically don't even talk to each other and we live in the same house. Be-
> cause I'm very bitter about the way that she loves her own father when he is so
> mean to her. . . . I've always been there and I've never, she's never really been
> close to me that way. . . . She'll walk into the house and not even say hi to me
> and I'll walk into the house and won't even say hi to her. I don't ask her how
> her day was; what's she doing or why. She doesn't have to ask me for permis-
> sion for anything because I don't really care what she does; I mean, I'm not go-
> ing to let her do something stupid, but if she wants to go down the street to her
> friend's house, she just walks out the door and goes. Because normally what she
> does is call us; she calls her mother right in front of me anyway, and has done
> that for a long time, probably led up to me feeling the way that I do. I was never,
> I never really understood what I was to her; I still don't. I felt, I've always felt
> like I should have been her father, but I never was, and I never will be.

From Monty's perspective Beverly's reluctance to perceive and respect him
like a father is displayed through her daily behaviors of ignoring him and
making a point of only recognizing her mother's authority. Although the
mother's presence may accentuate Beverly's refusal to acknowledge Monty's
fatherly presence, being alone with Beverly apparently doesn't alter her reluctance to see Monty as a father figure, and Monty's perception of being an
ineffectual outsider.

Introductions are one of the more obvious sites where men and children
have to negotiate the terrain of family language and, implicitly, relationship

identities. How do particular stepfathers introduce their stepchildren to others? In turn, how do children introduce to others the men in their lives who are treating them in a fatherly way? The conscious and unconscious distinctions individuals make between father and stepfather, dad and stepdad, son and stepson, and daughter and stepdaughter provide a frame for thinking about how individuals define others.

Juan, for example, describes how he was with his five-year-old stepson, Ivan, at a church when he ran into a "friend of a friend."

> We were talking and Ivan was there and he [the friend of a friend] asked me: "He is yours?" That was his question. I told him yes. . . . If I have a longer talk, a longer communication with someone, maybe if the issue comes or we talk about it, I'm going to explain. But I really don't feel that it's something that people have to know about or have to—it's something between us; it's not something that other people should care about. It's totally personal. The last thing I want is Ivan listening to me explaining that—because it could be not very good for him.

This scenario shows how Juan, as a stepfather, is conscious of different aspects of his situated experience as a stepfather and negotiates his identity, and indirectly his stepson's, accordingly. In the situation he describes, Juan is reluctant to divulge to others the "personal" information about his relationship with Ivan. On this occasion, he treats the information like a family secret. Because he perceives the conversation at the church to be a brief encounter, and Ivan is standing close enough to hear what Juan has to say, Juan makes a calculated decision to give a convenient reply, though not totally accurate, describing Ivan as his son. By doing so, he implicitly acknowledges that the public image conveyed by the word "stepson" is not as appealing as "son."

"People would come up to me and say like, oh, is this your son? I would tell them no, he's my wife's child. Even though I kind of wanted to say yes, but we were kind of dating so I had no right of saying that was my son." This is how Emmit starts to describe his experiences with being out in public with his five-year-old stepson, Jake, before he married the child's mother. It was common for people to tell Emmit that he and the child looked alike and even joke with Emmit, asking him whether he was sure he wasn't the father because of the physical resemblance. These comments would often lead Jake to look at Emmit and start laughing. With a sheepish grin, Emmit recalls a specific and more recent instance where Jake finally put him on the spot while Emmit was chatting with some of his parents' friends in a store during a trip back to his hometown. With Jake by his side, Emmit replied to the friends' question about whether Jake was his son. "This is my stepson, this is my wife's son." On hearing that, Jake looked up and said, "No, I'm your son." Ever since that day Emmit has always called Jake his son.

Some men are quick to pick up on the meaning of "step" and avoid it completely before its use can ever become a problem. Herman's perspective on introductions conveys his sense of how labels can signal different meanings about the claims people make about claiming children and taking responsibility for them. Herman professes not to introduce his fourteen-year-old "step" daughter as his stepdaughter, but rather as "my daughter." Herman is rather emphatic about seeing and calling this young girl his daughter. In Herman's eye the social element of a familial bond is as significant as the genetic tie.

Public introductions have also come into play with John, his wife, and his stepdaughter Harmony. When they run into Harmony's friends, she apparently doesn't always know whether to call John her father or stepfather. As John recalls, "She pauses, and I'm no dummy so I just put my hand out and say, 'I'm John; how you doing?' I don't want her to feel uncomfortable; she's still kinda, it's still building. We're still working on each other." John is sensitive to Harmony's predicament, which she captures when she says to him things like, "I don't know what to call you; I've got three dads [a biological father and a previous long-term stepfather]." They have talked about introductions and the larger issues of her having different men in her life who have treated her like their daughter. That they are becoming more comfortable with their situation underscores the notion that families that discuss these matters openly and frankly are likely to have the best chance of minimizing any potential awkwardness about how stepdads can be introduced.

Taken from the stepdad's perspective, he also has the option of using phrases that allow him to skirt around the distinction between saying "children" versus "stepchildren," or "son" versus "stepson," or "daughter" versus "stepdaughter." Several men describe that they typically refer to their stepchildren in public introductions or discussions as "my boy(s)" or "my girl(s)." This convenient vernacular provides the men an opportunity to manage the borders of familial life in public by conveying an intimate connection to the children. At the same time, they do not have to worry about the awkwardness or impreciseness that may result if they were to use more common labels such as "sons" or "daughters."

Other public instances where a stepfather can respond to the naming issues include situations where people refer to him or his stepchildren in a manner signifying that assumptions are being made about the relationship status. Perceptions may be that two people are father and daughter, or stepfather and stepson, and so forth. As a stepfather spends more time in a particular stepfamily, the chances will increase that he will confront these situations. Forty-two-year-old Mark notes that the language of "dad" is not important anymore when people in public refer to his stepdaughters as his daughters. He simply lets it go and responds as if no clarification is needed.

Mark's experience shows that a stepfather and others must sometimes negotiate their roles and identities on the fly when circumstances dictate. A stepfather and his stepchild may arrive at a common understanding of how they plan to relate to one another, but this obviously is not always the case. A child's willingness to buy into the idea that an adult man other than the biological father has a legitimate right to interact with him or her as a father figure, and the man's willingness to accept this status, will help to provide each with ready-made definitions to guide their perceptions and actions. Talking about and arriving at this understanding can ease the transitions a man and stepchild make when they move from private to public displays of the relationships they have with one another. The extent to which these issues can be discussed in a comfortable and effective fashion will depend on various factors, including the age of the child and the extent to which the mother supports the stepfather's having meaningful relationships with her child.

Although table 4.1 depicts scenarios where the stepfather and stepchild are both present, negotiations focused on the meaning of a stepfather's involvement with a stepchild in scenarios with and without other adults can also occur without the child being present. A man does not have to be with a child to express his stepfather identity; he can enter this mental space by discussing his stepchild with school teachers, neighbors, friends, grandparents, or other kids. Similarly, the private discussions a stepfather has with the birth mother could be seen as part of this more public context, though it seems reasonable to use the family unit as the reference point and interpret the discussions as being private.

Immediate and extended family members in various settings can influence a man's commitment to and style of stepfathering. When the stepfathers in my study comment on how their family and their partner's family treat them in their roles as stepfathers, they generally say that they feel okay about it. For example, Jesse increasingly has received positive signs for his involvement with his girlfriend's child, Shaun, from his partner's family as well as his own. Jesse parrots what Shaun's biological grandmother has said to make a point about how she feels toward Jesse: "You know, ever since you first started hanging out with Shaun, I've thought that you were a super good guy and that you would be a good quality father for Shaun." The support is equally positive on his side of the family. Reflecting on the way his parents have taken a liking to Shaun, Jesse details how they have made a place for him in their home—where Jesse lives as well.

It's kind of strange. You see all our furniture and then there's a football-shaped toy box and, like, how did that get here? And it's like my parents adjusted. There's apple juice in the fridge and baby yogurt and stuff like that. We don't have a baby in the house technically all the time, but they like buy groceries for

him and—because if he just stays over there and stuff. . . . My parents really like
having him around and so it's not awkward at my house.

By making some adjustments to their physical space, and creating an atmosphere where they role-play grandparents, Jesse's parents make it more convenient for Jesse to orient toward Shaun in a fatherly way. They help construct the grandparents' "place" where their son can parent.

Similarly, Carl remembers that his parents "had no problems with me having a small three-year-old tagging along and doing things." They eventually
adopted the roles of "Gram" and "Gramps" to his stepdaughter Vicky, whom
they first met five years ago. He also has felt at ease with the biological
grandmother. Talking about the grandmother and himself he makes the point
that "we've always both had Vicky's best interests in mind. We've always
gotten along with how those interests were to be doled out and there's never
a sense when I go there [grandmother's house] that I'm not important as part
of taking care of Vicky's life. . . . I'm not superseded by the matriarch position of the grandmother." For Carl, things apparently have worked out well
with all the grandparents because they have accepted Carl's strong commitment to Vicky and her mother from the beginning.

Although most of the stepfathers in my study feel supported by family in this
way, or at the very least they have not been aggressively challenged or harassed,
a few express serious concerns about how their family or their partner's family
have treated them. Involved in one of the most unpleasant situations is Thomas,
his wife Stephanie, her two teenage boys, and a four-year-old daughter they had
together. In a frustrated tone, Stephanie describes how she and Thomas have
been infuriated by the way his parents have treated her and handled the stepfamily arrangement. She first mentions how Thomas's family members would
introduce them to people they didn't know, presumably in domestic as well as
public settings. "'This is Thomas and his wife, Stephanie, and these are her
boys, Danny and Keith. But this is their daughter.' I mean, they would always
distinguish and differentiate who's was, this is hers and this is theirs." Stephanie
continues, demonstrating how Thomas confronted his family after the tension
got unbearable: "'This is my wife. And I love her very much. Those aren't my
boys, but they are my boys.' He would always say, 'They aren't mine, but they
are mine. And I love them very much too. And unless you can treat them like
family, then we just don't need to be around each other.'" Thomas apparently
has been true to his word, remaining estranged from his biological family because he feels they do not embrace his wife and stepchildren as family. For
Thomas, the blood tie was not as strong as the love tie.

Plenty of places provide the stepfathers opportunities for others to watch
and judge them as they interact with a stepchild. In some cases those doing

the watching know for sure that a child is not biologically related to the step-father and in other situations they will probably assume the child is his. One set of circumstances that can lead people to question a stepfather's relation-ship to a child in public involves the stepfather who is clearly of a different racial background than the birth mother, and most importantly the children. This is the case with the African American stepfather Eddie, whose wife and eight-year-old stepdaughter Rhendy are white. Eddie describes how he inter-acts with his stepchild by saying,

> When we're out in public she's a kid, so I drop to a kid's level. I'll put them in the buggy and I'll run around the store with them. Or I'll hide somewhere and they'll try to find me. We'll hug. I mean, I'll pick her up, I'll carry her. I'll let her ride on my back. It's just if—like I say, if it was me looking at me, I would say the only reason they would separate us is that she's white and I'm black. That's the only way. If we were both white, they would think I was her father. Stepfather wouldn't even cross their minds. It's just, this is how I am in public, I mean. I don't try to hide anything because her feelings are more important than everybody else's.

Eddie realizes that having a different racial background than his stepdaughter represents a red flag for others who will assume automatically that he is not the biological father. However, this does not appear to faze him much because he is content with the fun-loving relationship he has with Rhendy.

Ron, a stepfather of African American and Puerto Rican heritage, is more upset with how others treat him as being part of an interracial couple involv-ing white children.

> And every time we sit in a restaurant together, everybody looks at us because we are a black and white couple. . . . I might as well not even be here [restau-rant] because I don't even get responded to like I'm their dad.

Asked how it makes him feel, Ron is quick to reply, "It makes me feel like shit, of course." I sensed that Ron felt marginalized as a father figure in a va-riety of ways while finding it difficult to assume a full-fledged identity as a stepfather because others were not supportive, including the birth mother. Ron describes similar problems when he tried to live with his partner and her children at her mother's and brother's home for a short time after moving from the north. In Ron's opinion, these people were blatant racists, adding to Ron's dilemma. Reflecting on this period, Ron expresses his frustration:

> Where you're getting called racial remarks by your wife, and you have no con-trol of the kids. You're living in a house with her mom, where the kids can drop stuff all over the place and nothing be done. The kids can run over you and noth-ing will happen.

Ron's frustrations were clearly exacerbated by the fact that he had to live in someone else's home and at the same time be disrespected and denied any type of fathering presence by the kids and adults.

For some of the stepfathers, feeling as though others see and treat them in public (and private) as the father is rewarding. William, for example, responds to a question I ask about how he feels when he's out with his stepsons and fiancée, and how he believes others perceive him. "I feel good about it, even though I know it's not totally accurate, it makes me feel good. To be able to walk out among people and they look and they don't see mother, son, son, stepfather. They see father, mother, son, son. It makes me feel good." Having others see and treat him as the father is important to William, particularly when he's with his new family. Although he did not use any of these words explicitly, his demeanor and story suggests that he does not want to be perceived as an outsider, intruder, or an appendage. By placing himself at the head of the list of "father, mother, son, and son," William suggests that he would much rather see himself as the head of a nuclear style family.

In addition to those public sites where stepfathers construct their identities while in the company of their stepchildren, stepfathers can do identity work without their stepchildren being present. One such social setting that some of the stepfathers talked about involved their participation in parent–teacher conferences at school. Although some stepfathers left that responsibility up to their partner and sometimes the biological father, a number of stepfathers had gone to these meetings who had stepchildren old enough to be enrolled in school. On the whole, these men offered a range of responses to how they were treated by the teachers during the meetings. Some felt like they had been taken seriously and treated like an important adult figure in their stepchild's life, with some feeling as though they were treated as the father. A few felt more alienated from the process and treated in a marginal way. Similar types of situations can arise when stepfathers find themselves discussing their stepchildren's affairs with other adults who are responsible for their well-being.

FUTURE RESEARCH

Whether stepfathers act fatherly in the privacy of their homes or in public, alone with a stepchild or in the company of others, with the support of the mother or not, stepfathers have numerous situated opportunities to construct their identities in relation to stepchildren. Although not the main focus of this discussion, stepfathers also negotiate their identities in situations where their stepchildren are absent. These latter experiences may affect how stepfathers negotiate their identities while they're interacting with their stepchildren.

Throughout, I have emphasized that stepfathers construct their identities within contexts where either family members, most notably mothers, or others outside the family are involved. Thus, if stepfathers are to learn how to transition smoothly into stepfamilies and contribute to them in healthy ways, research and program initiatives can prove useful by providing insights and resources that take into account the individual, interpersonal, and community contexts affecting the multilayered process of stepfathering.

Among the forty different stepfathering contexts I have identified, and the additional permutations that easily can be imagined, some obviously are more common than others. In addition, certain scenarios are likely to be more consequential for how stepfathers construct and express their identities. Future research should initially focus on the most consequential and common sites. For example, scenarios 3 and 8 refer to stepfathers interacting with stepchildren in the physical setting of a home where other adult figures are not present. In the first instance biological children are not present, in the latter they are. Even though these two sites may not be the most common, the largely private stepfathering arenas warrant study because stepfathers have the opportunity to assert themselves without any immediate adult competition or challenges to their authority. Stepchildren may, of course, question the stepfather's authority, but the interpersonal dynamics associated with such a challenge are likely to have unique features if the stepfather is acting as an authority figure in the immediate context. These contexts may also provide stepfathers with important opportunities to engage in affinity seeking and maintaining strategies that influence how they construct their identities (Ganong, Coleman, Fine, and Martin 1999).

From a symbolic interactionist perspective, understanding fully the immediate context necessitates focusing on its nuanced, dynamic elements. For instance, little is known about how stepfather–stepchild interaction scenarios are shaped by the subjective realities connected to either stepfamily members' earlier experiences or expectations about the future. Research in this area also needs to clarify how individuals experience specific situations that are immersed in a larger physical/social context defined by various social conditions. For example, a stepfather may be interacting with his stepchild one-on-one in his house, but if they both know that the birth mother is at the neighbors' house next door the situation may be perceived quite differently than if the birth mother is on a five-day business trip hundreds of miles away. Interestingly, modern cell and computer technology may have altered the way stepchildren and stepfathers perceive their time together if the birth mother can be contacted directly despite her physical absence. This type of modern availability may be altering the extent to which and how physical conditions associated with certain stepfather–stepchild contexts are interpreted and influence interaction.

Scenarios 25 and 30 are particularly intriguing because they deal with venues where the biological father and stepfather are physically present along with the child. Even though these types of scenarios may not be particularly common for stepfamilies today, this may change as stepfamilies become a more institutionalized part of our cultural landscape. When these scenarios do arise, some occur within the confines of a family member's home, whereas others take place within a more public setting (e.g., school or recreational site). Those stepfathers who express themselves as a father ally toward the biological father are likely to experience these settings much differently than those who feel jealousy, animosity, or indifference toward the father. Research on how stepfathers negotiate their fatherly identity when the biological father is present should consider how gender-related conditions influence men's perceptions of and responses to various situations. What conditions enhance the likelihood that a stepfather and father will act cooperatively rather than competitively in a particular scenario? Research should explore the conditions and processes associated with cooperative dual fathering. When, for example, do stepfathers or biological fathers make a conscious effort to work on their relationship by having mature conversations about their relationship or the child's well-being, or initiate opportunities to spend time together in the presence of the child? Russ, a stepfather to a twelve-year-old boy, Samuel, illustrates this research domain. While discussing his feelings towards his stepson's father, he spontaneously comments, "Actually, Samuel has wanted for me and his grandfather and his dad to go fishing. I wouldn't even have a problem with that. . . . It would be weird. I would be kind of awkward, but . . . if that's what Samuel wants, I don't mind doing it." Noting this example several times during the interview, Russ implies that his affection for Samuel, and his desire to do the "right" thing for him, are sufficient grounds for him to experiment with sharing space and an activity with Samuel, the biological father, and grandfather. Whether he will initiate the contact necessary to make this outing happen is, of course, the critical question. Programmatic efforts designed to encourage such interaction while studying the outcomes for the stepfather, father, and child could produce intriguing results.

Another set of scenarios, 34 and 39, offer research opportunities to learn more about how stepfathers manage their identities in settings where friends and extended kin are a part of the social dimension defining particular physical sites. From a social psychological perspective, it is important to learn more about the extent to which these significant others can enhance or impede stepfathers' willingness and ability to adopt a fatherly identity in different types of settings.

Finally, the varied types of scenarios that involve stepfathering in public scenarios (20, 25, 30, 35, 40) are fascinating places to study how men construct and express their identities as stepfathers. Here, men will face numerous situations where they must navigate social situations that involve their being an adult authority figure for stepchildren in the presence of strangers and acquaintances, some of whom know very little about the men's specific relationship to the stepchildren. Under what circumstances do men approach these situations armed with preexisting definitions of the situation, and when do they spontaneously construct new ones? What conditions shape how men negotiate and express their identities in these situations? To what extent do these types of situations affect how men construct their more enduring identities as stepfathers that transcend a specific physical site?

Because stepfathers' identities are constructed in reciprocal role relationships, any full-fledged research agenda to understand stepfathers' situated experiences must take into account how stepchildren and birth mothers relate to stepfathers and perceive themselves. Learning more about how stepchildren, birth mothers, and stepfathers individually and jointly construct their identities should lead to a more complete picture of stepfathers' subjective lives.

Though it is beyond the scope of this chapter, features of the model outlined here could be modified relatively easily to make it applicable to nonresident and resident biological fathers. In particular, fathers who live apart from their children, like stepfathers, must grapple with a variety of challenges involving the navigation of physical space and the symbolic and social dimensions associated with it.

REFERENCES

Blumer, H. (1969). *Symbolic interactionism*. Englewood Cliffs, NJ: Prentice-Hall.

Cherlin, A. J. (1978). Remarriage as an incomplete institution. *American Journal of Sociology, 84*, 634–50.

Cooksey, E., and Craig, P. H. (1998). Parenting from a distance: The effects of paternal characteristics on contact between nonresidential fathers and their children. *Demography, 35*, 187–200.

Cooksey, E., and Fondell, M. (1996). Spending time with his kids: Effects of family structure on fathers' and children's lives. *Journal of Marriage and the Family, 58*, 693–707.

Ganong, L. H., Coleman, M., Fine, M., and Martin, P. (1999). Stepparents' affinity-seeking and affinity-maintaining strategies with stepchildren. *Journal of Family Issues, 20*, 299–327.

Ganong, L. H., Coleman, M., and Kennedy, G. (1990). The effects of using alternate labels in denoting stepparent or stepfamily status. *Journal of Social Behavior and Personality, 5*, 453–63.

Goffman, E. (1974). *Frame analysis: An essay on the social organization of experience.* New York: Harper and Row.

Hans, J. D. (2002). Stepparenting after divorce: Stepparents' legal position regarding custody, access, and support. *Family Relations, 51,* 301–7.

Hetherington, E. M., and Kelly, J. (2002). *Divorce reconsidered: For better or worse.* New York: Norton.

Hofferth, S. L., and Anderson, K. G. (2003). Are all dads equal? Biology versus marriage as a basis for parental investment. *Journal of Marriage and Family, 65,* 213–32.

Hofferth, S. L., Pleck, J. H., Stueve, J. L., Bianchi, S., and Sayer, L. (2002). The demography of fathers: What fathers do. In C. S. Tamis-LeMonda and N. Cabrera (Eds.), *Handbook of father involvement: Multidisciplinary perspectives* (pp. 63–90). Mahwah, NJ: Erlbaum.

Katz, S. N. (1999). Establishing the family and family-like relationships: Emerging models for alternatives to marriage. *Family Law Quarterly, 33,* 663–75.

Lincoln, Y., and Guba, E. (1985). *Naturalistic inquiry.* Beverly Hills, CA: Sage.

MacDonald, W. L., and DeMaris, A. (1996). Parenting stepchildren and biological children: The effects of stepparent's gender and new biological children. *Journal of Family Issues, 17,* 5–25.

Marsiglio, W. (2004). *Stepdads: Stories of love, hope, and repair.* Lanham, MD: Rowman & Littlefield.

Marsiglio, W., Day, R. D., and Lamb, M. E. (2000). Exploring fatherhood diversity: Implications for conceptualizing father involvement. *Marriage and Family Review, 29,* 269–93.

Marsiglio, W., and Cohan, M. (2000). Contextualizing father involvement and paternal influence: Sociological and qualitative themes. *Marriage and Family Review, 29,* 75–95.

Mead, G. H. (1934). *Mind, self, and society: From the standpoint of a social behaviorist.* Chicago: University of Chicago Press.

Nippert-Eng, C. (1996). Calendars and keys: The classification of "home" and "work." *Qualitative Sociology, 11,* 563–82.

Oxhorn-Ringwood, L., Oxhorn, L., and Krausz, M. V. (2002). *Stepwives.* New York: Simon & Schuster.

Palkovitz, R. (1997). Reconstructing "involvement": Expanding conceptualizations of men's caring in contemporary families. In A. J. Hawkins and D. C. Dollahite (Eds.), *Generative fathering: Beyond deficit perspectives* (pp. 200–216). Thousand Oaks, CA: Sage.

Palkovitz, R. (2002). *Involved fathering and men's adult development: Provisional balances.* Mahwah, NJ: Erlbaum.

Pleck, J. H. (1997). Paternal involvement: Levels, causes, and consequences. In M. E. Lamb (Ed.), *The role of the father in child development* (3rd ed., pp. 66–103, 325–32). New York: Wiley.

Pleck, J. H., and Masciadrelli, B. P. (2004). Paternal involvement by U.S. residential fathers: Levels, sources, and consequences. In M. E. Lamb (Ed.), *The role of the father in child development* (4th ed., pp. 222–71). New York: Wiley.

Strauss, A. L., and Corbin, J. (1998). *Basics of qualitative research: Techniques and procedures for developing grounded theory*. Thousand Oaks, CA: Sage.

Stryker, S. (1980). *Symbolic interactionism: A social structural version*. Menlo Park, CA: Benjamin/Cummings.

Thomson, E., Hanson, T. L., and McLanahan, S. S. (1994). Family structure and child well-being: Economic resources vs. parental behaviors. *Social Forces, 73*, 221–42.

Thomson, E., McLanahan, S. S., and Curtin, R. B. (1992). Family structure, gender, and parental socialization. *Journal of Marriage and the Family, 54*, 368–78.

White, L., and Gilbreth, J. G. (2001). When children have two fathers: Effects of relationships with stepfathers and noncustodial fathers on adolescent outcomes. *Journal of Marriage and Family, 63*, 155–67.

5

Nonresidential Fathers: Shifting Identities, Roles, and Authorities

Beth S. Catlett, Michelle L. Toews,
and Patrick C. McKenry

Divorce rates in the United States doubled between the late 1960s and the late 1970s, and have only slightly declined since the early 1980s (Teachman, Tedrow, and Crowder 2000). As these statistics illustrate, divorce has become an increasingly prominent feature in American families. And yet, although divorce has become commonplace and sometimes even described as a normative life transition (Price and McKenry 1988), there is relatively little information about fathers' experiences after divorce (Arditti 1995; Arendell 1995; Kruk 1994). What we know about divorce adjustment largely has been derived from the study of middle-class women (Kitson and Holmes 1992). For example, researchers and practitioners consistently have reported that women with custody of children, who have fewer economic resources and marketable skills, are at high risk for the negative consequences of divorce (Catlett and McKenry 1996; Clarke-Stewart and Bailey 1989).

Some limited inroads, however, have been made in assessing men's experiences with divorce. For instance, evidence indicates that sole physical custody by the mother with paternal visitation continues to be the most common custody arrangement after divorce, even in cases of joint legal custody (Braver 1998; Furstenberg and Cherlin 1991; Seltzer 1991). Accordingly, most divorced fathers experience the loss of physical custody of their children. This custody arrangement often involves the mother's retention of the predivorce family home and the divorced father's acquisition of new premises. This postdivorce family reorganization involving fathers' loss of primary family space may pose substantial risks and challenges for divorced fathers. (Dudley 1991; Kruk 1994). Indeed, studies indicate that men who experience the loss of their home and, perhaps more importantly, the loss of regular contact and shared physical space with their children suffer substantial emotional distress (Braver 1998). Moreover, nonresident fathers have been found to engage in impulsive and health compromising behaviors to a greater extent, and for a longer period of time, than fathers in any other family type (Umberson and Williams 1993).

In addition, marriage has been found to benefit men in terms of both emotional and physical well-being (Coombs 1991; Kiecolt-Glaser and Newton 2001). For instance, Nock (1998) contends that marriage is beneficial to men, in part, as a result of its meaning and implications for meeting societal ideals of masculinity. In a similar vein, Townsend (2002) concludes that men tend to define fathering very much in terms of marriage and sharing the same home with their children and their children's mother. This is a strong cultural construction, argues Townsend, and therefore can be helpful in explaining why divorce would be expected to prompt men's sense of despair and loss (Coombs 1991; Kiecolt-Glaser and Newton 2001).

Thus, although over the past decade progress has been made in exploring men's postdivorce lives as nonresidential fathers, there still exists a dearth of research based on father reports (Kruk 1994; Marsiglio 1995). Our study is a step toward addressing this gap. Using the understudied context of men in divorce transition, we explore the impact that postdivorce loss of shared family space with children has on men's symbolic constructions of fatherhood. Specifically, the purpose of this study is to examine how nonresidential divorced fathers perceive the loss of shared family space after divorce and to understand, from their point of view, how the lack of shared physical space shapes their postdivorce fathering roles and identities.

THEORETICAL FOUNDATIONS

We use both symbolic interactionism and feminist-informed gender theory to frame our exploration of men's postdivorce experiences as fathers. This theoretical model allows for an analysis of men's shifting identities and roles from a multilayered and interactive perspective. Specifically, we focus on those theoretical and ideological strains that form a coherent conceptual framework for thinking about how divorced fathers manage and perceive the transitions and constraints regarding postdivorce physical space.

In general, symbolic interactionist perspectives offer a frame of reference for understanding how humans, in concert with one another, create symbolic worlds, and how these worlds, in turn, shape human behavior (LaRossa and Reitzes 1993). Symbolic interactionists—and to a large extent feminist approaches—assume that meanings and actions are socially constructed. Meanings, then, are both experientially derived and culturally based (Arendell 1995). The conceptual tools of symbolic interactionism provide the foundation for an examination of men's definitions and symbolic understandings of divorce. This theoretical perspective is particularly useful in terms of understanding fathers' symbolic constructions and negotiations of physical space after divorce.

Feminist theoretical perspectives complement the symbolic interactionist assumptions, making them well suited to frame an exploration of fathers' postdivorce responses. Feminist theory highlights the overarching significance of gender in family life. Specifically, a feminist lens elevates the role of gender, viewing it as a process that underlies all behavior that is shaped by and reproduces social structure (Ferree 1990). Gender can be viewed as a fundamental category of social relations both within and outside the family. Moreover, a feminist conceptualization problematizes gender in families, recasting the family as a system of gender stratification situated in the context of a patriarchal social structure (Ferree 1990; Thorne 1992; Zinn 1990). Inequities in the larger society influence the differential access to resources and rewards for men and women in families (Allen and Baber 1994; Chafetz 1988). Gender power hierarchies, furthermore, are best understood as systematically related to other structures of power, including race, ethnicity, socioeconomic status, and sexual orientation (Collins 1990; Glenn 1987; Zinn 1990).

Thus, to understand fully the meaning men attach to postdivorce transitions in shared family living space, it is important to situate their interpretations within the larger social context. Life events occur within a social milieu that, to a large extent, structures men's and women's family roles in particular ways, and patterns the personal and social meaning attached to those roles. Moreover, large-scale social processes often shape the opportunities and constraints that fathers experience as they attempt to enact specific roles. Hence, it is important to view fathers' postdivore experiences of situated fatherhood as both socially patterned and individualistic in nature (Marsiglio 1995).

Connell's (1995) gender theory about multiple masculinities provides an interpretive framework to examine men's postdivorce responses. The masculinity forms align themselves in a quasi-hierarchical fashion with hegemonic masculinity at the apex. While this notion is most typically described with reference to men's dominance over, and subordination of, women, its most relevant manifestation for purposes of this study revolves around more general concepts of family power and authority. Hegemonic masculinity can be described as the form of masculinity that embodies the traditional hallmarks of successful manhood in this culture: attainment of wealth and of positions enabling men to exert power in business, government, athletics, and family. In essence, hegemonic masculinity involves men's dominant positions within, and authority over, their domains. Within this theoretical framework, the man who successfully attains hegemonic masculinity is able to enact the culturally dominant ideal of manhood in which men have a successful claim to authority and power.

The ways hegemonic masculinity is exhibited in fathers' multiple roles is particularly relevant for this study. A primary manifestation of hegemonic masculinity in the family is men's quest for head of household status. One aspect of this hegemonic masculine model is men's focus on their role as the primary provider of financial resources for their families. Historically, men's breadwinning not only has been a demonstration of their masculinity, but also the most unifying element in fathers' lives. Breadwinning and economic support of children are inextricably bound together in men's sense of the masculine self. As noted earlier, men often define fathering very much in terms of marriage and sharing the same home with their children and their children's mother. Thus men are seen as being afforded a variety of institutional and societal benefits in marriage. The loss of such marital benefits—in particular, the loss of primary shared living space with children—can be expected to prompt substantial shifts in men's sense of power and authority within their families.

METHODOLOGY

This study draws on data from two sources. First, we drew data from a larger project on conflict in the context of coparenting following marital separation and divorce. The sample population for this larger project was selected from (1) divorce court records of parents with a child under eighteen who divorced in the past two years in central Ohio and (2) newspaper advertisements. Then, for purposes of this study, in-depth interviews were conducted with twenty-four divorced fathers who reported high conflict with their former spouses during the separation process. Second, we examined in-depth interview data from twenty fathers who had been divorced between one and three years at the time of their interviews, and who were part of a larger study on the experiences of noncustodial fathers after divorce. This sample was selected from the files of all previous participants in a Marion County, Ohio, divorce education project. This project, known as Parents Education About Child's Emotions (PEACE), was one of the first in Ohio to be mandated for divorcing parents. It began in 1990, has served more than 5,000 individuals, and consists of a two-and-a-half hour seminar after filing but prior to the granting of the divorce decree.

Although the data are drawn from two distinct samples, the demographic profiles of these samples are nearly identical. Accordingly, it is reasonable to merge the data for purposes of this analysis. Our combined sample consisted of forty-four fathers who were predominately white (89 percent), ranging in age from twenty-three to fifty-one with a mean age of thirty-eight, and had approximately two children. They had been married an average of ten years, separated for one and one-half years, and divorced approximately one and one-half years at the time of their interviews. Regarding socioeconomic status, their annual incomes ranged from less than $10,000 to more than $100,000, with a median of $30,000 to $39,999.

The primary source of data collection was in-depth semistructured interviews conducted by four interviewers—two female and two male—and lasted from one to three hours. Questions generally were open-ended with follow-up probes designed to direct the participants' attention to the major domains of interest. Moreover, the interview guides were designed so that the participants could explore their experiences within a temporal framework—beginning with their marriages, then continuing through the process of marital separation, and concluding with an examination of life after the divorce.

The data analysis began with a verbatim transcription of the audiorecorded interviews. Once this was completed, the interview narratives were analyzed using the NUDIST program for analysis of qualitative data. Each transcript was examined by three independent coders for salient topics covered, as well as reccurring themes within and commonalities among the cases (Berg 1998; Bogdan and Biklen 1992; Denzin 1989). To represent these topics and themes, initial coding categories were developed. Next, the transcripts were coded into more specific and theoretically focused analytic themes (Bogdan and Biklen 1992) reflecting the study's grounding in symbolic interactionism and feminist perspectives on the fathers' negotiation of physical space after divorce. Our use of multiple coders helped enhance the reliability of our findings.

RESULTS

We begin by reviewing the fathers' descriptions of the ways in which they recollect their relationships with their children before divorce. Indeed, these recollections provide a critical context in which to consider questions about divorce and its influence on fathers' shifting and situated family roles. Next, we examine the transformations that divorce prompted in these men's fathering. Our particular focus is on the fathers' perception of physical space within the context of divorce, as well as on their perceived loss of family power and authority associated with shifting family uses of physical space. We also explore how the fathers' perceptions regarding shared family space, or lack thereof, provides a context for examining their shifting fathering identities after divorce.

Relationships with Children Prior to Divorce

The men in this study were asked to characterize their involvement and relationships with their children when they were married. In describing their predivorce relationships, the fathers discussed with great frequency issues involving their emotional connection to their children. The majority of the fathers in this sample reported that they felt very close to their children before the divorce. For example, in the course of exploring his life before divorce, one father described his relationship with his daughter in this way:

> Well, we've been close from day one. I mean hunt, fish, work on cars. . . . Yeah, you name it. It don't make any difference what we did, we done this as one more than as two. We was like my dad and I—we was almost inseparable.

Another father related his sense of devotion to his children to his vulnerable marital relationship:

> I was a real father and I really don't give a damn what anybody says or what anybody thinks. I knew what I did for my children. Completely, totally 100 percent. I gave as much as I possibly could. I gave much more than other fathers that I know. . . . In a sense because the relationship with my wife was failing, I put everything into the children.

One father described a sense of satisfaction about the intense emotional bond he and his daughter shared. Moreover, he characterized this bond as natural and almost effortless:

> I would term my relationship that we had as close to perfect as you can imagine.
> . . . We just had a tremendous . . . we did everything together. She's totally a daddy's girl. . . . It's been as close to perfect as I ever would have hoped for. . . . It comes very natural.

Postdivorce Transitions: Loss of Shared Family Space

Because sole custody by the mother with paternal visitation is still the most common custody arrangement (even in cases of joint legal custody), most divorced fathers experience the loss of physical custody of their children. This custody arrangement often involves the mother's retention of the predivorce family home and the divorced father's acquisition of new premises that are, by definition, shared as family space less often.

The fathers' custodial arrangements reflect this general trend. Specifically, twenty-one of the forty-four fathers defined themselves as the noncustodial parent; that is, these men's former spouses were awarded sole custody of their children, and the fathers visit their children on a schedule either set by the court or worked out with the former spouse through mutual agreement. Of the remaining twenty-three fathers, eighteen reported that they have joint legal custody of their children. In these cases, the fathers do not have physical custody of their children but do have legal decision-making authority. Thus the fathers with joint legal custody also maintain a visiting relationship with their children. Of the remaining five fathers, three have sole custody of their children and two described their custodial arrangement as joint physical custody.

From the perspectives of the majority of fathers participating in this study, the residential transitions associated with divorce—in particular, fathers' lack of consistently shared family space with children—represent a profound sense of loss. The men consistently reported a loss of access to and interaction with their children. This discourse of loss centered on fathers' lack of daily contact with their children. For instance, one father expressed his sense of pain and defeat when he said,

> I asked why a lot. You know, when you're used to coming home from work and your kids being there, you know, and then you come home from work and there's nobody there. That really hurts.

Another father portrayed his emotion in the face of the loss of a shared family home in this way:

> I see my kids a lot. Not every day, but I see them a lot. There are days when they come over but some of the things they say, where did you come up with that? I feel I missed these things. I don't see my kids to bed every night. I don't get the chance to give them a bath every night. I don't get the chance to sit down and eat dinner with them every day.

Other participants' sense of loss was exacerbated by the geographic distance between their new homes and their children's homes. One father articulated his feelings this way:

> I feel bad that I'm not able to be in their day-to-day lives. I feel bad that at a moment's notice I can't just watch them play soccer or go to their swimming lessons, whereas if they were local—I'm not saying I do it often, but occasionally I go see Logan at his swimming lessons. Or he played in a basketball league this past winter.

Another participant provides a powerful illustration of the challenges posed by geographic distance:

> You can't understand my life until you walk a mile in my shoes. I never would have understood. The sheer hopelessness, the pain, it's something you can't

describe. . . . I never feel the pain as intensely as the pain I go through with my own daughter even though I get to see her twice a month. I know she's there. I feel helpless in the fact that I can't just go over and take her out for an ice cream or whatever. I have difficulty even getting a hold of her on the telephone. She's twenty miles away and I can't go to her. I can't get through.

Beyond fathers' sense of pain in the face of the loss of day-to-day contact with their children, many men express the threat to their sense of personal integrity that the loss of the family home represents. The fathers' narratives demonstrate that fathers not only make spatial and residential adjustments after divorce, but that such transitions may well lead to a postdivorce utilization of living space in which men's perceived status is dramatically altered. For example, one father discussed what he considered to be a pitiable situation when he stated, "I didn't really have a permanent residence. I was just kind of living wherever. . . . I had [to have] my visitation at my mom's house." Several fathers mentioned how their children didn't see their new residence as a valid family space. One child told his father, "[Your] house is not that important to me." Another father drew links between the family home and personal accomplishment when he stated that

I'm not being very successful at this point in time but she's a good mother and then the fact at their house they also—again a real nice house, five bedrooms— they have their own bedrooms. See, here with me, my son sleeps in the bed with me, my daughter sleeps on a futon and the [other] two daughters sleep in a pull out sleeper sofa.

Not only did these men express their sense of personal loss and loss of status, but they also expressed the belief that postdivorce physical transitions and separations are detrimental to their children. In particular, one father reported considerable apprehension about the impact of joint physical custody arrangements on children:

I think it's utterly ridiculous, stupid to even consider shared parenting, meaning you go six weeks or six months with one parent or six months with the other, or a week or a month, because that's not fair to those children. They need to have a center. They need to have, I mean, they need to have a place. And to rip them up six months back, that's . . . what a terrible childhood to go through.

The report of another father lends support to the notion that moving from one family space to another may threaten children's sense of consistency and security. Specifically, this father reported that although his daughter had her own room, she insisted on sleeping with him because she was frightened by the unfamiliar environment.

As these narratives illustrate, fathers' sense of loss of daily contact and interaction with children, their perceived diminished status, and their concerns about the consequences of residential transitions on children are central themes in men's postdivorce family restructuring. Sentiments such as these illustrate the challenge that divorce—and the concomitant loss of shared private family space with children—poses for participants' sense of efficacy as men and fathers.

Loss of Familial Power and Authority

Another primary theme in the research participants' narratives was a symbolic construction of shared physical space with children, and perhaps more importantly, lack of shared physical space with children, in terms of authority, power, and control. According to these fathers, divorce, and the residential changes that it prompted, changed the nature of their relationships with their children, as well as with their former spouses. A substantial majority of the fathers in our sample discussed family living spaces in terms of loss with respect to their authority and influence in their children's lives. Moreover, they often described their new family position with reference to power struggles with their former spouses. They noted with great frequency the increasingly powerful and influential roles that their former spouses played in their children's lives because they shared family space with them. In essence, these fathers experienced postdivorce residential transitions as a realignment of family power in which their former spouses gained authority and power at their expense. One father's comment is particularly illustrative: "She got possession of the house and I couldn't go to the house [because] she changed the locks. I was the only source of income and now I couldn't even get in my own house."

Our findings suggest the fathers felt marginalized within their families. In addition, the loss of shared physical space with children, and fathers' perceived loss of power associated with shared physical space, were central to the way they negotiated their postdivorce fathering identity. In particular, the loss of shared physical space seemed to mirror or produce a shift in the fathers' identities. Without a daily shared family space in which they perceive themselves as head of household, these fathers were prompted to redefine their sense of themselves as fathers. This discourse of shifting identities and diminished family power and authority is evidenced in two primary topics embedded within these fathers' narratives: (1) visitation rights and (2) parental authority.

Visitation Rights

The vast majority of the fathers had a court-ordered visitation arrangement to see their children every other weekend and one additional day during the week. Moreover, the majority of fathers expressed a sense of resentment regarding their visitation arrangements and, in particular, over the power and control they perceived their former spouses to have in terms of controlling visitation with children. Indeed, the loss of consistent access to, or control over, the primary family space emerged as a central concern. One father characterized his situation this way:

> I was upset because of the situation with the kids. She liked to keep the kids away from me or I had to go to her house to see the kids and that did bother me considerably. She really dangled them over my head on many occasions.

Another father communicated a similar sense of frustration and powerlessness in the face of his former spouse's control of visitation:

> [My ex-wife makes visitation] a real control issue. You pick them up when I say, you bring them back when I say. And you have to live by these rules. Be there at eight or five or six or whatever. And basically I have to live—I need to be flexible but she doesn't. . . . I mean, I feel like she's the gatekeeper and I think she relishes that role.

Additional fathers echoed these sentiments saying things such as: "She has never ever given me one extra moment with the kids" and "There were times where she'd threaten to keep [my sons] away from me." One father even conveyed a story about how he stopped by his former wife's house one day and said to his children, "Come here guys, give me a hug." His former wife apparently responded, "No, you can't kiss them or hug them, it's not your day to see them," and then slammed the door. These same fathers stated that they wanted to "share more time" with their children; however, their former spouses "became very controlling."

As one might surmise from these emotionally charged accounts, the majority of the men in this study described the court system as biased in favor of women, and as privileging the mother's role over the father's in the post-divorce family. For fathers, loss of primary family space seems to be symbolic of diminished power. Moreover, in the absence of a consistently shared living space with children, men's provision of economic support is experienced as problematic. Specifically, numerous fathers reported feeling as if their parental status had been stripped from them by a legal system that sanctions problematic custody, visitation, and financial arrangements. As one father stated,

> I'm not asking for anything special. I'm not asking for anything more than just being fair and equal down the middle. To be treated as an equal parent which I was while I was married, but not the second I got divorced.

Others elaborated on this idea when they discussed being "reduced to a paycheck." One father illustrated,

> You go into a divorce being equal parents, as equal as you can be, and then all of a sudden one is a parent and one is a paycheck. A father isn't a parent in a divorce; he's an every other weekend paycheck, and it's sickening.

Similarly, another father stated that "the woman is given the kids and the man is told to pay the bills." One father clearly summed up the frustrations of many by stating, "There's a whole hell of a lot of us out there that want to be an active father and aren't allowed. . . . She's what they call the residential parent, so she got the control."

Parental Authority

Stemming from the perceived loss of power associated with lack of consistently shared physical space with children, the fathers perceived a loss of parental authority and control over their children's lives. One father, who had recently divorced at the time of our interview, clearly articulated the link between shared family living space and parental authority when he stated this fear:

> I was worried because I was afraid that they—even though I was very active in their lives and I had been trying to do whatever I could for them—I was afraid because they lived with their mother and they did not see me all the time, that there would be a split and it would show and it would really hurt me.

This fear seems to be manifested in many of the fathers' perceptions. For instance, one father felt that "truly parenting" his children had become close to impossible since the residential changes prompted by divorce. Asked about his role in his children's lives, this father responded,

> I have no involvement in their life other than being the guy that shows up every other weekend. That's what I wanted. I wanted some real involvement in my children's life. In which technically I have none right now. I have no control, no say so. . . . I'm being taken advantage of in a situation of which I have no control. . . . At this point my children know that I have no control, no say so, no input on anything they do. . . . I've talked with them, but they know their mother runs the show.

Other fathers discussed their diminished parental authority within the context of specific parental roles such as homework assistance, meal preparation, discipline, and so forth. Indeed, most fathers felt that fulfilling such roles had become nearly unattainable as a result of only intermittent shared family space with children. One father characterized his postdivorce family role in this way:

> I'm not a dad anymore. I see them four days out of the month. There's no time to be a father. There's just time to be a friend and I'm not going to spend my time arguing with my kids and bitching. Come on over, let's enjoy ourselves. Let's visit with each other and let's enjoy each other's company.

Another man reported on how he tried during visitation to help his children with their homework:

> It's really hard to sit down and work on the kids' school work during the week when you've got them for two hours. You have to feed them, and that's about it. I used to get them from 5:00 to 8:00. Last time I went back to court it was determined that 8:00 was too late for them. Now it's 5:00 to 7:00. You can't come home and cook dinner in that amount of time.

As we also discussed in terms of visitation, the fathers in our study perceived their loss of parental authority as the mothers' gain. For example, one father explained his concerns about his lack of parental authority after the divorce in a way that mirrored the sentiments of many fathers in the study: "She tells me that I no longer have a say in anything; . . . she tells me it's none of my business. She don't have to answer to me is what she says." And the comments of other men mirror this sentiment: "She's [his former wife] what they call the residential parent, so she's got much more control." Finally, another father noted, "She holds all the cards, all the aces."

Participants' narratives around issues of family power and authority after divorce, deliver a strong message about the salience of shared family space for fathers' sense of themselves as rightful parents to their children. Without the legitimizing context of shared family space, these men perceive that they are not able to parent effectively. Moreover, the loss of consistent access to, or control over, the shared family space emerged as central to fathers' sense of loss and perceived powerlessness in divorce.

DISCUSSION

These stories center on shifts in the physical location of fathering. The shifts in physical space seem to mirror (or produce) a transformation in fathers' identities and perceived roles. For men, divorce prompts a reorganization of family residences, and this in turn transforms family relationships and roles. From a gendered perspective, these transitions produce adjustments in the positions of relative privilege that men occupy when married. In other words, divorce, and the residential transitions that accompany divorce, calls men's family status into question (Catlett and McKenry 2004). In particular, the reorganization of living space and parenting roles following divorce can precipitate changes in fathers' prerogatives in the family. Thus the divorce process, and the residential shifts that it entails, redistributes power and may well lead to a postdivorce family structure in which men's perceived relative position is dramatically altered. Understood in this way, divorce represents a "crisis tendency" for men in families because it weakens the institutional foundation that sustains the legitimacy of their family power (Connell 1987; Messner 1997). That is, men tend to define fathering very much in terms of sharing the same home with their children (Townsend 2002). And without this legitimizing context of daily shared space and consistent access to their children, men's self-image may be dramatically altered.

Themes such as these illustrate the challenge that postdivorce shifts in the physical location of fathering poses for men's sense of connection to and authority within their families. Although a superficial examination of these men's narratives may imply that fathers' relationships with their children are dramatically changed as a result of the residential changes prompted by divorce, existing research suggests caution in drawing such a conclusion. For example, Furstenberg and Cherlin (1991) conclude that families after divorce look very much like families before divorce. In other words, because fathers no longer share living space with their children on a daily basis, divorce may merely expose the highly gendered patterns of parenting that existed even within the marriage. For instance, Allen and Hawkins (1999) argue that maternal gatekeeping in married families restricts father involvement, thereby limiting a close connection between fathers and their children. The work of Thompson and Walker (1989) and Coltrane (2000) takes a different position—these scholars contend that it is unlikely that maternal gatekeeping is the dominant influence on father involvement. Rather, they suggest that family involvement cannot be understood without a full examination of gender ideology, marital power, and both formal and informal market economies. These different explanatory perspectives notwithstanding, the notion that divorce disrupts the physical proximity of fathers and their children, and that as such, it illuminates highly gendered patterns of family involvement that may very well exist during marriage, finds strong support in the literature.

To understand fully the meaning of divorce in fathers' lives, one must consider the ways hegemonic masculinity is exhibited by fathers. In the hegemonic masculine model, fathers focus on their role as primary provider of financial resources for their families. In addition, because standards of fatherhood are fluid and changing, modern ideals assume that beyond providing, the "new father" will also be an involved, nurturant parent who is emotionally connected to his children (Coltrane 1996). During marriage, many men are able, at least on the surface, to present an image of attaining the societal ideal of a hegemonic, yet "new" father operating within the context of a shared family living space (Catlett and McKenry 2004). In this structure, they attain institutional authority from their status as head of a household—where mothers, fathers, and children live together—that our society has endorsed as the ideal (Thorne 1982; Townsend 2002).

Indeed, according to Nock (1998), marriage is one of the most basic and necessary requirements for adult masculinity. Marriage lays the foundation for a trinity of social roles that define masculinity. Specifically, masculinity is sustained when men are fathers to their wives' children, when they are providers for their families, and when they act as protectors of their wives and children. This is a strong cultural construction and provides a valuable framework in which to understand our participants' resentment regarding being "reduced to a paycheck" after divorce. Perhaps when fathers' role as financial provider is separated from their role as resident father, the former role becomes a source of resentment and perceived victimization rather than a demonstration of culturally sanctioned masculinity.

The narrative themes from our study provide strong support for viewing men's adjustment to the postdivorce nonresidential parenting role as a sort of crisis in gender relations of power in their families. Certainly these men feel disempowered because divorce removes them from their role as head of the household. Because these men no longer occupy shared family living space with their children on a daily basis, they believe that they are unable to fulfill their fathering roles. This shift, in turn, precipitates men's perceived loss of parental status and authority, a position to which many of these men feel entitled.

IMPLICATIONS FOR POLICY

Before drawing any conclusions from this study, three distinguishing features of the research are important to consider. First, the sample was quite narrow in terms of race and even socioeconomic status; it should be noted, however, that the demographic profile of this sample reflected the two counties from which it was drawn. Second, over half of our sample was composed of men who reported high conflict with their former spouses during the separation process. This feature may have shaped the research results in meaningful ways. For instance, the men's powerful depictions of their disempowered and marginalized status as live-away fathers may have been influenced by a variety of factors that were related to their highly conflictual relationships with former spouses. Finally, this study relied on the responses and perspectives of the male participants only; former spouses reports could affect our results substantially.

These limitations notwithstanding, our data provide insights for those interested in effecting policies that would facilitate the reorganization of family systems after divorce. The legal systems surrounding divorce should be examined and perhaps adjusted to promote more effectively mothers' and fathers' cooperation and continued coparenting after divorce.

One of the central issues in the divorce process is the decision about child custody. Many jurisdictions already have opted for joint legal custody or shared parenting as the preferred custody arrangement after divorce. Some scholars suggest that men adjust better to divorce when they have joint legal custody because this custody arrangement formally validates fathers' influences in their children's lives (Bertoia and Drakich 1995; Coltrane and Hickman 1992). Our data suggest the need to further examine the issue of joint custody. In particular, for most of the men in our study joint legal custody entailed a new role as nonresident father, and a sense of profound loss in access to and control over shared family space with children. These distinct custody arrangements—joint legal custody and joint physical custody—can be expected to have a differential impact because of the powerful symbolic meaning of shared living space with children for fathers.

Thus debate over standards of custody should continue. Braver (1998) argues that joint legal custody, combined with substantial—although not identically equal—access time for both parents, is a fair standard. Our research certainly supports the notion that the access of fathers to their children must be protected. At the same time, however, increased rights for fathers must go hand in hand with increased responsibilities (Czapanskiy 1991). Pasley and Minton's (1997) work on fathers' individualized efforts to redefine their fathering identity after divorce is instructive here. Fathers who think more flexibly and creatively about how to best father after the residential transitions prompted by divorce are likely to negotiate this transition most effectively. Our research suggests that a central element of this redefinition should center on fathers renegotiating their sense of themselves as men so that they no longer equate masculinity with status as head of household in which they live with their wives and children. An important theme is the reorganization of family relationships around issues of power and emotional connectedness (Fox and Blanton 1995), and encouraging fathers to focus on the personal connections and responsibilities that fathering entails even when daily physical contact is not possible.

FUTURE RESEARCH

The theoretical insights that emerge through this study's narrative data suggest several pathways for future research. In general, future research should develop a more nuanced sense of fathers' perceptions of physical space issues as they relate to postdivorce fathering, as well explore how fathers manage their family lives by taking into account physical space.

Toward this end, this study's findings suggest grounding future work in a theoretical framework that makes gender a central analytic category. Our study touches on gender relations of power as they relate to issues of house and home for men after divorce. Future research can build on this foundational knowledge and explore how men's concerns concerning physical space and postdivorce fathering relate to their constructions of themselves as masculine individuals. Moreover, efforts at capturing the intersectionality between gender and other systems of stratification such as race, class, and sexual orientation also are greatly needed. For example, future research should include more diverse populations to explore the influence of social status on men's postdivorce utilization of family space and the meanings attached to those uses. Much can be gained by examining both cultural influences and structural constraints on men's perceptions of the importance of shared physical space with children. Evaluating these influences, both individually and collectively, and studying different populations, should allow us to build a body of research on situated fathering that is more cumulative, inclusive, and complete.

Collins's (2004) interaction ritual chains model also would provide a valuable theoretical perspective to frame examination of how changes in physical space influence the prospects for, and quality of, various kinds of father–child rituals. Simply put, Collins' theoretical model focuses attention on interpersonal interaction rituals that create meaning for individuals and families in terms of constructing their personal biographies. Future research could incorporate this theoretical framework to examine how fathers and their children construct a sense of "we-ness" in postdivorce living spaces. One might explore the various conditions within which fathers are able to navigate postdivorce transitions in physical space effectively, as well as those cases in which fathers experience problems in resituating their fathering and persistently attempt to repeat previous family rituals, roles, events, or activities.

Implementation of new theoretical models such as these should involve examination of the experiences of fathers, mothers, and children, allowing them to be understood in relation to each other. For example, our finding that the loss of consistent access to and control over shared family space was perceived as men's loss and their former spouses' gain warrants future research that incorporates fathers' and mothers' reports. In addition, future research should attempt to understand children's perceptions of their fathers' living spaces; questions such as whether children view fathers' new living spaces as home and how properties of physical space (e.g., size, safety, neighborhood/community, social status) shape father–child relationships postdivorce deserve scholarly attention.

Another application of this inclusive approach would be to explore the experiences of nonresident fathers within distinct subgroups of fathers. For example, we could learn a great deal about how space patterns fathering styles by concentrating on fathers who become fathers outside the institution of marriage, gay fathers, stepfathers, and so on. Analyzing the influence of nonresident father status within such groups has the potential to sharpen our insights on fathers' situated roles and identities.

In a related vein, nonresident fathers who retain the family home after divorce are a relatively small group. Nevertheless, research with this subgroup of fathers will allow researchers to explore the experiences of men who father in their former primary family residence. Moreover, future research should explore the experiences of fathers with different types of custody arrangements and ask questions about how space considerations factor into their fathering experiences in different or similar ways.

REFERENCES

Allen, K. R., and Baber, K. M. (1994). Issues of gender: A feminist perspective. In P. C. McKenry and S. J. Price (Eds.), *Families and change: Coping with stressful events* (pp. 21–39). Thousand Oaks, CA: Sage.

Allen, S. M., and Hawkins, A. J. (1999). Maternal gatekeeping: Mothers' beliefs and behaviors that inhibit greater father involvement in family work. *Journal of Marriage and the Family, 61,* 9–212.

Arditti, J. A. (1995). Noncustodial parents: Emergent issues of diversity and process. *Marriage and Family Review, 20,* 283–304.

Arendell, T. (1995). *Fathers and divorce.* Thousand Oaks, CA: Sage.

Berg, B. L. (1998). *Qualitative research methods for the social sciences* (3rd ed.). Boston: Allyn & Bacon.

Bertoia, C. E., and Drakich, J. (1995). The fathers' rights movement: Contradictions in rhetoric and practice. In W. Marsiglio (Ed.), *Fatherhood: Contemporary theory, research, and social policy* (pp. 230–54). Thousand Oaks, CA: Sage.

Bogdan, R. C., and Biklen, S. K. (1992). *Qualitative research for education: An introduction to theory and methods* (2nd ed.). Boston: Allyn & Bacon.

Braver, S. L. (1998). *Divorced dads: Shattering the myths.* New York: Putnam.

Catlett, B. S., and McKenry, P. C. (1996). Implications of feminist scholarship for the study of women's postdivorce economic disadvantage. *Family Relations, 45,* 91–97.

Catlett, B. S., and McKenry, P. C. (2004). Class-based masculinities: Divorce, fatherhood, and the hegemonic ideal. *Fathering, 2,* 165–90.

Chafetz, J. S. (1988). The gender division of labor and the reproduction of female disadvantage. *Journal of Family Issues, 9,* 108–31.

Clarke-Stewart, K. A., and Bailey, B. L. (1989). Adjusting to divorce: Why do men have it easier? *Journal of Divorce, 13,* 75–94.

Collins, P. H. (1990). *Black feminist thought: Knowledge, consciousness, and the politics of empowerment.* New York: Routledge.

Collins, R. (2004). *Interaction ritual chains.* Princeton, NJ: Princeton University Press.

Coltrane, S. (1996). *Family man: Fatherhood, housework, and gender equity.* New York: Oxford University Press.

Coltrane, S. (2000). Research on household labor: Modeling and measuring the social embeddedness of routine family work. *Journal of Marriage and the Family, 62,* 1208–33.

Coltrane, S., and Hickman, N. (1992). The rhetoric of rights and needs: Moral discourse in the reform of child custody and child support laws. *Social Problems, 39,* 400–420.

Connell, R. W. (1987). *Gender and power: Society, the person, and sexual politics.* Stanford, CA: Stanford University Press.

Connell, R. W. (1995). *Masculinities.* Berkeley: University of California Press.

Coombs, R. H. (1991). Marital status and personal well-being: A literature review. *Family Relations, 40,* 97–102.

Czapanskiy, K. (1991). Volunteers and draftees: The struggle for parental equality. *UCLA Law Review, 38,* 1415–81.

Denzin, N. K. (1989). *Interpretive interactionism.* Thousand Oaks, CA: Sage.

Dudley, J. R. (1991). Increasing our understanding of divorced fathers who have infrequent contact with their children. *Family Relations, 40,* 279–85.

Ferree, M. M. (1990). Beyond separate spheres. Feminism and family research. *Journal of Marriage and the Family, 52,* 866–84.

Fox, G. L., and Blanton, P. W. (1995). Noncustodial fathers following divorce. *Marriage and Family Review, 20,* 257–82.

Furstenberg, F. F., and Cherlin, A. J. (1991). *Divided families: What happens to children when parents part.* Cambridge, MA: Harvard University Press.

Glenn, E. N. (1987). Gender and the family. In B. B. Hess and M. M. Ferree (Eds.), *Analyzing gender* (pp. 348–80). Newbury Park, CA: Sage.

Kiecolt-Glaser, J. K., and Newton, T. (2001). Marriage and health: His and hers. *Psychological Bulletin, 127,* 472–503.

Kitson, G. C., and Holmes, W. M. (1992). *Portrait of divorce: Adjustment to marital breakdown.* New York: Guilford.

Kruk, E. (1994). The disengaged noncustodial father: Implications for social work practice with the divorced family. *Social Work, 39,* 15–25.

LaRossa, R., and Reitzes, D. C. (1993). Symbolic interactionism and family studies. In P. G. Boss, W. J. Doherty, R. LaRossa, W. R. Schumm, and S. K. Steinmetz

(Eds.), *Sourcebook of family theories and methods: A contextual approach* (pp. 135–62). New York: Plenum.

Marsiglio, W. (1995). Fatherhood scholarship: An overview and agenda for the future. In W. Marsiglio (Ed.), *Fatherhood: Contemporary theory, research, and social policy* (pp. 1–20). Thousand Oaks, CA: Sage.

Messner, M. A. (1997). *Politics of masculinities: Men in movements.* Thousand Oaks, CA: Sage.

Nock, S. L. (1998). *Marriage in men's lives.* New York: Oxford University Press.

Pasley, K., and Minton, C. (1997). Generative fathering after divorce and remarriage: Beyond the "disappearing dad." In A. Hawkins and D. Dollahite (Eds.), *Generative fathering: Beyond deficit perspectives* (pp. 118–33). Thousand Oaks, CA: Sage.

Price, S. J., and McKenry, P. C. (1988). *Divorce.* Newbury Park, CA: Sage.

Seltzer, J. A. (1991). Relationships between fathers and children who live apart: The father's role after separation. *Journal of Marriage and the Family, 53,* 79–101.

Teachman, J. D., Tedrow, L. M., and Crowder, K. D. (2000). The changing demography of America's families. *Journal of Marriage and the Family, 62,* 1234–46.

Thompson, L., and Walker, A. J. (1989). Gender in families: Women and men in marriage, work, and parenthood. *Journal of Marriage and the Family, 51,* 845–71.

Thorne, B. (1982). Feminist rethinking of the family: An overview. In B. Thorne and M. Yalom (Eds.), *Rethinking the family: Some feminist questions* (pp. 1–24). New York: Longman.

Thorne, B. (1992). Feminism and the family: Two decades of thought. In B. Thorne and M. Yalom (Eds.), *Rethinking the family: Some feminist questions* (rev. ed., pp. 3–30). Boston: Northeastern University Press.

Townsend, N. W. (2002). *The package deal: Marriage, work, and fatherhood in men's lives.* Philadelphia: Temple University Press.

Umberson, D., and Williams, C. L. (1993). Divorced fathers: Parental role strain and psychological distress. *Journal of Family Issues, 14,* 378–400.

Zinn, M. B. (1990). Family, feminism, and race in America. *Gender and Society, 4,* 68–82.

6

The Haunted Hero: Fathering Profiles of Long-haul Truckers

Jeremy P. Sayers and Greer Litton Fox

The U.S. trucking industry provides the backdrop for this study of fathers who are long-haul or over-the-road (OTR) truck drivers. OTR truckers travel across states in large tractor-trailers carrying anything from cogs to cars. In 2002 over-the-road truckers logged nearly 100 billion miles of driving in eighteen-wheel trucks alone. For the typical OTR driver, job requirements mean being away from home for five or more consecutive days, often for weeks at a time. Truckers are glorified as mysterious rebels, "the most literal descendants of the cowboy" (Ouellet 1974, 104). We see this mythology in advertisements featuring truck drivers, and it is echoed repeatedly in the music drivers prefer.

This chapter focuses on one particular aspect of the long-haul trucker's life—his dual role as over-the-road truck driver and as father to his children. More often than not, research focusing on fatherhood has emphasized middle-class men who live relatively traditional lifestyles; references to working-class or blue-collar fathers are rare and often speculative. Although there is some research on blue-collar men, very little addresses the unique set of challenges associated with being an over-the-road (OTR), long-haul truck-driving father. The scarcity of research on blue-collar fathers, and specifically the lack of research on the OTR dad, presents a significant gap in the research literature when one considers that almost 7 million men are employed as truck drivers, most of whom have children (U.S. Department of Labor 2002). By exploring how the nature of fatherhood is shaped by the spatial circumstances that define the work and family life of twelve OTR fathers, we hope to fill a gap in our understanding of fathering among OTR truckers. Specifically relevant to this volume, we will illustrate how spatial limitations of long-haul driving restrict men's ability to fulfill their fathering roles.

Trucking offers a unique opportunity to study situated fatherhood in that time and distance—two spatially relevant variables—are tremendously salient in the majority of a driver's fathering behavior. Typical drivers spend weeks at a time thousands of miles away from their children. The OTR drivers spend only a fraction of the time at home that blue-collar men in other occupations spend with their families. This is especially important (and problematic) against the backdrop of blue-collar, class-wide reliance on family connectedness. In this chapter we show how OTR fathers, as blue-collar men, internalize ideal notions of fatherhood and how these idealized notions are often shattered by real spatial limitations.

THE IDEAL AND THE REAL:
BLUE-COLLAR FATHERS, THE PROVIDER ROLE,
AND THE CHALLENGE OF THE NURTURANT FATHER MODEL

This study of OTR fathers can be placed in a larger context of research on blue-collar men. Komarovsky's (1962) pioneering work on blue-collar marriage describes the taken-for-granted quality of the provider role in husbands' and wives' construction of the part men play in family life. Indeed, her poignant descriptions of the cascade of marital strains caused by provider role failure remain timely today. Rubin's (1976) analysis of the "worlds of pain" of blue-collar families provides a clear picture of the differences by social class in the sorts of problems experienced by and solutions available to families occupying different rungs in a class hierarchy. According to Rubin, middle-class professionals' work requires too much personal investment while blue-collar workers' jobs requires too little. The middle-class father may compensate for his overinvestment in work with an accumulation of material possessions while the blue-collar man more often turns for meaningful connection to his family and community to compensate for the dullness and routine of his daily labor. Bellah et al. (1985), too, argue that family connectedness is cherished by the lower class for its protection against the alienation of the blue-collar work world. Lamont's (2000) work on blue-collar men found similarly that family connectedness is a source of pride; providing for and protecting the family against uncertainty and danger are two central tenets in the morality of the blue-collar workers she interviewed.

The centrality of men's provider role has its roots in traditional American culture (Hareven 1982; LaRossa 1997; Zaretsky 1976) and is of "continuing importance to men's understanding of what it means to be a father" (Fox, Bruce, and Combs-Orme 2000). This is especially true for blue-collar fathers who are quick to define their family worth in terms of the good provider role

(Komarovsky 1962; Loscocco 1990). For these men, the drive to provide supercedes all other aspects of fathering and, in fact, to provide well is equated with fathering well (Lamont 2000).

Even though it is assumed that fathers provide (Cohen 1993), and that this provision is valued on a cultural level, at the level of family the story may be quite different. Christiansen and Palkovitz (2001) argue that the value of providing ascribed to the father by his culture is rarely matched by members of his family; providing is expected but not appreciated. Further, because parenting is usually assumed to require direct involvement with the children, economic providing per se is robbed of any association with fathering and "is often seen as competing with involvement or, more severely, creating a lack of involvement" (Christiansen and Palkovitz 2001, 86).

A model of "involved fathering" now urges fathers to participate more regularly in nurturing opportunities with their children at home (LaRossa 1988; Robinson and Barret 1986; Rotundo 1985). The good father, while still expected to provide, must also share the roles of family protector and care giver of children with the mother (Fox et al. 2000; Gerson 1993; Marsiglio 1995), and there is evidence that the model of nurturant fathering crosses class lines (Fox, Sayers, and Bruce 2001; Gerson 1993; Lamont 2000). For the blue-collar father the impetus for nurturant fathering may come from class expectations of family cohesion as opposed to middle-class cultural expectations of "androgynous fathering" (Rotundo 1985, 20).

Although the importance attached to fathers' "providing" versus "nurturing" may be contested on a cultural level, there is plentiful evidence that the provider role continues to matter to men on a personal level. It seems likely that fathers from different classes value the provider role for different reasons, but most every father worries more about his ability to provide adequately for his family than he does about most other aspects of fathering (Lamont 2000). Further, fathers worry more about providing than do mothers (Fox et al. 2000). In examining the provider role, Fox and colleagues report that fathers of newborns "feel especially burdened by performance expectations in precisely the area in which their performance is most taken for granted" (p. 126). Not only are fathers anxious about their ability to provide, but also they often receive criticism if their efforts to provide are perceived to be interfering with their at-home fathering. And how can providing not be associated with neglecting nurturant fathering at home? Since the industrial revolution, providing has involved leaving the family home for at least forty hours a week (Christiansen and Palkovitz 2001). The problem is that the new nurturant father may be more ideal than real: a product of our culture that is simply not a part of the practice of fatherhood for many fathers (LaRossa 1997). The need to provide, however, is real.

With the father's providing expected but not respected, his work can become a necessary evil. Especially for the blue-collar man whose family rests precariously near poverty, providing is needed for survival. For these fathers, a few days of missed work to participate in the birth of a child could prove financially devastating. According to many different studies, the "evil" part of "necessary evil" lies in that a father's seemingly *necessary* adherence to the notion of fathering as providing prohibits or constrains him from being involved in the culture of the new "nurturant" father (Blankenhorn 1995; Christiansen and Palkovitz 2001; Gerson 1993; Palkovitz, Christiansen, and Dunn 1998; Robinson and Barret 1986; Roy 2004). Gerson (1993), for example, in an analysis of the commitments men make to work and family, notes that among men who found success and gratification in their jobs, their commitments to family and work came to compete with one another in a zero-sum game: their increased hours on the job meant proportionally less time at home and less energy once they were home. Roy (2004) notes, similarly, that men who are at the *lowest* rungs of the work force, often working two or more jobs to support their families, are also faced with the same trade-offs, such that attending to the provider role severely limits family time and family involvement. In an era in which the expectations for "good" fathering were met by consistent economic support of the family, noninvolvement with children was understood as an acceptable trade-off. For contemporary fathers, such a trade-off is less tenable. In this study we focus on how over-the-road fathers, whose work requires them to be away from their homes for much of their work life, manage this trade-off between providing and nurturing.

OVER THE ROAD DRIVERS AS BLUE-COLLAR FATHERS

Despite the dominance of trucking as a blue-collar occupation, there is surprisingly little research on truck drivers who are fathers. We note two studies here. In an innovative comparison of how family time is experienced by commercial fisherman and truck drivers, Zvonkovic, Manoogian, and McGraw (2001) identify four phases (departure, separation, homecoming, and reunion) experienced by families with extended periods of father absence. Perhaps because of the indeterminacy and unpredictability of their absences, the fisherman families evolved different responses to the four phases as compared to the truck drivers and their wives. The fact that the drivers were employed by a trucking firm that provided regular routes and a regular five-day work week, such that they were at home every weekend, may account for why the shifts in conjugal roles and the adjustments required of family members were less marked for the truck driver as compared to the commercial fishing families. In our study, the OTR fathers more closely resembled Zvonkovic and colleagues' fishermen with their prolonged and unpredictable periods of absence.

The second study is a pioneering work on the lives of truckers. In this study, Ouellet (1974) identified three distinct trucker types, based on the men's personalities and bargains with family and work: supertruckers, workers, and truckers. We have found Ouellet's typology useful in our analysis and discuss it in detail later in this chapter.

METHOD

This study was designed to be an exploratory, qualitative study. Following two pilot interviews, research interviews were conducted by Sayers with twelve men who were, at that time, over-the-road truck drivers with at least one child. The average age of the respondents was thirty-six years old with twelve and a half years of fathering experience and two children. Of the twelve men, ten had been divorced at least once and ten were white.

The interviews were conducted in the eating area of a busy truck stop along Interstate 40 just outside Knoxville, Tennessee, during a four-week period shortly after Christmas 1998. The truck stop was an interesting place, especially as it facilitated drivers' family life. There were a dozen phone booths, phone card vending machines were prominent, and every wall was lined with shelves full of gifts for children and spouses, from knickknacks to stuffed animals and toy cars.

Interviews were semistructured, designed to explore the experience of being an OTR driver and father. Specific questions were presented consistently to each interviewee, although participants were encouraged to explore and discuss their experiences in each area in as much depth as seemed appropriate. Typically, conversations flowed from one topic to the next, as all participants seemed eager to share their perspectives and the details of their lives.

Following the work of others, we rely on the notion of thick description of concepts (Gilgun 1992; Weiss 1994). Interviews were transcribed, and, from the pilot data, two independent readers developed a preliminary inventory of themes and ideas, and coded textual raw materials into thematic concepts. As additional interviews were conducted, we searched for and noted repetition of existing themes and emergence of new themes. For example, the notion of providing as fathering was a constantly recurring theme as were references to despair over a sense of failed fatherhood. The successes and failures attributed to spatial limitations were also noted as thematic material. Using these notes and frequently returning to the transcriptions, we used a constant comparative method to analyze the emerging themes.

A Typology of Truck Drivers

We relied on Ouellet's (1974) categorization of drivers into supertruckers, truckers, and workers, and in the following paragraphs we present his typology briefly and note how we divided our OTR fathers into the three types of drivers he identified.

Supertruckers

Two of our twelve respondents were supertruckers, the stereotypical driver who, according to Ouellet, sees himself as the king of the road, the asphalt cowboy. This driver places great importance on the job he performs, the equipment he uses, even the load he hauls. Supertruckers typically own their own trucks and are known as owner-operators. This type of driver is consumed with driving and spends time at home working on the truck, cleaning the vehicle, and resting, with little time left for family. This driver "strikes or forces a bargain with his family in which it is understood that the vast majority of his time will be devoted to his job" (Ouellet 1974, 199). In our study men were coded as supertruckers in large part based on their use of signal words to describe what they do, such as "last of the cowboys" and "king of the road." Further, a man's passive and uncaring attitude toward failed attempts at fathering and accounts of feeling betrayed by the family made it easy to identify the men who considered themselves, above all else, the kings of the road.

Workers

The worker's sole motivation for being a truck driver is to provide financially for his family as best as he can (Ouellet 1974). The worker is not overly enamored with the freedom of the road nor the machismo often associated with long-haul drivers. To the contrary, his focus is on providing his family with a middle-class living, and he is willing to sacrifice whatever is necessary in order to accomplish this. Seven of the twelve respondents fit clearly the "worker" designation. Respondents were coded as workers based on their self-reports of being primarily providers for their children. Workers voiced a keen dislike for their jobs while claiming that driving provided the best possible income for their families.

Truckers

The trucker falls somewhere in between the worker and supertrucker; however, his situation is often the most complicated. Unlike the other two types of drivers, the trucker does not have clear arrangements with his family about the apportionment of work and nonwork time; that is, the allocation of the man's time and energy between job and family is continually contested. "The truckers' family sees someone who wants or acknowledges a duty to spend as much time as possible with them, but whose notions differ from their own as to what is possible" (Ouellet 1974, 205). Of the twelve men interviewed, three have been truckers throughout their careers and one other moved from worker to trucker after losing all connections with his family. We classified respondents as truckers based on their more active involvement than supertruckers in staying connected to and involved with the family. Truckers worked within their spatial limitations in a directed effort to be a father while on the road and at home. Classifying fathers as truckers required some speculation on our part, but in general truckers reported detailed accounts of efforts to do fathering while at the same time evincing a much stronger commitment to OTR driving than we found among the men classified as workers. Truckers would call home to talk with the kids about their day and to make plans for the future, whereas supertruckers and workers called home only when they had a chance and then only to say hello. Truckers were the most actively involved in fathering.

In analyzing data from the interviews with the twelve drivers, we found that each respondent fit into one of these three types. Each type demonstrated a clear and distinct pattern of family interactions as well as a unique attitude about the dual roles of driver and father. That is, each type of driver's identity was shaped by differing responses to situational limitations of time and space. For example, supertruckers embraced distance from their family as a factor necessary for the good of the driver and thus his family. Workers, on the other hand, saw their situation as an unfortunate drain on the driver and his family but necessary for the financial good of the family. Truckers looked at spatial factors as variables that could be manipulated for the better of the family as a whole.

This three-part categorization proved useful in organizing the data from the interviews and in describing the lives of the drivers. While interest in situated fathering is relatively new, Ouellet's thirty-year-old typology based on men's attitudes toward work and family provides an excellent framework for a study on time and space and their relationship to blue-collar fatherhood.

FINDINGS

Kings of the Road: OTR Fathers as Supertruckers

Supertruckers, like all drivers, spend the majority of each month on the road. The difference between supertruckers and other drivers rests in their motivation for staying on the road and their attitude about the consequences of spatial and temporal distance on the family. Supertruckers enjoyed being on the road and thought that being away helped them be better fathers: from Edgar, "It pulls you away from your family but on the positive side you got it to look forward to, to spend that quality time." And for Dylan fulfillment of his personal goals was a prerequisite for being a good father: "The last of the cowboys, that's what I wanted to be . . . but there's a price you have to give up. . . . There's a stable home life to give up to be the king of the road, but you got to make that decision and you got to live with it."

Unlike other drivers, who shared some decision making with their wives, responsibilities for child rearing and financial matters were handled entirely by the supertruckers' wives while they were on the road. As one driver put it, "Everyday decisions, that's hers. . . . They're the ones eating the food and wearing the clothes" (Dylan). And again, "She'd get the check in the mail. . . . She cashes it, or she puts it in the check book. It was taken care of" (Dylan). For Edgar, "Should something arise while I was at home, then I was the one who dealt with it, [but] she handled everything while I was out on the road" (Edgar). As these quotes illustrate, situational factors that kept the supertrucker fathers away from their families were not viewed as limiting factors. Thus, strategies to bridge work-related absence and fathering behavior were unnecessary to these men. While supertruckers often kept in touch with "the family back home," they did not do so out of a sense of fatherly responsibility. The supertruckers gave the impression during the interviews that they considered phone calls home as tedious, favors they bestowed on the family. When supertruckers did touch base with home, contact was made via the phone, although one driver reported having an Internet connection in his truck that allowed him to stay in touch with his family and with an elementary school classroom that used his travels to study U.S. geography. The other supertrucker confined his on-the-road fathering to collecting postcards and taking pictures of geographical points of interest to take back to his son. But, primarily, for the supertruckers, fathering was equated with providing, or in Edgar's words: "I made the money."

Spatial separation from the family constitutes the greatest portion of a driver's life, but there is also a time for return. For the supertrucker, returning home was less like switching hats and more like hanging up the hat. While some time at home was spent doing what the wife wanted to do, much of the supertrucker's time at home was spent resting or working: "The first thing I did when I got home was take a shower and go to bed" (Dylan). Edgar described quality time with his son as watching his son clean his rig in exchange for spending money. For Dylan, who no longer lived with his family, special arrangements often had to be made: "I have to reschedule my route—that's why I'm looking at the map—I'm going to Houston now, so I'm trying to get a load going down to Tampa to see my kid" (Dylan). However, earlier in his child's life, Dylan was virtually uninvolved with his child because "Jr. was three years old, so we couldn't take him a whole lot of places—like a father and son thing, you know."

Unlike the workers who described feelings of sadness when departing, supertruckers adopted a more detached, unfeeling attitude. To them, they were just doing their job, and it wasn't their fault if their wives and kids couldn't handle it: "She didn't like [that I was leaving] so I told her, you married a trucker, you knew me before we got married, you knew what the life is like" (Dylan). And for Edgar's wife, "It got real lonely for her . . . but, you know, this is my livelihood, this is what I do for a living" (Edgar). As was true for the workers, over time their continual prolonged absences resulted in the loss of family; but unlike the workers, the loss for supertruckers was not problematic. Supertruckers were quick to blame both the wife, for failing to take responsibility for the family, and also the companies that employed them: "Trucking companies have this thing about sending you home. . . . They don't want to do it" (Dylan).

Supertruckers are wont to point out that they have done their part in providing for the family—a sufficient condition for claiming to be a good father. Of all the drivers, supertruckers earned the highest income. But instead of recognizing and making an effort to manage the difficult balance between involved fathering and providing, the supertrucker kicks the fulcrum out from under the balance and claims the two are the same, end of discussion. As we will discuss next, the worker tends to pick up the pieces and keep going. The supertrucker denies there are any pieces to pick up. Firmly embedded in the mythology of the truck driver, he is more likely to cast himself in the role of victim, as having been abandoned by his own family for simply doing his job. Thus, the supertrucker may be the king of the road and a hero in his own mind, but he has distanced himself from cultural expectations for family involvement, is without love, and in his less defensive moments, struck us as lonely.

Picking Up the Pieces: OTR Fathers as Workers

In Ouellet's typology, workers were family men, and this family focus was construed by the men in our study as being a good provider first and foremost. These men also uniformly gave voice to feelings that fulfilling their provider role obligations necessitated such a high degree of absence from their families that it led to a detrimental lack of involvement in the lives of their children. Roberto typifies the worker. For eighteen years he beat the roads with his truck, back and forth, repeatedly leaving, then coming home; and now, according to Roberto, there were no happy returns. Typical of many of the men, he had gradually lost touch with his family, and now, in his words, "I am on the road all the time . . . cause I have nothin' to go home to. There's the truck and it's my life, and it destroyed my marriage." For eighteen years of his twenty-two-year marriage, Roberto had worked on the road more than three weeks per month to pay the bills and placate his family. Now, with his daughters out of the house and only a sixteen-year-old son at home, his marriage was ending and his children were reticent: "[They say,] 'If I see you, Dad, I see you. If I don't, I don't.'" His home is his truck, and driving is all he has. Roberto is a homeless man with a job.

The worker spends more time on the road than any other type of driver. More than 90 percent of his average month is spent away from his wife and kids. Six of the seven drivers we classified as "workers" were divorced from the mothers of their children. While they were on the road, workers left all family responsibilities in the hands of their wives: "When you're gone you can't really do it" (Marcus). All reported that their wives were responsible for the handling of finances and had free reign to spend the family money in whatever fashion they deemed necessary, and some added that any unanticipated spending needs would be discussed over the phone. While the men were on the road, the wives handled discipline of the children as well. Some men feared that their children were being allowed to "slide" a bit when the wives were in charge: "When they do something wrong, Daddy ain't getting a hold of them" (Terry). But the workers accepted this as unavoidable if unfortunate: "Sooner or later the kids start losing track of Dad . . . because Dad's not there to supervise. . . . The kids just start doing things on their own without thinking about Father" (Roberto). Unlike supertruckers, the workers looked on, and freely discussed, the erosion of family connectedness due to situational absence as problematic and a source of sadness.

The workers kept in closer contact with their families while on the road than did the supertruckers. Not surprisingly, the sole means of maintaining this connection was the phone: "I called every night, I still call every night" (Marcus). And again, "I call my wife every day" (Moses). For some divorced workers no longer living with their children, efforts to stay emotionally connected with their kids involved phone calls: "On the weekends when I'm home, I call my daughter. . . . I get visitation with her every other weekend, so in order to get visitation on the other weekends, I call her" (Moses). Keeping in touch via phone was "one of the most important things for a truck driver because, until you get back home, you're around nobody but strangers" (Bill). Most fathers mentioned buying phone cards and calling late at night in order to make this more affordable. Typically, the workers called once a day, sometimes at prearranged times. For most workers, calls were made whenever there was time: "I just pick up the phone and call . . . when I'm getting loaded or when I stop and get fuel" (Moses). Even with such regular phone contact, workers felt that their responsibilities were eroding with the passage of time: "A lot of times, I didn't find out about decisions until it's like a month later" (Rudy). And in Roberto's words, "It got to the point where my opinion didn't matter anymore. . . . That's just how it ended up. . . . It just started going downhill." Eventually, this worker's children developed problems in school, and when Roberto tried to discuss this with them, their response was, "Well, Dad, you were never home."

Especially for the men described as workers, being at home meant being a dad: "I'm not a truck driver now, I'm a dad and I'm home" (Bill). During the interview most workers became quite animated when asked to talk about at-home fathering. We suggest that this is because workers have divided their fatherhood into two distinct situational realms: distant fathering and at-home fathering. The attitude of most workers towards fathering on the road seemed one of helplessness and passivity. They attributed their loss of connection and failure as fathers almost entirely to situational constraints of distance. Fathering at home was also a source of frustration and failure for the workers, but it was their best opportunity to succeed as fathers.

We saw their description of a transitional phase between on the road and at home as a strategy to bridge the worlds of work and family. Returning home involved active preparation: "You got to get ready to be Dad again" (Bill). The driver returns from an environment of solitude and hard driving to an emotionally charged family life where prolonged absence is made up for in a short period of time. Most workers recall time at home as being entirely devoted to unquestioningly doing whatever the rest of the family wanted to do. Workers also reported taking time at home to plan for the upcoming weeks of father absence. Most workers and their wives attempted to take care of as much as possible while both parents were present, leaving little guess work for the wife at home. Even so, for some workers, all planning and family management was left to the wife: "She runs the house. When you're gone, you really can't do it. I guess that's why we're divorced" (Marcus).

Several workers used technology to their advantage in an attempt to keep up with important events in their children's lives. This was different from the contact that supertruckers maintained with their families in two significant ways. First, workers used technology as a tool to incorporate events that happened while on the road into at-home fathering. Three different men told of how their wives videotaped ballet recitals, football games, and wrestling matches that occurred when the driver was on the road. For these men, part of the time at home was spent proudly reviewing these performances with their children. Second, in contrast to the supertruckers, workers saw a need to find ways of making fathering a more active and involved process despite, and because of, their spatial separation while on the road.

As the time to leave home approached, many workers described a process of mental preparation. Several men described the pain of pushing away from "clingy" children and wives who try to understand but remain lonely. Especially for fathers of young children, there were always questions about why Dad has to leave. For every worker, leaving was replete with pain and anxiety for the whole family. As Bill observed, "I'd say it's a bad situation for any father. . . . The child doesn't get the full effect of you being a father, and you don't get the full effect of being a father. I still cry when I leave my kids." Even so, for the worker the call to provide always trumped the desire to be more involved as a father. For many men, financial anxiety kept them on the road longer than they wanted, picking up extra loads when they were available, and for most it was a precipitating factor for their divorces.

For the worker, then, we see that there is indeed a problem with the allocation of time between work and family. In the face of such time constraints, Daly (1993; Daly and Dienhart 1998) has suggested that some men may discard the ideal notion of father altogether and flee from involvement. Not so for these drivers. The workers in this study did what they could to stay involved. Time at home was spent selflessly on the family, and when they were on the road, communications were kept open via the telephone. Nonetheless, the reality was that, after being gone for so long, the men found that they just couldn't get caught up. These drivers were honest in reckoning their family problems. These men believed that they had made a choice that would better their life and the lives of their families. Workers believed that they could keep connected with their spouses and children, but they were mistaken, as their record of failed marriages attests.

The worker blamed himself for his troubles and seemed to trace his problems back to faulty decisions on his part, such as overreaching and stretching his finances too thinly for his wages. The workers managed despair by continuing to drive and to provide for their estranged children without the reward of family connectedness. Some of the men started over with another wife or girlfriend, hoping that this time they could make it work. However, like Rubin's (1976) blue-collar men, the worker's social position and occupation created problems in the family, problems whose potential solutions were limited by the job's required absence from the family.

Fragile Balances: OTR Fathers as Truckers

Both the worker and the supertrucker demonstrate a work spillover into family life that "interferes negatively with family life" and "leads to less available energy with which to pursue nonwork activities" (Small and Riley 1990, 52). The men denoted as truckers, on the other hand, seem to have found some compromise that keeps them committed to both work and family with fewer negative consequences in both arenas. In this study, truckers spent the least amount of time on the road (81 percent of an average month, or 10 percent less than workers averaged) and more time directly involved in their children's lives.

As was true of the other drivers, for the trucker the telephone was the primary means of connection between father and family. Two truckers carried a cell phone, which was unusual at the time of the interviews, to maximize the amount of contact they could have with their families. Truckers, moreover, were purposeful in their phone calls: they used this time to participate actively in family decisions and to talk with their children.

Two truckers also reported taking their children with them over the road during summer vacations as a way of bonding. Doug reported that he takes his teenage daughter with him for at least one month every year: "She likes to go, and I like to have her along" (Doug). Other drivers had mentioned child ride-alongs as a long-term goal, but only the truckers had actually made it happen.

More so than for workers, returning home for truckers was truly shifting gears. These men verbalized a reentry process of mental preparation, so that when they arrived home they were physically present and emotionally available. One trucker, James, described stopping for a bite to eat and a cup of coffee whenever he pulled into town just before he returned home. This break acted as a transition period to buffer any negative spillover from the fast pace of OTR driving.

Truckers were clearly more involved with their children when at home than were other drivers. Their descriptions of at-home activities were richer and more detailed. Truckers reported spending time with each child individually, saying prayers, reviewing homework, playing ball, and engaging in meaningful conversations about private issues like dating and friendship. James talked about family meetings where "we do everything jointly and try to hash them out where they suit not just one person more than the other but suit the family so that the outcome is for the best."

Along with the rest of the blue-collar world, truckers believed that one of their primary roles as father was breadwinner. Therefore, they would head back to work just as did the rest of the drivers. While there were sadness and tears when it was time to go, for the truckers and their families leave-taking seemed more manageable. An understanding and acceptance of why he was leaving seemed to have facilitated this easier departure, as in Gil's words: "They understand what it is I'm trying to do—supply for our needs."

The truckers were happy to get back on the road. Part of their contentedness lies in not "leaving a lot of unfinished business at home" (James). They reported being able to go out and fulfill their provider obligations knowing that they had an emotionally rich father relationship to return to. And, like the supertrucker, there was some magical feeling to being on the road, doing something different than in-home fathering. Truckers reported enjoying and even needing the solitude of OTR driving in order to have a good family life.

The trucker is the driver who has most successfully balanced the dual demands of father and provider. He has done this by drawing a clear line between the two while still being able to do both at the same time when necessary. When the trucker is home, he is firmly involved in his role as father, and when he is on the road and away from home, he is still able to act like a father. Yet, he is on the road because he loves his job and because, like his family, it is an important part of his identity. Most importantly, for the trucker, providing may be a necessary condition of fathering, but it is not a sufficient condition of being an OTR dad.

Behind each of the truckers was a supportive and understanding family. The truckers always mentioned their somewhat lonely but devoted wife and older children. Marital harmony manifested itself in concerted efforts to stay out of debt, budget, and make other similarly reasoned choices together. Financial peace seemed to make it easier for the driver to become a trucker rather than a worker. Unlike the workers we interviewed, the truckers had managed to avoid debt and other financially burdensome choices.

DISCUSSION

Each of the three types of drivers demonstrated distinctive approaches to managing the spatial challenges of father and caregiver responsibilities while on the road and to reestablishing themselves as fathers when returning from the road. Each type of driver exhibited different classes of problems, and correspondingly different attitudes, regarding how to manage the dual status of father and long-haul driver. Workers, driven by financial necessity, despaired over their necessary absence from their family and typically experienced a gradual loss of connection with their wives and children. Supertruckers also lost touch with their families, but to them this was an acceptable loss and simply an unavoidable part of being an asphalt cowboy. Truckers created a working balance between their dual lives that minimized conflicts. An extra day at home and a higher quality of fathering behavior made all the difference for these men. What conflicts did arise were managed through complex and multidimensional problem solving.

Despite their differences, several common themes were apparent. This is not surprising given that every driver, regardless of type, had chosen the job of OTR driver and was consequently away from home almost constantly. We address three of these themes here: bridging strategies, space and time, and the struggle with and resolution of the issue of provider role as father identity.

Bridging Strategies

One of the primary bridging strategies that truck drivers used to cover the gap between work and family was through technological means. Technology played a large role in many of the drivers' efforts to stay connected to their families and to "do fathering." Not surprisingly, all drivers used telephones to keep in touch and some utilized cell phones, now almost universally affordable, to make this connection more available. A few drivers even had computers with e-mail capability and used this to touch base with family members. Technology made it easier for men to reestablish their fatherly presence in their children's lives on return as well. Several of the men spent time at home watching home movies of events and milestones they had missed while on the road; these recorded images at least partially made up for not being there in person.

The Problem of Space and Time

The relationship between the dual roles of provider and engaged father was often cast in terms of the control of space and its consequence for time. Good time management in the context of spatial estrangement often made for better fathering while still adequately providing for family welfare.

Conversely, failure in being a good father was often explained in terms of mismanaged time and overwhelming problems associated with nearly constant spatial separation. And, just below the surface of the interview conversation was the hint that the men thought their wives harbored different conceptions of time. In contrast to the predominant attitude among the drivers that family time was measured only in at-home time and thus was a scarce commodity was the more complex understanding of time shared by their wives. When a driver took on his wife's perspective and focused on quality of time regardless of spatial separation as opposed to quantity of at-home time, outcomes were usually positive. Their efforts to do fathering while on the road were often rewarded with more positive father–child relations in general. However, more commonly, the drivers heard only their wives' complaints about their frequent and extensive absences and what the men had failed to take care of in the brief periods they were at home. The men internalized the shortcomings described by their wives, creating incongruity between the ideal fathering self and the actual fathering self. This, in turn, frequently led to discarding any notions of the ideal in favor of adopting a provider role account to justify their limited father roles. For many of the drivers, providing food and shelter was—or came to be—defined as a sufficient condition for being a good father, at least to themselves.

Related to this is the idea of individual control of space and time. Similar to the men discussed in Daly's (1993) study of middle-class men, the fathers in this study employed varying attitudes towards the control of time on a *humanistic* to *fatalistic* continuum. With what little unscheduled time was available to OTR drivers, some exerted a great deal of control over their time while others, more fatalistic in posture, entered into their time commitments on the basis of obligation, compulsion, and coercion. While all OTR drivers faced serious constraints on their time and job related spatial estrangement, attitudes about time and space did play a role in the successes and failures of men's attempts to do fathering. We note that a few of the drivers acknowledged their wives' efforts to organize and facilitate productive use of their at-home time. They saw "a good wife" as enabling them to be successful husbands and fathers.

It is not uncommon for working-class fathers to express a desire to be more involved with their children and families. But because of the salience of the provider role and time demands created by real economic necessity, many do not have the opportunity for much at-home interaction (Palkovitz et al. 1998). Nowhere was this more evident than among the drivers we categorized as workers in this study. Many of these men incurred significant debt early in life, were compelled to work long hours to pay down this debt, and then lost their wives and gained child support payments in the process. This anticipates the third overarching theme among the drivers, the equation of fathering with providing.

Embracing the Provider Role

Earlier research on blue-collar fathers pointed to two overriding factors that governed their construction of family life: the desire to provide a degree of financial stability for their families, and a drive to be a "family man" and maintain a high degree of connection and presence with their families, including spending time in the familiar spaces of home. In fact, however, those in blue-collar occupations who wish to provide well often must sacrifice the culturally valued time at home. Some blue-collar men are seemingly required to sacrifice their families and to "expect a divorce" in their efforts to provide (Roy 2004). For truck drivers, "doing well" may involve being able to own their own rig, to provide a home for their family, and to buy nice things for the children. However, their attempts to achieve financial success carry a high cost in terms of required spatial distancing and thus time spent away from the family. This defines the dilemma these men confront. Over-the-road fathers find it difficult to do fathering while working at the jobs they hold, and so their efforts to achieve a middle-class family life end up eroding family connectedness, often destroying their families in the process.

Nearly all of the men in this study held some form of the belief that being a good provider was a necessary, and often sufficient, condition for fathering. However, it is important to note that when these same men became fathers they expected to be nurturant, involved fathers, albeit in blue-collar fashion (e.g., outings to NASCAR-type race tracks rather than soccer fields). Similar to the middle-class men of other studies (LaRossa 1988; Daly 1993), the OTR drivers quickly found themselves falling short of their own fathering expectations and failing similar expectations held by wives and children. The resulting personal dissonance between ambitiously adopted cultural expectations of fathering and the actual fathering they accomplished resulted in a number of interesting outcomes. Although a few manipulated their use of time, resisted spatial distancing, and restructured their family lives to allow living more fully with their family, most of the drivers simply abandoned the ideals. Ideals about being a "new nurturant" father were replaced with the safer, more familiar, and certainly more accommodating belief that providing alone is tantamount to good fathering, as was true of men of their fathers' generation. Like Rubin's (1976) blue-collar men, our truck drivers often redefined success so that it was more compatible with their modest accomplishments as fathers. For some, being the hero of the road was enough, or became defined as enough, and thus low levels of aspiration in familial roles were acceptable to them. In turn, these narrowed down expectations of self became powerful shapers of the men's evaluations of their lived experience. For example, despite a nearly 100 percent divorce rate and near total absence from their children, these men deemed their fathering performance as good.

FUTURE RESEARCH

The many ways in which this study was limited led to suggestions for needed research. Because of its small scope and its recruitment method, no data were gathered directly from the wives or the children of the drivers. Without a doubt, interviews with the wives and children of OTR drivers would provide a valuable alternative understanding of the unique problems of nearly constant father absence, and this promises to be a fruitful avenue for future research. A sample selection strategy that targets equal numbers of currently married and nonmarried OTR fathers would elicit valuable information on differences in managing the constraints of space and time on family relationships.

Topics were raised in the interviews that need to be more thoroughly explored. For example, religious beliefs were alluded to by a few of the drivers and could be explored in detail as a potential factor in the negotiation of work and family conflict. Other topics, such as the use of performance-enhancing drugs, alcohol, and the temptations of sex on the road—all part of the mystique of the trucker—could be explored as threats to the marital and parental bonds.

What kind of support truckers receive for their family roles while on the road remains to be explored. In the particular truck stop we used as the setting for this research there were many reminders of family in terms of goods to purchase and access to telephones facilities and in the monitoring of the overnight parking areas to discourage prostitution and other illicit behaviors. Whether this is the case in the majority of rest stops and truck stops frequented by OTR drivers is not known. Nor is it evident that truckers engage in family talk with one another while on the road or during their rest stops. The trucker culture is hyped as a macho, loose-living, free and easy one with little room for acknowledging, much less sharing with other drivers, a man's concerns with loneliness, homesickness, worry over children or a marriage that is in trouble. The willingness, indeed eagerness, of the twelve men in this study to spend a little time talking about their families led us to believe that many of the men hungered for an opportunity to talk about home.

We saw in this study that a few of the fathers had developed strategies for moving into and out of disparate cultures as they moved from their trucks and "the road" to home and back. Some of them eschewed the rough "roadie" culture altogether, while others relished that aspect of their jobs and seemed to be stuck in the situational definitions of the mythical trucker even at home. Conditions that foster the relative ease of the transitions the men made from one setting to another, and their ability to respond to the demand characteristics of the situations in which they find themselves, is of particular interest for further exploration in the case of OTR truckers, given the incompatibility of the trucker culture with a family culture.

The developmental stage of children as a condition for fathering needs to be taken into account more explicitly than we were able to do in this study. All fathers face challenges of parenting children of different ages and needs. How trucker fathers do so at extremes of distance and time is of interest. For example, it is far more difficult for very young children than for older children to create and maintain a sense of "daddy" as a continual presence in their lives. Fathers who are gone for lengthy periods can have no object permanence for very young children, and a distant voice on the telephone is not likely to be meaningful to children younger than three. How new fathers and mothers can maintain the idea of "daddy" with infants and toddlers during the trucker's long absences from home merits exploration. Middle-age children characteristically grapple with self-expression. It is difficult for preteens, who need almost limitless time and parental patience as they work out ways to express their often inchoate ideas, to quickly find the vocabularies they need to condense their ideas and compress their conversations into fleeting telephone calls with a faraway father. OTR fathers provide a laboratory for testing the limits of quality versus quantity time and the potency and limitations of physical presence versus psychological presence in parenting. Adolescents' needs, in particular those for parenting in real time, presage difficulties for trucker parents who must ask their teens to postpone sharing their concerns and their successes until a road trip is concluded. It is encouraging that a few of the drivers were able to establish and maintain supportive relationships with children over time and despite the difficulties inherent in long-distance relationships. Whether relationship maintenance becomes easier or more difficult over time or as children mature remains to be explored.

In sum, there are numerous avenues for the pursuit of additional research in the lives of OTR fathers. Beyond the purely academic interests in the work–family interface of the men and women who choose long-haul trucking as an occupation lie the needs for evidence-based recommendations for the drivers and their families, the companies who employ them, and the policy makers—in unions and in government settings—who establish industry regulations. Recommendations are needed for both formal and informal strategies that could enhance the capability of OTR truckers to become more fully the men and fathers they aspire to be.

REFERENCES

Bellah, R. N., Madsen, R., Sullivan, W. M., Swidler, A., and Tipton, S. M. (1985). *Habits of the heart.* New York: Harper and Row.

Blankenhorn, D. (1995). *Fatherless America: Confronting our most urgent social problems.* New York: Basic.

Christiansen, S. L., and Palkovitz, R. (2001). Why the "good provider" role still matters: Providing as a form of paternal involvement. *Journal of Family Issues, 22,* 84–106.

Cohen, T. F. (1993). What do fathers provide? Reconsidering the economic and nurturant dimensions of men as parents. In J. C. Hood (Ed.), *Men, work, and family* (pp. 1–22). Newbury Park, CA: Sage.

Daly, K. J. (1993). Reshaping fatherhood: Finding the models. *Journal of Family Issues, 14,* 510–30.

Daly, K. J., and Dienhart, A. (1998). Negotiating parental involvement: Finding time for children. In D. Vannoy and P. J. Dubeck (Eds.), *Challenges for work and family in the twenty-first century* (pp. 111–22). New York: de Gruyter.

Fox, G. L., Sayers, J., and Bruce, C. (2001). Beyond bravado: Redemption and rehabilitation in the fathering accounts of men who batter. *Journal of Marriage and the Family, 32,* 137–63.

Fox, G. L., Bruce, C., and Combs-Orme, T. (2000). Parenting expectations and concerns of fathers and mothers of newborn infants. *Family Relations, 49,* 123–31.

Gerson, K. (1993). *No man's land: Men's changing commitments to family and work.* New York: Basic.

Gilgun, J. F. (1992). Definitions, methodologies, and methods in qualitative family research. In J. F. Gilgun, K. J. Daly, and G. Handel (Eds.), *Qualitative methods in family research* (pp. 22–39). Newbury Park, CA: Sage.

Hareven, T. K. (1982). *Family time and industrial time.* Cambridge: Cambridge University Press.

Komarovsky, M. (1962). *Blue-collar marriage.* New York: Random House.

Lamont, M. (2000). *The dignity of working men: Morality and the boundaries of race, class, and immigration.* New York: Russell Sage Foundation.

LaRossa, R. (1988). Fatherhood and social change. *Family Relations, 37,* 451–57.

LaRossa, R. (1997). *The modernization of fatherhood: A social and political history.* Chicago: University of Chicago Press.

Loscocco, K. A. (1990). Reactions to blue-collar work: A comparison of women and men. *Work and Occupations, 17,* 152–77.

Marsiglio, W. (1995). Fathers' diverse life course patterns and roles: Theory and social interventions. In W. Marsoglio (Ed.), *Fatherhood: Contemporary theory, research, and social policy* (pp. 193–218). Washington, DC: Urban Institute.

Ouellet, L. J. (1974). *Pedal to the metal: The work life of truckers.* Philadelphia: Temple University Press.

Palkovitz, R., Christiansen, S. L., and Dunn, C. (1998). Provisional balances: Fathers' perceptions of the politics and dynamics of involvement in family and career development. *Michigan Family Review, 3,* 45–64.

Robinson, B. E., and Barret, R. L. (1986). The developing father: Emerging roles in contemporary society. New York: Guilford.

Rotundo, E. A. (1985). American fatherhood: A historical perspective. *American Behavioral Scientist, 29,* 7–25.

Roy, K. (2004). You can't eat love: Constructing provider role expectations for low-income and working-class fathers. Unpublished working paper. Purdue University.

Rubin, L. B. (1976). *Worlds of pain.* New York: Basic.

Small, S. A., and Riley, D. (1990). Toward a multidimensional assessment of work spillover into family life. *Journal of Marriage and the Family, 52,* 51–61.

U.S. Department of Labor (2002). Http://www.dol.gov/ and ftp://ftp.bls.gov/pub/specialrequests/ lf/aat12.txt

Weiss, R. S. (1994). *Learning from strangers: The art and method of qualitative interview studies.* New York: Free Press.

Zvonkovic, A. M., Manoogian, M. M., and McGraw, L. A. (2001). The ebb and flow of family life: How families experience being together and apart. In K. J. Daly (Ed.), *Minding the time in family experience: Emerging perspectives and issues* (pp. 135–60). Oxford, UK: Elsevier Science.

Zaretsky, E. (1976). *Capitalism, the family, and personal life.* New York: Harper and Row.

7

"Until the Ball Glows in the Twilight": Fatherhood, Baseball, and the Game of Playing Catch

Ralph LaRossa

> Baseball is fathers and sons playing catch, lazy and murderous, wild and controlled, the profound archaic song of birth, growth, age, and death.
>
> Donald Hall (1985)

It has been said, "Whoever wants to know the heart and mind of America had better learn baseball" (Barzun 1954). It may also be said that whoever wants to know the heart and mind of American fatherhood—the pattern of meanings associated with fatherhood—had best be familiar with the symbolism connected to a father teaching a child how to catch and throw a ball. In certain segments of the population, the game of playing catch not only is indispensable to learning the fundamentals of baseball, but also is instrumental to being defined as a caring dad (Rosenblatt 1998; McCormack 1999–2000).

How did baseball and the game of playing catch come to be associated with fatherhood? Drawing on a range of written and iconographic texts (e.g., newspaper and magazine articles, books, cartoons, films), I document the historical link between the institution of baseball (America's "national pastime") and a fleeting but important component of father–child interaction. Focusing on the question of who, where, when, how, and why (as in, "*who* plays the game?" and "*where* does the game take place?"), I show how ecological contexts (backyards and sunsets) and gender-specific meanings (definitions of fatherhood and athleticism) have transposed a seemingly mundane activity into a sacred and memorable moment; and how the moment itself is constructed through a combination of talk (or silence) and geometry (distance between the players). Ultimately I aim to demonstrate, via the game of playing catch, how physical and social realities are intertwined.[1]

BASEBALL AND FATHERHOOD

As one observer put it, "Chances are good that if you're a baseball fan, your dad had something to do with it—and your thoughts of the sport evoke thoughts of him" (Anonymous 2001). Baseball, however, was not always a part of America's social landscape; nor was it always central to fatherhood. How, then, did it become so?

Who invented baseball is open to debate, but lore has it that the sport was a variation of the English game of rounders and that it first became popular in the 1800s (Litsky 2004; Pennington 2004; Steele 1904). In its infancy, baseball was mainly the province of the upper middle class, but by the late 1800s, it had spread to the working class. Contributing to the diffusion was (1) the arrival of large urban parks or fields (rural havens in the city; Barth 1980); (2) the growing preoccupation with health and exercise (America went "sports crazy"; Dubbert 1979, 175); and (3) the increasing belief that sport was an effective response to America's turn-of-the-century "crisis of masculinity" (sport was a "place where manhood was earned"; Adelman 1986, 286) (Kimmel 1990).[2]

Thirteen major league fields were built or reconstructed between 1909 and 1915 (Bluthardt 1987), and the presence of major league ballparks in populated areas helped make professional ballplayers objects of admiration and emulation. Children were afforded opportunities to see baseball skillfully played; and fathers, more often than not, were the ones who took their kids to their "first game"—a phrase that, technically, can refer to any baseball contest seen for the first time, even if played on a sandlot, but that symbolically has come to be defined almost exclusively as a child's first visit to a major league venue.

Looking for early references to baseball and fatherhood, I examined over three hundred popular magazine articles published between 1900 and 1960, which were categorized under the heading of "fatherhood," "fathers," or "father–child relationships" in the *Reader's Guide to Periodical Literature*.[3] If popular magazine articles are any indication, commercial media accounts of fathers taking their kids to a ballgame or teaching them how to play baseball were rare in the early twentieth century. The first article that I discovered was published in *The Outlook* in 1914. A father reported that he had escorted his eleven-year-old son to a baseball game every afternoon the previous summer, in an effort "to take seriously the business of being a companion to the boy." He said that he had bought a baseball glove for himself, so that he and his son could play. "I mean to be closer to him in the next ten years than any other companion—to be a bigger influence in his life than any of the influences that are outside our control. He's going to be a better man than I am, if

I can make him so" (Barton 1914). Eight years later, a father writing in *American Magazine* declared that if he did not help his ten-year-old son "grow up right," he would consider himself a "failure," no matter how much money he made or how big a reputation he achieved. So when his son asked him to play catch ("Dad, come on and peg me a few"), he immediately interrupted what he was doing and went outside. "Is that the swiftest you can throw," the boy asked. "Do you want them faster?" the father replied. "Sure, burn 'em in," the boy answered.

> Now I thought I knew that boy. I fancied I could tell anyone all about him. Yet it had been almost a year since I had tossed a baseball to him. . . . To my surprise he could handle his mitt with ease and grace. He was not afraid of the ball and he caught what little speed I have left without flinching. (Guest 1922)

And in 1923, in *Ladies Home Journal*, a father talked about how he and his two sons would drive into Boston to see the Red Sox or Braves play and that "for a time baseball would absorb [them]." He also mentioned precisely how he played with his children. "I used to lay down a glove to represent second base, station the boys on either side as shortstop and second baseman, and bat or throw . . . leaving it to them to make the instant decision who would go for the ball and who would cover . . . [the base]" (Merwin 1923).

The four-decade span of the 1920s to the 1950s generally is known as baseball's "golden years." Radio and later television began to broadcast the games, and arenas grew even larger. (Some 74,200 fans were in attendance when Yankee Stadium opened in 1923; Yankee Stadium History, n.d.) Prior to the 1920s, baseball was mainly a game of singles and doubles, batted balls that would advance base runners and add to a team's score. While this strategy continued to be important, the interwar years marked the glorification of the home run, wherein a ball would be hit over an outfield fence. The changing social meaning of the "long ball" not only altered how kids viewed the physical world of baseball but also reconceptualized their own performances on and off the field. "Swinging for the fences" became a prized strategy in the sport as well as an aphorism for striving for success in life.

From 1932 to 1937, *Parents* magazine ran a series of monthly articles under the banner "For fathers only." Curiously, only two articles mentioned baseball. The first, published in 1932, talked about the importance of positive reinforcement, using the game of catch to illustrate the point: "A father who has been doing a little quiet research concludes that when parents adopt the 'do' attitude, few 'don'ts' are necessary. . . . 'Don't be afraid of the baseball' can be translated into 'Do show me how well you can catch'" (Motherwell 1932). The second, published in 1933, offered the observation, "It is frequently only when a son becomes interested in baseball that a father begins to see a chance for companionship with his boy." The article went on to offer advice on how to teach a child who was just learning the game.

> If a father tries to get his son interested in baseball, he must be prepared to maintain poise and gentleness in the face of the boy's acting babyish, crying and complaining about a hurt finger, placing himself in a ridiculous position by making silly faces and gestures as he misses catch after catch, or slamming down his glove and sulking because of errors. (Rademacher 1933)

After Pearl Harbor and America's entrance in World War II, the question arose as to whether baseball should be temporarily suspended. The commissioner of baseball wrote to President Roosevelt to seek his advice. The president "responded the next day with what has become known as 'the green light letter,' offering . . . his personal opinion that baseball should continue." Roosevelt felt that "the benefits of the game would provide a much-needed morale boost to those on the home front and to American service personnel overseas" (Percoco 1992). As the war progressed, a number of professional baseball players were drafted into the armed forces but were replaced by others eager to play. It was during this time also that the All-American Girls Professional Baseball League was formed. The historical significance of the "Girls" league is that it gave women the opportunity to play baseball professionally. Although fans initially seemed to enjoy the women's competitions, interest waned after the war ended. The league was disbanded in 1954 (Peterik 1995).

Little League Baseball, founded in 1939, expanded during the war, as well (Little League Online, n.d.). Although organized youth leagues existed in the 1920s and 1930s, none of them equaled Little League in popularity. (The leagues were thought to be an effective antidote to juvenile delinquency; Hurley 1935; Speaker 1939.) The growth of Little League put more pressure on children to learn the sport and more demands on fathers to instruct their kids in the intricacies of the game (Fine 1987).

Since the 1960s, baseball has become an even larger and more complex entertainment industry. Whereas before, professional teams were located mainly in the industrial North and the Midwest, major (and minor) league baseball now is played in cities and towns throughout the United States and Canada. Baseball also has taken hold in other areas of the world, especially in Japan and Latin America. Video games, sports television networks, and the further expansion and bureaucratization of youth baseball now encourage children to both learn and consume the game. (Profits on the sale of baseball paraphernalia are considerable.) Although baseball continues to be a game played by boys and men *for* boys and men, it is increasingly common for girls to play youth ball, and some women have played high school or college ball, on the same team as their male classmates.[4]

At the same time that baseball has grown, its share of the sports pie has shrunk. Over the past forty years, major league baseball has had to contend with the mounting popularity of other sports (Mandelbaum 2004). For example, fathers, who grew up in the 1950s and 1960s loving and playing baseball, have had children who enjoyed playing other sports more. Looking forward to the day they would play catch with their kids (as their own fathers did or did not do with them), men raised in the postwar era often have discovered that their sons and daughters would just as soon practice the deft footwork that soccer requires—a skill that the men may not have learned and thus cannot teach.[5]

THE GAME OF PLAYING CATCH

A baseball enthusiast once remarked that although playing catch is called a game, "there is really no game to it" because "nobody wins or loses" (Rosenblatt 1998). The fact is, however, that while playing catch may not be a game in a conventional sense, it *is* a game, in a sociological sense, because the social institution of baseball penetrates the heart of the activity. So does the institution of fatherhood. Thus it can be said that the community of baseball and fatherhood "exercises control over the conduct of its individual members" (Mead 1934, 155). To put it another way, "America surfaces in a ball park" (Geertz 1973, 417)—and sometimes in a backyard.

What is the social nature of the game of catch? To answer this question, I initiated a series of bibliographic and Internet searches to find as many references to playing catch as I could. (I also had kept a file on the subject for several years.) Relying on these texts, I endeavored to dissect the game. I was interested in five basic questions: *Who* plays catch, and *where*, *when*, *how*, and *why* is the game played?

Who

Although nothing prevents several players from forming a circle and tossing around a ball, in the texts that I reviewed, playing catch almost always was described as a two-person game. What seems to make the game special—and memorable—is the opportunity the game affords to have private time, not just with "any other," but with a "significant other." Structurally and experientially, playing catch is a to-and-fro dance—a pas de deux, prized for its intimacy ("just you and me").

The fact that playing catch often involves two people who are at different skill levels is important, too. The game can be dangerous and does demand concentration. The adult must be careful not to throw too fast, so as not to hurt and/or embarrass the child. The child, especially if new to the game, must remember how to hold the glove to avoid getting hit in the face. As players get older, however, skill levels may reverse. One of my children, for example, is now a better fielder than I ever was, and the velocity of my "fast ball" diminishes with each passing year.

Playing catch also is generally talked about as a game between fathers and sons. However, recent texts have included references to fathers and daughters, as well as to mothers and sons.[6] A daughter exclaimed, "My dad is way, way cool. . . . He taught me to believe in myself and be fair. He taught me how to throw a baseball" ("My dad is way, way cool," 2003).[7] A son reported, "I played catch with my father, of course, but also with my mother. She would borrow my father's big glove late on a summer's weekend afternoon" (Lichtenberg 1993). (Note the "of course," when the son talked about playing with his father.) A man spoke of the special relationship he had with his two girls, both of whom played softball: "I've been doing it [playing catch] for over twenty-five years with my daughters. It binds us together, connects generations, widens our appreciation of some of the old-fashioned virtues of America just as much as boys with their fathers." He also reminisced, "Almost every day, when I would come home from work, one or the other, or both, would say 'come on, Dad, let's play catch.' It was our special time together. 'We can do it,' they seemed to be saying, 'we can do it just like boys; we're no wimps'" (Cummins 2001).

Where

Not every recent reference to playing catch happened to mention where the activity took place. But of the cases in which location was identified, it was a yard or, more specifically, a *backyard* that was mentioned most of the time.

Notably, the yard as a location to toss a ball (or bat it) was not talked about much in the pre–World War II articles that I reviewed. I did find several postwar articles that included pictures of fathers and children playing ball, but the texts rarely specified where they were playing. One that did was a 1952 article in *Woman's Home Companion*. It had a photo of a father pitching a ball to his son in a yard in what appears to be the back of a house ("Today's Father," 1952). A 1950 *Snookums* comic strip, published in the *Atlanta Journal and Constitution*, depicted a father taking his toddler son "out in the yard" (far enough away not to "break any windows"), hoping to "get him interested in baseball." And a *Sparks* strip, published in 1956 in the *Chicago Defender* (an African American newspaper) portrayed a father and son playing catch in an open, but indeterminate area. ("I wanna see how ya like this new fast ball I've developed . . . Daddy!" "Okay! Let 'er fly!")

Recently published texts included more references to playing in a back-yard. As some saw it, the game was something that *naturally* took place there: "It's an American ritual for a father and son to grab a ball and glove and go out in the backyard to play catch" (Ward 2003). In one case, when both a yard and playground were mentioned, it was the backyard game that was the better remembered of the two: "Many professional ballplayers . . . have come and gone since the days in the mid-1950s when my father and I played ball in our backyard or at Mohawk school across the street from our house. . . . Dad is 82 and I just turned 56, so obviously it has been many, many years since we played pitch-and-catch *in our backyard*" (Hart 2002, emphasis added).

Where a game of catch happens to occur is significant. The availability of a backyard increases the likelihood that fathers will be engaged in the activity, since it does not take much effort to walk out the door to play. Playing catch in the backyard is, as one author put it, "an easy thing to do—you don't need to have access to something like a basketball hoop and you don't have to strap on a ton of gear" (Codding 2002). A backyard also can make it more difficult for a father to deny a child's request. In the popular song about generational alienation, "Cat's in the Cradle," a son's appeal to his father ("Thanks for the ball, Dad, come on let's play"), is heart-rending because we assume that the boy simply is asking his father to step outside. The father's reply ("Not today, I got a lot to do") comes across as insensitive, because playing catch does not seem to be too much to ask. (After all, a few days earlier the son had been given a ball on his tenth birthday.) The father's refusal to make room for his son ultimately comes full circle when, later in life, his son refuses to make room for him ("I'd love to see you [son] if you don't mind." He said, "I'd love to, Dad, if I could find the time") (Chapin and Chapin 1974).

An ecological variable that may have contributed to the popularity of the game of catch was post–World War II suburbanization. The backyards of suburban homes were marketed as family-friendly areas, perfect for weekend barbecues and evenings of tossing a ball around. Suburban spaces also were designed to be safe places to play. In *Fathers Playing Catch with Sons*, the poet Donald Hall recalled playing catch with his father in the 1930s and 1940s, but he spoke about doing so near a busy street.

[At first] I threw straight. Then I tried to put something on it; it flew twenty feet over his head. Or it banged into the sidewalk in front of him, breaking stitches [on the ball] and ricocheting off a pebble into the gutter of Greenway Street. Or it went wide to his right and lost itself in Mrs. Davis's bushes. Or it went wide to his left and rolled across the street while drivers swerved their cars. (Hall 1985, 28) [8]

Hall and his father were playing in traffic (literally), where a misthrown ball could put a child or father in serious danger. Suburban yards eliminated, or at least minimized, these risks.

Needless to say, not everyone can live in suburbia—or wants to. Fathers who reside in the city either by choice or circumstance, and who desire to play catch, may have to dodge cars, much like Hall's father was forced to do. Or they may invest more energy and time trying to find a safe place to play (e.g., walking or driving to a nearby park). Separated or divorced suburban dads, living in an apartment that does not have a yard, may discover that extemporaneous games of catch are not as easy to arrange as they once were.

Where family members engage in sports activities also is connected to spatial and temporal privacy. A backyard large enough to throw a baseball back and forth affords the players a space where they can interact without necessarily being observed. A child learning the intricacies of baseball thus may take solace in the fact that his or her mistakes are not open to scrutiny. Equally if not more important, the quality of a Little Leaguer's performance under the watchful eyes of his or her teammates may hinge on the opportunity he or she has to practice in what may be called a backstage region (Goffman 1959). A backyard also provides a measure of temporal privacy, because it reduces the likelihood that others will interrupt the game (Zerubavel 1981). Locked in a temporal bubble, a parent and child can more easily manufacture "quality time," in which the sport itself becomes subordinate to the emotions engendered between the players.

When

Assuming a place to play can be found, throwing and catching a baseball can occur whenever people can get together. Two other factors, however, impinge on whether or not a game is played. The first is visibility. Without artificial illumination, playing catch is an activity that can happen only in daylight or lowlight (e.g., twilight). The second factor is the set of commitments that a parent and child might have. For a father, there is work; for a child, there may be school. These commitments often relegate playing catch to weeknights and weekends, but even this schedule assumes that the father is working from 9:00 in the morning to 5:00 in the late afternoon and has Saturday and Sunday off. (A father who works evenings and/or nights, and/or weekends, or is a stay-at-home dad, operates within different temporal constraints.)

Despite the number of possible permutations, playing catch typically was described in the texts that I reviewed as an activity that occurred not so much on the weekend as toward the end of the day, after the father had come home from work.

It is almost evening, and I have just settled into my spot on the couch. I want nothing more than to slip off my shoes and be totally, blissfully idle.

Suddenly my baseball mitt comes flying from behind and lands in my lap. "Wanna play catch?" It's Dash, my ten-year-old son, the boy never seen without his baseball cap, the boy who sleeps with his mitt.

"It's almost dark," I tell him. "And I'm worn out."

He doesn't say anything, just gives me the look that says: SOMEDAY WHEN YOU ARE OLD AND I AM GROWN, YOU'RE GOING TO REGRET EACH DAY YOU DIDN'T PLAY CATCH WHEN I ASKED YOU.

I put on my shoes. "Grab a ball."

"Already got one." He grins and flips it to me.

And the arc is renewed. The ball. The toss. Fathers playing catch with their sons. (Morris n.d.)

What is intriguing is the length of time referred to in the above excerpt. The father indicated that it was almost dark when his son asked him to play, which meant that they did not play for all that long. Later on in the article, the father talked about playing catch with his own father. He and his dad would go "out back beyond the orange trees" and "spend hours and hours just tossing the ball back and forth" (Morris n.d.). The fifty-six-year-old author (cited earlier), who reminisced about playing "pitch-and-catch" with his father, also spoke of "the hours" that they spent together "after a long hard day at work" (Hart 2002). And another writer spoke affectionately of fathers and sons playing catch "until the ball glows in the twilight"—a phrase that implied playing after the sun went down and suggested, too, a sacred quality to the act (Cozine 2003).

The chronological dynamics in playing-catch discourse is revealing of how the game is contemplated. The symbolism conveyed is that when fathers and children play catch, time becomes irrelevant. The moment is all there is.

How long fathers and children *actually* play catch is harder to decipher. If playing catch requires a certain degree of natural light, and if indeed the game can be played in twilight, how much time is there at the end of the day to play? The answer is a matter of both history and geography.

The father who recalled playing catch with his dad in the mid-1950s said that he grew up in Scotia, New York, which is just north of Schenectady. According to the U.S. Naval Observatory, sunset was at 7:38 and twilight ended at 8:13 on July 1, 1955, in Scotia. If we assume that the father worked from 9:00 to 5:00 and would get home by 5:45, that would leave approximately two hours of direct sunlight and about a half hour of twilight to engage in an outside game. The author spoke of "the hours" that he and his father spent together playing ball at the end of the day. If indeed that were the case, the two would have had to begin playing as soon as the father got home and continue playing until just about dark. Dinner would have had to wait. This very well may have been the family's pattern. Then again, it may not. It could be that most games of catch in the 1950s lasted no more than forty-five minutes, maybe an hour, but that because the time devoted to playing was limited, the activity itself became more precious in the child's mind and also more memorable. It is possible, as well, that the wistfully recollected "hours" of postwar fathers and sons playing catch is more emblematic of what baby boomers wanted, but rarely received.

The situation, however, is not the same today. In 1966, the Uniform Time Act was passed and signed into law. This act was an attempt to establish one pattern of Daylight Saving Time from April to October across the country. Up until then, daylight saving time was based on local laws and customs. (There are communities that, by state law, are exempt from DST, but they are few.) ("Daylight Saving Time" n.d.). On July 1, 1966, in Scotia, sunset and the "end of civil twilight" were at 7:38 and 8:13, respectively, precisely when they were in 1955. But on July 1, 1967, both occurred *one hour later*, at 8:38 and 9:13. Thus after the Uniform Time Act was enacted, there was more daylight at the end of the day in the spring and summer and early fall (the baseball season) for families to play outdoors. Because of the implementation of daylight saving time, a father and child playing catch may have become more common in the *immediate* wake of the change.[9] As for comparisons between now and twenty or thirty years ago, the longer commutes between work and home and the overall "frenzied temporal climate" (Daly 1996) may mean that contemporary fathers are playing catch less often with their children than their fathers played with them. In other words, the historical pattern, with regard to the frequency of the game, may be curvilinear (i.e., first a rise, then a decline).

Sunlight patterns also vary by latitude and longitude, creating different opportunities for playing outside in the evening. In midsummer, the sun sets in Boston at 8:25, in Atlanta at 8:52, in San Francisco at 8:36, and in Los Angeles, at 8:09 (USNO times for July 1, 2004). Thus, in general, fathers in Boston may play catch less often, and for shorter periods of time, than fathers in Atlanta; and fathers in Los Angeles may play less often, and for shorter periods of time, than fathers in San Francisco.

How

How to play catch is influenced, to some extent, by the amount of space available to the players and by the rules of baseball. A small yard or the presence of trees may limit "pop-ups," balls thrown high in the air by one player and caught on the way down by the other player, while a yard with shrubbery in the middle may limit "grounders," balls skipped across the grass or dirt. Needless to say, trees and shrubs, as well as other obstacles, may be cut down or eliminated to "make room" for the game, which raises the question of how often fathers build or craft physical sanctuaries to facilitate play. In the tongue-in-cheek book, *How to Dad*, the point is made, "Playing Catch with the Old Man involves more than merely tossing a ball back and forth. . . . It is a ritual that connects one generation to the next and should make you feel compelled to build a lighted domed stadium in your backyard (Boswell and Barrett 1990, 16). While building a baseball park is well beyond the reach of the average father, we certainly can envision the space around a home being modified to accommodate one sport or another. I recall cutting the grass in our backyard more frequently when our sons were young to make the terrain more suitable for our ball games.

It is not unusual, when playing catch, for fathers and children to pretend they are pitching to a batter, in which case they may mark off the official distance between the "pitching rubber" (with which a pitcher's foot must always be in contact) and "home plate" (behind which the catcher crouches). In Little League, the distance between the pitching rubber and home plate is 46 feet. In high school, college, and major league baseball, it is 60.5 feet. While a backyard may be available, it may not be large enough to accommodate throwing across these distances. If it is not, players may still "pitch" to each other, but they will do so under artificial spatial conditions. (Imagine having a basketball hoop in one's driveway, but at lower than regulation height.)

The geometry of the game of playing catch is less contingent on institutional rules. The game can involve nothing more than repeatedly throwing and catching a baseball, with the players standing 20–30 feet apart. As the game ebbs and flows, the distance between the players will expand or contract, depending on how they feel at the moment (how much they are *in* the moment). In this scenario, it is the relationship between the players that determines the game's spatial parameters, rather than vice versa. For some who have played catch, this is the game they remember most and the game that captures best the game's aesthetics: "We fell into the timeless pace of throw and catch and throw and catch: we found the timeless place of playing catch" (Littlefield 2002).

Clearly how people play is linked to the *meanings* they attach to the activity. Take, for example, whether players should talk to each other. According one view, playing catch is optimal when quiet prevails.

> The best part of the game is the silence. . . . Once I happened to be on the field of Yankee Stadium before game time when the players were warming up. . . . Every easy toss was delivered at a speed greater than a good high school fastball pitcher could generate. *Thwack, thwack, thwack* in the leather.

And the silence between the men on the field. It was interesting to note that even at their level, this was still a game of catch. We do what we can as parents, one child at a time. . . . The trick, I think, is to recognize the moments when nothing needs to be said. (Rosenblatt 1998)

To others, however, talk is essential to the game. A writer who grew up playing catch with his father and his mother argued that conversation between a parent and child is crucial—*but not just any conversation.*

My mother had nothing to teach me about the techniques of baseball. I threw the ball to her, she threw it back to me. Her chat was observation, not praise or prescription. My father called: "Nice grab!" or "Two hands!" or "Keep your eye on it!" She'd say, "That was a high one." I had to ask her to throw me grounders and explain to her what they were. "You know, grounders. On the ground. Like a ground ball. *Grounders.*" My mother smiled at me, half apologetic, half amused. I could hear as I talked baseball to her that, like her, I was new at this, not eloquent and authoritative like my father. I couldn't make every detail of skill and strategy seem like an absolute truth. As I explained to her a bit of what I'd recently learned from him, I could hear something a boy might otherwise miss: *baseball was strange.* Why would an intelligent person engaged in throwing a ball back and forth want the ball aimed at the ground? . . . What she threw me wasn't the official Dad stuff, but it was fine on its own terms. . . . For boys and their fathers, baseball follows an established progression, from instructional games to catch to stickball or Little League, then school teams with fatherlike coaches, and finally employment, with "team players" and "hardball," whether literal or figurative. But my mother and I had only a pickup game she offered to invent with me as we went along. . . . Catch for me was preparation. My father was keeping in practice for the pickup softball games he loved. But my mother never played softball. When my father threw with me it was as if to say, *This is how we do what we do.* Not with my mother. Our "we" was not yet defined. She was not saying, *This is what we do.* She was saying: *Don't leave. We'll figure something out.*" (Lichtenberg 1993, 28–29)

Another man, recalling his relationship with his dad, said, "As I grew older and more distant (the way sons too often become with their fathers), playing catch was sometimes the only way we could talk. Or try. The turf between us seemed wider than ever, our only connection the path of a ball" (Morris n.d.).

If every act of verbal and nonverbal interaction ultimately says, "This is how I see myself . . . this is how I see you . . . this is how I see you seeing me," and so forth (Watzlawick, Beavin, and Jackson 1967, 52), then the game of playing catch has as much to do with interpersonal relations as any other form of communication might have. The silence and the talk are ingredients in the mix, defining who we are, and would like to be.

Why

It is interesting that the game of catch is called "catch," when the game entails not only catching but also throwing. For many, in fact, learning how to throw the ball is the most difficult part of the game.

With arrival of youth baseball leagues, teaching children how to throw the "right way" became a key reason to play catch. A boy who threw without the proper arm motion or, worse, "threw like a girl" could be the object of ridicule, both on the field and off.[10] A father could be taken to task, as well. ("What kind of father would not teach his son how to throw?") A man who knew how to "correct" his son's throwing, on the other hand, could be a hero. Said one author, recalling his youth:

> I'm 8 years old and I'm playing Little League Baseball for the first time and my dad's the coach! It's my first tryout/practice and it's an exciting, confusing, scary affair, with what seems like hundreds of boys. . . . Later at home, my father informs me that there are two boys on the team who throw like girls, and that I, unfortunately, am one of them! By the next practice, he tells me, we will have corrected that problem. That evening, with glove and cap securely in place, I anxiously face my father on the front lawn. And we play catch. For quite a while, I am concentrating, working hard to throw correctly ("like a *man*"), pulling my arm back as far as I can and snapping the ball overhand, just past my ear. When I do this, it feels very strange—I really have very little control over the flight of the ball, and it hurts my shoulder a bit—but I am rewarded with the knowledge that *this is how men throw the ball*. If I learn this, I won't embarrass either myself or my father. (Messner 1995, 46–47)

The professional baseball player Harmon Killebrew once talked about how he and his brother would play ball with their father and how his mother would admonish them for tearing up the lawn. Killebrew's dad reportedly would reply, "We're not raising grass. We're raising boys" (cited in Kennedy 2003, 3D). In some people's minds, the whys and wherefores of playing catch have less to do with baseball than with gender and masculinity. Through the game, boys are shown "how men throw" (i.e., how "real" men *behave*).

Rationales for playing catch have not been constant, however. If we take a historical look at the texts, we can discern a shift. In the early twentieth century, a common justification for playing catch was that playing with a child would help a father to get to know that child. Playing catch thus was placed in the same category as playing marbles or playing hide-and-seek. ("To know a boy you must play with him"; Guest 1922.) Then, in the mid-twentieth century, as more children got involved in organized youth sports, playing catch became an instructional activity. Learning how to throw and catch "correctly" grew in importance. (Recalling what it was like to grow up in the 1950s, a former Little Leaguer said, "I was lucky to have a dad who cared enough to teach me the basics"; Hart 2002.) In the late twentieth century, the meaning of playing catch appears to have taken yet a different turn. The game is still about play and instruction, but also it has been transformed, at least for some, into a celebration of fatherhood (e.g., "There's something about a father playing catch with his son that is just so pure, so iconic, so American"; Kennedy 2003). Playing catch, in addition, may now be perceived to be about *multiple* generations of fathers and sons, and through a process of temporal extension, the game has been reified; for example, "I played catch in the backyard with my dad, as kids have done and dads have done *since baseball first arrived"* (Littlefield 2002, emphasis added); *"for 100 years and more now*, fathers have been playing catch with sons" (Codding 2002, emphasis added).

Hollywood also has embraced this theme. Perhaps the best example is the 1989 film, *Field of Dreams*. The film's story is about a man who lives with his family on an Iowa farm about to go bankrupt and who repeatedly hears a voice telling him, "If you build it, he will come." He interprets the message to mean that he should build a ballpark in his cornfield, which he does. (Anything is possible in fiction. By the way, few fatherhood and baseball films merge the physical and the social as well as *Field of Dreams* does.) Eventually the 1919 Chicago White Sox show up to play. This is an infamous team that included several members who were charged with deliberately losing that year's World Championship. Many baseball fans, however, feel that at least one of the players, "Shoeless" Joe Jackson, was wrongly accused. The "he" who "will come," however, turns out to be neither Jackson nor any other public figure, but the main character's dad. (An underlying premise is that the farmer and his dad were estranged.) When the father shows up on the "field of dreams," the son meekly asks, "Hey, Dad, you wanna have a catch?" The film closes with the father and son lazily throwing a baseball back and forth to each other. The game is meant to symbolize paternal bonding. ("It is through baseball, America's game, that father and son are reconciled, that the pain of both father and son is finally healed"; Aronson and Kimmel 2001.) Men have confessed that they cried while watching this scene. I will admit that I have.

Field of Dreams was based on the novel *Shoeless Joe*, by W. P. Kinsella (1982). The film basically repeated the plotline of the book, but with one important exception. The final scene of the father and son playing catch was added. Apparently, the film's producers and writers felt that the new scene would resonate with fathers. Looking at films that have come out since 1950 and that have baseball and fatherhood as a theme, we see that films increasingly have used the connection between baseball and fatherhood, and between fatherhood and playing catch, to tell a heartwarming story. *The Natural*

(1984), *City Slickers* (1991), *Hook* (1991), *Free Willy* (1993), *The Sandlot* (1993), *Sleepless in Seattle* (1993), *Three Wishes* (1995), *Liar Liar* (1997), and *My Dog Skip* (2000)—among others—all rely on these connections.

Why did playing catch become more strongly associated with fatherhood in the late twentieth century? One can only speculate, but a combination of both the physical and social would seem to be involved. It could be that the growing popularity of Little League baseball, and other youth baseball leagues, in the postwar suburban (more available space) era created a generation of kids who enjoyed playing ball. These kids then grew up to be fathers (and writers, artists, producers, etc.) in the late twentieth century, just when another wave of "New Fatherhood" was encouraging men to "be there" for their children. (An earlier wave of "New Fatherhood" was evident in the early twentieth century; LaRossa 1997.) The spread of major and minor league baseball venues (imposing physical edifices) and the ubiquity of baseball on television also may have increased children's desire to be baseball proficient and to emulate their sports heroes. Along with these factors, the passage of the Uniform Time Act in 1966, which created more daylight (temporal space) at the end of the day, afforded greater opportunities for fathers to play the game in the 1970s and 1980s. It appears that playing catch may occur less frequently today than twenty or thirty years ago, in part because of the growing physical distance between home and work in automobile-oriented America. But this turnabout actually may have elevated the game's nostalgic (remembrance of things past) value and further solidified its sacralization in contemporary popular culture.

FUTURE RESEARCH

The game of playing catch clearly is central to the social meaning of fatherhood in America. It is not an activity, however, that researchers have chosen to explore to any great degree. Relying on a variety of written and iconographic texts, I have pieced together a picture of how the symbolism attached to the game changed over the course of the twentieth century, but there is much that still remains unknown. Consider, for example, what we could learn from an interview study of men born in different decades. Such a study would be valuable in that that it would allow us to uncover the subtleties of the game in the 1980s and 1990s (and beyond), relative to its subtleties in the 1940s and 1950s, and 1960s and 1970s. An important question would be whether the ecology and geometry of the game have changed over the years. What effect did suburbanization have? How exactly has the game been played under different physical and social contexts? Being retrospective accounts, the narratives also would shed light on how the game is remembered from one generation to the next. What do the stories—or, more specifically, the plotlines—suggest about children's feelings toward their fathers?

Comparisons between playing catch and other activities deserve scrutiny, as well. For some families, "the game" they revere is centered not on throwing a baseball but on passing a football, or kicking a soccer ball. For others, it is playing one-on-one basketball ("shooting hoops"). Still others enjoy bowling or tennis, ice or street hockey. Studies that systematically examine the "who, where, when, how, and why" of these games could be very revealing of family dynamics, particularly if they focus on the definitions that parents and children attach to the play and the physical realities that demarcate the interaction.

It is worth noting, for instance, that the game of playing catch is enacted outside and is flexible enough to allow the players to move closer and farther apart, as they wish. Rarely, however, do they touch one another. Basketball can be played either outside or inside, with players staying in close proximity, moving vigorously, and often pushing off each other (if it is a competitive game). Physical contact also can be part of a one-on-one football game. I remember the times my sons and I would wrestle with each other on our living room floor while in the midst of watching a televised football game. Pretending to carry a ball toward an imaginary goal line, one or the other of us would be "thrown for a loss" or "break a tackle" to score. Times like these provided an opportunity for us to be close.

The game of playing catch also is generally a noncompetitive activity. If a parent and child pretend that they are playing in an actual event, they often will imagine themselves on the same team. ("It's a grounder to the shortstop [child], he flips to the second baseman [father] who then rifles it to the first baseman [child] for a double play.") One-on-one basketball, bowling, and tennis, however, generally develop into a competition. ("I finally beat you!") What difference does this make to families? What difference does it make to the flow of conversation during and after the game?

The role of talk in family sports indeed can be crucial. Bowling, for example, is played generally in a public setting with onlookers nearby (sometimes only a foot away). Marked lanes dictate where the players stand and deliver the ball. The same parameters are operative when fathers play tennis with their children at a public park. The chance to have a private chat is minimal. One could hypothesize that there are fewer heart-to-heart talks when parents and children bowl or play tennis than when they play catch. No one, to my knowledge, has done a study that examines whether there is a connection between the kinds of one-on-one sports activities that fathers and children have engaged in (and how often) and the perception of the quality of their relationships. This would be a worthwhile project.

Finally, it is imperative to explore how sport activities and the social construction of space are connected to socioeconomic status, race, ethnicity, and nationality. Whereas some groups perceive backyard baseball as a thing of beauty, others view cityscape basketball or open field soccer that way (Mandelbaum 2004). Our propensity to see an object "glow in the twilight" depends on the "thought community" to which we belong (Zerubavel 1997).[11]

NOTES

I would like to thank Elizabeth Cavalier, Regina Davis-Sowers, Maureen Mulligan LaRossa, William Marsiglio, Kevin Roy, Cynthia Sinha, and Frank Whittington for their assistance with this chapter.

1. The texts tell us more about the culture of fatherhood than about conduct of fatherhood. By that I mean the texts reveal more about how fatherhood, baseball, and catch are *portrayed* rather than about how they are *performed*. Still, while the connection between culture and conduct should never be presumed, neither should it be denied. Thus there are times when, on the basis of cultural evidence, bits and pieces of conduct are inferred. (For a discussion of the distinction between the culture and conduct of fatherhood, and how the two may or may not be related, see LaRossa 1988, 1997, 2004.)

2. Commenting on the perceived crisis of masculinity, Kimmel (1996, 157) notes, "By the beginning of the twentieth century, testing manhood had become increasingly difficult. The public arena was crowded and competitive, and heading west to start over was more the stuff of fiction than possibility. What was worse, many believed, a new generation of young boys was being raised entirely by women, who would turn America's future men into whiny little mama's boys. Men sought to rescue their sons from the feminizing clutches of mothers and teachers and create new ways to 'manufacture manhood.'"

3. A more thorough survey would have included articles published in the nineteenth century, as well. My search was limited to articles indexed in *The Reader's Guide to Periodical Literature*, which begins in 1900.

4. Although men historically have dominated baseball, a number of women, over the years, have loved baseball, too. The All-American Girls Professional Baseball League of the 1940s and early 1950s is but one illustration. The historian Doris Kearns Goodwin wrote a memoir about her infatuation with the Brooklyn Dodgers in the 1940s and 1950s. She began, "When I was six, my father gave me a bright red scorebook that opened my heart to the game of baseball. After dinner on long summer nights, he would sit beside me in our small enclosed porch to hear my account of that day's Brooklyn Dodger game. Night after night he taught me the odd collection of symbols, numbers, and letters that enable a baseball lover to record every action of the game" (Goodwin 1997, 13).

5. Youth soccer has become very popular in the United States ("Youth Soccer" n.d.). A disjunction between fathers' and children's preferred sports also may have occurred in the 1940s and 1950s. Fathers who grew up in the 1920s and 1930s but did not play organized youth sports may not have been as adept as they would have liked at teaching their Little League sons how to throw, catch, and bat.

6. Mothers and daughters playing catch are rare but could become more common, given the number of single women raising girls who are interested in competitive sports.

7. A father whose six-year-old daughter is playing Little League baseball reported, "She practices with me in the backyard too, but she can hit a lot better than her daddy. I hope she has the time of her life playing the great game of baseball and has lots of 'Kid-type' memories, too!" (Piszek 2003).

8. Hall's 1985 book, *Fathers Playing Catch with Sons*, probably has done more to promote the *culture* of the game of catch than any other text. Other authors who have written about the game often reference (and revere) the book. The lead chapter, "Fathers Playing Catch with Sons," originally was a 1974 article (in *Playboy* magazine), but it is the 1985 book that has become synonymous with the game's sacralization.

9. The passage of the Uniform Time Act raises another interesting possibility. Fathers who had children in the 1970s and 1980s indeed may have played catch with their children more than their own fathers played with them. But they also may have forgotten that, prior to the act's passage in 1966, sunset came "sooner" at the end of the day, leaving less time to play outdoors in the evening. That is, their fathers were operating under different ecological circumstances.

10. A skilled player's arm operates like a catapult to hurl the ball. A whip of the wrist can provide additional spin and speed. The connotation of "throwing like a girl" is almost always negative. The denotation is harder to pin down. (What does "throwing like a girl" look like?) The negative label often appears to be associated with an arm motion that *stops* just as the ball is released, as opposed to allowing the arm to *continue downward*, while finely timing the ball's release.

11. In a study of Korean and Vietnamese immigrant children, one son said, "I love my dad but we never got to play catch. He didn't teach me how to play football. All the stuff a *normal* dad does for kids" (Pyke 2000). Baseball and football are integral to American culture. Some see understanding these games, and learning how to play them, as a benchmark of assimilation.

REFERENCES

Adelman, M. L. (1986). *A sporting time: New York City and the rise of modern athletics, 1820–1870*. Urbana: University of Illinois Press.

Anonymous. (2001). Book description accompanying *The final season: Fathers, sons, and one last season in a classic American ballpark* by Tom Stanton. Retrieved November 6, 2003, from http://amazon.com

Aronson, A., and Kimmel, M. (2001). The saviors and the saved: Masculine redemption in contemporary films. In P. Lehman (Ed.), *Masculinity: Bodies, movies, culture* (pp. 43–50). New York: Routledge.

Barth, G. (1980). *City people: The rise of modern city culture in nineteenth-century America*. New York: Oxford University Press.

Barton, B. (1914, May 2). When your son is a fool. *Outlook, 107,* 37–40.

Barzun, J. (1954). *God's country and mine: A declaration of love spiced with a few harsh words*. Boston: Little, Brown.

Bluthardt, R. F. (1987). Fenway Park and the golden age of the baseball park, 1909–1915. *Journal of Popular Culture, 21,* 43–52.

Boswell, J., and Barrett, R. (1990). *How to dad*. New York: Dell.

Burwell, B. (2003, August 17). Dad knew best: You can't strike out when it comes to baseball. *St. Louis Post-Dispatch*. Retrieved October 20 2003, from http://web.lexis.nexis.com

Chapin, H. and Chapin, S. (Music and Lyrics). (1974). Cat's in the cradle. On *Verities and Balderdash*.

Codding, J. (2002). Do I really need a reason? Bullz-eye.com: The Guys' Portal to the Web. Retrieved October 23, 2003, from http://www.bullz-eye.com/codding/2002/041701.htm

Cozine, G. (2003). Pop fly in the son. *Elysian Fields Quarterly*. Retrieved October 20, 2003, from http://www.efqreview.com/NewFiles/v20n2/myturnatbat.html

Cummins, P. (2001). Fathers playing catch with daughters. *Santa Monica Mirror*. Retrieved July 26, 2003, from http://www.smmirror.com/volume3/issue12/fathers_playing_catch.asp

Daylight saving time. (n.d.). Retrieved July 18, 2004, from http://webexhibits.org/daylightsaving/e.html

Daly, K. (1996). *Families and time: Keeping pace in a hurried culture*. Thousand Oaks, CA: Sage.

Dubbert, J. (1979). *A man's place: Masculinity in transition*. Englewood Cliffs, NJ: Prentice-Hall.

Fine, G. A. (1987). *With the boys: Little League Baseball and preadolescent culture*. Chicago: University of Chicago Press.

Geertz, C. (1973). *The interpretation of cultures*. New York: Basic.

Goffman, E. (1959). *The presentation of self in everyday life*. Garden City, NY: Anchor/Doubleday.

Goodwin, D. K. (1997). *Wait till next year: A memoir*. New York: Touchstone.

Goodwin, M. (1984, October 7). On common ground. *New York Times Magazine,* 79.

Guest, E. A. (1922, August). My job as a father. *American Magazine, 94,* 13–15, 124.

Hall, D. (1985). *Fathers playing catch with sons*. New York: North Point.

Hart, A. (2002, December 24). The man who made it Christmas one day in May. *Times Union*. Retrieved October 31, 2002, from http://web.lexis-nexis.com

Hurley, R. J. (1935, August). A city builds teams from gangs. *Recreation, 29,* 256–57.

Kennedy, L. (2003, June 12). Having a ball with dad. *Rocky Mountain News,* p. 3D. Retrieved October 31, 2003, from http://web.lexis-nexis.com/universe/printdoc

Kimmel, M. S. (1990). Baseball and the reconstitution of American masculinity, 1880–1920. In M. A. Messner and D. F. Sabo (Eds.), *Sport, men, and the gender order: Critical feminist perspectives* (pp. 55–65). Champaign, IL: Human Kinetics Books.

Kimmel, M. S. (1996). *Manhood in America: A cultural history*. New York: Free Press.

Kinsella, W. P. (1982). *Shoeless Joe*. Boston: Houghton Mifflin.

LaRossa, R. (1988). Fatherhood and social change. *Family Relations, 37,* 451–57.

LaRossa, R. (1997). *The modernization of fatherhood: A social and political history.* Chicago: University of Chicago Press.

LaRossa, R. (2004). The culture of fatherhood in the fifties: A closer look. *Journal of Family History, 29,* 47–70.

Lichtenberg, G. (1993, November 7). About men: To catch a mother. *New York Times Magazine,* 28–29.

Litsky, F. (2004, May 12). Now Pittsfield stakes claim to baseball's origins. *New York Times.*

Little League Online. (n.d.). Little League Baseball historical timeline. Retrieved July 8, 2004, from http://www.littleleague.org/history

Littlefield, B. (2002). The game of catch. *Only a Game* (from NPR and 90.9 WBUR Boston). Retrieved October 23, 2003, from http://archives.onlyagame.org/archives/2001/06/0606comm.shtml

Mandelbaum, M. (2004). *The meaning of sports: Why Americans watch baseball, football, and basketball and what they see when they do.* New York: Public Affairs.

McCormack, D. (1999–2002). How to teach your child to play catch. *Long Island Parent Stuff.com.* Retrieved October 31, 2003, from http://www.libabystuff.com/inspire/kids.shtml

Mead, G. H. (1934). *Mind, self, and society.* Chicago: University of Chicago Press.

Merwin, S. (1923, July). A father's relation to his children. *Ladies Home Journal, 40,* 15, 28.

Messner, M. (1995). Ah, ya throw like a girl! In P. S. Rothenberg (Ed.), *Race, class, and gender in the United States: An integrated study* (pp. 46–48). New York: St. Martin's.

Morris, B. (n.d.). An enduring game of catch. Retrieved July 26, 2003, from http://www.legendsmagazine.net/37/endurcat.htm

Motherwell, H. (1932, November). For fathers only. *Parents Magazine, 7,* 4, 39.

My dad is way, way cool: Kids tell us why their fathers are best. *The Columbus Dispatch.* Retrieved October 20 2003, from http://web.lexis-nexis.com

Percoco, J. A. (1992, summer). Baseball and World War II: A study of the Landis-Roosevelt correspondence. *Organization of American History Magazine of History, 7.* Retrieved July 9, 2004, from http://www.oah.org/pubs/magazine/sport/percoco.html

Peterik, A. (1995). Women's baseball during World War II. *Illinois History.* Retrieved July 9, 2004, from http://www.lib.niu.edu/ipo/ihy950452.html

Pennington, B. (2004, September 12). Baseball's origins: They ain't found til they're found. *New York Times,* 1, 23.

Piszek, B. (2003). The Little League Baseball experience: Daddy's memories. *The World of English*. Retrieved October 31, 2003, from http://www.woe.edu.pl/2003/2_03/littleleague.html

Pyke, K. (2000). "The normal American family" as an interpretive structure of family life among grown children of Korean and Vietnamese immigrants. *Journal of Marriage and Family, 62,* 240–45.

Rademacher, E. S. (1933, August). For fathers only. *Parents Magazine, 8,* 6.

Rosenblatt, R. (1998, July 13). A game of catch. *Time*, 90.

Speaker, T. (1939, April). Diamonds in the rough. *Rotarian, 54,* 22–25.

Steele, J. L. (1904). How the national game developed: Some baseball reminiscences. *Outing, 44,* 333–36.

Today's father. (1952, August). *Woman's Home Companion,* 112–14.

Yankee Stadium History. (n.d.). Retrieved July 10, 2004, from http://newyork.yankees.mlb.com/NASApp/mlb/nyy/ballpark/stadium_history.jsp

Ward, L. (2003). Like father, like son. *Ahwatukee Foothill News*. Retrieved November 6, 2003, from http://www.ahwatukee.com/afn/sports/articles/010502c.html

Watzlawick, P., Beavin, J. H., Jackson, D. D. (1967). *Pragmatics of human communication: A study of interactional patterns, pathologies, and paradoxes*. New York: Norton.

Youth soccer. (n.d.). *SoccerNova*. Retrieved October 29, 2004, from http://www.soccernova.com/working/youth/youth.htm

Zerubavel, E. (1981). *Hidden rhythms: Schedules and calendars in social life*. Chicago: University of Chicago Press.

Zerubavel, E. (1997). *Social mindscapes: An invitation to cognitive sociology*. Cambridge, MA: Harvard University Press.

8

"Nobody Can Be a Father in Here": Identity Construction and Institutional Constraints on Incarcerated Fatherhood

Kevin Roy

I shouldn't have been smoking and partying and hanging with the wrong crowd. But being incarcerated is a little too much. They took a victimless offense and my boys are victims of it. Last time I talked to them, one was like, "Daddy, when do you get out of that work place, when's your boss gonna let you go?" I just want to be a father to my children. I want them to grow up right. Nobody can be a father in here.

                                                                                                Chad, 36

Most studies of fatherhood locate men in familiar physical and social spaces, where parenting is a visible and socially recognized activity. What about men who parent their children in nontraditional settings? Correctional facilities have become important locations for fathering of children in low-income and/or minority families (Nurse 2002). The evolving war on drugs and legacy of mandatory minimum sentencing laws dramatically increased the population in prisons throughout the 1980s and 1990s (Hairston 2001; Hallinan 2001). In 1999, 55 percent of state and 63 percent of federal prisoners reported having a child under eighteen, resulting in approximately 1.5 million minor children with incarcerated parents (U.S. Dept. of Justice 2000).

We know little about the parenting experiences of fathers and families who move through correctional facilities. Thus I examine how the unique physical and social contexts of correctional facilities—in this case, work release programs and their site-based policies—shape men's experiences and identities as incarcerated fathers.

LITERATURE REVIEW

Fathering Inside Correctional Facilities

Symbolic interactionist and related social constructivist approaches can inform the study of how physical and social spaces affect men's fathering when it is regulated and redefined by correctional powers (Daly 1995; Marsiglio 1995). Fathers' identity work inside correctional facilities and in isolation from children is unique and seldom discussed. Incarcerated fathers are assigned to a spatial context that guarantees a degree of liminality (defined as a suspension of commonplace rules), an intermingling with strangers in strange settings, a heightened sense of uncertainty, and a sense of mobile circumstances (Turner 1967, 1969). They move through a transitional program that isolates them in a state of rehabilitation prior to reintegration into their families and communities as ex-offenders. During this time, men are likely to encounter ambiguous social expectations as fathers from family members, correctional personnel, and representatives of the justice system.

When fathers are incarcerated, the fabric of interdependencies that keeps men embedded in family relationships is damaged (Currie 1985). Hairston (1995) found that almost none of 126 surveyed fathers were active with their children, and most nonresidential fathers were ill-served by existing fatherhood programs. Economic, psychological, and interpersonal problems for the entire family system result from sudden, involuntary separation of families (King 1993). For example, men's absence from their children's lives can have long-term and serious consequences (McDermott and King 1992). Many children experience feelings of rejection, abandonment, depression, and anger, as well as other emotional, somatic, and other externalizing problems (Fritsch and Burkhead 1981; King 1993). They are often not told the truth about their father's absence and experience anxiety and confusion over the situation (Hannon, Martin, and Martin 1984). Their school performance may be negatively affected as a result.

Many families are economically disadvantaged before incarceration, and afterwards these families often fall into poverty (Arditti, Lambert-Shute, and Joest 2003). As sole providers and decision makers for their families, wives experience depression, loneliness, demoralization, and frustration with their incarcerated spouse (King 1993; Hannon et al. 1984). Particularly over the first six months of confinement, marital relationships deteriorate (Brodsky 1975). Many men fear a "summer shake," in which girlfriends and wives seek alternative partners while men serve time in facilities (Nurse 2002). Hairston (1995) found that nearly 75 percent of inmates who were married at the time of arrest in her study were subsequently divorced while in prison.

As for men themselves, fatherhood becomes displaced and routinized, and men face a type of social and cultural limbo. Those with the poorest parent–child relationships appear to have the greatest potential to develop negative psychological consequences while incarcerated (Lanier 1993). Often the loss of family support results in feelings of guilt and shame (Toch 1975), demoralization, helplessness, and dependence on others in the outside world to do what they should be doing as fathers (Hairston 1995). Incarcerated fathers may retreat emotionally from their children as a means of dealing with the pain of separation (Palm 1996). Both "hard timing," cutting off social ties with the outside world, and sudden loss of temper, or "flashing," are common as fathers deal with separation from children (Nurse 2002).

However, for some men, "time to think" about reforming family relationships (as noted in Nurse 2002) may be the most positive aspect of fathering behavior in correctional facilities. Families can provide bridging networks (Ekland-Olson, Supancic, Campbell, and Lenihan 1983), as well as a supportive stability zone that "softens the psychological impact of confinement" (Toch 1975). In a rare qualitative study of low-income men of color, Hughes (1998) showed that respect and concern for their own children was related to lower rates of recidivism. Many fathers become increasingly aware of special responsibilities as parents, acting in a more prosocial manner both behind prison walls and in the free world (Lanier 2003).

Work Release as a Unique Sociospatial Context

A related ecological systems perspective locates relationships in larger arenas of interaction between families, communities, correctional systems, schools, workplaces, and social policies. Arditti (2002) argues that this perspective is vital to understanding the full effect of incarceration on families. To view the daily challenges incarcerated fathers and their families face, researchers are compelled to attend to the ways in which physical contexts craft social relations. The "situating" of values, customs, and daily routines of local moral worlds allows us to grasp how behavior unfolds in context (Hopper 2003). In particular, an ecological approach provides insight into systemic regulation of criminal behavior, as well as strategies that fathers employ to sustain involvement despite limits on physical mobility and social interaction (Roy 2004a).

In his consideration of historical social structures of abeyance, Mizruchi (1987) suggests that hybrid institutions, such as workhouses, almshouses, asylums, and police stations, absorb excess capacity from the labor market and serve as a warehouse for cheap labor and a monitoring system for otherwise unengaged working men. Similarly, work release programs promote the functional equivalent of work for people who might pose a threat to social order (Hopper 2003). Through the 1970s and 1980s, work release programs were first created as local hybrid abeyance institutions to serve as emergency population release valves for jail. Typically, these programs are segregated facilities for upwards of 100 men and fewer numbers of women. Programs house and monitor offenders of nonviolent crimes (inability to pay child support or alcohol and drug related violations, such as public intoxication, OWI, DWI, or DUI).

Work release programs require offenders to work in the community in order to pay rent and related expenses. Fathers are isolated from their families but are integrated into workplaces, giving them limited but defined presences in communities. For example, a program in Alabama encouraged, "Any business or individual looking for workers can go to the work release facility in the prison, or a bus from prison will deliver and pick up inmates to and from their work location" (Cox 1995, A8). Inmates were housed in trailers on state land, next to a poultry plant, where inmates worked because it allowed them the opportunity to earn money for their inmate account. Work release programs cost less per day than jail programs and offenders' work is used to offset correctional costs in maintenance of facilities themselves, making these programs a boon for local taxpayers and judicial systems.

They are also minimum-security sites, given that offenders must pass in and out of the facility on an hourly basis to go to work. The open physical design of a work release program allows for constant monitoring of offenders' activity. Work release programs also extend monitoring of inmates into local communities. Here, inmate-workers are aware of surveillance of their work activities, have limited social interaction, and must follow defined transit routes. Work release programs, in this regard, have evolved into full-service institutions, as disciplinary and monitoring units, employment enforcers and brokers, banking systems, and arbiters of family relationships. Although many work release programs focus exclusively on men's participation in work as a measure of rehabilitation, other programs have based program goals on reintegration, rehabilitation, and preparation for transition.

In summary, incarceration experiences intimately affect an entire range of family relationships, including father–child ties. However, it is difficult to generalize about typical ways incarceration affects fathering without reference to the nature of a facility, level of crime and length of sentence, program rules for contact with families, or a sense of men's isolation or integration with nonincarcerated populations.

METHODS

Qualitative approaches are particularly well suited for the study of incarcerated fatherhood. They are especially sensitive to issues of context, dynamic processes, and subjective perspectives (Burgess 1982; Denzin and Lincoln 1994). Qualitative approaches can frame involvement in context by revealing individual, group, and neighborhood processes and patterns that are missed or obscured by less intensive methods (Jarrett and Burton 1999). Qualitative researchers can learn the meaning systems that undergird paternal roles, how meaning systems are socially constructed, and how deeply held beliefs and values are influenced by opportunities and constraints (Jarrett, Roy, and Burton 2002). Qualitative methods "may play a crucial role in developing a rich understanding of cultural context and interpersonal processes associated with . . . how fathers are directly or indirectly involved in their children's lives" (Marsiglio, Amato, Day, and Lamb 2000, 1179). These methods offer "an ethnographic corrective" to acontextual analyses of fatherhood by "keeping things complicated" (Hopper 2003).

Samples and Research Context

As a facilitator of "life after incarceration" curriculum, I spent eighteen months directing weekly workshop sessions with men involved in a work release program in a small metropolitan county in Indiana. These men were serving sentences of up to two years for charges of driving while intoxicated, possession of illegal substances, nonpayment of child support, and fighting or domestic violence. Men in this facility were mandated to pay for their boarding so they worked at one or more jobs each day in the local community, but were formally restricted to the facility during nonwork hours. Fathers in the Indiana program encountered relatively consistent opportunities for employment in factories, construction teams, and the service sector. Despite the loss of jobs and decreasing real wages in recent decades in Indiana (Perrucci, Perrucci, Targ, and Targ 1988), the area still boasted a base for manufacturing jobs.

Our team of three male facilitators/researchers (two European Americans and one African American) identified forty men with children from our weekly sessions and asked if they would volunteer for an interview about father involvement. The sample of men included twenty-eight European American fathers, ten African American fathers, as well as one Asian American and one Native American father. The sample was diverse in terms of age, with seventeen of the men age 23–28; fourteen men 29–40, and nine men over 40. The average father had 2.18 children, with eight men with only one child, twenty-two men with two or three children, and six men with four or more children. Four of the fathers were expecting a child or were social fathers of their partner's biological children.

Data Collection

Multiple methods of data collection were utilized for this study. Participant observation allowed firsthand accounts of specific ecological conditions affecting fathers and families. By spending multiple hours each week at the fatherhood program or the correctional center, the research team developed field notes detailing men's accounts of how work and family roles changed over time. We also reviewed information on multiple Web sites to establish how the local work release program related to similar programs around the United States.

We drew on both structural and phenomenological approaches to the social construction of fatherhood (Lupton and Barclay 1997). Interviews were conducted and recorded during two-hour sessions in small classrooms in the correctional facility. Using a life history protocol, we asked men to discuss various turning points in their lives, including relationships in family of origin and procreation; employment and education; residence; and periods of incarceration. During the interviews, we plotted timing and sequencing of these turning points onto life history calendar grids, a methodological technique that enhances the validity of longitudinal data (Freedman, Thorton, Camburn, Alwin, and Young-Demarco 1988; Scott and Alwin 1998). We asked fathers to consider how their turning point experiences related to their understanding of their own fatherhood. Our interviews also focused on how the men's fathering was shaped by contextual opportunities and constraints.

We established trustworthiness in data collection through reliance on a range of established criteria (Lincoln and Guba 1985). Data credibility was enhanced through prolonged engagement and persistent observation in the field. Triangulation of multiple sources of data (including myself, program staff, and fathers themselves), along with multiple methods of data collection, helped to meet criteria for both credibility and dependability of data. We also used member checks (in-person discussions with fathers some weeks after their interviews) to validate preliminary notions of how neighborhood conditions affected social interaction.

Data Analyses

Interviews were tape-recorded, transcribed, and both interviews and field notes were coded for fatherhood themes with the QSR NUDIST qualitative data analysis program. Using the basic elements of grounded theory approach (Strauss and Corbin 1998), we reread interview texts and developed a simple coding scheme using sensitizing concepts (Patton 2002), which included fathering shaped by site-specific family policies (blue pass, phone calls, etc.), shifting role expectations, and generativity scripts. During a wave of axial coding, we developed profiles for each father that allowed us to consider differences and commonalities among the fathers. We focused on their experiences and narratives concerning site policies and physical constraints, as well as their opportunities for fathering. Finally, a conceptual framework for selective coding was developed that linked patterns between and within cases to core categories (as defined by Strauss 1987). These core categories, *liminal identities* and *physical space*, are considered to be the main themes of the analyses. They integrate case patterns and reflect the "dense and saturated" relationship between physical space and social meaning.

From the first days of participation in interviews and program activities, the research team recognized that the institutional environment and policies affected men's behavior and activities as parents. We noted that men were not permitted to see their children while on their jobs, and that on-site visitation facilities were minimal, leaving short "blue pass" releases as the only time in which inmates could interact with their children. Staff monitored men during their lunch hours and during evening activities for which they received release, such as AA meetings or counseling. Men did not receive meals except through their own purchase of vending machine food in the day room, which was typically expensive fast food. Finally, we observed the stressful interactions and limited family discourse in the day room and the nightly calls on pay phones men placed to their partners and children. These observations, and related interviews, led us to develop the notion of liminal fathering, in which men sought to create identities and either maintain or establish family relationships in interstitial spaces during transitions between work hours and evening confinement.

FINDINGS

Fathers' interaction with their families was a contested negotiation between work release programs and men themselves. Although physical contexts and site-specific policies shaped that interaction, fathers resisted constraints and worked to create new opportunities to express their fatherhood. I focus on three dimensions to examine more closely this process of negotiation in a work release context. First, I describe and discuss institutional policies regarding family interaction, and how these policies affected men's experiences. Second, I show how policies affected the physical context of the work release site. In this section, I note men's varied contact with their families, resistance to policies, and efforts to turn constraints into positive inducement to change. Finally, I explore notions of fathers' liminality, as expressed by courts, children, and men themselves.

Policies toward Family Interaction

The Indiana work release program explicitly focused on men's participation as workers in local communities as the priority for reintegration. The facility itself was not equipped for extensive visitation by children and families (see figure 8.1). Inmates were granted the opportunity to have one visitation session per week on Sundays. Visitation period began at 1:00 P.M. and ended at 4:00 P.M., lasted fifteen minutes per session, and included a maximum of three visitors. The visitation room was small and very seldom used by program participants. Children and family members were not permitted to visit men at the work site, during time off, during the lunch hour, or in the transition process from the facility to work or work back to the facility. Each family member

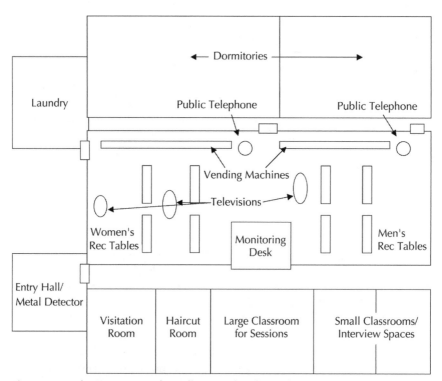

Figure 8.1.   The Dayroom at the Indiana Work Release Site

noted the program's monitoring and regulatory dimensions. For example, Rock, a fifty-four-year-old ex-accountant and submarine commander with a history of alcohol abuse, was dropped back off at the facility after a short visit with his daughter and grandchildren. His three-year-old granddaughter commented to Rock that "here we are, Grandpa—back to your day care place. Except that it's night time."

Some men wrote letters to their children, but this type of communication was underutilized. The only other physical sites for interaction with families were two public pay phones, located in the day room immediately outside the doors of two large shared dormitories. After men returned from work at 6:00 P.M. each night, long lines for phone calls were commonplace and overheard conversations could be a source of frustration and stress. Andy, a soft-spoken thirty-two-year-old father of three preschool age children, had worked as a manager at a shipping company and had struggled with a drinking problem and a pending divorce. He was frustrated by dependence on the telephone as the basis of his relationship with his children.

> I've been wanting to draw closer to them, but I've never been one of those guys that can really talk through a phone. I have a hard enough time face-to-face anyways, 'cause sometimes I have something to say and, I just, don't know, I'm too scared to say it or something. And being on the phone in front of everyone, in the day room and everybody running around, the TV blaring in your ear.

Other fathers encountered difficulty contacting their children by phone if families deterred calls at home. Charles, a forty-three-year-old father of two young adult sons, was transferred from prison and had not spoken to his children or partner in almost one year. He found that his sons' phones had blocks placed on them and he did not have their addresses. The two school-age sons of Chad, a divorced thirty-six-year-old father, lived with their mother and her boyfriend, who had shut the phone off because Chad called too often to speak with his children. He had few options, declaring, "What the hell else am I . . . I want to talk to my kids." Although telephones did not guarantee substantial communication, most fathers were content with speaking to their children on a frequent basis. For example, Devon, a twenty-six-year-old father of two young children, relied on the phone to develop his relationship with his three-year-old son.

> He knows my voice, and he's been a real problem for my mom when I called down there a few days ago. He'd been sick and what he wanted was just to hear Dad's voice. He laid down on the floor and laid his head on the phone and went right to sleep. My mom said she'd been trying to get him to go to sleep for the last twelve or thirteen hours, and he wouldn't do it. She just had to slide a pillow in where the phone was.

When men had served a month without violating work release policies, they were permitted to apply for a blue pass, which allowed them a furlough to visit their families inside the county. They could receive up to two blue passes per month that varied in duration (two hours, four hours, and eight hours) contingent on the amount of time served in the facility (ninety days, six months, and one year, respectively). Fathers used passes to throw themselves—willingly—into the rhythms of children's days. With younger children, blue pass visits usually entailed a few hours of playtime. Pat was an auto mechanic and the father of a three-year-old girl placed in foster care with her grandmother. He had not been able to establish a relationship with her prior to incarceration due to his drinking problem and conflict with his ex-partner, who was serving time in prison. Pat used the pass visit to introduce himself to his daughter.

> She knows who I am. I took her up and got her ice cream and pizza. We went back to the house and she wants to show me all her tapes, she wants me to keep picking her up so she can put in the Barney tapes. Then she says, "Lay down with me," she says, "Well, cover up," 'cause she doesn't want me to leave. That's kind of hard. I have to go back and I don't really want to leave, but I got to leave anyway.

Visits with older children were usually more fast-paced and at the mercy of children's high expectations "to do everything at once." After more than nine months at the work release program, Lionel, a forty-two-year-old father, had established a blue pass ritual with his two school-age children and his wife. With two four-hour passes each month, he insisted that

> I do whatever they want during those four hours. They always have a movie, popcorn, fix something for dinner and this and that. I can't go out, be walking around and stuff like that; they know that. They understand the rules that I have to go by as far as me having passes to go home.

Transit time was a contested aspect of blue pass policies. In general, work release participants were allowed up to half an hour of transit time to work and half an hour from work each day. They were not permitted to stop and leave their vehicles to enter a building to buy cigarettes or food. Some managed to push the limits of the policy and stop by fast food drive-up windows to purchase food as an alternative to vending machine fare. To maximize their blue pass visit, men struggled to secure quick transportation to traverse extensive distances. Marley, a thirty-two-year-old father of two children who lived with his ex-girlfriend and her husband, "couldn't help himself" from seeing his children.

> I have two hours on my first blue pass next week. They have this stupid rule: if somebody picks you up then you get extra travel time, but if you're on your own you get half hour travel time to and from. I'm running around with my head cut

off looking for somebody to borrow me a moped next week, just to have an extra forty-five minutes to spend with my children.

Lombardo, a thirty-year-old tree cutter and roofer who was serving in work release for domestic battery, faced even greater time constraints. He devised a mad dash around town to collect three children from various households and to rendezvous at his parent's house, which sat on the outskirts of the county. He admitted that "it's hard to do anything really significant in the two hours that I end up having by the time everything gets together."

The limited set of policies designed to regulate men's interactions with their children and families served only as a starting point for the negotiation of incarcerated fatherhood. With an open-door policy in work release facilities, efforts to interact with family members inevitably went beyond on-site visitation or phone calls, which are typically the limits of family policies in prison and jail settings. The dispersed spatial context of work release allowed men room for creative strategies to act fatherly—but it also sent mixed messages to families and fathers themselves about what is permitted and what the costs of some types of interaction could be.

Fathering in Constrained Physical Space

The work release facility in Indiana housed over one hundred male inmates and multiple female inmates. Given most inmates' struggles to find and maintain low-wage, short-term jobs (Roy 2004b), as well as overcome addictions to drugs and alcohol, public spaces in the facility were scenes of great stress and occasional outbursts. Although often unspoken, a contributor to these stressful interactions was separation from familiar and trusted family members. Trent, a young father of four preschool children, expressed his stress by shedding forty pounds and becoming "sick, really sick, since I've been away from my family." Marley, admitted into work release for drug possession, acknowledged the stress of prison-like rules and separation from his children, which manifested itself with every gesture and movement between inmates.

> Sometimes I feel like a walking time bomb. I don't like this place, man. I'm sick of being judged every day, for who I'm not. I'm frustrated and I cannot vent. I have to come in here and deal with this, and I have to deal with my kids, the everyday things and I miss them, and I can't see them.

Contact with Children

Under limited family policies, a regime of intensive work participation, and even a minimum-security monitoring system, the quantity and quality of

fathers' contact with children inevitably deteriorated. Keith was released during the course of the study, and his contact with his two toddlers increased to
a common amount among nonresidential fathers: fifty-two hours each month
during weekend and weekday visits. Newly committed fathers could spend
only four hours per month, and even after a year in the facility, fathers could
only manage sixteen hours per month of contact time. Keith also received
calls at two or three in the morning from the mother of his children, asking
him to help his son go to bed "because he has school tomorrow." Keith felt
that he was able to act like a responsible father and support his children in
those early morning phone calls, but fathers in the work release facility did
not have access to the public phone at these hours. As other examples illustrate, in reaction to limited contact, fathers salvaged and savored every count-
able hour with their children. Pat even worried that the timing and sequencing of his visits would give his young daughter the impression that he could
visit frequently. "I had a blue pass last Thursday, and I'm getting another one
this Thursday," he said. "I don't really want them spaced that close together,
because I don't want her to think, you know, she's starting to recognize times
and stuff like that."

Serving in work release programs translated into missed opportunities to
witness important events in children's lives. Jimmy could only console his son
after his loss in the state wrestling championship; as a proud father, he had
only a videotape to watch, and he had to cope with the knowledge that he
could not be there to support his son. Rusty, a thirty-year-old father of six children, also missed a sporting event, in which his daughter's team won second
place in a softball tournament. "It was hard, I cried, I was real upset," he admitted. "It's my own fault I'm in here, but I wanted to be there, I wanted to see
her. She even hit a home run in this one, five years old and already hitting
home runs." Other fathers faced greater challenges in their absence. Fathers
envisioned themselves as protectors of their children, which were roles they
could not fulfill while serving in work release. One father worried about being
unable to protect his children from racism. Another father was fearful of the
physical abuse that his sons faced living with their mother and her boyfriend,
both of whom used drugs.

> I'm really scared for my boys, especially since I'm in here and can't really do
> anything about it. Derek told me the guy hits him. And Donny has bruises on his
> butt. They tell the boys to leave the house when they do cocaine. When I get out
> of here, things are going to change.

Limited contact with fathers provoked different responses from children,
often according to their ages. Younger children could react with anger at their
fathers' absence. Ronald's fourteen-month-old daughter was unaccustomed to

the ups and downs of sporadic contact with her father. After daily play and care giving activities with her as an infant, he did not see her at all for four months. "Now she just acts scared around me. I call and try to talk with her, but she can only say a few things. I've been out of her life the whole time, and last weekend she wouldn't go with me, threw a fit." Lombardo acknowledged that the absence "hasn't made much difference" for his daughters, but his renewed efforts to use blue passes has made an impression on his son. "To Jack, it means a lot. He used to be quiet because he didn't know how to act around me, but now that I'm coming around more regularly, he's starting to understand that I want to see him."

Finally, it is important to note that fathers had to rely on other family members to ensure contact with their children. Family members, particularly men's mothers, sometimes purposively brought children to see their fathers or arranged for fathers to visit at their homes. Devon noted that "every time my mom picked me up for work, she had [my boy] with her—so I got to see him a few times [when I was first incarcerated] in work release." Family connections were fragile as well, however, and many fathers simply lost contact because they had no one who would facilitate their relationships with their children.

Distance and Being Out Of Reach

Under work release program policies, the range of men's activities could only extend so far outside of the physical facility without jeopardizing monitoring. For example, with only a two-hour release, men could travel up to thirty miles before they used up most of their visit time in transit. Roland, a forty-year-old father of four teenagers and former steel worker, had no use for a blue pass, as his children lived over an hour away.

> They're too far away, they're too young to come up here on their own. I was just starting to catch up with them, and they're like, "Oh, Daddy's doing good, Daddy got a car and he's living out of town, he got a house, he's coming to see us get us, take us shopping," and they're telling their little friends. Then I called them and told them I was in work release, and they said, "Daddy, damn."

Public pay phone calls to households outside of the county were expensive propositions, which curtailed many fathers' motivation to contact their children. Ironically, in a world of cyberspace technology, men were not permitted to use e-mail in the facility. This could be particularly difficult for men confronted with urgent family matters, such as immediate health concerns, or those who struggled to maintain contact with family members residing beyond permitted boundaries of travel.

Resistance to Separation from Children

Although fathers adhered to work release policies that regulated family interaction, they also crafted creative strategies to bend these rules in order to spend more time with children. Their resistance to enforced separation from their children usually unfolded in transition or during open and unmonitored spaces outside of the work release facility. Fathers depended on family members for transport to work, and the work release facility could not regulate who was in the car when fathers caught rides to and from work. For example, Alcoholics Anonymous meetings were suitable public space to spend time with children. Jimmy's daughter would travel with his wife to attend Thursday night AA meetings with him, and "it's an open meeting, so we'll spend a little time before and after it."

Fathers had the most chances for interaction with their children during breaks and lunchtime at their worksites. Coworkers and managers often turned their heads when men's children came to visit, as long as it did not interfere with work duties. Pat noted that "I can't stop my sister from bringing her car to be looked at, at my shop, and if she's watching my daughter that day, well . . ." Marley was so desperate at times to see his two children that he called up his ex-girlfriend and told her, "Bring them over, sit down and eat. I'll pay for it. Let me just see my kids. If I get caught, I get caught. It's worth it for me. And she's pretty cool about that." But this interaction could also be a risk, as it was prohibited by work release. Jake, a thirty-two-year-old father with seven- and nine-year-old sons, could not convince his ex-girlfriend to pick him up for work, but seeing his kids might offer his ex-girlfriend the chance to report him.

> I wouldn't be in violation if she came and picked me up and took me to work, and the kids were in the car, but she won't do that. I'm afraid that she's going to tell on me because I'm not to have any visitors or visit people while I'm in the program.

As participant-observers at the work release facility, the research team found that staff most likely knew about fathers' extra yet limited interactions with their children at the workplace, yet they tolerated them. However, fathers could push the restriction rules too far. During the first warm weeks of spring, one father arranged with his children's mother to meet him in a park after work, to play catch for a few minutes while in transit back to the facility. A work release staff member was also at the park and reported the father to the facility. As a result this inmate was "violated," moved from work release to the prison structure up the street, and became subject to an extended sentence, enhanced security, and more severe limits on family interactions.

Desistance from Drugs and Improved Family Relationships

In comparison to incarcerated men in prisons, who have large amounts of unstructured time on their hands, fathers in work release had a fluid daily schedule. They lived in dormitories that segregated men far from the edge of town, with a rare chance for permitted "practice" reintegration with children in their own homes. In this way, work release participants could be physically and temporally ensured of an opportunity for positive turning points in their lives. Most inmates were incarcerated on a drug- or alcohol-related offense, and time and space apart from the stress of everyday family life and friends who used substances, offered men the chance to desist.

Fathers found time and space for reflection that was qualitatively different than the unrealistic expectations or fantasies about return to children and families of men in prison (Nurse 2002). They took small but real steps to improve family relationships through regular communication. Jimmy noticed that his children were forced to become more independent without him.

> As a result of being here, we'll discuss a problem, and before they'd use their mom, she'd tell me, and I'd tell them the result, period. It wasn't no communicating there. Now, since I've been gone away from them, they're a little bit older, more mature. They take responsibility for themselves.

Under the difficult conditions of incarceration, children and extended families pulled together to support men in work release. Remy, a twenty-seven-year-old father, had not secured a consistent job and struggled to remain involved in the lives of his three school-age children. He was surprised to find his family unified in support of his time in work release.

> The family has been very supportive, and that's what's been getting me through. There's been no unaccepted calls, no unaccepted letters, or returned letters. They help me out as much as they can. It's just grown more since I've been locked up because it just took me to realize that [the family] was really there.

In summary, physical contexts of the work release program provided both institutional constraints and opportunities for negotiation of incarcerated fatherhood. In the midst of heightened stress in the facility itself, fathers coped with limited contact and missed opportunities to witness their children's growth or to protect their children and family's health and safety. Physical separation provoked a range of responses from children, some complicated relationships, others strengthened precarious ties. Men's reliance on other family members to act as catalysts for father/child relationships could place fathers at risk. Finally, fathers resisted restrictions on interaction by strategizing to see their children in the interstices between worksites and work release facilities. Some also crafted preliminary scripts for new fatherhood roles, through enhanced communication, desistance from substance use, and commitment to future interaction—not withdrawal—from children.

Liminal Status, Liminal Space

In spite of the range of negotiations over interaction and role expectations that fathers faced each day in the work release program, transitions were so prevalent that men's identities as fathers were placed in "holding patterns." Work release programs can be considered interstitial sites because they transport offenders out of their everyday worlds and into a facility in which some normative interactions hold, and others do not. By definition the work release program was neither prison nor probation, and its relatively short term (two weeks to eighteen months) discouraged men from adapting too completely to the facility's norms. As a result, fathers struggled with ambiguous expectations and constantly shifting paternal identities. Multiple transitions in place and time were marked by daily movements between community (for work) and facilities (for surveillance), punctuated by occasional visits to familiar home settings. In effect, men's work trajectories often continued unabated, whereas men's family life was disrupted. Ultimately the work release program placed fathers in a social limbo in which some of their routine activities were supported and others were grounds for violation.

The challenges of men's liminal status as parents in work release were echoed in many aspects of men's experiences. Judges and court personnel were often confused as to the status of men's sentences, given their short term and the courts' focus on efficiency. Children were frequently confused about their father's status as well. This led many of them to suspect the worst for their fathers, as Chad's four-year-old son did.

> The first time I was out of jail, I went to Wal-mart to see my children and go shopping. My little boy comes running, screaming, "Mommy, Mommy! My Daddy's alive, he's alive!" He thought I was dead. I don't want them to ever go through that again.

Ronald's son, at five years old, understood where his father lived, and how his participation in work release involved some degree of negotiation with legal authorities. He was intent on his father's attendance at normal family holiday rituals.

> Every time my son brings me back he wants to come in, or Thanksgiving or Christmas, "Daddy, why can't you ask the police if you can come over here for a little bit?" What the hell kind of answer do you say to that? "Why can't you

come over here and watch me open my presents? Ask the police if you can come over here for a little bit." That's just hard when a five-year-old asks you that.

What remained for many fathers, after a short but disruptive stay in work release, was a lack of recognition from children. As Roland stated, when he returned to see his children after his release, he expected them "probably to look at me kinda strange, like 'who is you, man?'"

Living with ambiguity for many months left fathers themselves grasping for an explanation for who they were and what they had done to land themselves in work release. Chad (quoted above) felt strongly that incarceration was an extreme consequence for a "victimless offense" that ultimately punished his children more than anyone. Lionel stressed honesty with his children but could not make sense out of his sentence in a prison-like environment for noncriminal activity. He and his children developed an unspoken code about the work release system and how it took him away from his family.

> I don't keep nothing from them about my troubles. It was alcohol related, not like I was out robbing and shooting people and fighting and stealing and all that shit. I might not know how to explain it to them, but we have an understanding as far as me being in here and needing to be here.

Unable to make sense of the advanced monitoring and discipline structure in which they landed due to noncriminal activity, some fathers incorporated a notion of precarious balance into their timeworn identities as fathers. While promoting better communication and closer relations with his children, Jimmy cautioned himself and his children that their family life was fragile at best. Although he realized the need for his stay in work release to deal with his substance abuse, he recognized a new level of vulnerability that he lived with as a father.

> All in all, I think it's to the best. Not my time away from them, not knowing when I'm gonna be able to see them. But I told them, you can't blame anyone but me. I was locked up in DOC for driving drunk. I'm your daddy and I'm the one that booked on you. They may violate me tonight, it could ruin everything, or I can lose everything because I can't catch up on my bills, you know. Either way I stand a chance of losing.

With short sentences in work release, most men settled for living with liminal statuses and constantly shifting fathering roles. For other fathers, liminality was threatening, and their choice became whether to "knife off" past failures (Laub and Sampson 2003) and make a change in their lives by leaving children and partners. Ben was a successful contractor who had abused drugs and, as a result, served time both in prison and the work release program. His one desire was to move on from his mistakes and inability to resolve contradictions about who he once was—and who he had become—as a father.

> There are just places that I don't really wanna go. I'm not trying to go backwards here. About my kids coming to visit me in prison, that's all in the past, and I don't want to live in the past. I don't want to bring it up because it upsets me. If you weren't around your kids for two years, wouldn't it be a sensitive question to you?

DISCUSSION

Work release programs offer unique contexts to theorize about the overlap of physical and social space of men's parenting. First, physical space constrained the parenting activities of these forty fathers. They were housed in a correctional dormitory and were restricted to specific daily routes between this facility and their workplaces. Contact with children and family members was regulated, both in terms of amount of contact time and form of communication. A monitoring system secured the spatial boundaries of these routes, both through surveillance of men's employment activities and of their relationships with their families. Apart from homeless shelters and related institutions, few fathers encounter this degree of physical restriction on their parenting. Many fathers are physically distant from their children due to the demands of their jobs (such as military personnel, truckers, and traveling business people). Few fathers encounter higher levels of parental monitoring, except for the possible exception of parents who have lost their children to foster care systems or who are under observation by courts for unfit parenting practices.

Specifically, the constraints of physical space crafted men's social relationships. Most men "never missed a beat" in familiar and expectable daily interactions with coworkers and employers who were required in the work release program. However, they lived in a physical setting that called their status as fathers into question on a regular basis. Fathers were forced to justify their motivation as incarcerated parents in applications for blue passes and in long waits for phone calls. Fathers and children both desired regular rhythms of family life and the physical aspects of interaction (such as playing with toys or kisses and hugs). Without mundane knowledge of each other's daily lives, men appeared to be "lost" or "dead" to their children (see Boss 2000 on ambiguous loss).

Incarcerated men tried to navigate these ambiguous relationships and manage liminal father identities. In historical periods of transition, father roles for all men are ambiguous and shifting (Griswold 1993). For men who remained workers but lost their roles as fathers, the sense of liminality was exacerbated. They did "what they can when they don't know what to do" in order to cope with undefined, or redefined, parental roles. They bridged spatial boundaries and made phone calls in order to maintain contact with their children.

In turn, many fathers developed strategies of resistance to manipulate physical space and to restore their social relationships. They increased contact with family members in interstitial spaces between work and the facility, outside of institutionalized monitoring. In car rides back and forth to work, they orchestrated brief moments and spaces in which they did not need to justify their fatherhood. On blue passes or on lunch breaks, "fathers could be fathers" based on preexisting normative expectations of their behavior as parents. Many fathers in the Indiana work release program relied on their own mothers and children's mothers to provide spaces and social support for their continued father involvement (see Dyson 2003; Morgan 2003). Similar findings are reflected in related studies with paternal kin, who can secure safe spaces for men's interactions with their children in risky urban neighborhoods (Roy 2004a).

Fathers also used regulated spatial contexts to promote positive changes in their lives, such as desistance from use of drugs and alcohol and commitment to quality relationships with family members. Identity work (Gubrium, Holstein, and Buckholdt 1994) can be a relentless, daily task of construction and reconstruction of identity for individuals in liminal settings and institutions of abeyance, such as homeless shelters, unemployment lines, supportive housing, or correctional facilities (Roy, in press; Snow and Anderson 1987). Marginalized individuals employ makeshift strategies to locate material for both physical survival and identity construction (Hopper, Susser, and Conover 1985). Arditti (2002) notes that coping with layers of stigma, due to racial discrimination, poverty, substance abuse, mental illness, or lack of education, makes identity construction a complex task. In effect, an identity as a father may "fit" one day, yet may need to be abandoned on another day as shifting expectations and institutional constraints require a different understanding of one's role with others.

FUTURE RESEARCH

Researchers increasingly promote more intensive study of the contours and constraints of men's parenting in prison (Day 2003; Lanier 1995; Palm 2001). As an exploratory case study, this analysis details an understudied intermediate correctional program, sitting between the extremes of prison and house arrest. Limitations of this study may help to identify future directions for research. Although I noted different experiences among the variety of men in the program, comparison of men's experiences in different work release programs could illustrate the advantages and disadvantages of focuses on reintegration, rehabilitation, preparation for transition, and socialization to work. An examination of a range of correctional settings (including work release, house arrest, and maximum security jail/prison facilities) would offer insight into how different physical spaces shape different social contexts for parenting.

I chose to limit my research to reports and experiences of incarcerated men. Researchers may continue to develop more expansive study designs that include reports from multiple members, such as partners, children, and extended family members (see Arditti et al. 2003). Research should explore how incarcerated men's social relationships with their children change—or remain unchanged—due to men's marital/relationship status, as well as their varied experiences of residence with their children prior to incarceration. As demonstrated in this study as well as others in this volume, men's ability to bridge physical distance often depends on effective communication patterns and technological access. Although I noted a range of communication processes between fathers and children, access to technology for this group was relatively limited. Future studies of incarcerated fathers, as an alternative, may compare and contrast how e-mail access, phone access, and visitation conditions, such as availability of family playground facilities, influences men's roles as fathers. Experimental designs may help us understand which technological or social "bridges" are effective at promoting more integration and closer relationships between fathers and children, even when men are incarcerated.

This study hints at some potential outcome measures for father–child relationships. Systematic collection and coding of men's compliance with conduct codes, instances of violation, court experiences, and criminal records would offer in-depth understanding of reasons for and experiences during incarceration. Reported changes in closeness between fathers and children during and after incarceration would indicate some of the consequences of correctional policies around parenting. Ultimately, researchers could work closely with correctional programs to utilize follow-up services and measure recidivism rates in relation to measures of men's incarceration experiences and changing family relationships.

The lack of policies to support incarcerated fathers' generative behavior could prove problematic in the long run for correctional systems (Maruna, LeBel, and Lanier 2003; Palm 2001). Advocating generative parenting requires shifting from a deficit paradigm to recognizing that individuals play crucial roles in the lives of others (Lanier 2003). Programs that focus less on work requirements and more on parenting classes, support meetings, resources for fathering, volunteering, and more quality contact with children (Lanier and Fisher 1990) may reduce recidivism and promote reintegration and family preservation (Arditti et al. 2003). They would also offer incarcerated fathers opportunities to contribute to prosocial attitudes of future generations (Toch 2000).

REFERENCES

This study was conducted with support from the National Institute for Child Health and Human Development under Project no. 5 R03 HD 42074-2 and the Purdue Research Foundation at Purdue University in West Lafayette, Indiana. I would like to thank Keith Cross, Omari Dyson, Melissa Morgan, and Miki Cochran for assistance in data analyses.

Arditti, J. (2002). *Ecological nightmares of the worst kind: The effects of incarceration on families*. Paper presentation at the Theory Construction and Research Methodology Workshop, National Council on Family Relations annual conference, Houston, TX.

Arditti, J., Lambert-Shute, K., and Joest, K. (2003). Saturday morning at the jail: Implications of incarceration for families and children. *Family Relations, 52,* 195–204.

Boss, P. (2000). *Ambiguous loss: Learning to live with unresolved grief*. Cambridge, MA: Harvard University Press.

Brodsky, S. (1975). *Families and friends of men in prison: The uncertain relationship*. Lexington, MA: Lexington Books.

Burgess, R. (1982). *Field research: A sourcebook and field manual*. London: Allen & Unwin.

Cox, M. (1995, June 6). Can work release really benefit all? *Montgomery Advertiser,* A8.

Currie, E. (1985). *Confronting crime: An American challenge*. New York: Pantheon.

Daly, K. (1995). Reshaping fatherhood: Finding the models. In W. Marsiglio (Ed.), *Fatherhood: Contemporary theory, research, and social policy* (pp. 21–40). Thousand Oaks, CA: Sage.

Day, R. (2003). Book review of *Handbook of Father Involvement,* C. Tamis-LeMonda and N. Cabrera (Eds.), *Fathering, 1,* 182–84.

Denzin, N., and Lincoln, Y. (1994). *Handbook of qualitative research*. Thousand Oaks, CA: Sage.

Dyson, O. (2003). *Low income men of color's changing relationships with their families during incarceration.* Master's thesis. Purdue University, West Lafayette, Indiana.

Ekland-Olson, S., Supancic, M., Campbell, J., and Lenihan, K. (1983). Postrelease depression and the importance of familial support. *Criminology, 21,* 253–75.

Freedman, D., Thorton, A., Camburn, D., Alwin, D., and Young-Demarco, L. (1988). The life history calendar: A technique for collecting retrospective data. *Sociological Methodology, 18,* 37–68.

Fritsch, T., and Burkhead, J. (1981). Behavioral reactions of children to paternal absence due to imprisonment. *Family Relations, 30,* 83–88.

Griswold, R. (1993). *Fatherhood in America: A history.* New York: Basic.

Gubrium, J., Holstein, J., and Buckholdt, D. (1994). *Constructing the life course.* Dix Hills, NY: General Hall.

Hairston, C. (1995). Fathers in prison. In K. Gabel and D. Johnston (Eds.), *Children of incarcerated parents* (pp. 31–40). San Francisco, CA: Lexington.

Hairston, C. (2001). Fathers in prison: Responsible fatherhood and responsive public policies. *Marriage and Family Review, 32,* 111–35.

Hallinan, J. (2001). *Going up the river: Travels in a prison nation.* New York: Random House.

Hannon, G., Martin, D., and Martin, M. (1984). Incarceration in the family: Adjustment to change. *Family Therapy, 11,* 253–60.

Hopper, K. (2003). *Reckoning with homelessness.* Ithaca, NY: Cornell University Press.

Hopper, K., Susser, E., and Conover, S. (1985). Economies of makeshift: Homelessness and deindustrialization in New York City. *Urban Anthropology, 14,* 183–236.

Hughes, M. (1998). Turning points in the lives of young inner-city men forgoing destructive criminal behaviors: A qualitative study. *Social Work Research, 22,* 143–51.

Jarrett, R. and Burton, L. (1999). Dynamic dimensions of family structure in low-income African-American families: Emergent themes in qualitative research. *Journal of Comparative Family Studies, 30,* 177–88.

Jarrett, R., Roy, K., and Burton, L. (2002). Fathers in the 'hood: Qualitative research on low-income African-American men. In C. Tamis-LeMonda and N. Cabrera (Eds.), *Handbook of father involvement: Multidisciplinary perspectives* (pp. 211–48). New York: Erlbaum.

King, A. (1993). The impact of incarceration on African American families: Implications for practice. *Families in Society: The Journal of Contemporary Human Services*: 143–51.

Lanier, C. (1993). Affective states of fathers in prison. *Justice Quarterly, 10,* 49–66.

Lanier, C. (1995). Incarcerated fathers: A research agenda. *Forum on Correction Research, 7,* 34–36.

Lanier, C. (2003). Who's doing the time here, me or my children? Addressing the issues implicated by mounting numbers of fathers in prison. In J. Ross and S. Richards (Eds.), *Convict criminology.* Belmont, CA: Wadsworth.

Lanier, C., and Fisher, G. (1990). A Prisoners' Parenting Center (PPC): A promising resource strategy for incarcerated fathers. *Journal of Correctional Education, 41,* 158–65.

Laub, J., and Sampson, R. (2003). *Shared beginnings, divergent lives: Delinquent boys to age 70.* Cambridge, MA: Harvard University Press.

Lincoln, Y., and Guba, E. (1985). *Naturalistic inquiry.* Beverly Hills, CA: Sage.

Lupton, D., and Barclay, L. (1997). *Constructing fatherhood: Discourses and experiences*. Thousand Oaks, CA: Sage.

Marsiglio, W. (1995). Fathers' diverse life course patterns and roles: Theory and social interventions. In W. Marsiglio (Ed.), *Fatherhood: Contemporary theory, research and social policy* (pp. 78–101). Thousand Oaks, CA: Sage.

Marsiglio, W., Amato, P., Day, R. D., and Lamb, M. (2000). Scholarship on fatherhood in the 1990s and beyond. *Journal of Marriage and Family, 62,* 1173–91.

Maruna, S., LeBel, T., and Lanier, C. (2003). Generativity behind bars: Some "redemptive truth" about prison society. In. E. de St. Aubin, D. McAdams, and T. Kim (Eds.), *The generative society: Caring for future generations*. Washington, DC: American Psychological Association.

McDermott, K., and King, R. (1992). Prison rule 102: "Stand by your man": The impact of penal policy on the families of prisoners. In R. Shaw (Ed.), *Prisoner's children: What are the issues?* (pp. 50–73). London: Routledge.

Mizruchi, E. (1987). *Regulating society* (2nd ed.). Chicago: University of Chicago Press.

Morgan, M. (2003). *Maternal gatekeeping: Mothers' encouragement and discouragement of paternal involvement of incarcerated fathers*. Unpublished honors thesis. Purdue University, West Lafayette, Indiana.

Nurse, A. (2002). *Fatherhood arrested: Parenting from within the juvenile justice system*. Nashville, TN: Vanderbilt University Press.

Palm, G. (2001). Parent education for incarcerated fathers. In J. Fagan and A. Hawkins (Eds.), *Clinical and educational interventions with fathers* (pp. 117–41). New York: Haworth Clinical Practice Press.

Palm, G. (1996). Understanding the parent education needs of incarcerated fathers. Paper presented at the National Council on Family Relations annual conference, Kansas City, MO.

Patton, M. Q. (2002). *Qualitative research and evaluation methods*. Thousand Oaks, CA: Sage.

Perrucci, C., Perrucci, R., Targ, D., and Targ, H. (1988). *Plant closings: International context and social costs*. New York: Aldine de Gruyter.

Roy, K. (In press). Father stories: A life course perspective on paternal identity for low-income African American men. *Journal of Family Issues*.

Roy, K. (2004a). Three block fathers: Spatial perceptions and kin-work in low-income neighborhoods. *Social Problems, 51,* 528–48.

Roy, K. (2004b). You can't eat love: Negotiating provider role expectations for low-income fathers and families. *Fathering: A Journal of Theory, Research and Practice about Men as Fathers, 2,* 253–76.

Scott, J., and Alwin, D. (1998). Retrospective versus prospective measurement of life histories in longitudinal research. In J. Giele and G. H. Elder Jr. (Eds.), *Methods of life course research: Qualitative and quantitative approaches* (pp. 98–127). Thousand Oaks, CA: Sage.

Snow, D., and Anderson, L. (1987). Identity work among the homeless. *American Journal of Sociology, 97,* 1337–71.

Strauss, A. (1987). *Qualitative analysis for social scientists*. New York: Cambridge University Press.

Strauss, A., and Corbin, J. (1998). *Basics of qualitative research: Techniques and procedures for developing grounded theory* (2nd ed.). Thousand Oaks, CA: Sage.

Toch, H. (1975). *Men in crisis: Human breakdowns in prison*. Chicago: Aldine.

Toch, H. (2000). Altruistic activity as correctional treatment. *International Journal of Offender Therapy and Comparative Criminology, 44,* 270–78.

Turner, V. (1967). *The forest of symbols*. Ithaca, NY: Cornell University Press.

Turner, V. (1969). *The ritual process*. Ithaca, NY: Cornell University Press.

U.S. Department of Justice. (2000). *Bureau of Justice Statistics Report*.

9

Situating Fatherhood in Responsible Fatherhood Programs: A Place to Explore Father Identity

Elaine A. Anderson and Bethany L. Letiecq

Much of learning, personal development, and achievement occurs in social contexts (Adler 1998). Parenting also takes place to varying degrees in social contexts, and some have asserted that fathering is more "contextually sensitive" than mothering (Doherty, Kouneski, and Erikson 1998, 287). Yet the social context of fathering—or fathers' "situatedness"—has received little attention in the parenting literature. For example, little is known about the ways in which various institutions and settings (e.g., public schools, Head Start programs, fatherhood programs, child support agencies, employment) promote or hinder fathers' capacities to nurture, give care, and provide for their children.

Moreover, not all contexts are based on equality or foster the realization of one's fullest potential as a parent. For low-income African American fathers, their social context is riddled with unequal access to education, employment, political power, commercial goods and services, and social resources (Coley 2001; Lazur and Majors 1995). In general, African American families are ten times more likely than European American families to live in neighborhoods where at least 30 percent of residents are poor (Duncan, Brooks-Gunn, and Klebanov 1994). African American families are also disproportionately represented in neighborhoods characterized by high levels of joblessness, violence, crime, and drug activity (Chase-Lansdale and Gordon 1996; Sampson, Raudenbush, and Earls 1997).

Low-income African American families are often characterized as "father absent" families as many fathers have never married their child's mother or lived in the same household with their children (Ventura and Bachrach 2000). Moreover, many low-income fathers have failed to meet their child support obligations for any number of personal, relational (e.g., conflict with the child's mother), and contextual (e.g., unemployment, incarceration) reasons (Anderson, Kohler, and Letiecq 2002). Perhaps because of their residential and financial absence from their families, African American fathers are often viewed by the larger society as deficient and inadequately prepared to perform roles as fathers (Allen and Connor 1997). However, there is some evidence that the "absent father" stereotype is a misleading portrayal of black family life as many unwed fathers are involved early on in their children's lives regardless of their residential status (Carlson and McLanahan 2002). Coley and Chase-Landsdale (1999), in their study of urban African American families, suggest that approximately half of nonresidential fathers had regular contact and provided some financial support during their children's preschool years. Further, in another study of low-income African American fathers of preschoolers living in high-violence neighborhoods, Letiecq and Koblinsky (2003) found that both residential and nonresidential fathers were actively involved in attempting to protect their children from community dangers.

Qualitative studies of low-income African American fathers further reveal the complex and myriad roles played by these men in family life (Anderson et al. 2002; Hamer 1998; Jarrett, Roy, and Burton 2002; Letiecq and Koblinsky 2004). These studies suggest that definitions of fatherhood have been too narrow and should comprise both economic and relational components (such as providing financially for children and spending "quality time"). These studies also recognize that many fathers go to great lengths to fulfill their roles while simultaneously coping with tremendous sociocultural barriers (Nelson, Clampet-Lundquist, and Edin 2002). Although a majority of African American fathers are nonresidential, approximately 40 percent live in the same home as their children, including 4 percent who are the sole parent (U.S. Census Bureau 2000). Such evidence suggests that many fathers are present in young children's lives in some capacity. What remains to be understood is how fathers' situatedness in larger social contexts affects their identity as fathers and their interest and ability to perform their father roles.

The new theoretical model of situated fathering offered by Marsiglio, Roy, and Fox (chapter 1) provides a framework to examine fathers' social contexts, where men's subjective processes and behaviors are interwoven with social life. Marsiglio and colleagues note that men construct their identities and are involved with their children in diverse settings that often have interrelated physical, social, and symbolic dimensions. Key concepts in the model include an examination of the *symbolic meanings* fathers give to their experience within a given *place and time*. Situated fathering recognizes that the physical location of fathers may influence the level of power, privilege, knowledge, and resources they have to draw on when engaging in their roles as fathers. Additionally, where a father is located will influence what policies, practices, and personal power and control he may employ in his "fatherwork."

In the current study, we examine the symbolic meanings low-income African American fathers give to their experiences while participating in a Responsible Fatherhood (RF) program. Specifically, we explore how place—being situated in a RF program—allows these men to create a discourse about being men and fathers. In other places—at home, at work, during recreational activities—such discourses are unlikely. Thus this study offers a unique opportunity to examine the salience of place in understanding the fatherwork conducted by a group of men historically ignored in most social contexts, and particularly in contexts directly related to parenting.

BACKGROUND OF RESPONSIBLE FATHERHOOD PROGRAMS

Over the past decade, public discourse began focusing on low-income families and welfare reform (Anderson et al. 2002; Curran and Abrams 2000; Roy 1999). Rather than perpetuating single mothers' dependence on the state, policymakers turned to the biological fathers in (or on the periphery of) these family constellations and looked to increase their economic and social responsibility to their offspring. One result of this shift in public discourse was the demonstration and later institution of fatherhood initiatives.

Early work on young unwed fathers was reported by Achatz and MacAllum (1994) in a compilation of ten working papers that reviewed data to identify program and policy issues concerning these men. The authors generally agreed that establishing paternity was the first step to acknowledging paternal responsibility. Further, they argued that unemployment was a major barrier to fathers being able to provide financial support to their children. Thus discussion ensued that identified the importance of developing programs that would establish paternity and address parenting challenges, job skills, and employment opportunities for young unwed fathers.

One of the early government funded fatherhood programs to speak to the needs of low-income noncustodial fathers was the Parent's Fair Share demonstration (Johnson and Doolittle 1996). This pilot program identified as their primary goals: (1) the implementation of peer support groups, which addressed such themes as parenting, relationships, communication, and racism, and (2) employment and training services, which included job search assistance, on-the-job training, education, and skills training. Child support enforcement was tackled by offering a temporary reduction or adjustment of the father's child support order while he was participating in the program. And finally, mediation of disputes between the custodial and noncustodial parents was offered.

Johnson, Levine, and Doolittle (1999) reported the initial effects of the Fair Share program, stating that there were a range of personal, social, and economic gains made by the participating fathers. Although failures occurred when programs fell short of identifying fathers' specific needs and ways to help them address such needs, these pilot programs generally succeeded when there was a match between the recognition of noncustodial fathers' needs and the services made available to facilitate fathers' functioning and well-being. Subsequent to the Fair Share program, the Partnership for Fragile Families and the Office of Child Support Enforcement Responsible Fatherhood Demonstrations were established (Mincy and Pouncy 2002). Drawing on earlier demonstrations, these programs provided a range of services from a variety of community agencies. For the first time, child support and nurturing were both recognized as equally important in the provision of services for fathers.

The common goal of today's Responsible Fatherhood (RF) programs is the promotion of men's financial and emotional involvement in their children's lives, although programs may differ in the activities offered to achieve this goal. Some programs encourage the development of relationships and marriage as a way to connect fathers to their children, whereas others make the fathers more attractive by choosing to emphasize human capital through offering parenting classes, job training, and education (Tamis-LeMonda and Cabrera 1999). Many of these programs teach fathers communication skills through the peer support groups in which they participate (Curran and Abrams 2000). Situated within the fathering group, the caseworker, along with other male group members, typically monitor each father's activities and provide guidance and support to each other. Some have suggested that the most important effect of these programs is the peer support group in which fathers learn to interact with other men and provide emotional support for their children (Curran and Abrams 2000).

RF programs may attempt to improve the quality of fathers' relationships with their children by offering parenting classes, counseling with their children, or organized programs involving children, such as homework help sessions or extracurricular recreational activities. Programs may also sponsor father–child groups that include parenting activities on play, discipline, and day-to-day child care (Curran and Abrams 2000). Some programs may facilitate fathers' reconnection with the mothers of their children and work to improve their relationships with former partners. Sometimes fathers' motivation of reestablishing relationships is to get back together with their partners, whereas others desire to have a better relationship in order to enhance communication about their mutual children. Thus fathers may attend joint therapy sessions with their partners and work on enhancing their conflict management skills.

Fathers who join RF programs may meet with counselors who help them assess their current life situation and determine what goals they will work on to enhance their well-being. Fathers may work on obtaining their general education degree or seek additional training for a given area of work. Programs may work with fathers to identify and make contact with potential employers and prepare for interviews. Further, programs may work with fathers to address on-the-job problems to enable them to maintain employment. Fathers who have substance abuse problems may begin to identify those issues and work towards resolution of their dependencies. Most RF programs have a specified place and time during which fathers are involved in program activities. Although the length of programs varies, most last between six months to a year.

Regardless of the specific components offered by RF programs, these programs reflect the ultimate of spatial dictates. These programs provide a unique physical and social space for men to define the meanings of fatherhood and father involvement, to explore their roles as fathers and nurturers of children, and to gain relationship and employment-related skills. Drawing on the situated fathering model (chapter 1), we examine how place—in this case, an RF program—can create an environment where low-income men of color, stereotypically on the margins of families, can construct their own meanings and discourse about fatherhood and ultimately make changes in their lives that better fit with these new constructions. To capture these men's stories and the transitions they experienced while participating in an RF program, we employed qualitative focus group methodology.

METHOD

Sample

Twenty fathers participated in focus groups between May and October of 1999. Fathers came to the RF program through several sources: some were referred through the courts, others learned about the program through social service referrals, and finally some came to the program through the suggestion of other neighborhood fathers. The twenty participants had various levels of involvement with the RF program at the time of the focus groups. Eight participants were at the entry level of the RF program, five were currently enrolled in the fathers' groups, and seven had "graduated" from the program and were involved in an ongoing support group. The ages of the fathers ranged from seventeen to forty-eight (M = 31.2, SD = 9.19), with fourteen in their twenties and thirties. All but one was African American and fifteen had never married. Their education levels ranged from nine to fifteen years. Thirteen fathers were employed at the time of the focus group and nearly all of the fathers had been employed at some point in time. Thirteen of the fathers also graduated from high school or obtained a GED. Participants had an average of three children each. All fathers reported having either their names on their children's birth certificates or having established legal paternity. The fathers in the study had a total of fifty-two children, twenty-three of whom lived with their fathers. Half of the fathers reported having at least one of their children living with them.

Procedure

Four focus groups were held at the RF program site, which was located in an urban, low-income community in the Baltimore, Maryland metropolitan area. Three cofacilitators (two white women and one male African American RF program graduate) led the groups. Once the participants had been greeted and informed consent was obtained, they were asked a series of questions using a focus group guide developed by the research team. Questions pertained to the fathers' attitudes about and experiences of becoming fathers, involvement in the RF program, current financial and emotional involvement with their children, relationship quality with the mothers of their children, challenges in supporting their children, and impressions of the program. The focus group lead moderator began the group session by introducing himself, stating his age, children's names, their gender and ages, and how many of them he was supporting. By beginning the focus group sessions in this fashion, the lead moderator provided a useful demonstration of what he expected of others and established a sense of equality in the group. Focus groups lasted approximately two hours and were audio taped for transcription. Trained research assistants also recorded participant responses and noted fathers' nonverbal communication to further enrich and validate the transcription. All participants were compensated $40 for their involvement in the study.

Focus groups were chosen because they can capture the perspectives of the participants in their own language, while offering a respectful way to encourage uninhibited discussion of potentially sensitive issues. The process promotes group interaction, evokes candid opinions, facilitates the sharing of a variety of experiences, and encourages members to consider and perhaps find commonalities with, or differentiate their ideas from, others (Krueger and Casey 2000). Focus groups seem particularly well suited for exploring the situated context of the lives of these fathers within the RF program.

Data Analysis

Data were analyzed using a hermeneutic phenomenological methodology. Hermeneutic phenomenology is an interpretive approach that seeks to understand the essence of everyday lived experiences and the meanings constructed from them (Patton 1990; van Manen 1990). The analytic goal of this study was to illuminate and better understand the symbolic meanings participants assign to being a father and how their experiences within the RF program have had an impact on their fathering capacity. Specifically, we examined RF participants' experiences and life changes in light of the five primary properties of situated fathering identified by the Marsiglio model, including (1) the *physical condition* or setting of the RF program, (2) the *temporal dynamics* or the "when" of father activities, (3) the *symbolic meanings* or ready-made definitions given to the fatherhood program, (4) the *social structural* expectations of the program for fathers, and (5) the *private and public* spaces where these men perform their fatherwork and how the program facilitates and/or empowers such work. When appropriate, we also incorporated the model's secondary properties (i.e., institutional and cultural conditions, transitional elements, personal power and control, gendered attributes, and fatherhood discourses) into the analysis and discussion to further explicate the primary properties.

Data analysis occurred in two phases. The first phase involved carefully reviewing each transcript to identify thematic categories reflective of the situated fathering model. Members of the research team read the transcripts and noted themes that emerged, using an open coding procedure to label portions of each transcript for their meanings. The team members then met to discuss the results and to ensure that all conceptually valid themes were captured. Next we discussed the themes and subthemes as they related to the situated fathering model. Having identified these thematic categories, direct quotes were highlighted that represented each theme (and possible subtheme). This step provided a rich description of the phenomena and enhanced the trustworthiness of the analysis (Lincoln and Guba 1985).

RESULTS

Physical Conditions

According to the model devised by Marsiglio and colleagues, fathering experiences are connected to a wide range of physical locations, such as housing units and buildings occupied by families. The physical setting itself can determine what kinds of fathering activities occur. The RF program examined in this study was in a building that housed several social services that participants could take advantage of, including a food stamp office, a health clinic, and a child care facility. This building was on a centrally located and well-trafficked street, close to bus stops and parking. The facility included two large rooms with tables and chairs that could be moved to hold different kinds of meetings. There also were several counselor offices where men could meet privately with staff. Finally, there was an entry space where the program secretary resided and where chairs for congregating were placed. The area felt spacious, was clean, and was nicely painted and appointed. It felt welcoming and active. Typically there were several people regularly coming in and out of the facility; consequently one felt like "things were happening."

In this study, we found that the RF program offered fathers a physical space to spend time together, let down their guard, share their experiences with one another, and discover what it means to be a father. "Coming to the program, by not expectin' anything, I found my place there. I found myself and could be the kind of father I needed to be for my children," one father shared. Another father stated, "Once I came and started seeing other men like myself wanting the same thing . . . we dropped the masculine thing, the mask that says, 'I'm hard, I'm not gonna share this.' And it was about being there for each other." Or as another said, "You see all these grown men putting their business right out front. . . . Even the things you don't want to deal with, you will have to deal with. . . . Guys were really being honest."

The physical setting of the RF program not only enabled fathers to have peer interaction and exchanges with other fathers, but also provided a place for men to interact with the mother of their children, engage in activities with their children, and hence increase their feelings of belongingness. As several fathers suggested, the program met a need in their lives and extended their sense of family: "[The] men's center [is] like a sanctuary for men. . . . I just needed some positive people . . . to talk to" and "These programs become like an extended family . . . [which] is very important to me." When explaining why he wanted to continue with the RF program after graduation, one father said, "I didn't want to lose what I had gotten here, . . . The staff was comforting, reassuring; . . . they were attentive. And we found ourselves helping each other, not just ourselves, and I didn't want to lose that especially since I've got no [extended] family here."

Beyond offering fathers a physical space to explore their father identities and feelings of connectedness, the RF program also provided a social space where the staff and peer mentors served as catalysts for changing the men's roles as fathers. Staff regularly challenged men to reorient their lives during private counseling sessions and support group meetings. Some men actually moved from no fathering to fathering their children for the first time after becoming involved with the program. This transition is captured by one father when he said, "It took me a coupla times to get locked up before I realized that if you goin' in and outa jail . . . you can't be a father to your child. You're not teachin' your child the right thing." Other fathers were able through interaction with peers and attendance at program offerings such as father/child gatherings and holiday celebrations to reframe the notion of parenting and feel for the first time that they could perform as parents. One father expressed his transition this way:

> When I first heard about the [RF] program . . . I considered it a blessing because when I got my second son, it was a very scary feeling to me. . . . I didn't know nothin' about parenting. Didn't know how to be a parent. Wasn't sure if I was grown up enough, man enough to handle it. I came down to this building here . . . and talked to one of the coordinators. I felt like I had some hope then.

Finally, some fathers recognized the transitions they were making while in the RF program. As one father shared, "When I was a dope fiend, I was mentally into instant gratification. [My RF facilitator] told me, 'The man who succeeds in life is able to delay gratification.' I've also been incarcerated. I've learned that that was a process then and this is a process now." Thus the RF program appeared to offer a place—often a safe and nonjudgmental place—for men to explore fatherhood, establish supportive relationships with other fathers, make transitions in their lives, and begin to see their fathering roles and experiences as a process for growth and change.

Temporal Dynamics

Temporal dynamics were regularly addressed in the Responsible Fatherhood program. This social construction addressing *when* men act as fathers appeared to facilitate fathers' newfound understanding of their paternal roles and develop new strategies for implementing them. Not unlike many parents, the fathers in the RF program discussed the challenges of juggling the time they allotted to work, having personal space, and still finding quality time to be with their kids. Managing all of the daily life tasks and the stresses often accompanying those tasks was an area that the RF program worked on with participating fathers. As one father said,

> This is not going to be easy. This is gonna be a process. . . . Some days my son might be sick. Some days I might be sick. I got car troubles now. . . . But goin' through all that, I still gotta do what I have to do for me so I can grow.

Beyond focusing on the challenges of balancing work and family demands, the program also promoted the importance of fathers spending time with their children. As one father stated,

> [There was] a time where I would have time to myself or might play Play Station and wouldn't want to bother with 'em [his kids], or if they tryin' to tell me

something, I'd be like, wait a minute. So [the RF program] taught me more to listen to my kids and pay more attention to them and play with them when they wanna be played with.

Through their involvement with the program and contact with other fathers, these RF fathers were learning the necessity of spending time with their children, which sometimes meant addressing their child's needs before their own. Further, discussing one's children with other fathers helped the men realize how important they and their behaviors are to their children as reflected by the following statement:

> One night I was feeling bad and didn't want to be bothered by anything. My daughter said, 'You just not yourself today, Daddy. You need to smile.' By her sayin' that, I kinda caught myself. In the program, we talk about how we act affects our children.

Once the men recognized how instrumental their time in the RF program was for enhancing their work on issues involving their children, their expectations for themselves and their parenting roles changed. The following examples reflect some of those changed fathering expectations at various stages of children's development. "Child support is getting up at three o'clock in the morning. Feeding your child. . . . Those are the things that make you feel like I am man, like I'm being a father," or as another father stated,

> Giving them [his kids] support and guidance that I did not get as a child. My intention is to give them the guidance they need to make decisions. I want to be with my sons and to hear what they are thinking about decisions they might make and to support them on those decisions. Without having a father there to support me . . . I fell short on some of the activities that I should have finished. I didn't have him there to drive me, to keep me going. . . . I'll be there to back them up being that it's the right thing.

Another father proudly stated,

> I really felt like a man and a father when I was takin' him to school in the mornin' and he would say, 'Daddy, I'm gonna get a star today.' . . . It's very important for me to see my son everyday. 'Cause it makes me feel like I'm doin' the right thing.

Finally, one father said, "I'm taking a computer class now. . . . And I sit down and do my homework with my kids. And I study with my kids. . . . So we're interactin' and we're all doin' homework. They say, 'That's cool, Dad's doin' homework with us!'" Thus, as fathers spend time in the RF program, some appear to shift their participatory roles from that of a previously disengaged father to that of a connected father engaged with his children. They have changed how they "do fathering" and manage family time.

Symbolic Meaning

As stated in the model, when fathers encounter a new setting, they are likely to come equipped with "ready-made definitions" of it or they will form judgments while there (Marsiglio et al., chapter 1). Many fathers come to Responsible Fatherhood programs voluntarily; however, others are mandated by the courts to attend the program. Thus fathers sometimes enter the program with pretty strong views. One said, "I thought it [RF program] would be a bunch of, uh, BS at first." Another father stated, "When I first heard about the program . . . I thought it was gonna be where we all sit in the classroom and somebody stands up in front of the class saying, 'You do this with your child, you do that.' But when I got here, it was totally different." Fathers' perceptions of the RF program ranged from the notion of wasting their time, "I thought it was going to be sittin' here and listenin' to other people talk and not nobody askin' me what I thought," to acknowledging the positive benefits the program offered such as facilitating a father's sense of connection and hope, "[The RF program] helped to open my mind, rebirth, open my social skills, integrity, honor, and respect, helping others and teaching others."

The six months or more that many of the fathers spent in the supportive environment of the RF program allowed their perceptions about the program, as well as about fathering, to evolve. Some fathers mentioned how they had changed their view of fathering during the time they were in the program. One father said,

> To be honest . . . I didn't understand a lot about it [the RF program]. . . . I didn't know if it would work for me or nothin' like that. But I went anyway just to see. In part, I figured it was the best thing I could do. Here we are with a bunch of men talking about being fathers, being responsible fathers and stuff like that. I said, "Hey! This is what I need!"

Another father acknowledged,

> When I first came down here [to the RF program], I wasn't really into it, but as time went on, I grew on the program and the program grew on me. And I just started coming back all the time. And anticipating new things, going places with them . . . learning about myself, and being a man. And it gave me a better understanding of how to raise my son.

Finally, this father stated, "You are only going to get what you put into it [the RF program]. If you come in the same way and leave the same way, you never even tried. If you haven't given away anything, you haven't learned anything."

As a result of their participation in the RF program, men's perceptions also seemed to shift and change regarding the way they understood masculinity and the gendered attributes of parenting and fatherhood. In essence, the program helped fathers understand that, while some environments accentuated a masculine style of interaction, the RF environment was a place where fathers could explore more expressive and nurturing parenting styles. As one father noted,

> I was with them [his kids] physically but not mentally. After they would tell me about a situation, the program taught me to ask them, "Well, what did you think about that?" It helped me open up to them mentally. Now I'm not afraid to tell them I love them because I do love them. I'm not just doing only that masculine thing.

The RF program, as a place that exuded a softer, gentler side of fathering, also appeared to facilitate fathers' acknowledgment of their personal need for connection, information sharing, and expressions of emotions. As one father reflected,

> The information I find in this group really helps me out in a lot of different ways, more than just parenting . . . and it's a challenge for me to come here . . . [but] I really don't feel it would be in my best interest to disconnect myself. . . . I'll be defeatin' myself if I do that.

Another father expressed what the program meant to him by saying,

> You talkin' about the program to [people] and they'll say, "I don't need nobody to tell me how to raise my kids or give me information." But . . . that's not what the program tryin' to do. They tryin' to help you and guide you and give you good advice.

Finally, fathers' newfound connections and ability to express feelings (as promoted by the RF program) was articulated by one father speaking at the program's graduation ceremony. He reflected, "I had a chance to tell my story. . . . I thought I was the only one that [felt] my pain over what I went through . . . and then I looked around and I see all these women in the audience crying and it really done something to me." Clearly the fathers grew more comfortable talking in social settings about their lives and families and the meanings they ascribed to their experiences.

Social Structural

According to the situated model, "each setting has some type of negotiated normative order associated with it that helps individuals determine how they are expected to relate to each other" (Marsiglio et al., chapter 1). Fathers were able to express fairly well the numerous personal growth experiences the RF program offered them and, consequently, what was expected and what they might get from the program. One father suggested the program afforded him the opportunity to feel better about himself when he stated,

> When I joined the program, they built up my confidence within myself and motivated me a lot. And we went out on several outings . . . we talked to young teens and young adults about the Young Fathers Program. . . . It really built my self-confidence up a lot.

Several fathers indicated the RF program showed them better ways to interact with their child. These positive actions were expressed by one father, who stated,

> We never take the time out to really sit down . . . listen to our kids . . . play with them, take them places. . . . As long as we give the baby's mother some money, we done our job and that was the type of attitude at first I had about my son. But now since I been in the [RF Program], it gave me a better opportunity to expand my thinking . . . show my appreciation and love to my son.

Some fathers talked about the work opportunities they were offered that made them feel like they had more power in their lives. A father said,

> It [RF program] helped me get a coupla jobs. . . . I ain't never had no job until I got into the program. [The] counselor really support me on that right there. . . . And like he told me, you got to take your steps, one by one, don't try to just grab everything at one time. So I worked myself from the bottom and went up.

Further, regarding jobs and expectations in the workplace, one father said,

> They [RF staff] gave me information on how to keep a job . . . how to work along with other people in my work area and [develop] good relations with people and *respect* for my supervisor. . . . Because I always could get a job. I had many jobs over the years but for some reason I always ended up losing 'em. And I learned . . . that nobody ever fires you . . . you fire yourself.

Finally, as a result of meeting the expectations of the RF program, some fathers expressed how certain experiences changed them and increased their levels of knowledge, power, and privilege. As one father shared, "The most memorable [experience from our RF program outings] was volunteering for the homeless shelter. That really did something to me . . . reachin' out helpin' someone and serving someone." Or as another father said, "The program has really helped me to advance socially and emotionally. . . . I was exposed to different types of experiences. That facilitator was very good at helpin' me see things in a way different than I was used to thinking." As these examples illustrate, focus group fathers were able to reflect on their internal shifts and personal growth as they moved through the RF program and gained insights into the program's expectations of them as fathers to their children and members of their communities. These men appeared to learn new ways of being fathers and engaging in their communities as they internalized the complex meanings of "responsible fatherhood."

Private/Public

Finally, Marsiglio and colleagues' situated fathering model suggests that men act as fathers in settings that vary in degrees of privacy. In this study, much of the fathers' parental work took place in the public eye, as they were intimately involved with their extended kin and in-laws, social services, child support enforcement agencies, health care services, prison systems, and the family courts. For many men, they were learning to be fathers and creating new father identities in a very public arena through the support groups and activities offered by the RF program.

Related to the concept of "public fatherhood," as presented in the situated fathering model, institutional and cultural conditions (e.g., visitation policies, health care practices, discrimination) may influence the degree to which men can operate as fathers. One of the primary goals of RF programs is to assist fathers as they navigate through the various public institutions that regulate paternal involvement (e.g., family courts, child support enforcement agencies). As RF fathers became more invested in being involved with their children (as a result of program participation), they often were faced with challenges related to visitation or custody disagreements with the mother of their child. These often public displays of parental conflict, largely through the courts, were exemplified by fathers in the following manner:

> My fifteen-year-old, he and I have never really been close; for like twelve years I didn't see him at all. And child support had a lot to do with that 'cause I owed money. Every time I would make an attempt to see my son, his mom would complain to support enforcement . . . and I ended up getting locked up for being behind in my child support. So even though they say child support and visitation have nothing to do with each other, in actuality they do.

Another father stated,

> I'm going through changes with his [son's] mother, now. 'Cause when he was born, we broke up. It's been about thirteen years we've been apart from each other. But we going through changes. I'm in the process of going to court—back to court—I'm gonna try to see if I can get joint custody.

Health care settings also brought fathering experiences out into the public arena, sometimes in the form of discrimination. As one father said,

> A lot of us men have to put up with a lot of suspicion and prejudice when we behave as independent, responsible fathers. For example, when I take my child to get medical treatment, I'm told, "Well, you have to bring the mother." They would accept a mother saying she was being both the mother and the father, but not the father.

Fathers felt that they were perceived in the public arena, sometimes because of their involvement with the RF program, as unfit fathers. One father expressed this sentiment when he said, "When we're [fathers in RF program] introduced as bad, bad, bad people, I know we're not bad people, so it shouldn't bother me. . . . Except that this is how they see me. Who wants to go through that?"

Given the many public arenas that low-income nonresidential fathers often have to navigate in order to express themselves as fathers—and their sense that others view them in a negative way—it appears that another function of RF programs is to empower fathers and support their attempts to access and rear their children. As one father noted, "I was assisted with legal problems. I had a court case and the program helped me with a letter. And some transportation was provided to me to go." Another father stated,

> When I first learned I was gonna be a father, I was incarcerated at that time. I felt real proud of being a father [but] I didn't understand how to be a father, 'cause my father wasn't there for me for twenty-one years. . . . When I came home [after incarceration] there wasn't no help for me. So I felt I had to do everything myself. But I decided that I couldn't do everything by myself. I told him [RF advocate] that I'd come and check it [RF] out.

One father also discussed his newly found sense of empowerment as a "dangerous commodity" as the program enlightened men regarding their custodial/ visitation rights and responsibilities in family life. This father went on to say, "You know, it's like, the more that you know, the more potential you have to take the child back." RF programs, with their focus on relationship quality issues, also appear to empower fathers in their personal relationships. One father, discussing prior visitation disagreements between him and the mother of his child, stated, "The child becomes a pawn when they [mothers] can use the child to their advantage. . . . But since I been in the program, our relationship has turned around tremendously." Perhaps one father summed up the positive changes reflected from his experience in the RF program best when he said,

> We all bring something of value to the mix. It's not like you all come in here and listen to us because we're older. It's not like you listen to the coordinator because he's the coordinator. Because I know when I do groups, I learn something every night . . . and I take that stuff home and not only do I empower myself, I empower my family.

In essence, RF programs offer these men a place to "take the power back" in their fathering roles, promoting a sense of personal power and control in public arenas where they may have once felt demoralized and dismissed.

DISCUSSION

Much of the discourse on low-income African American fathers has traditionally focused on the deficits and negative attributes associated with these men—with little regard for their social contexts and the sociocultural barriers they face in performing their roles as fathers (Allen and Connor 1997; Nelson et al. 2002). Drawing on a new theoretical model of situated fathering, we explored how place can stimulate discussion of and new understandings about low-income African American males' experiences as fathers. Thus this study offered a unique view of low-income fathers of color participating in a RF program who were engaged in a dialogue about the meanings of fatherhood. Based on study results, the RF program appeared to empower participants to identify and, in many cases, meet their fatherhood goals and to be more invested in their fathering roles and better prepared to meet their family needs.

Situating fathers within an RF program, we found that the program facilitated transitions and significant life changes. Prior to joining the program, it appeared that many participants had not fully conceptualized the meaning and significance of their fathering roles. However, over the course of their participation, many fathers began to understand for themselves the salience of being a father. What did it mean to them to have or not have a father figure in their own lives? How did they want to be different for their children and what was it going to take to make the necessary changes to get there? What could they draw from other fathers' experiences within the group to enhance their own positive parenting functions?

The RF program seems to have engendered a new discourse among fathers that could produce positive outcomes for fathers and their children. For example, as a result of the program, some fathers were challenged by program leaders and other fathers to reexamine counterproductive masculine conceptualizations of fatherhood. They were encouraged to explore alternative, gentler ways of fathering. As several fathers noted, the RF program helped them to open up to their children and tell them that they loved them, thus allowing for new expressions of warmth and closeness in the father–child dyad. Parental warmth and nurturance is critical to the well-being of children, as nurtured children likely develop secure attachments to their parents, which serve as important emotional foundations for later development (Chase-Lansdale and Pittman 2002). Moreover, children and adolescents whose parents are warm and supportive have healthier peer relationships, higher levels of self-esteem and social competence, and lower levels of depression, anxiety, and behavior problems (Shumow, Vandell, and Posner 1998; Weiss and Schwarz 1996). Thus the RF program appears to have supported fathers' movement toward more positive parenting.

Applying the situated fathering model also helped us recognize that place can indeed promote fathers' identity development and personal growth. Fathers in this study appeared to cultivate a more expansive identity for themselves as fathers. Further, the RF program appeared to facilitate fathers' acquisition of self-confidence regarding their fathering ability and, in many cases, their ability to negotiate personal relationships, manage time, perform in the work setting, and/or navigate the social systems that often dictate how they can be with their children. Fathers in the RF program seemed to confront the stereotypical notions of black fatherhood and challenge the negative images conjured up by terms like "absent father" or "deadbeat dad" that they themselves may have internalized when they became unwed fathers. Developing a positive father identity through their participation in the RF program may increase the likelihood that these fathers will engender healthy familial and civic relationships. This identity work may also be important to the mental health and well-being of low-income men of color who may experience depression or substance abuse problems related to a negative sense of self or internalized racism (Anderson, Kohler, and Letiecq 2005).

We found that the secondary properties of the situated fathering model (institutional and cultural conditions, transitional elements, personal power and control, gendered attributes, and fatherhood discourses) helped us grasp how fathers changed during their program participation. In other words, these properties aided our understanding of the apparent internal psychological processes or changes that enabled fathers to address some of the cultural inequalities they had experienced in the public arena, to enhance their personal power and control over their relationships with their children and the children's mothers, and to simply engage in new discourses about their fathering roles. We heard fathers discuss the gendered notions of masculinity and what it meant to be a man and a father when one drops that "masculine thing." Such discussions seemed critical to fathers' ability to redefine their roles and reformulate their gender identity. These discussions also helped fathers conceptualize how they might interact with various social systems differently in order to make the systems better work for them. As one father noted, the RF program made them "dangerous commodities" because they had gained insight, skills, and ultimately personal power in social realms previously foreign and disempowering to them.

Each facet of the situated fathering model allowed us to gain insights about the complex ways in which fathers reframed their roles. By examining the RF program's physical setting, we saw how the actual place—the "safe haven" offered by the RF location and fostered by program staff—facilitated change. Likewise, when we examined the elements of time, social structure, and public/private arenas, we better understood how the program encouraged participants to develop new expectations for themselves while enhancing their ability to negotiate their fathering roles, as well as navigate the public arenas to achieve their fathering and family goals.

Although we have focused most notably on the positive aspects of the RF program and the changes fathers experienced while participating, it is also important to note that not all fathers succeed in RF programs. These men have numerous needs and one program cannot be all things to all fathers. In our study, some fathers struggled with finding employment and were frustrated by the program's inability to ensure job success. Others wanted the program to do more to help them navigate the various social systems that regulated their father involvement. Ideally, as these RF programs mature and grow, they will continue to grapple with their complex and often competing goals of (1) facilitating fathers' ability to provide financially for their offspring and (2) promoting fathers' positive involvement in their children's lives.

In sum, by focusing our research on fathers' "situatedness," indeed the very places where men do their fatherwork, we expanded our understanding of the needs of low-income fathers of color: a *place* to practice fathering and develop new, more expansive father identities; adequate *time* to parent their children, especially when living apart from them; a safe space—both physically and emotionally—to explore the *meanings* of fatherhood and to challenge traditional notions of masculinity without judgment; social structural *expectations* of fathering that are achievable given one's social context and access to power and resources; and finally, skills to navigate the not-so-father-friendly *public arenas* that oversee many aspects of low-income nonresidential fathering.

When we meet fathers where they are, listen to their stories, and attempt to understand the symbolic meanings they ascribe to their experiences, we as researchers, practitioners, and policymakers may be better positioned to promote positive changes in fathers' lives and empower them to meet their family goals.

FUTURE RESEARCH

Although this study provides insight into the salience of place for a group of low-income fathers of color participating in a RF program, many questions remain unanswered. For example, because little demographic data were collected from participants, we cannot extensively describe the participants' family relationships, particularly the nature of their relationships with the mothers of their children. Recent research (e.g., Bumpass and Lu 2000) revealed that many parents in supposedly "single-parent" families are either romantically involved or cohabiting, especially around the time of a child's birth. Additional research on the fathering experiences of low-income men involved in a variety of relationship and family constellations is an important next step. Such work could inform program development and service delivery because the needs of fathers who have and have not continued romantic involvements with the mothers of their children are likely to differ considerably.

Findings from this study also suggest a need to reconceptualize the relevance of place in fathers' lives. How does one's location—both physical and social—influence one's definition of and experiences with fatherhood? How does a RF program's location in different neighborhoods or types of facilities influence fathers' participation rates? Further, how might the setting influence fathers' level of involvement in the program and do certain types of activities (e.g., child's play, homework, or daily child care tasks) influence fathers' program involvement? Studying men's perceptions of and experiences with these activities could be a direction for future research.

Several research questions could address the impact of social space on the fathers. What strategies do program staffs use to connect with fathers and how do those strategies affect program success? Studying the different motivational strategies program staffs use to increase fathers' commitment to the program could be useful. Because many of the fathers have been involved with the courts due to child support challenges, researchers could examine whether fathers' RF program participation enhanced their communication skills and interactions with the court. In addition, learning more about the support and friendships fathers garner from their participation in the program seems important for understanding how fathers maintain positive relationships with their peers and children.

Future fatherhood programs should acknowledge their unique opportunities to address the inequalities low-income fathers of color may experience regarding their children. RF programs can provide a safe place for fathers exposed to the dangers of inner-city life to explore their relationships with others. Practitioners and researchers might consider the intersections of place and culture. Additional research is necessary to answer how practitioners and the physical settings in which they work could further enhance the various cultural experiences participants bring to the program, and how "situatedness" might promote or hinder cultural ways of knowing that are important to positive fathering practices.

Further, it seems important to follow these RF fathers over time to assess how their newly established relationships with their children and families change. Research regarding RF programs should address the importance of long-term follow-up and maintenance activities for participants. Research with RF low-income fathers of color should explore how they manage their family activities and grapple with work-related challenges. Ultimately, perhaps the most important question is, Do children experience discernable benefits when their fathers balance their nurturing and child support roles more effectively?

REFERENCES

This research was supported by a grant from the Department of Health and Human Services Administration for Children and Families administered by the Maryland Department of Human Resources (DHR) Community Services Administration in collaboration with DHR's Child Support Enforcement Administration and Family Investment Administration. We would like to acknowledge Ellen Schultz for her assistance with the data analysis and Dr. Sandra Hofferth for her thoughtful comments to improve the manuscript. We are also indebted to Dr. Gwen Wallen, Kenneth Hunt, Stan Bain, and Patti Most for their assistance with this research and to the fathers who shared their stories with us.

Adler, A. (1998). *Social interest: Adler's key to the meaning of life* (C. Brett, trans.). Oxford, U.K.: Oneworld Publications. Original work published in 1938.

Achatz, M., and MacAllum, C. (1994, Spring). *Young unwed fathers: Report from the field*. Philadelphia: Public/Private Ventures.

Allen, W., and Connor, M. (1997). An African American perspective on generative fathering. In A. J. Hawkins and D. C. Dollahite (Eds.), *Generative fathering: Beyond deficit perspectives* (pp. 52–70). Thousand Oaks, CA: Sage.

Anderson, E. A., Kohler, J. K., and Letiecq, B. L. (2005). Predictors of depression among low-income, non-residential fathers. *Journal of Family Issues, 26,* 547–66.

Anderson, E. A., Kohler, J. K., and Letiecq, B. L. (2002). Low-income fathers and "responsible fatherhood" programs: A qualitative investigation of participants' experiences. *Family Relations, 51,* 148–55.

Bumpass, L., and Lu, H. (2000). Trends in cohabitation and implications for children's family contexts in the United States. *Population Studies, 54,* 29–41.

Carlson, M., and McLanahan, S. (2002). Fragile families, father involvement, and public policy. In C. S. Tamis-LeMonda and N. Cabrera (Eds.), *Handbook of father involvement: Multidisciplinary perspectives* (pp. 461–88). Mahwah, NJ: Erlbaum.

Chase-Lansdale, P. L., and Pittman, L. D. (2002). Welfare reform and parenting: Reasonable expectations. In M. K. Shields (Ed.), *Future of children, vol. 12, no. 1: Children and Welfare Reform* (pp. 167–83). Los Gatos, CA: David and Lucille Packard Foundation.

Chase-Lansdale, P. L., and Gordon, R. A. (1996). Economic hardship and the development of 5- and 6-year-olds: Neighborhood and regional perspectives. *Child Development, 67,* 3338–67.

Coley, R. L. (2001). (In)visible men: Emerging research on low-income, unmarried, and minority fathers. *American Psychologist, 56,* 743–53.

Coley, R., and Chase-Lansdale, P. (1999). Stability and change in paternal involvement among urban African American fathers. *Journal of Family Psychology, 13,* 1–20.

Curran, L., and Abrams, L. (2000). Making men into dads: Fatherhood, the state, and welfare reform. *Gender and Society, 14,* 662–78.

Doherty, W., Kouneski, E., and Erickson, M. (1998). Responsible fathering: An overview and conceptual framework. *Journal of Marriage and the Family, 60,* 277–92.

Duncan, G., Brooks-Gunn, J., and Klebanov, P. (1994). Economic deprivation and early childhood development. *Child Development, 65,* 296–318.

Hamer, J. (1998). What African American noncustodial fathers say inhibits and enhances their involvement with children. *Western Journal of Black Studies, 22,* 117–27.

Jarrett, R., Roy, K., and Burton, L. (2002). Fathers in the hood: qualitative research on low-income African-American men. In C. S. Tamis-LeMonda and N. Cabrera (Eds.), *Handbook of father involvement: Multidisciplinary perspectives* (pp. 211–48). Mahwah, NJ: Erlbaum.

Johnson, E., and Doolittle, F. (1996). *Low-income parents and the Parents' Fair Share Demonstration; an early qualitative look at low-income noncustodial parents (NCPs) and how one policy initiative has attempted to improve their ability to pay child support.* New York: Manpower Demonstration Research Corporation.

Johnson, E., Levine, A., and Doolittle, F. (1999). *Fathers' Fair Share: Helping poor men manage child support and fatherhood.* New York: Russell Sage Foundation.

Kreuger, R. A., and Casey, M. A. (2000). *Focus groups: A practical guide for applied researchers* (3rd ed.). Thousand Oaks, CA: Sage.

Lazur, R. F., and Majors, R. (1995). Men of color: Ethnocultural variations of male gender role strain. In R. F. Levant and W. S. Pollack (Eds.), *A new psychology of men.* New York: Basic.

Letiecq, B. L., and Koblinsky, S. A. (2003). African American fathering of young children in violent neighborhoods: Paternal protective strategies and their predictors. *Fathering: A Journal of Theory, Research, and Practice about Men as Fathers, 1,* 215–37.

Letiecq, B. L., and Koblinsky, S. A. (2004). Parenting in violent neighborhoods: African American fathers share strategies for keeping young children safe. *Journal of Family Issues, 25* (6), 715–34.

Lincoln, Y. S., and Guba, E. G. (1985). *Naturalistic inquiry.* Beverly Hills, CA: Sage.

Marsiglio, W., Roy, K., and Fox, G. L. (2005). Situated fathering: A spatially sensitive and social approach. In W. Marsiglio, K. Roy, and G. L. Fox, (Eds.), *Situated Fathering: A focus on physical and social spaces.* Lanham, MD: Rowman & Littlefield.

Mincy, R., and Pouncy, H. (2002). The responsible fatherhood field: Evolution and goals. In C. S. Tamis-LeMonda and N. Cabrera (Eds.), *Handbook of father involvement: Multidisciplinary perspectives.* Mahwah, NJ: Erlbaum.

Nelson, T., Clampet-Lundquist, S., and Edin, K. (2002). Sustaining fragile fatherhood: Father involvement among low-income, noncustodial African American fathers in Philadelphia. In C. S. Tamis-LeMonda and N. Cabrera (Eds.), *Handbook of father involvement: Multidisciplinary perspectives* (pp. 525–53). Mahwah, NJ: Erlbaum.

Patton, M. Q. (1990). *Qualitative evaluation and research methods* (2nd ed.). Newbury Park, CA: Sage.

Roy, K. (1999). Low-income single fathers in an African American community and the requirements of welfare reform. *Journal of Family Issues, 20* (4), 432–57.

Shumow, L., Vandell, D. L., and Posner, J. K. (1998). Harsh, firm, and permissive parenting in low-income families: Relations to children's academic achievement and behavioral adjustment. *Journal of Family Issues, 19,* 483–507.

Sampson, R., Raudenbush, S., and Earls, F. (1997). Neighborhoods and violent crime: A multilevel study of collective efficacy. *Science, 277,* 918–24.

Tamis-LeMonda, C. S., and Cabrera, N. (1999). Perspectives on father involvement: Research and policy. *Social Policy Report, 13,* 1–26.

U.S. Census Bureau. (2000). *Statistical abstract of the United States: 2000* (120th ed.). Washington, DC.

van Manen, M. (1990). *Researching lived experience.* Albany: State University of New York Press.

Ventura, S., and Bachrach, C. (2000). Nonmarital childbearing in the United States. 1940–1999. *National Vital Statistics Report, 48* (16). Hyattsville, MD: National Center for Health Statistics.

Weiss, L. H., and Schwarz, J. C. (1996). The relationship between parenting types and older adolescents' personality, academic achievement, adjustment, and substance use. *Child Development, 67,* 2102–14.

10

Military Fathers on the Front Lines

*Shelley MacDermid, Rona Schwarz, Anthony Faber,
Joyce Adkins, Matthew Mishkind, and Howard M. Weiss*

Approximately 1.5 out of every 100 male workers in the United States serves on active duty in the military (Military Family Resource Center 2002; U.S. Census Bureau 2003). One additional male out of every 100 serves in the national guard or reserve (Military Family Resource Center 2002; U.S. Census Bureau 2003). More than eighty-nine times between 1975 and 2001, U.S. military members were deployed to locations around the world to serve as peacekeepers (e.g., Operation Joint Guardian in Bosnia), to provide humanitarian aid (e.g., Operation Avid Response in Turkey), or to engage in armed conflict (e.g., Operation Desert Storm in Kuwait) (Center for Defense Information 2004). At the time of writing, estimates are that over 150,000 military members are deployed in the Middle East ("US forces" 2004). Although many of these members are mothers, this chapter focuses explicitly on fathers because their deployments have received far less attention with regard to parenting.

Children who grow up in military families experience multiple separations from their military parent lasting anywhere from a few days to many months. About 44 percent of active duty military members and 38 percent of members of the guard and reserve have children, about two-thirds of whom are younger than fourteen. Today, more than 750,000 children in the United States are under age fourteen and have a parent serving in the military (Military Family Resource Center 2002).

During deployments, military fathers become "nonresidential." They both resemble and differ from other nonresidential fathers in important ways. Like long-haul truckers and commercial fishermen, deployed military fathers are repeatedly separated from their families, sometimes for prolonged periods of time, because of work demands. Like incarcerated fathers, deployed military fathers are not free to visit their families when they wish. And like divorced fathers, deployed military fathers depend heavily on mothers for contact with children. Unlike any of these fathers, however, deployed military fathers are expected to be prepared to risk their lives engaging in armed combat. As has been the case with studies of other nonresidential fathers, we have only a limited understanding of deployed military fathers. They are rarely studied because they are difficult to recruit and retain as research participants, and military duties during deployment can be intense. Studies of the effects of deployment on children often conceptualize fathers simply as "absent" (e.g., Amen, Jellen, Merves, and Lee 1988; Hiew 1992; Jensen, Grogan, Xenakis, and Bain 1989).

The editors of this volume have proposed a framework for understanding how "physical sites and social settings" (Marsiglio, Roy, and Fox, chapter 1) affect men's thoughts and actions as fathers. Military deployments offer a provocative and instructive opportunity to learn about the power of settings, with the potential to generate insights about how fathers encounter and deal with challenges to their involvement as parents. In this chapter, our goal is to use the editors' framework to understand the experiences of fathers recently returned from military deployments. We document the experiences of these fathers, discuss their connections to fathers' thoughts and behavior, and speculate about the utility of the framework for future research.

METHODS

Data were gathered through focus groups conducted with twenty-seven fathers at Walter Reed Army Medical Center in Washington, D.C. over a four-day period in the summer of 2004. Participants were recruited through announcements made at morning and afternoon formations, occasions where all soldiers were required to assemble. Interested soldiers were screened to ensure they met the following eligibility criteria: U.S. military service member, father of child(ren) younger than eighteen, returned from a deployment within the past twelve months, no life-threatening or incapacitating injury or cognitive impairment due to illness, injury, or medication. Eligible soldiers then were scheduled for a focus group. The number of participants in each focus group ranged from two to six individuals. Each focus group lasted approximately two hours and consisted of a series of open-ended questions used to stimulate discussion. Participants referred to themselves and to one another using pseudonyms they chose; those pseudonyms are also used in this chapter.

Most of the participants were military police in the Army, who had recently returned from deployments to the Middle East (n = 22), Guantanamo Bay, Cuba (n = 3), or in the United States (n = 2). All of the participants had been evacuated from their deployments for medical reasons; hence their presence at Walter Reed Army Medical Center. None of their physical conditions was life-threatening or incapacitating (e.g., arm injuries, herniated disks). Although the sample was small and homogeneous in terms of military job, the participants were diverse in terms of their military and marital histories, ages of their children, and locations of service. Most participants had been deployed multiple times—up to five—but ten had just completed their first deployment. Most participants (n = 15) were members of the national guard, seven were reservists, and one was active duty (four participants did not report their status). Most participants were African American (n = 22), and most were married (n = 21); the remainder were divorced (n = 4), separated (n = 1) or engaged (n = 1). Most participants had more than one child or stepchild (ten had two children or stepchildren, ten had three or more children or stepchildren). Children ranged in age from one to twenty-six.

The design of the focus group protocol was based on the conceptual framework proposed by Marsiglio, Roy, and Fox (chapter 1). For example, to get at the issue of transitional elements, we asked fathers, "How do you switch roles, from combat to peacetime, from warrior to father, and back?" The focus groups were audiotaped and transcribed verbatim. N6 software (QSR International Pty Ltd 2002) was used for analyses. Each author coded transcripts for the elements of the conceptual framework. Early in the process a coding meeting was held to discuss the conceptual clarity of the data associated with each element and to make coding decisions. For example, we decided that infrastructure for communication was a "physical condition," while rules for access to communication were "institutional policies." We then returned to the transcripts and coded each for all elements. Each author then wrote a summary of a subset of elements and read them to the group. Group discussions were held to ensure once again that each element was as conceptually distinct as possible and that the descriptions fairly represented the transcripts.

FINDINGS

Not surprisingly, there is considerable overlap among the various physical, temporal, and social elements of settings. For this reason, we group elements of the conceptual model in our presentation of findings. We begin with the spatial and temporal elements of the setting, which also includes the juxtaposition of public and private spaces.

Space and Time

The experiences of deployed fathers are heavily defined by both space and time. Space includes not only immediate physical conditions but also location on the planet. In turn, location on the planet had a great deal to do with the degree to which time posed challenges for fathers.

Physical Conditions

The fathers stationed in Iraq experienced primitive living conditions, especially those soldiers who arrived early in the war or were members of mobile units. The extreme heat, sand storms, and sand fleas made it difficult for soldiers to stay focused on their job or to sleep, particularly after twelve- to sixteen-hour workdays.

As American forces became more established in Iraq, more permanent base camps were established, with bathroom facilities and tents equipped with cots, wooden floors, and—sometimes—air conditioning. For fathers deployed to Guantanamo Bay, living conditions were less austere from the beginning. There, the soldiers in our focus groups lived in townhouses with air conditioning, cable television, and Internet access. Regardless of location, the fathers described their military duties as unpleasant and dangerous. Soldiers in the war zone reported constantly feeling in danger, as did Gator, a divorced reservist father of two children and veteran of three deployments.

> One time I let down my guard thinking that it was just a little bit safe but got a quick reality check. A soldier was shot right in the neck in the Market Square and that was deemed a secure zone. So you never know.

Fathers' access to communication with their families varied widely as a function of physical location and conditions. Communication facilities were very sparse for soldiers who arrived early in the Iraqi conflict, for whom weeks or even months passed without talking to their families. According to Roy, a national guardsman with three children on his first deployment,

> A lot of us had laptops but we had no way to hook up to the Internet, and then once a signal came in we had to fight for the signal. . . . We went almost the whole year without contacting our families.

Land mail sometimes was not delivered because of attacks on convoys and theft along the way, and slow when it was delivered, taking an average of two months. Fathers accustomed to daily contact with their children found the isolation difficult to tolerate.

As conditions improved, satellite phones and computers were installed at some base camps. In addition, soldiers who were stationed at more permanent locations or whose job required the use of computers, such as supply sergeants, had access to the Internet, video cameras, and cell phones. Despite the improved infrastructure, however, soldiers reported having to wait in line for six or seven hours to be given only ten to fifteen minutes of use, or to be denied access entirely by telephone malfunction or by enemy attacks.

Temporal Dynamics

Fathers deployed to Iraq faced many challenges in timing their military duties with their contact with families, including the time difference, constant movement from one location to another, and work schedules.

> It's like a six-hour difference, if you call at 3:00 in the morning the kid sometimes dead asleep. A lot of times I had to wake my kid up at 3:00 in the morning just to talk to him because, the flip side of it, the other times, I'm trying to protect my life. (CJ, national guardsman with a five-year-old son and two grown daughters)

> It's hard to catch up to a soldier if you're moving. If you're constantly moving they can't, sometimes they don't even find you, takes 'em months to find your unit. So it [communication] really takes a long time. . . . So, the gap between there, lots of things could happen that you didn't pick up on that were going on at home. (Rock, national guardsman with twenty-one years and five deployments, father of four children ages one to seventeen)

Fathers in Cuba had an easier time because they had more communication facilities, more predictable work schedules, and were located in a time zone closer to home. Nonetheless, their communication time was rationed, making it difficult to juggle communications with every family member. CJ described rationing the two 15-minute telephone calls he was permitted each week:

> You try to talk to the grandson and my wife at home and then you try to talk to your daughter away at school, you know, and then I have my oldest daughter; if I don't get to talk to her, she's feels left out even though she's twenty-six years old. You see what I'm saying, it's unfair.

Fathers expressed some ambivalence about contact with their families. On the one hand, they craved contact as an important source of emotional support and a connection with the outside world. But family contact also caused tension because it had the potential to distract soldiers while they were on patrol.

Several soldiers, among them the father of four children younger than fourteen quoted below, commented that it took significant amounts of time to decompress from phone calls before they were fit for a mission.

> Because you have to refocus again after you get off that phone. Because then you get up and you're like missing he's crying on the phone, wife is crying on the phone, so you limit those calls home—as much as you want to, you don't want to. . . . At one time I was sitting there and my friend was like "come on, we gotta go on a mission" and I'm like "Can I go later?" because I didn't recuperate from that phone call and then I finally had to go back out again. Because when you got out you want to be focused, because if you're not focused the slightest thing will, your life or your buddy's, so you're responsible.

Private/Public

Because deployed soldiers are almost never truly off-duty or alone, they operate almost exclusively in public space. Most soldiers complained about the lack of privacy and the omnipresence of strangers watching and listening; with twelve and sometimes even seventy people in one tent, accommodations were tight and soldiers did their best to construct privacy for family conversations. Rock explained,

> Every time, I kind of like, looked around the guys were always like this [he covered his head and bent down and covered himself up and tried to muffle the sound so that people wouldn't hear what he was saying on the phone]. You're like, it doesn't matter, you can have this big, this big room but if you pick up the phone in Iraq, everybody was like this on the phone, just huddled in like one little corner.

On the other hand, the lack of privacy could sometimes be beneficial in that it promoted the sharing of stories, advice, and discourse about fathering with other fathers in the unit. According to JC, a national guardsman who had been deployed four times,

> Other dads will come up to you and say, "What should I do?" you know, "You think I should do this?" What would I do, I would do this, what would he do? I don't know. It does get, bonding, yes, is it natural, yes.

Fathers' public and private worlds collided to affect their parenting in two major ways. First, fathers experienced the tension between wanting to answer their children's difficult questions and reassure them, but needing also to avoid revealing information that could compromise the safety of the fathers themselves. CJ said,

You can say, "Hello, how are you doing in school?" and that kind of thing but if they start to ask you questions that you can't answer and you're sitting on the other end looking stupid like, "Okay, my kid is asking me a difficult question here and I can't answer it because of the security reasons." And you know you go through a thousand briefings about what you can say and what you can't say. . . . It's hard to communicate with your family and tell them what they really need to know so that they can have kind of have some kind of closure, or some kind of understanding of what you're doing.

Public and private domains also collided when television news brought the public events of the war into the private space of the home with vivid images of military action. The existence of twenty-four-hour news frequently dictated how fathers conversed with their children. Again, this illustrates the dual role of soldier—trying to maintain security—and father—trying to respond to children's questions. T, a married national guardsman with twenty years of experience and one deployment, wanted to manage the exposure of his fifteen-year-old child:

One of the main problems I was having was he [son] was watching the news a lot, and I told his mother to keep him away from it 'cause I don't want him . . . to try to see . . . 'cause he knows I drive trucks and a lot of convoys are getting hit.

The fathers in this study who were deployed under combat or wartime conditions, particularly on the front lines of armed conflicts, focused heavily on basic necessities of life—safety, sleep, and hygiene. The physical conditions of their deployment were unpredictable and unstable. Accommodations depended on whatever was available at their location, and fathers in Iraq moved frequently with little notice. Fathers who experienced such isolation and uncertainty seemed particularly invested in contact with their families, providing detailed and emotional descriptions of both the importance and the risks of such contact. For fathers with access to computers and the Internet, cyberspace in the form of electronic mail, Internet video, and cellular telephones supplemented more conventional modes of communication. In many ways, the online environment functioned as "psychological space" (Suler 2002), stretching the definition of fathers' presence. Especially in Iraq, the temporal features of deployment were particularly striking. Fathers' job duties were extensive, demanding, and frequently changing. Fathers had little control or foreknowledge of their schedules, and the time difference between Iraq and home made it very difficult to reliably reach children.

Deployed fathers must negotiate fatherhood without access to private space and without sharing physical space with their children. Nonetheless, fathers' public roles as soldiers and their private roles as husbands and fathers repeatedly came head-to-head, challenging fathers to simultaneously serve two masters, caring for their children but also fulfilling their responsibilities for safety and security.

Sociocultural Context

Marsiglio, Roy, and Fox (chapter 1) describe the social structural aspect of settings as a "negotiated normative order," a description particularly apt of the military. A total institution, the military requires 24/7 availability of its members and imposes a myriad of regulations and resources in areas ranging from housing to health care to family preparation for deployments. As such, the military is both a culture—with macrolevel policies, traditions, and expectations—and an institution driven by policies and programs. For military members deployed to isolated areas with few resources, distinguishing between the culture and the institution must be nearly impossible because of their total reliance on the military for life's necessities.

Social Structural

When asked to characterize the culture of the military regarding soldiers' families, the fathers we spoke with offered slogans they had heard repeatedly from military leaders or colleagues. The most common example was "Mission first, family second." Another example was, "If the army had meant for you to have a family, it would have issued you one."

Although it would probably be a mistake to conclude that the military is more hierarchical than large private employer organizations, it certainly has an explicit and visible hierarchical social order. Nonetheless, it was also clearly a negotiated order. Fathers' accounts suggested that commanders had considerable discretion to act supportively or unsupportively toward family issues (we use "commander" as a generic term for military superiors, not as an indication of any particular rank or level in the organization). Because of the frequent rotations of leadership that are common across the military, some fathers had a good basis for their observations, like A, a veteran of two deployments:

> I worked for one guy and he came and introduced himself, said "You know what? This is how I feel. I'm going to tell you. I been to wars, I got kids—don't care about them, don't care about their mother, don't care how long we gonna work." I've been with some that on Fridays he would try to get, if the people that were married, you know, and had a little kid, they would try to get you all [off], but he would also compensate the single people also. So it just depends on who you work for.

In fathers' accounts, both they and commanders connected family concerns directly to performance of military duties, as opposed to treating them simply as a morale issue.

> Some leaders will say, "Well, you know if your family's not right then I can't use you. You need to go take care of that and then when you come back. Until your family is taken care of you ain't no good to me." (C, a married national guardsman with one child)

Commanders' actions directly impacted not only soldiers but also their families when commanders made decisions about soldiers' travel home for family reasons. Fathers told stories of being denied permission to travel home to be with an ill spouse or to be present for the birth of a child. At the other extreme, one commander involved his wife in sending e-mails to update soldiers about administrative matters that were being pursued on their behalf. Participants in our focus groups rarely distinguished between superiors immediately above them and superiors at higher levels of the organization, but when they did, it was to give examples of inconsistency, or policy decisions at one level being contradicted by decisions at another.

Culture also is constructed with coworkers and peers. Here, too, there was diversity, but, in general, fathers described supportive and sympathetic treatment by colleagues. Here is an example by D, a married reservist with two children:

> The people that I was dealing with . . . we had an understanding. If there was something wrong with your child or something wrong at home, we'd be like, "Okay, go handle your business, we'll cover for you." But then you have some people who say burn the bridge at both ends, constantly using that excuse.

L, a married guardsman with two children, noted that single people in Iraq had volunteered to give up two-week leaves so that married soldiers could visit home.

Institutional Conditions

According to Marsiglio, Roy, and Fox (chapter 1), institutional conditions comprise "explicit or informal organizational policies about how space is to be used and how fathers can navigate within it." Certainly the military does not suffer from a lack of policies. Fathers specifically mentioned policies related to pay and military allowances, which affected wives' effort in the labor force; redeployment, which could result in very short intervals between deployments; and family visits, which made it difficult to know whether or when they could see their families or to afford to do so.

Because military policies are so comprehensive, they tend to extend and reify the privileges of military rank. For active-duty soldiers, access to on-base housing, various financial allowances, and housing standards all become more generous at higher ranks. Perhaps as a result, fathers had much to say about social disparity, although less from the perspective of their status as fathers as from their statuses as frontline soldiers and members of the national guard. During deployment, access to communication and conveniences were key ways that privilege was made evident:

> Commanders had the phones; they were using them constantly all the time. They had computers they were using we were not allowed to use. So, communication in my unit really sucked. (Mr. T., married father of four children)

Fathers in the national guard also objected to discrepancies in their treatment vis-à-vis active duty troops. One father with eleven years' service said the guard is treated as "a stepchild until the nation needs us."

Personal Power and Control

In some ways, military life seems to be a lesson in lack of control. Military members may have little choice about their duties, or where or when they must go to carry them out. Fathers commented that they had just a few days to a couple of weeks to get everything in order before being deployed, which caused hardship for their families and delayed activities like family vacations and children's events.

> My first deployment was for a year and it was at the Pentagon. Just when I thought I was going home, they hit me with a deployment to Cuba with no break or anything; a week later I was going to Cuba. It was tough on everybody, my wife, my children. You think you'll be back at work at your civilian job and, you know, back to your normal life, and it's like you get deployed but this time you're overseas and it's like nothing you can do about it. How can you fight it? (X, a national guardsman with eleven years' service and three deployments, married with two children)

We asked fathers about their experience of fathering from a distance and the degree to which they felt any control over their children's behavior during deployment. In general, fathers reported feeling little control over their ability to discipline or comfort their children, but there was considerable diversity in how fathers responded. Some fathers resigned themselves to the situation, as did T-bone, an engaged reservist father of two:

> You just have to let it go. At first you think maybe the first couple of weeks I still can play that role and then reality sets in where you just have to let it go.

Say, hey, you can't do nothing about it, you're here and there is nothing you can do about it.

Other fathers confronted feelings of powerlessness by developing strategies for active involvement. A few regularly contacted their children's teachers to check up on how their child was doing in school and work with the school on getting their child help if needed. Another father secretly told his family's friends and neighbors about tasks or errands that they could do to help his wife and children. Yet another father had his daughter e-mail him her future math assignments, which he would work on during down time and then be able to help her when he talked to her. T-bone described how many fathers turned to technology.

A lot of people started buying the video cameras and they started buying the camera phones. And a couple of people came in and we had a computer guy who was really great and would set your camera or your video cam into that computer; he would program it in, so you could get a live feed, but a lot of times you would have to call them, tell them to get online, but it was like you was on a time limit, so you had to do these things like quickly, but it did work out.

Some fathers were particularly purposeful and creative. One recorded himself reading children's stories before he was deployed. Then each evening his wife would play the video tape to his daughter so each night he was still able to read his daughter a bedtime story. Hadji, a married reservist with five children on his fifth deployment, found a way to "be at home" with his family even while he was in Iraq.

[to his wife on the phone] "I'm just listening—just leave the phone there and you can put it on speaker phone and I'll tell you when I have to go and I'll just listen, kind of like you were there." So I had the headset on working at my desk typing or doing something getting ready for another mission and I could hear them all in the background playing, talking, and everything. Then I'd finally have to say, "gotta go" and turn around and go take off and do what you need to.

For the military fathers we spoke with, personal power and control appeared to have a great deal to do with their thoughts and actions as fathers. Some deployed fathers felt as though they had no ability to control anything about their children's lives and resigned themselves to a distant, disengaged relationship. Other fathers, perhaps in different circumstances at home or at work, viewed the lack of control and power as a challenge to develop new techniques and strategies for active fathering.

The explicit and thoroughly institutionalized hierarchical structure of the military reinforced a variety of social disparities, according to our participants. Although they felt clearly disadvantaged as guardsmen and reservists, and members of lower ranks, the messages they received about their status as fathers were sometimes more positive, depending heavily on the views of particular superiors. Perhaps not surprisingly, the sheer size of the military bureaucracy, combined with the privileges of rank, provided commanders considerable latitude in granting soldiers access to their families, at least in the eyes of these fathers. Once again, uncertainty was an enormous factor in fathers' lives, because fathers knew that unless they took action they would be treated 'as a number.' As a result, fathers devoted considerable energy to negotiating their positions and one of the ways they described doing so most actively was with regard to family visits. A, a father of two children, seventeen and twenty-three, shared,

> Five months from the time we got into the country, my chain of command knew that I had a soldier whose wife was going to have a baby in a [month]. The whole time, "Yeah, we're working on it, we're working on it." . . . I checked on it weekly, daily, you know, "Lieutenant, what'd you hear? You find anything out from the commander?" "Yeah, we're working on it, we're working on it." We got back into Kuwait and it was, his baby was born [date], and we got back into Kuwait, it was like [seven days before] and he still didn't get to go home. . . . He's on R&R [the whole week] and they would not send him home! For no reason, because he's a number. Everybody's a number.

Interpersonal Context

Against the backdrop of the social and institutional context, we considered how fathers' ready-made definitions of and experiences with fathering influence the way they expressed themselves as fathers while deployed. Here we focused on fathers' perspectives about the symbolic elements of military service and how gender affects their attitudes.

Symbolic/Perceptual

Surprisingly, and perhaps because of the wording of our questions, fathers spoke very little about the symbolic meaning of military service, despite multigenerational involvement with the military in some families. Several fathers shared with Gator both his military heritage and his socialization by several members of his extended family.

> I lost my father at an early age, but he was a Navy man, so I got a good eight years, you know, being the first one, so I knew what discipline was about and as far as responsibility. And after he died, my mother, her two aunts, and my one uncle raised us, you know, and we turned out pretty fine because we had strong family values and that's where I got it from and still continue on.

Despite strong connections between the soldier and father roles (described below), fathers typically did not mention discussing the symbolic meaning of military service with their children. Instead, fathers' descriptions (and children's questions) tended to focus on very concrete and explicit aspects of daily experience—their safety, their location, their physical circumstances, and their duties.

Gendered Attributes

In general, fathers expressed strongly gendered views of their family roles, focusing primarily on themselves as authority figures and/or providers. Although several fathers focused explicitly on disciplining children and their ability to be more effective than their wives, being deployed significantly limited their options in this regard. Fathers also clearly saw themselves as providers for their families, both of economic and other resources. Consistent with military expectations of careful preparation by families for deployment, C focused on making arrangements for financial stability, as well as preparing his wife and fourteen-year-old daughter for the impending separation:

My method was before I left I was trying to make, put things in place so things can go smoothly while I was gone. I would spend more time, I would switch, you know, maybe this Sunday . . . allow her to go away with her friends because then she can get used to me not being around her a lot. Then when it came down to the financial side of the house, that's when I dug in and saved money so, you know, I didn't have to worry about, you know, what's not getting paid at home. And then I can focus on what I'm doing here so I can get back. So I set myself up in a way that everybody can be comfortable when I am gone.

Despite their somewhat traditional views about the authority and provider elements of their roles, fathers also acknowledged flexibility in allocating their previous family responsibilities to their wives during deployment. But responsibilities within families also evolved over time, as D, a married reservist with two children, described.

During my first deployment I was pretty much the person that did everything as far as paying the bills, because when we married she was pretty young, she was nineteen. So, I was like, I was basically doing everything. And then after that first deployment I showed her how to pay the bills and take care of everything and when I came back I found that my wife was more mature after I had gotten back after that first deployment. She had the kids' school work and she'd paid all the bills so she had grown up. So, when the second deployment came up it was no problem for her as far as taking care of the household and running things.

Fathers also described changes over time in their view of their parental roles, toward greater involvement in traditionally feminine tasks:

> Everyday I would pick [them] up from the sitter's, I come home and I cook dinner, you know, feed the kids and give them their baths, you know, just the routine everyday. . . . I give them that quality time outside, we play around for a while, . . . big joke about me being the house mom, but, you know, I'm proud of that house mom role, I ain't going to lie. It's just spending time with them, because, just because of the last deployment we did, you know, I wasn't even with my son, I wasn't really involved too much, you know, . . . as far as spending the time that I wanted to spend with him. I didn't get a chance to do it, you know, because the deployment came up real fast. So I'm proud of myself with the last one, that I was going to be more with him and spend a lot more time. (B, a married guardsman with two deployments and two children, one and three)

During deployment, fathers depended on their wives for support and assistance. Several fathers commented that supportive spouses could make things much easier—and unsupportive ones could cause great difficulty. One way that this played out was in wives' actions to support or limit communication with children. Some wives acted as stage setters, explained L, a guardsman with eight years in the military and two children, eight and ten:

> Everybody has been very supportive. . . . My wife makes sure if I would call or communicate that they [the children] would be there or they would be up, you know. I would usually let her know when I was gonna call, and so she would prearrange with them, you know, with the boys so I could talk with them.

Fathers also reported, however, that wives acted as gate keepers, purposely withholding information about children's problems to avoid distracting or worrying them. One father in this situation was T, a married national guardsman with twenty years of military experience:

> The only thing I have a problem with her is, she don't want to tell me everything what he's not doin', you know. He's like staying up like fifteen, like fourteen (years old) staying out till one or two o'clock in the morning and she didn't tell me. . . . I have a problem with that.

Fatherhood Discourses

The discourses that contributed to fathers' understanding during deployment were those that occurred with their children and with other soldiers. Given the hierarchical nature of military life, it is perhaps not surprising that the soldier role sometimes flowed over to shape fathers' approaches to parenting, in particular regarding discipline; we label this "soldier as father."

> I don't have to raise my voice. . . . You can use the soldier part of it but use it in terms we all know how to be disciplinarians. Not like the old movies where you have your son/daughter marching and all that. It is just the discipline part of the lessons instilled in you; you can convert that into everyday discipline of your kids or praise your kids. (B, a national guardsman with two deployments, father of two children, one and three)

We were more surprised by the degree to which fathers articulated how their experiences as fathers influenced their actions as soldiers. Sometimes this was an uncomplicated positive experience, such as when fathers felt they were able to be especially supportive of a younger soldier because of the patience and understanding they developed as parents. In other instances, the connection was much more complicated, presenting fathers like Mr. T, a father of four, with simultaneous but competing urges to care for young Iraqi children, soldiers under their command, and their own children (by preserving their own safety).

> I used to separate the two. It's like when you leave . . . and you go out on a mission, now you're a soldier. Now you're responsible; if you're a gunner, you're responsible for those two inside the vehicle. And when you would drive out there you would see them little kids; that hit you, like, that's the same age as my son. He's like four and he's standing there in the hot sun—I can't even take the heat—145°, barefooted on the black tar, just standing there, "Mister, mister, mister, mister, food?" Now you're like, you've got to play a little father role and go back to the soldier and be like, you gotta do a flip like real quick. Because then you can't buy into it. Because from when, it never happened to me, but they were saying that they were using the kids to distract you and then they got you. So I would look around real quick and MREs [meals ready to eat] that nobody was eating I would give it to them and it's like, "Thank-you, thank-you," and they would run. They don't eat it right there, they take it home and I guess they share it. . . . So you had to flip those two roles, father role, soldier role; you just can't get caught up out there, out on the wire, being a father in a situation like that. You just, you're going to be in trouble. You're going to cost everybody their life.

The fathers' military training and often stern parental figures appeared to contribute an interest in respect, responsibility, and authority that they sought to teach their own children. In contrast to the traditionally masculine attitudes of wanting to lead and provide for their families, many of the fathers had been trained by female relatives during childhood to be competent at traditionally feminine tasks like household work and child care. Also, the shift schedules of their civilian jobs and the repeated deployments of their military jobs demanded that fathers and their partners display some flexibility in allocating responsibilities over time. For most participants, their father and soldier roles tended to meld, challenging fathers to monitor and manage a boundary between them for their own safety and the quality of relationships with their children.

Coming Home: Transitional Elements

In contrast to fatherhood experienced in discrete physical settings, transitions explore how men negotiate fatherhood when moving from one site to another. Such transitions involve a change not only in physical, but also psychological and interpersonal, space (Cowan 1991).

The deployment experience and the reunion that follows are examples of normative transitions in military family life. When fathers return from deployment, the whole family needs to readjust to changes and new expectations associated with the return to civilian life. One of the biggest challenges military fathers face is how to reestablish a relationship and close bond with their children. As one soldier put it, "Each time we see each other it's like a getting back to know each other again." Fathers in this study employed a number of strategies to reconnect with their children, depending on the age of their children, their deployment history, how long they had been away, and the nature of the father–child relationship(s) before and during deployment. Fathers with infants reported the most difficulty since many of them got deployed before they had an opportunity to grow attached to their children.

> My son had just come home, my wife had just had him and [then when] we got home I got deployed. So the only thing he had to remind him of me was I went out and took a picture of myself in uniform and I let her hang in on the refrigerator so when she walks past she just says, "There's daddy," so when I got home, well . . . when I walked in the door, my son like flipped. He saw a ghost. He started screaming. It was a whole month before I could touch him.

Fathers acknowledged that it would require considerable time and patience and that the process of gaining their children's trust could not be rushed. Fathers talked about "letting them come to me" and "not forcing myself onto my children . . . but let them feel comfortable enough to come to me." Or, as another father described, "He didn't want to come close to me, he just stayed away from me for like the whole [time]. You just stay back and stay back until I took him to the toy store and that's how we got back."

Overseas deployments and their accompanying reunion represent one type of major transition that fathers and their families experience. Perhaps equally stressful, however, were the frequent moves that these injured and ill fathers made back and forth from their private lives at home to their public role as soldiers at the Walter Reed Army Medical Center. Even though their short-term leaves were appreciated, fathers described their children as having difficulty with the ambiguity and anxiety associated with the multiple arrivals and departures.

> When you're overseas, they know you're over there; there's no chance of you coming over for a week or a couple of days. Over here, like, they release us, like, on Friday and we have a pass, or we go home for that certain amount of days and we come back, or we go leave and come back. So that gives the kids mixed emotions, too; it's like you're leaving then you come back, you're leaving then you come right back, so and I know that bothers my daughter tremendous. She always says, "Daddy, well, why don't you just stop coming and going, either stay or leave." (W, a married national guardsman with eight years' experience and two deployments, with three children, nine, eleven, and thirteen)

A number of fathers reported that even after they had been home, children repeatedly kept asking, "Are you going back, are you going back?" and despite reassurances from one father, it took them about two weeks to realize that he wasn't going back. In another case the father was unable to reassure his child, stating, "I don't know. I ain't trying to go back but you know I can't say yes, I can't say no." Consistent with other research (e.g., Bell and Schumm 1999) short-term leaves, while appreciated, were also stressful.

In addition to the need to reconnect with their children, the transition of returning home also demanded that fathers reassume their parenting roles. Not surprisingly, the ease or difficulty of doing this depended on many factors, but particularly upon the child's developmental age. Those who were more successful generally had more deployment experience and older children, such as Gator.

> Mine, she's fifteen and . . . I've been through several deployments, too. Just had to change tactics a little bit. . . . She's going through those changes as a woman, young female things of that nature. I just let her tell me what's going on. I approached it from that angle as far as easing back into it and not just stepping back in, instead of just jumping back into the role and taking over.

Typically, however, fathers stated that reentry into the fathering unfolded over time, ranging from two weeks to several months. Lengthy deployments and limited communication seemed to make some fathers unprepared for the changes in their children, even fathers with considerable military experience like Clark, a veteran of five deployments:

> I found my daughters had grown up. . . . I've been deployed for about two and a half [years], and . . . no boy wasn't around and you wasn't dropping no notes

off at no boy. Now I'm like, "What happened?" I done missed two years of
something. . . . You know, there's a big difference now . . . and they talking more
out of their mouth and there's a big difference if you're with girls and you left
and they wasn't menstruating two and a half years ago and you come back and
they're menstruating now.

One of the reasons for difficulties with the reunion/readjustment process,
particularly after a lengthy deployment, might be fathers' style of interacting
at home. Some fathers reported that they had to be reminded by their wives
that they "weren't talking to any prisoners, . . . any punks, . . . [or] any soldiers." Fathers mimicked their children's comments and questions: "Dad's
back home, he's still in the bossy mood, he's used to ordering people around
so it'll take a while for him to get out of that again. . . . Dad why you gotta
be so mean?" or "Dad's back, what's wrong with Dad?"

Despite the frequent challenges in navigating the reciprocal transitions between military and civilian life, not all transitions were stressful or problematic. Nor were all children reluctant to interact with their long-absent fathers.
Indeed, as one father stated, "Once I got back I couldn't even sit and rest because they wanted me to go everywhere and do everything with them." Many
reunions were happy joyful events in which "kids were all over you, basically
just running up to you, hugging and stuff."

DISCUSSION

We aimed to document the experiences of deployed fathers as a function of
the physical, temporal, and social elements of their settings. The fathers were
deployed great distances away from their families, for long periods of time,
with limited and unpredictable access to communication with their families
and limited ability to speak freely even when they were in contact. Many fathers devoted considerable effort to maintaining contact but at the same time
expressed ambivalence about its effects on their ability to concentrate on their
military duties.

Military culture, especially fathers' commanders, conveyed mixed messages to fathers about their family's importance. Some commanders were
very supportive, interpreting family problems as potential threats to the performance of military duties; others admonished soldiers to keep family issues
out of the workplace. Fathers attributed a variety of social disparities related
to rank, gender, and active versus guard or reserve status to the military's organization and policies. Some fathers struggled with their inability to control
family events.

Although deployed fathers expressed strongly gendered views, emphasizing their roles as authority figures and providers, they also described flexibility and evolution in their roles over successive deployments. They relied on children's mothers not only for access to children but also for maintenance of the household. Fathers often experienced complex juxtapositions of their roles as soldiers and fathers, which sometimes persisted into the transition home.

What were the implications of deployed fathers' experiences for involvement with their children? Clearly, deployment imposed severe limitations. Using Lamb and colleagues' (1987; see also Pleck and Masciadrelli 2004) definition of involvement, fathers were not easily accessible and had very limited opportunities to engage in direct interaction with their children. Despite and perhaps because of their lack of accessibility and limited engagement, many deployed fathers expressed a strong sense of responsibility for what was happening to their children. Of course, this is not the same as being physically present, but deployed fathers appeared to be far from absent from their families, despite being labeled as such in prior research.

Deployment is a stressful experience for families. In part, this may be because so much about deployment is uncertain and unpredictable (e.g., Eastman, Archer, and Ball 1990; Jensen, Lewis, and Xenakis 1986). Ambiguity associated with a family member's absence is a situation or event that Boss (2002) refers to as ambiguous loss; how the family perceives this ambiguous loss is called boundary ambiguity. Military deployment is a good example of ambiguous loss with the potential to cause boundary ambiguity. Families adjust to deployment by reallocating responsibilities and reorganizing boundaries. When the military member returns, families must "reopen" their boundaries, reallocating and reorganizing once again.

From fathers' accounts, the uncertainty and ambiguity associated with fathers' arrivals and departures were particularly stressful for young children who lacked the cognitive capacity to understand time (i.e., the difference between long and short absences) and space (i.e., the difference between deployment in Iraq and medical treatment at Walter Reed). Existing research suggests that children's well-being during deployments tends to be very much a function of the well-being of the parent at home (Jensen 1992). Findings also show that separation from deployed fathers is just as important for children's outcomes as separation from deployed mothers (Applewhite and Mays 1996). The social cultural environment of the military is similar to that of divorced fathers in terms of rule and regulations that limit the amount of control or involvement they may have with their children (Pasley and Minton 1997). However, military fathers may have more motivation to remain involved in their children's lives than do divorced fathers. For military fathers, staying connected and involved in one's family may provide a source of support to combat the harsh physical conditions of war.

Finally, we found Marsiglio and colleagues' framework (chapter 1) useful because of the detail it contains. Of course, the elements of any setting are very interconnected and any attempt to consider them separately will seem arbitrary at times. Nonetheless, we experienced some difficulty in our coding with regard to the social/structural and institutional/cultural elements. In part this was because the military is both a social system and an institution for deployed fathers. We might be inclined to reorganize these elements as social/cultural and institutional/structural. Designations of properties as primary or secondary were not always intuitive.

FUTURE RESEARCH

Although this small study offers new insights about deployed military fathers, a group that has received relatively little prior attention, there are significant limitations. We spoke with only a small number of fathers, most of whom were military police serving in the army. Some fathers may have emphasized some points of view in focus groups more than they would have in private interviews. We also have only fathers' retrospective perspectives, with no corroborating evidence from their wives or children. Nevertheless, this study can inform future research about both civilian and military nonresidential fathers.

Although characteristics of the physical setting shaped communication by influencing the availability of and access to technology, individual fathers responded differently to these constraints. Thus future research should explore the frequency, methods, and content of communication and their implications for the deployment and reunion experiences of parents and children. For example, experimental studies could manipulate the availability of particular technologies to understand their influence on fathers' well-being, contact with their children, military commitment and performance, and the ease of reentry to life at home. Prospective longitudinal studies could track father–child relationships prior to deployment and then changes in those relationships as a function of the nature of communication during deployment.

Given fathers' uncertainties about what information they should share with their children, future research also could focus on the implications of communication content for relationships during and after separation. For example, what issues do fathers and children stress in their letters, e-mails, and phone calls? How do fathers "do fathering" by what they include or exclude, and how do these decisions differ as a function of children's gender, age, status as biological or stepchildren, or other characteristics? How do children with particular characteristics respond to particular types of communication? In general, there is an urgent need for studies of the cumulative effect of deployments on military children and their relationships with their fathers. We were struck by some fathers' disengagement and wonder if long gaps in communication early in deployment have a chilling effect on later interactions during and after the deployment.

Clearly the reunion journey of military fathers varies widely as a function of both fathers' and children's characteristics, and also the behavior of children's mothers. Understanding the process more clearly would help military policymakers and educators who design intervention programs and parent-training models to better prepare parents and children for deployment and reunion (Lamb, Chuang, and Cabrera 2003). Researchers could interview parents and children during separations, then track changes in parents' well-being and their strategies for managing children's behavior. We also know little about how fathers manage the transitions between being a warrior, husband, father, and peacetime worker.

Future study of nonresidential military fathers may offer useful insights regarding the involvement of civilian fathers with their children and vice versa, helping to better explain why some fathers appear to abdicate their relationships with their children (Seltzer and Brandreth 1995). For example, fathers' relationships with the mothers of their children, both in terms of legal status and amicability, are important influences on fathers' relationships with their children, and this is likely to be especially true for deployed military fathers.

REFERENCES

Preparation of this manuscript was supported in part by the Military Family Research Institute with funding from the U.S. Department of Defense (DASW01-00-2-0005, S. MacDermid and H. Weiss, coprincipal investigators). The opinions expressed are those of the authors and do not necessarily represent the official position or policy of the Department of Defense. We appreciate assistance from Walter Reed Army Medical Center, the editors and reviewers, and our colleagues at MFRI, including Eric Welch and Andrew Behnke. Thanks also to the fathers who participated. Address correspondence to Shelley MacDermid at: Purdue University, 101 Gates Road, West Lafayette, IN 47907 (shelley@purdue.edu).

Amen, D. G., Jellen, L., Merves, E., and Lee, R. E. (1988). Minimizing the impact of deployment separation on military children: Stages, current prevention efforts, and system recommendations. *Military Medicine, 15,* 441–46.
Applewhite, L. W., and Mays, R. A. (1996). Parent–child separation: A comparison of maternally and paternally separated children in military families. *Child and adolescent social work journal, 13,* 23–39.

Bell, B. D., and Schumm, W. R. (1999). Family adaptation to deployments. In Peggy McClure (Ed.), *Pathways to the future: A review of military family research* (pp. 109–33). Scranton, PA: Marywood University.

Boss, P. (2002). *Family stress management: A contextual approach* (2nd ed.). Thousand Oaks, CA: Sage.

Center for Defense Information. (2004). U.S. military deployments/engagements. Retrieved August 19, 2004, from www.cdi.org/issues/USForces/deployments.html

Cowan, P. A. (1991). Individual and family life transitions: A proposal for a new definition. In P. A. Cowan and M. Hetherington (Eds.), *Family transitions* (pp. 3–30). Hillsdale, NJ: Erlbaum.

Daly, K. J. (1995). Reshaping fatherhood: Finding the models. In W. Marsiglio (Ed.), *Fatherhood: Contemporary theory, research, and social policy* (pp. 21–40). Thousand Oaks, CA: Sage.

Eastman, E., Archer, R. P., and Ball, J. D. (1990). Psychosocial and life stress characteristics of navy families: Family Environment Scale and Life Experiences Scale findings. *Military Psychology, 2,* 113–27.

Hiew, C. C. (1992). Separated by their work: Families with fathers living apart. *Environment and Behavior, 24,* 6–225.

Jensen, P. S. (1992). Military family life is hazardous to the mental health of children: Rebuttal. *Journal of the American Academy of Child and Adolescent Psychiatry, 31,* 985–87.

Jensen, P. S., Grogan, D., Xenakis, S. N., and Bain, M. W. (1989). Father absence: Effects on child and maternal psychopathology. *Journal of the American Academy of Child and Adolescent Psychiatry, 28,* 171–75.

Jensen, P. S., Lewis, R. L., and Xenakis, S. N. (1986). The military family in review: Context, risk, and prevention. *Journal of the American Academy of Child Psychiatry, 25,* 225–34.

Lamb, M. E., Chuang, S. S., and Cabrera, N. (2003). Promoting child adjustment by fostering positive paternal involvement. In R. M. Lerner, F. Jacobs, and D. Wertlieb (Eds.), *Handbook of applied developmental science* (Vol. 1, pp. 211–25). Thousand Oaks, CA: Sage.

Lamb, M. E., Pleck, J. H., Charnov, E. L., and Levine, J. A. (1987). A biosocial perspective on paternal behavior and involvement. In J. B. Lancaster, J. Altmann, A. S. Rossi, and L. R. Sherrod, (Eds.), *Parenting across the lifespan: Biosocial dimensions* (pp. 111–42). Hawthorne, NY: Aldine de Gruyter.

Marsiglio, W., Roy, K., and Fox, G. L. (2005). Situated fathering: A spatially sensitive and social approach. In W. Marsiglio, K. Roy, and G. L. Fox (Eds.), *Situated fathering: A focus on physical and social space.* Lanham, MD: Rowman & Littlefield.

Military Family Resource Center. (2002). *2002 demographics profile of the military community.* Arlington, VA: Military Family Resource Center.

Pasley, K., and Minton, C. (1997). Generative fathering after divorce and remarriage: Beyond the "disappearing dad." In A. J. Hawkins and D. C. Dollahite (Eds.), *Generative fathering: Beyond deficit perspectives* (pp. 118–33). Thousand Oaks, CA: Sage.

Pleck, J. H., and Masciadrelli, B. P. (2004). Paternal involvement by U.S. residential fathers. In M. E. Lamb (Ed.), *The role of the father in child development* (pp. 222–71). Hoboken, NJ: Wiley.

Seltzer, J. A., and Brandreth, Y. (1995). What fathers say about involvement with children after separation. In W. Marsiglio (Ed.), *Fatherhood: Contemporary theory, research, and social policy* (pp. 166–92). Thousand Oaks, CA: Sage.

Suler, J. (2002). The basic psychological features of cyberspace. In *The psychology of cyberspace.* Retrieved August 14, 2004 from www.rider.edu/suler/psycyber/basiccfeat.html (article orig. pub. 1996).

U.S. Census Bureau. (2003). *Statistical abstract of the United States: 2003* (123rd ed.). Washington, DC: U.S. Census Bureau.

U.S. forces order of battle—15 August 2004. (2004, August). Retrieved on August 23, 2004, from www.globalsecurity.org/military/ops/iraq_orbat.htm

III

FATHERING IN COMMUNITY SPACE

11

Farm Dads: Reconstructing Fatherhood, the Legacy of the Land, and Family in the Fields of the Midwest

Gregory Peter, Michael M. Bell, Susan K. Jarnagin,
and Donna Bauer

In 1845, while Henry David Thoreau was living the simple single life among the farm families of Concord, Massachusetts, he witnessed farm families next to him struggling to make ends meet with challenges from their livestock, weather, pests, weeds, and adopting the new John Deere plow. Yet he helped perpetuate the rural myth. As Coward and Smith stated in 1982, "The myth that is perpetuated portrays country living and family life as simple, pure, and wholesome; slower paced; free from pressures and tensions; and surrounded by pastoral beauty and serenity. In reality, rural life seldom matches this popular characterization, and many family scholars believe that it rarely did" (77).

Rural sociologists like Coward and Smith have moved beyond Thoreau by systematically analyzing the individual, social structural, and cultural aspects of rural family life. They made policy suggestions, provided outreach, and applied their research to real life-situations. Much of this research has appeared in the journal *Rural Sociology* since 1937. Sixty years since that first issue, Janet Bokemeier (1997), in her presidential address to the Rural Sociological Society, called for a greater research and applied focus on rural families and households.

Recent research in rural areas has taken heed of this call on several exciting paths such as documenting the challenges rural families face with changing rural gender ideologies (Campbell and Bell 2000; Meares 1997; Peter, Bell, Jarnagin, and Bauer 2000), an increase in poverty rates in rural families and female-headed households (Brown and Lichter 2004; McLaughlin, Gardner, and Lichter 1999; Snyder and McLaughlin 2004), changing rural family structure and stresses (Albrecht and Albrecht 1996; Conger and Conger 2002; Kassab, Luloff, and Schmidt 1995), the health care challenges for rural families, the opportunities and constraints for parental involvement, and the effects of the changing structure of agriculture on the family (Lorenz, Elder, Bao, Wickrama, and Conger 2000; Chan and Elder 2001; Israel, Beaulieu, and Hartless 2001). While much rural sociology research has focused on the entire household unit, family scholars increasingly have focused attention on aspects of fatherhood (Marsiglio, Amato, Day, and Lamb 2000a). This research informs our analysis of farm fathers by drawing attention to the significance of gender ideologies in shaping family life (Hobson 2002), the complexities of father involvement, challenges between fatherhood and work, and the social construction of the culture of fatherhood

Using interpretive analysis, we explore the challenges farm fathers face in interacting with their children, including variations in the market, environment, weather, seasons, technology, and structure of agriculture. Indeed, farm fathers' socially constructed identities are intimately tied to their family roles, as well as their land, livestock, and livelihood. Farming is an occupation that is a cultural way of life permeating multiple levels of empirical analysis. In our ethnographic study of farm fathers, we detail the difficulties they encounter juggling work and family life. We argue that in order for farm fathers to overcome these obstacles and stay completely present in family life, they must socially reconstruct their identities, the legacy of the land, connection to space and place, and the meanings of farm and family. We merge rural sociology and family studies literatures to provide a framework for understanding how farm fathers negotiate fatherhood.

IN THE FIELD

From 1994 to 2002, we gathered data from farm families in Iowa. Iowa has more prime agricultural soil than any other state and has the highest percentage of land under cultivation. Each member of the research team brought to the project different levels of familiarity with Iowa, agriculture, and a farm organization called the Practical Farmers of Iowa (PFI). Since it emerged in 1985, during the 1980s farm crisis, PFI has developed into Iowa's principal farmer-based sustainable agriculture organization. By 1995 membership in PFI had grown to nearly 750 members. PFI sponsors field days that are field trips to a farm that presents on-farm research trials in collaboration with Iowa State University Extension.

We conducted seventy face-to-face interviews ranging in length from one hour to five and a half hours, and utilized what we call co-structured procedures—we were open not only to the directions the researchers wanted to take the conversations but to the directions the participants wanted to take. As a team, we conducted taped interviews with individuals from thirty-five PFI households and thirty-five non-PFI households. All names in this chapter are pseudonyms to maintain strict confidentiality and follow human subjects guidelines for research.

Beyond the taped interviews, we came to know the farm households in more informal ways through farm stays of varying lengths. We helped bale hay, plant beans, slaughter chickens, fix refrigerators, repair jammed augers, repair planter wheels, and feed horses; sometimes we spent the night on participating farms.

This study of farm families was primarily ethnographic. Ethnography is a way of studying the social world that requires researchers to immerse themselves in the community. We realize that our presence in the field as social scientists affects the people and processes we study. Thus we minimized this infamous Hawthorne effect by having multiple researchers, varied sources of information, multiple levels of analysis, prolonged engagement, and member checking. We also are aware that the Becker principle applies to most social situations—the social structure persists whether the researcher is present or not. Ethnographer, Mitch Duneier (1999, 338), explains the Becker principle: "Most social processes have a structure that comes close to insuring that a certain set of situations will arise over time. These situations practically require people to do or say certain things because there are other things going on that . . . are more influential then the social condition of a fieldworker being present." Nevertheless, we realize that in the postmodern sense of human knowledge we may have only captured partial truths in this research (Clifford 1986). Historical processes and hegemonic power that are sometimes beyond our own awareness shape the interpretive lenses researchers apply.

Our ethnographic work is based primarily on an inductive approach. We did some initial background research on farm families, went into the field and gathered evidence, analyzed the evidence, came up with more questions, then went back into the field to do more research. In this chapter, we use this qualitative evidence, literature review, and our own theoretical grounding to analyze the social, environmental, and economic challenges farm fathers face. We conclude with suggestions for future research.

The Legacy of the Land

As already noted, we are far from being the first to explore the complexities Thoreau once noticed in farm families. In deconstructing the origins of the term "family farm," sociologists argue that both words are historically located. Just as the myths about ideal families of the 1950s have been smashed (Coontz 1997; LaRossa 2004, 1997), so, too, have the rural myths been destroyed regarding Grant "Woodish" farmers living on picture perfect fields of green, with well-trimmed houses and smiling families (Coward and Smith 1982; Flora, Flora, Spears, and Swanson 1992; Strange 1988). As family sociologists further debate the meaning of family, rural sociologists take on the changing definition of farm. Students in introductory rural sociology classes at land grant universities across the United States all memorize the four revolutions in the structure of agriculture ranging from the mechanical, petrochemical, and biogenetic to the managerial (Buttel, Larson, and Gillespie 1990; Bonanno 1994; Strange 1988). In previous research, we have shown how these revolutions have changed not only the structure of agriculture but also the social construction of self, family, community, and environment (Bell, Jarnagin, Peter, and Bauer 2004). Furthermore, we have argued that the gendering of the farm defines farmer identity as male while affecting the division of labor on the farm, ideologies of work, connections to nature, and the transition to what is called sustainable agriculture (Bell et al. 2004; Peter et al. 2000). In this section, we argue that a farm father's identity is reconstructed by the legacy of the land, his performance at work, and role strain. A field example clarifies our research goals.

Sue interviewed Clayton, a young PFI farmer in his early twenties, and his young bride in their rather rundown home in central Iowa. Sue noted their age and early marriage in her field notes as an indicator of rural farm cultural socialization. Clayton described his perception of family farm life.

> Being a farm family has a lot of stress is involved. The hours a farmer keeps sometimes, during harvest and during planting time, will tend to put stress on the marriage or on the parent/child relationship. It's tough sometimes . . . when the prices are not so good. You get a bad crop. There's a lot of worry where the money is going to come from.

Family farmers have basic concerns similar to their urban counterparts or nonfarm families such as health care, job security, and child care. However, rural studies show that family farmers often face greater financial instability, chronic stresses, inadequate housing, and less access to basic services such as health care, which often affects farm family well-being (Albrecht and Albrecht 1996; Conger and Conger 2002; Bokemeier and Garkovich 1991; Kassab et al. 1995). Sue's interview indicates that Clayton knew full well how family life can be affected by these stressors and that the agro-ecological processes of growing crops do not wait. The crops must be fertilized, planted, cultivated, and harvested at certain times of the season and in tune with local weather patterns. Clayton recognized these spatial and temporal constraints and the challenges they present to a farm father's life. Asked what he thought were important issues facing America today, Clayton responded,

The family thing. That's one of the things I'm concerned with. The way society goes and how it's going to be in ten to fifteen years when I'm raising children. I worry about the life and culture my kids grow up in.

Clayton, at twenty-one, is planning on having children and is also planning ahead for the challenges farm fathers face. He is also reflecting on the way he was socialized in his own family growing up. Sue did not ask him about having children, nor about family in this question; she was asking about America and the world, yet Clayton's world clearly includes children in the future. Asked where he gets his information on farming, he replied, "Personally, my best teacher has been my dad. I learned most of what I know from him." From a sociological point of view, Clayton is already forming his procreative and fatherhood identity—his understanding of what it will mean to be a father someday (Fox and Bruce 2001; Marsiglio and Hutchinson 2002).

As in Clayton's case, farm fathers often pass on farm knowledge to their sons, and it is not uncommon for a farmer to be working on the same piece of land his grandfather farmed. In Iowa, there are many century farms, farms that have been in the family for over one hundred years. This connection to geographic space and cultural place is another important part of a farm father's identity.

Sue interviewed Ryan, a non-PFI farmer in his forties, and his spouse at the kitchen table of their old farmhouse. They have five children and openly talked about their background. Ryan explained how he started farming:

We started out helping my father. He was—his health wasn't the best for farming anymore. He had some health problems so I had to kind of fill in, and then, basically, we started taking it over. I guess we just kind of moved into it because my Dad was wanting to retire, and all the other kids were moved and married and gone away. None of them were farmer candidates.

Elsewhere, we have documented how farming is almost an ethnic identity passed on from generation to generation (Bell et al. 2004). With this identity comes great investment, not only in physical labor but in the legacy of the land passed on to the next generation. Ryan was more or less pulled into taking over the family farm, rather than choosing to do so freely. Because of this, Sue explored Ryan's connection to the identity of "farmer" by asking him if he considered himself a farmer.

Yes, I do. I love to farm. I don't know if it's in my blood or it's just growing up doing it with my grandpa and my dad, but to just work with the soil. Yeah, I consider myself a farmer.

Ryan clearly connects his farmer identity to his father and grandfather before him, as well as the soil he depends on to make his living. In this sense, letting the farm get sold to someone else would have been turning down the legacy of the land that has been passed onto him.

Jeff, a PFI farmer in his forties, has three children ranging in age from seven to nineteen. Interviewed along with his wife, he responded to a question about whether he had the same farm as his father.

> Yeah, that's something that's kind of changed over time, too. I'm sure it is hard when you retire, and he's done it like this for forty years, along comes this kid who wants to do it differently. You know, I farmed with my Dad for several years, crop share, and it was . . . it's tough. I can get along with my Dad. Well . . . it really is tough 'cause I got into ridge tillage, and I contoured everything. My dad just thought I was nuts.

Compared to his father's forty-year-old farming practices, Jeff was trying out new environmentally friendly farming methods. His Dad may have thought he was nuts, but he was willing to let him try it anyway. Sue probed to discover if Jeff ever convinced his father that his way of farming the land was acceptable.

> Well, yeah, eventually I did. I think he's all for it now. In fact, recently, when we've gone to visit relatives or something—far away—and he'll be talking about it, he'll say, "Jeff has done this and this," and it really makes me feel good because he wouldn't have done that fifteen years ago. That's been rewarding. I think he likes the way I farm now.

Jeff was initially putting a strain on his relationship with his father but also taking a chance with the legacy of the land, something deeply rooted in both of their socially constructed identities. This is a different dynamic for farm fathers than fathers in some professions. For example, while a university professor may pass on the love of knowledge and teaching to his children, he cannot pass on his post at the university and most likely would not even be concerned about passing on the house and the yard the children grew up on. For the university professor, the legacy may be different from the land. For Jeff's father, however, the legacy is safe, and he is free to brag to the relatives about it. But what about when Jeff retires in twenty years? According to the 2002 USDA Census of Agriculture, the age of Iowa farmers is increasing, with over half being over fifty-five. We found great concern out in the fields about the rural brain drain, which involves young people being raised on the farm, going off to college, and not returning to claim their legacy to the land. Jeff wants someone to take over the family farm, but if his children decide not to, there may be no family on this farm in the future.

Mike interviewed Carl at his kitchen table in their newly remodeled farm-house. In his late fifties, Carl has two grown sons in agriculture. Asked about the challenges farmers face today, Carl shared,

> The business of farming is . . . a person has to be very optimistic. You wouldn't dare go into farming if you weren't an optimist because you have everything thrown at you: the markets which you have no control over, you got mother na-ture which you have no control over, you have insects you have no control over. What the government does, you have no control over. There are so many factors out there that the farmer has no control over.

Farming for Carl is a challenge because there are so many factors he has no control over, factors that affect his roles as farmer and father. Family stud-ies clearly indicate that a father's role identity influences his behavior, in-cluding his performance as a father (Fox and Bruce 2001; Minton and Pasley 1996; Pasley, Futris, and Skinner 2002). Carl has role strain as a farmer and may also feel strain as a father. In addition, Carl may experience conflict be-tween statuses. Interestingly, Carl does not mention family as a problem area, perhaps because he exerts more control over this domain.

Other interviews indicated that farm identity was synonymous with family identity. We argue that the struggles in farming are simultaneously struggles to retain an identity as a farm father. One farmer stated, "A good farmer is one that cares for his property, livestock, and family. Not necessarily in that order. And he cares for his community." Another said,

> I can say spending more time with my family than like, say, a nine-to-five job. I mean there are times of the year where I don't see my family a lot. In the fall or in the spring. But I feel that I make up for that time in my off season in the winter more. I kind of like that quality of life. It's being more family [oriented]. I have the time to spend with my family.

A third said, "In other words, I enjoy putting in long working hours, but I'm not going to give up family life, social life, recreation off the farm for the sake of just being this, what I think is a good sustainable farmer."

If the family loses the farm, the legacy of the land is lost. Certainly the cul-tural pressure to have a family on the farm still runs deep in the fields of Iowa. An interrelated element of a farm father's identity is his connection to space and place.

SENSING SPACE AND PLACE

As mentioned earlier, farm fathers have a strong connection to geographic space and cultural place. This is especially true on the century farms. In his article, "After the Flood," essayist Scott Russell Sanders talks about a land-scape evoking strong memories for him and it being "a place by which I measure every other place" (1992, 158). This sentiment is evident in the growing body of literature using social psychological and cultural perspectives to help explain people's connection to space and place (Bell 1997; Cuba and Hummon 1994; Gieryn 2000; Lobao 2004; Orum 1995; Snyder, Brown, and Condo 2004). As Lobao (2004, 7) forcefully argues, "Rural sociologists have always grappled with conceptual questions about space that have only more recently permeated much general sociology."

In this literature, place not only is a physical construct, a geographic location but has an ideational quality that takes root in people's minds and hearts. Thus we argue that connection to place has a great impact on a farm father's identity, his relationship to the environment, and his legacy to his children.

Farm fathers have a strong sense of place and are eager to pass this legacy down to their children. This does not mean they would never leave the homestead, but, as mentioned earlier, there is a strong cultural connection to the house one grew up in and the soil that has been passed down from generation to generation.

Brian, a PFI farmer in his forties, farms the same land his grandfather and father once owned. He explained his connection to the house in which he and his ancestors have lived. Although Brian and his spouse, Karen, have remodeled the house a bit to fit their own personalities, it is essentially unchanged from Brian's childhood.

> The only reason I would move would be the simple fact it'd be easier for Karen. She's given up things for the family, and, I guess, if that would make her feel more at peace, I would move. I realize it's the home place, but yet, for the sake of preserving my family, I would walk away from it. I would probably look at preserving my family's happiness versus holding onto something that would ruin it.

Even though Brian feels a deep connection to the house, as well as the land that has been part of his family for generations, he is willing to sacrifice this connection. *It's the home place* for Brian, but he would give it up for his family if need be. The cultural connection to place is strong but does not supersede the connection to family. Although he realizes his connection to the home place could be a conflict someday in his marriage, the ideal for Brian is if the family feels that same connection that he does.

Another place connection for farm fathers is their connection to the environment. One of the ongoing debates in rural sociology focuses on sustainable versus industrial agriculture (Allen and Sachs 1991; Bell et al. 2004; Beus and Dunlap 1990; Buttel et al. 1990; Chiappe and Flora 1998; Kloppenburg, Lezburg, De Master, Stevenson, and Hendrickson 2000). The debate revolves around farmers taking a long-term perspective on the environmental, social, and economic aspects of agriculture (sustainable agriculture) versus viewing agriculture primarily through the lens of economic production and the culture of capitalism (industrial agriculture). We found this balance hard to reach for some farmers and often explored this in our questioning.

Mark, a PFI farmer in his forties with two children, defined sustainability:

> I think a sustainable farm, what separates them from conventional farmers, is that sustainable farmers are trying to farm more environmentally sound and more socially sound. . . . It means there's going to be biological life in the soil. It means diversity of crops and livestock. It means wildlife habitat. It means seeing more beneficial insects, and it means seeing a variety of wildlife. It means a family working together on some farming jobs. It means seeing people outside working.

For Mark, farming sustainability means farming with the family. It also means passing on a cultural connection to place and the environment. It means the family must be working together outside, a Goffmanesque performance for all to see as they drive by. This could also be interpreted as a means of reconstructing family values around place. The social construction of this performance happens in the family but also in a broader sense of place. Mark continued,

> There's a saner way, a healthier way. It's a way that's going to be better for our future generations if we're even going to survive at all. I think it has to be a very deep spiritual thing as well. Being a good farmer has spiritual connotations, because I guess I view the earth as definitely something that didn't just happen by coincidence. We are a part of the lowliest microbe. . . . I think that should humble us, and it should give us a very deep spiritual message that we have to take care of this earth because it's the only place we got.

Mark feels that connection to place as one that is healthier and better for his children and their children. For him, a sense of place also has a spiritual connection. It connects him to something larger than his own personal identity. In fact, for him it goes well beyond his own farm or his own lifetime. This sense of place is important to Mark and something he is sure to reconstruct in his children. Further in the interview, he recognized the role generations play in place making:

> I feel like that my dad is up there giving me some spiritual guidance. I can feel that, and I'm sure that I didn't know my grandpa, but I'm starting to think more about what was my grandpa like? And, how did he view farming in the land and

so forth? So I think there is some continuity there that we don't understand, and we've gotta have that. We can't know the future for sure, but we can try to work toward ensuring that we have some sort of future that we think is good or have a vision.

The continuity of place, as well as attempting to ensure it by making a goal or plan for the future, is very important to Mark. This connection is socially constructed and reconstructed in interaction, and it takes a conscious effort to keep it going.

Interviewed at their farm, Jay and Sally, both PFI members in their sixties, reflected back on when they were growing up on the farm. Jay described how it was when he was a child.

> Our weekend was. "Okay kids, get your sled, and we're going to get in the wagon, and we'll go up to this timber." And we would cut wood, and we would slide in the hills because we had to use the wood for heat. We all had a good time. And they still talk about it. The best things in life are still free. We'd say let's go down to the river. We're going to build a bonfire, and Mom gets some hotdogs and a few marshmallows if we could buy them. If we couldn't, just to sit there and watch nature. Mother Nature hasn't changed that much. She can be greatly appreciated if we do it.

Growing up with an appreciation of nature was important to Jay. Nature, place, and work were valued, but the economic stresses were downplayed. As he saw it, *the best things in life are still free . . . a few marshmallows if we could buy them*, a sentiment possibly reflecting the embedded nonmaterialistic value of the environment Jay found important enough to mention. Perhaps he was also making a statement about how our values have changed in recent years.

Roger and his spouse, Wendy, non-PFI members in their thirties with a toddler and an eight-year-old son, responded to our quality-of-life question. Roger began:

> Probably, like our two brothers, you know, they live pretty high. I guess, if they would look at us, they would say, "Oh I can't believe they are sitting in this space, you know, like that." They make large sums of money. The sad part of that is, if that money would get cut off they're going to be so lost. What are they going to do? They don't have the values.
>
> [Wendy agreed] And they don't spend time with their kids. Their kids go from this to this to this, and it's too much. The Jones kids are in band, basketball, baseball, soccer, football—I think the best thing you can give is yourself to them. That's the way it should be, and a lot of them are putting them in everything they possibly can just to get them out of their hair.

[Roger added] I really think so. Bret's eight and Brad's three, and when we go down the road, I talk about weeds, corn, and pigs, and they know. "Dad," Bret said, "that guy didn't cultivate his corn." It's probably kind of dumb, but they know the environment. We went camping and we were back in the woods, way back there, and there were some thistle plants. Bret said, "Dad, look, that guy didn't spray those thistles." [They know] I'm bad on weeds. If I see a weed, I gotta spray it. And his cousin is the same age; he had no idea of his surroundings.

Roger is proud that his sons *know the environment,* and he knows that his legacy and knowledge are being passed on to the next generation. Again, it may be wise to be critical of the Foucaultian power implications that knowledge possesses. If knowledge is power, lacking knowledge about the environment may be also be viewed as lacking the power to adapt to it. Farmer knowledge and understanding of the environment also play a strong role in how farm fathers view work.

HOME SWEET WORK

Fathers face challenges to their traditional socially constructed identity as breadwinner and may even face role overload by taking on too many responsibilities (Crouter, Bumpus, and Head 2001; Edwards 2001; Hood 1993; Perry-Jenkins, Repetti, and Crouter 2000). Hochschild (1989) documented the unequal division of labor that often occurs in U.S. households, noting many women's tendency to assume a "second shift" at home. In this vein, we found that most farm families today experience more than a second shift, but also third shift with a job away from the farm, and a fourth shift involving community and church activities. We also found that the tensions individuals experience between career versus family also resonate strongly with farm fathers, only the distinction for them is farm versus family. Although initially it may seem that farm fathers have plenty of opportunity to spend time interacting with their children since they work at home, we found this to not always be the case. Overall, farm fathers have a strong work ethic. They struggle to balance farm and family, share shifts, and try to find a way to be fully present in family life.

As farm fathers socially construct the balance between the world of work and home for their children, their children are socialized with a distinctive work ethic. We found a strong work ethic to be a very important part of a farm father's cultural legacy to his children. Ryan, a non-PFI farmer in his forties with five children, discussed the division of labor on his farm:

All the family is involved in it. I mean, they all work out there. Even the little ones go out and help. That's been great for our family. It's interesting, but it's good to get everybody out there because today we've got to clean the farrowing house [birthing structure for pigs], and they all have to do their part. That's great for family. Then we can all go out and have pizza or whatever. They complain, but we make them do it. They've got to learn how to work just like everybody else. That was their biggest feather in their cap wherever they went; wherever anyone employed them, they said, "Don't quit, because we know you can work." That's what they hear every time. So, the work ethic is very important, extremely important.

Ryan values a strong work ethic, recognizing its meaning in the larger community as well. Much farmwork is performed outdoors for all to see, and this performance is recognized in other settings. Thus Ryan sees his children's commitment to work as a *feather in their cap.* His children know how to work; more importantly, others draw attention to their efforts and reward them accordingly. However, some farm fathers may place too much emphasis on work, prompting some children to leave the farm forever.

Phil and his spouse, Sarah, non-PFI members in their forties, were interviewed at their kitchen table with their college-age son. Jason did not intend to return to the farm after college (the brain drain mentioned earlier), and this was a point of contention in the family. At one point in the interview, Sue asked Phil what he sees as a good quality of life: "Like my dad said, 'Life's too short and don't use it all working.'" At this point Sue took advantage of having Jason at the table and tested Phil's statement by asking Jason directly, "I wonder. How do you feel about not having enough time with your dad? Did you ever feel that?" "No," Jason replied. "I don't think I did." At this point, Jason's mother jumped into the conversation.

> He wasn't deprived. . . . Kids can go out with you. The kids can be out in the tractor with you. They can be out if you're doing chores. They can come out and help you do this. They can talk to you for hours while you're fixing the combine. But like your neighbors in town, if they had a second job it would be, say, McDonald's, well the kids are still at home. So Dad has gone to the first job and the second job. So, where is Dad? This is a whole lot different.

Although the tension between work and family is clear in this conversation, family may not have won out. While Phil was trying to justify the amount of work he has to do to keep the farm going and plan for retirement, Sarah was arguing that farm kids actually have more interaction with their fathers than city kids do. She punctuated her point by rhetorically asking: *So, where is Dad?* The social interaction of farmwork is in the field, fixing machinery, doing chores, all time that could be well spent between fathers and their children. In this sense, farm fathers may have ample opportunities to interact with their children even while they are working long hours. However, in our study, not all farm fathers took advantage of those opportunities.

To explore this tension further, one of our interview questions for every farm father was: Is farming a business or a way of life? Although we wanted to hear their answers, we knew that, as with every dualism, the answer probably lies somewhere in between. Which way a farm father leaned helped us understand how he prioritized work and family.

Greg interviewed John, a PFI farmer in his forties with two children, while riding on the wheel well of John's tractor as he cultivated his soybeans. Responding to a question about whether farming was a business or a way of life, John said,

> It's both. It's a way of life. It's a business to create a way of life that you want to live. It's made me realize that to separate a family life from the business is a struggle I've been going through in the last year or so.

John's struggle between family and career is well documented in family studies (Crouter et al. 2001; Edwards 2001; Hochschild 1989; Hood 1993; Rubin 1994; Hays 1996). We found that while the flexible schedule and opportunities to interact with children are often touted by the farm father as ideal, the reality may be different. Home is sweet but can also be endless acres of planting and hog pens full of work.

While visiting Carl, a non-PFI farmer in his fifties, Mike asked him if he worked with his sons on the crop farm.

> I don't work with them too much anymore. I did help them get started. And I got to the point where somewhere along the line they had to strike out on their own. Because their enterprise is too risky, it got to the point where I could not continue cosigning notes because, if something would happen, it would have taken me down. So, I made the decision a few years back, "Boys, you're on your own." It was kind of like the bird kicking the young'ns out of the nest.

Because of the changing structure of agriculture, many farm fathers struggle with Carl's role strain. On the one hand he wants his sons to be farmers and is proud of that. On the other hand, he needs to stay in the increasingly commodified business of farming. This affects a farm father's ability to interact with his children and be fully present in their lives, and it ultimately affects the structure of the family. "Kicking the young'ns out of the nest" seemed to be the best way to balance farm and family to Carl. It also seemed to us to be a decision he made himself without consulting his spouse or their children. Carl continued,

> Like I told them they were young enough that they could do something else. I wasn't . . . I like to say it was me that got wounded during the mid '80s, but I

survived, and at that time we decided that each of the boys should grow up on their own. . . . Dad is going to be separate.

The 1980s are often referred to as the farm crisis period. Whether this period was worse than others or now is debatable, but there is no question that farmers across the country *got wounded,* as Carl stated, and are still getting wounded now—some of them to death. Carl's family is not alone, nor do we want to blame the victim of a personal problem when the problem is clearly what C. W. Mills (1959) called a public issue. Since the 1980s, there has been an increase in rural family poverty rates and female-headed households as well as changes in rural family structure and stresses. Although farm policies in the United States attempt to solve these public issues, they are often applied on a personal basis (Lasley, Leistriz, Lobao, and Meyer 1995). For Carl, his farm is his identity but in the larger picture of agriculture, it is also a business struggling to survive. In this case, maybe the farm won over the family. Yet the family still exists. Carl explained,

> It takes a whole family to work nowadays. The wife has to work. The man has to work. Maybe not one or two jobs, maybe three jobs. Actually, there's four sources of income if you look at it. There's a check from Allied Electronic that she draws, the check from Mobil that he draws, the check from the crops that he draws, and also the check from the custom feeding. Back when I started, we only needed one source of income and that came off this particular unit itself.

Carl uses industrial terminology to explain that a farm is a business first. Everything he described about the work: *their enterprise, units, sources of income, drawing checks*, all of this language is external to the identity of farmer. Carl's sons have socially reconstructed a way to stay in farming, but the business end has been difficult for their families. Not all farm families are like Carl's, although similar tensions are there; some seemed to balance family and farm in a different way.

Harold and Joyce, a PFI couple in their early forties with three children ranging from seven to thirteen, own a hog farm. Harold and his brother started farming with their Dad, and when he retired, they took over the family farm. Though Harold and Joyce were very busy, they made it clear that their children come first in every decision, even if the farming has to wait. Harold offered,

> In recent years, I think the biggest thing has been kind of a *shift of priorities*. I grew up in a farm where the farm was first. Everything else came second. I saw the conflict in that once we had a family. The family really was something that was awfully important, and I struggled a lot with that the last few years. I think there's been a *shift of priorities* more toward family being the most important. Farm sort of has to come second. Our philosophy was you deal with things when

the problem comes out, and there have been days when I spent half a day counseling [our] kids and when you knew you should have been doing something
[else]. Dad's priority was Farm First; our priority was Family Too!

The shift of priorities Harold talked about may reflect a generational shift.
Shifting priorities has been difficult for Harold because it involved changing
his work identity, work ethic, and father involvement. But it may make working at home sweeter for him and his family.

FUTURE RESEARCH

We have argued that farm fathers today are socially reconstructing their identities toward work, the legacy of the land, and their sense of place through the
institutions of family, agriculture, church, and school. In the field, we learned
a great deal from the families we interacted with and that interaction has
changed us. Perhaps it will continue to change others as well. Until then, as
long as farmers still work in the fields and families still live on the farm, farm
fathers will not live Thoreau's notions of quiet desperation, rather they will
struggle to find ways to be involved in their children's lives and sustain their
family farms.

As family farms continue to evolve with the times, researchers have intriguing opportunities to study how the physical and symbolic features of this
setting influence fathers' involvement with their children. Researchers should
explore the gendered features of how fathers and their children react to the
physical landscape. While each family socially constructs a division of labor
on the farm, these patterns may be shaped by gender-related norms. For example, are fathers more likely to incorporate their sons compared to daughters into everyday shared experiences having to do with working the farm? To
what extent do fathers teach their daughters, as well as sons, to operate and
fix farm machinery? When are fathers willing to teach their daughters the
business aspects of running a farm?

The physical attributes of farms and rural areas, coupled with the cultural
ethos of rural living, may foster unique experiences for farm fathers. Do fathers spend more time doing certain types of things with their children because the children are less apt to be playing with neighbors? From a sociology of leisure point of view, it would be fruitful to analyze whether farm
fathers spend more time with their kids outside doing various things (playing catch, hunting, fishing, hiking, snowmobiling, etc.) compared to fathers
living in urban settings who may be more likely to participate in commodified leisure (going to movies, restaurants, the mall). What about fathers' expectations of children's work versus play time? Are farm fathers, compared

to urban or suburban fathers, more likely to expect their children to be responsible and to play less? How do these experiences affect child development? Does being part of a farm family offer fathers a more diverse set of opportunities than most fathers to teach their children various practical skills and life lessons? Are farm fathers better at multitasking than nonfarm fathers? Does farm land and the surrounding rural area provide special opportunities for fathers and their children to create shared memories and attachments that are linked to the natural physical environment?

Finally, research could explore the complexities of "fathering" versus "farming." Although our study was in Iowa where the structure of agriculture is mostly corn, soybeans, and hog production, comparing farm fathering from other states could clarify how the structure of agriculture interacts with family processes. Some modes of farming may call for individuals to work cooperatively on particular facets of a project, but other forms may be more easily accomplished by segmenting the work, allowing family members to do their chores away from one another. In some instances, though, fathers may structure work tasks to facilitate more direct involvement with their children. When and how does this occur?

The issues noted above illustrate several ways scholars can begin to think more systematically and theoretically about men's experiences as farm fathers. We also encourage those interested in these and related issues to consider how the application of family research out in the fields can inform the design of interventions to help farm families address their unique challenges.

REFERENCES

We are grateful to all collaborators on this project, including the Practical Farmers of Iowa, their neighbors, our own academic neighbors, our families, and the editors of this book. Partial funding for this research came from SARE grant LWF 62-016-03517 and a UW-Madison/UW Colleges Summer Research Grant.

Albrecht, D., and Albrecht, A. (1996). Family structure among urban, rural, and farm populations: Classic sociological theory revisited. *Rural Sociology, 61* (3), 446–63.

Allen, P. and Sachs, C. (1991). The social side of sustainability: Class, gender, and ethnicity. *Science as Culture, 2,* 569–90.

Barlett, P. (1993). *American Dreams, Rural Realities: Family Farms in Crisis.* Chapel Hill: University of North Carolina Press.

Bell, M. M., Jarnagin, S., Peter, G., and Bauer, D. (2004). *Farming for us all: Practical agriculture and the cultivation of sustainability.* University Park: Pennsylvania State University Press.

Bell, M. M. (1997). Ghosts of place. *Theory and Society, 26* (6), 813–36.

Beus, C., and Dunlap, R. 1990. Conventional versus alternative agriculture: The paradigmatic roots of the debate. *Rural Sociology, 55,* 590–616.

Bokemeier, J. (1997). Rediscovering families and households: Restructuring rural society and rural sociology. *Rural Sociology, 62* (1), 1–20.

Bokemeier, J., and Garkovich, L. (1991). Meeting rural family needs. In C. Flora and J. Christenson (Eds.), *Rural Policies for the 1990s* (pp. 114–27). Boulder: Westview.

Bonanno, A. (Ed). (1994). *From Columbus to ConAgra: The globalization of agriculture and food.* Lawrence: University Press of Kansas.

Brown, B., and Lichter, D. (2004). Poverty, welfare, and the livelihood strategies of nonmetropolitan single mothers. *Rural Sociology, 69* (2), 282–301.

Buttel, F., Larson, O. and Gillespie, G., Jr. 1990. *The Sociology of Agriculture.* New York: Greenwood.

Campbell, H., and Bell, M. (2000). The question of rural masculinities. *Rural Sociology, 65* (4), 532–46.

Chiappe, M., and Flora, C. (1998). Gendered elements of the alternative agriculture paradigm. *Rural Sociology, 49,* 183–209.

Clifford, J. (1986). Introduction: Partial Truths. In J. Clifford and G. Marcus (Eds.), *Writing culture: The poetics and politics of ethnography* (pp. 1–26). Berkeley: University of California Press.

Coontz, S. (1997). *The way we really are.* New York: HarperCollins.

Conger, R., and Conger, K. (2002). Resilience in Midwestern families: Selected findings from the first decade of a prospective, longitudinal study. *Journal of Marriage and Family, 62* (2), 361–74.

Coward, R., and Smith, W., Jr. (1982). Families in rural society. In D. Dillman and D. Hobbs (Eds.), *Rural society in the U.S.: Issues for the 1980s.* Boulder: Westview.

Crouter, A., Bumpus, M., and Head, M. (2001). Implications of overwork and overload for the quality of men's family relationships. *Journal of Marriage and the Family, 63* (2), 404–17.

Cuba, L., and Hummon, D. (1994). Constructing a sense of home: Place affiliation and migration across the life cycle. *Sociologia Ruralis, 8* (4), 547–72.

Daly, K. (1993). Reshaping fatherhood: Finding the models. *Journal of Marriage and the Family, 14* (4), 510–30.

Duneier, M. (1999). *Sidewalk.* New York: Farrar, Straus & Giroux.

Edwards, M. (2001). Uncertainty and the rise of the work–family dilemma. *Journal of Marriage and the Family, 63* (1), 183–97.

Flora, C., Flora, J., Spears, J., and Swanson, L. (1992). *Rural communities: Legacy and change.* Boulder: Westview.

Fox, G. L., and Bruce, C. (2001). Conditional fatherhood: Identity theory and parental investment theory as alternative sources of explanation of fathering. *Journal of Marriage and the Family, 63* (2), 394–404.

Gieryn, T. (2000). A Space for Place in Sociology. *Annual Review of Sociology, 26,* 463–96.

Hays, S. (1996). *The cultural contradictions of motherhood.* New Haven, CT: Yale University Press.

Hobson, B. (Ed). (2002). *Making men into fathers: Men, masculinities and the social politics of fatherhood.* Cambridge: Cambridge University Press.

Hochschild, A. (1989). *The second shift.* New York: Avon.

Hood, J. (Ed.) (1993). *Men, work, and family.* London: Sage.

Israel, G., Beaulieu, L., and Hartless, G. (2001). The influence of family and community social capital on educational achievement. *Rural Sociology, 66* (1), 43–68.

Kassab, C., Luloff, A. E., and Schmidt, F. (1995). The changing impact of industry, household structure, and residence on household well-being. *Rural Sociology, 60* (1), 67–90.

Kloppenburg, J., Jr., Lezburg, S., De Master, K., Stevenson, G., and Hendrickson, J. (2000). Tasting food, tasting sustainability: Defining the attributes of an alternative food system with competent, ordinary people. *Human Organization, 59* (2), 177–86.

LaRossa, R. (2004). The culture of fatherhood in the 1950s. *Journal of Family History, 29* (1), 47–70.

LaRossa, R. (1997). *The modernization of fatherhood: A social and political history.* Chicago: University of Chicago Press.

Lasley, P., Leistritz, F. L., Lobao, L., and Meyer, K. (1995). *Beyond the amber waves of grain: An examination of social and economic restructuring in the heartland.* Boulder: Westview.

Lobao, L. (2004). Continuity and change in place stratification: Spatial inequality and middle-range territorial units. *Rural Sociology, 69* (1), 1–30.

Lorenz, F., Elder, G., Bao, W., Wickrama, K. A. S., and Conger, R. (2000). After farming: Emotional health trajectories of farm, nonfarm, and displaced farm couples. *Rural Sociology, 65* (1), 50–71.

Marsiglio, W., and Hutchinson, S. (2002). Sex, men, and babies: Stories of love, hope, and repair. Lanham, MD: Rowman & Littlefield.

Marsiglio, W., Amato, P., Day, R., and Lamb, M. (2000a). Scholarship on fatherhood in the 1990s and beyond. *Journal of Marriage and the Family, 62* (4), 1173–92.

Marsiglio, W., and Cohan, M. (2000). Contextualizing father involvement and paternal influence: Sociological and qualitative themes. *Marriage and Family Review, 29* (2–3), 75–95.

Marsiglio, W., Day, R., and Lamb, M. (2000). Exploring fatherhood diversity: Implications for conceptualizing father involvement. *Marriage and Family Review, 29* (4), 269–93.

McLaughlin, D., Gardner, E., and Lichter, D. (1999). Economic restructuring and changing prevalence of female-headed families in America. *Rural Sociology, 64* (3), 394–416.

Meares, A. (1997). Making the transition from conventional to sustainable agriculture: Gender, social movement participation, and quality of life on the family farm. *Rural Sociology, 62* (1), 21–47.

Mills, C. W. (1959). *The sociological imagination.* New York: Oxford University Press.

Minton, C., and Pasley, K. (1996). Father's parenting role identity and father involvement. *Journal of Family Issues, 17* (1), 26–45.

Orum, A. (1995). The urban imagination of sociologists: The centrality of place. *Sociological Quarterly, 39* (1), 1–10.

Pasley, K., Futris, T., Skinner, M. (2002). Effects of commitment and psychological centrality on fathering. *Journal of Marriage and the Family, 64* (1), 130–39.

Perry-Jenkins, M., Repetti, R., and Crouter, A. (2000). Work and family in the 1990s. *Journal of Marriage and the Family, 62* (4), 981–99.

Peter, G., Bell, M. M., Jarnagin, S., and Bauer, D. (2000). Coming back across the fence: Masculinity and the transition to sustainable agriculture. *Rural Sociology, 65* (2), 215–33.

Rubin, L. (1994). *Families on the fault line: America's working class speaks about the family, the economy, race, and ethnicity.* New York: HarperCollins.

Sanders, S. R. (1992). After the Flood. In Martone, M. (Ed.), *Townships* (pp. 156–64). Iowa City: University of Iowa Press.

Snyder, A., Brown, S., and Condo, E. (2004). Residential differences in family formation: The significance of cohabitation. *Rural Sociology, 69* (2), 235–60.

Snyder, A., and McLaughlin, D. (2004). Female-headed families and poverty in rural America. *Rural Sociology, 69* (1), 127–49.

Strange, M. (1988). *Family Farming: A New Economic Vision.* Lincoln: University of Nebraska Press.

Thoreau, H. D. (1937 [1854]). *Walden.* New York: Random House.

12

"Gotta Protect My Own": Men Parenting Children in an Abandoned City

Jennifer F. Hamer

Few social scientists have explored how vastly impoverished environments may affect how fathers act to protect their children from the violence and danger that pervades these places. How do low-income and poor men in abandoned African American communities define the potential harms to their children? How do they act to negotiate a safe space for their daughters and sons? In this ethnographic case study, I investigate how low-income African American men actively attempt to mitigate the negative impact of neighborhood disadvantage in cities long ago abandoned by corporate and state leaders. What I find is that an assessment of fathers' perceptions of the potential harms to their children requires us to expand traditional notions of violence and danger. Fathers who live in poor places must develop strategies to protect their children from not only personal violence, such as assault and gang activity, but also broader state-abetted perils.

ABANDONED PEOPLE, ABANDONED PLACES

Paychecks are only part of what is lost when men and women lack family-wage jobs or career opportunities. Communities and families suffer as well. Cities experience a loss of revenue that leaves them unable to adequately support infrastructures. Municipal buildings crumble. Public facilities such as libraries, zoos, and parks receive reduced attention in city and county budgets—threatening the city's cultural and recreational environment. City trash pickup, street and stoplight maintenance, and pothole repairs are curbed and abridged for other community needs. Police and fire departments make reductions in personnel, equipment maintenance, and purchases—threatening the safety and protection of citizens. Schools must reduce the costs of staff and faculty. They cut academic and extracurricular programs and charge families more for book rentals and other supplies. This occurs at a time when families in the city have less to spend. By the 1970s, former manufacturing centers such as Gary, Indiana; Newark, New Jersey; East St. Louis, Illinois; and many other Midwestern cities began to show the signs of cities beleaguered by disproportionate poverty, lost tax dollars, and diminishing living-wage jobs.

Current family policy makes low-income fathers more accountable for the health and safety of their children. However, studies suggest that what fathers do as parents is negotiated in a larger ecological context. What men do as parents is influenced by, among other variables, men's relationships with others, access to education, low-wage jobs, joblessness, commutes to and from work, proximity from children, and having several sets of children (Carlson and McClanahan 2002; Hamer 2001; Johnson 2001). Stable employment and good relationships with the mothers of their children, for example, help men maintain a paternal role (Carlson and McLanahan 2003). In contrast, men's parenting is hindered by divorce and by the time it takes to continue higher education and work at multiple jobs (McLanahan, Garfinkel, and Mincy 2001; Lerman and Sorensen 2000). But, contrary to popular belief, good fathering is not limited to those who reside in the same households as their children. Recent studies tell us that many African American fathers actually do maintain close relationships with their children—especially when children are very young (Amato and Gilbreth 1999; Coley and Chase-Lansdale 1999; Hamer 2001).

Many men who live away from their children spend time with them, serve as role models, offer guidance, and provide financial support. It appears that poor black fathers who are unable to meet paternal financial responsibilities are emphasizing their social and emotional obligations to their children (Hamer 2001). Some African American low-income fathers are responding to the growing incidence of child neglect, maltreatment, and incarceration among mothers by assuming the full-time care of their children (Coles 2002; Hamer and Marchioro 2002). African American fathers are more likely than other men to be a full-time single parent (Coles 2002; Hamer and Marchioro 2002). Overall, it seems that many fathers believe that it is their paternal obligation to provide support, security, and protection for their children.

But how do they maintain and protect the well-being of their children in abandoned communities? Recent studies have begun to explore the strategies that parents develop to protect themselves and their children from traditional definitions or forms of violence. Researchers argue that children's exposure to violence takes three major forms: "The first is child maltreatment, which constitutes a direct physical assault on a child by a caregiver; the second is exposure to maternal assault in the child's immediate family system; and the third is exposure to violence in the larger system of neighborhood or community" (Mohr, Fantuzzo, and Abdul-Kabir 2001, 75). Statistics indicate that these forms of violence are on the rise, especially in low-income urban areas.

Researchers argue that parents can mitigate the ill effects poor neighborhoods have for their children. In a small study of ten African American women, Mohr et al. (2001) discovered that a group of mothers did not look to traditional institutions, such as the police or shelters, to rescue them or their children from potentially violent partners or community circumstances. Rather, they looked to themselves, peers, and neighbors to keep men at bay and to keep trouble from their doorsteps. Other studies found that mothers especially went to great lengths to protect their children (Jarrett 1997; Fordham 1996; Burton 1995; Brodsky 1996). Similar to mothers, fathers also seem to be developing strategies to protect their children from violent members of the community. Findings from a study by Letiecq and Koblinsky (2004) indicate that fathers attempt to protect their children by educating them about safety, offering constant supervision, and directly confronting alleged troublemakers in their communities (see also Anderson 1990). In general, poor families routinely create strategies to safeguard their sons and daughters (Duncan 1996; Jarrett 1997).

The traditional definition of violence in black neighborhoods consists primarily of African American mothers and fathers harming their children, African American men abusing and assaulting African American women, or black people in the community injuring black neighbors. Thus solutions to the problems tend to center on programs that emphasize the agency of individuals and individual households. But the formal definition of violence often used by researchers is limited and fails to capture the everyday perils of the public sphere that jeopardize the health and safety of African American children in low-income urban communities. Too, it fails to capture the many parents who act to protect their children from more pervasive sources of poor health and welfare that may be directly linked to large-scale state neglect. On the whole, it appears that abandoned cities, neighborhoods, and communities may pose a particular challenge to men's parental efforts to protect children.

METHODS: AN ETHNOGRAPHIC CASE STUDY

Why do black men and fathers seem to live and function so differently than mainstream America does? This question, more than any other, has guided ethnographic research on poor black urban men and fathers. In fact, many would argue that this body of literature provides us with the richest and most holistic explanations for understanding the lives of people in poor communities. Traditional ethnographies offer detailed descriptions of settings. They tend to emphasize culture (values and norms) of the poor and working class and actually minimize the analysis of structural factors. Even researchers who have recognized structures don't analyze how these systems impact, shape, create, and bind the choices that poor and working people make about family. Ultimately such an approach reifies arguments about the culture of poverty and underclass theses (Lewis 1975; Wilson 1989). It does so by naturalizing conditions of inequality. They leave uninterrogated power relations of race and class and do not account for how these conditions have evolved through the decisions of corporate and state leadership.

From these studies one could easily assume that there is little hope, no structure or order left in these cities or communities, and no interaction between residents here and the wider society. Equally problematic, analyses are often overlaid onto field descriptions that nowhere demonstrate how macrostructural forces come to impact life inside poor communities (Wacquant 2002). In other words, there is a poverty of ethnographic literature on the circumstances and behaviors of black men and fathers in poor communities. Family and work life have been inadequately theorized—even among research that appears sympathetic to these populations. Past research generally neglects to analyze fully the larger-scale urban processes that directly and indirectly impact the everyday lives of poor people.

Bringing Structure into the Analysis

Any examination of black families is incomplete if it does not adequately take this larger structure into account. Values and behaviors are negotiated in the broader context of the state. What role does it play in creating the environment in which black men understand their circumstances and then make decisions about children? In other words, people may live in poverty but the state has a role in creating these conditions. How do people negotiate life when they are disposable and the state, industry, and institutions have abandoned their needs for other interests?

To address the limitations of past research, especially traditional ethnography, I use a mixed qualitative methodology consisting of both ethnographic and case study approaches. This approach enabled me to (1) discover the attitudes and actions of these fathers regarding aspects of their father roles and (2) situate their paternal behaviors in broader urban processes so that links between lived experiences and institutionalized policies and responses could be more easily observed.

Between 1996 and 2003, I spent many days, weeks, and months on the streets, in the churches, hospitals, parks, and many private spaces in the city of East St. Louis. I am an African American with family roots in the area. However, it is difficult for any researcher to be an insider in this city. Residents here voiced concerns about past exploitation by university groups and others looking to make fame and fortune off of the stories and circumstances of those living in this place of poverty. Findings and discussion for this chapter are based on interviews with and observations of twenty-nine fathers who, at the time of my fieldwork and data collection, lived with their children in a marital or cohabiting arrangement or as single parents—though some of these arrangements changed over the period of time I spent in the field. Most of these fathers had completed high school or a GED, and their ages ranged from twenty-four to fifty-seven. Regardless of their level of education, all reported annual incomes below $20,000. All but two spent their childhood in East St. Louis. We met on bus benches, in parks, hospital clinics, restaurants, and occasionally walking down the street. I visited their homes and shared their meals. I visited their churches and participated in their various workshops and organized activities. In the case study tradition, I utilized multiple sources of data that were rich in information, such as newspapers, local and regional archives, and interviews with local leaders and authorities. I set about to describe the setting of East St. Louis, to understand issues of parenting from the perspective of fathers; and then to explore the processes that link everyday parental behavior to the elements of poor urban areas.

NEGOTIATING A SAFE SPACE IN THIS ABANDONED PLACE

Regardless of their low educational, occupational, and employment status, many men raise children here and know all about the harshness of life in this community. They believe that men should provide for and protect their children. They believe that the most important element of their parental role is the time they give their children—guiding them through a safe childhood and toward productive older years. In the remainder of this chapter, fathers discuss the varying issues that confront their parenting on a daily basis. Fathers protect young ones from traditional notions of peril and violence often associated with urban areas. They try to protect their young daughters from sexual encounters and their boys from drug-related activities. Although some of their concerns fall into the categories of personal violence, others were more inclusive of the extensive dangers that make up the physical environment of this city.

Shielding Girls and Raising Boys

Carlos used to like "young women," he explained. He used to seek them out in clubs, in the malls, or on the street after the Lincoln High School bell released the adolescents for the day. He liked women who did not require deep conversation or a lot of time, had "tight" bodies, and were easily impressed by his "style." In those days, in his early twenties, he would drive around in his uncle's Cadillac. His job at McDonald's and later as an office clerk at his uncle's law firm enabled him to purchase fashionable shoes and clothing. He lived with his mother and had no bills. Thus he always had spending money in his pocket. He'd say, "Girl, let me take you to Red Lobster," or "Let me buy you a new sexy dress at the mall." In this city, he explained, "these young girls eat it up . . . they'll do anything for a brotha if you give them some food, buy them something, you dig? It's easy for a brotha with a little bit of money in his pocket to get some play from these girls here." But when Carlos's daughter began to develop breasts and a shapely figure, he became "overly protective" of her and her friends. "I know how these men be looking at these young ladies. That used to be me. I'm ashamed to say, but that used to be me. So I feel like me, better than anybody, know how to protect her from these niggas out here."

Other men here agree. Seducing young women is "like a game here." Ty Johnson provided some detail: "Every brotha is constantly looking out for the sweetest young thing to come around—then you get her and that's that [snaps his fingers]. Some wanna turn her out. You know make some quick cash off her. But some of us are just in it for the game. That's entertainment. Shit, we ain't got nothing better to do for free. . . . But really, that's one of the major ways that you can say, 'I'm a man.' Get these young things to open up to you." They explain that part of being a man here is the ability to attract women—very young women who can make a man feel important and older women who can pay a man's way—buy him clothing, food, maybe even a car, and provide him with a place to live. "The thing of it," Carlos explained, "is that these girls, if they don't have nothin' else going for them, then they susceptible to men like that." From his experience, girls whose fathers were in jail or otherwise lived out of the home were vulnerable. Girls whose mothers had full-time jobs and were away from home for lengthy periods of the day were vulnerable. Girls who lived in impoverished households were vulnerable. And in this city, these characteristics defined the bulk of households. This set of circumstances, resulting in their vulnerability to men who lusted after them, was part of their environment. Men with little means for well-paying employment stood outside daily looking at young girls playing and walking by. Young girls attended school looking for a way to have all of the nice things that mall stores offered and television entertainers seemed to possess—

no different from middle-class youth in urban suburbs. But in this city, over half the population lives in poverty and most girls and boys live in single-mother households. Nearly 70 percent of the children here are born to single mothers and almost one-quarter are born to adolescent girls (U.S. Census 2001).

How do men here understand these statistics? Many felt that high levels of unemployment created a population of men who had "nothing better to do but hustle women." Some of the men themselves placed their activities in this category. However, the popular public rhetoric made its way into their explanations. They blamed mothers for not practicing strict discipline and teaching appropriate morals. They blamed church ministers for selfishly having relationships with young women in their congregation and taking money from poor households to line their own pockets with a "Cadillac fund." They blamed fathers for not spending enough time with their children, for going to jail, and for not providing support to single parenting mothers. From many men's perspective, in this environment, girls need a parent who is always present, who diligently monitors clothing and friendships because the steady stream of jobless men interested in their daughters seems endless.

Fathers worried about boys as well and practiced protective strategies that were similar to those that were described for girls. However, for fathers, the primary hazards for boys in this city were forms of deadly personal violence. Fathers were concerned that boys would get into fights at school or on the street. They were concerned that boys would begin to hang around with the wrong kids and begin to make money performing illegal activities and engage in violent activities associated with the business. They provided supervision to boys and made sure that they were too busy to get into trouble. Damian Carver, for example, made certain that his son was actively involved in church activities such as the youth choir, ushering, and Sunday school. Prince Gerry, the unemployed father of ten-year-old David, walked his son to and from school on a daily basis. He offered his reasons: "Won't no bully mess with him cause they see his daddy is going to be waiting for him after school. When I'm around, that'll discourage any nonsense." Supervision and extracurricular activities were not always successful. Nor did all fathers practice these methods. Adolescent boys seemed to grow weary of their fathers constantly standing over their shoulder. According to one,

> He [father] has got to let me be my own man one day. At some point, I'm going to have to fight somebody. What's gonna happen if he ain't around then, huh? I'm gonna get my ass kicked, that's what.

Other fathers felt that offering advice, rather than supervision and intense engagement, was the best means to protect boys. "He's my son so I gotta teach him how to be a man. I tell him how to back out of a bad situation but when it come down to it, then he's gotta make a decision about what to do, you understand?"

Protection *from* the Police

Fathers in East St. Louis also emphasized the importance of warning and educating their children about the perils associated with area police. Their anxieties were often premised on their own negative experiences. East St. Louis, similar to many low-income black urban areas, had an infamous public reputation. Residents in surrounding cities identified it as a space for prostitution, welfare mothers, unruly children, and drug dealers. These men surmised that being a black man from East St. Louis affected all interaction outside of the city. "If you go to Target in Fairview, they gonna look at you funny, they gonna follow you around the store, make sure you ain't putting nothing in your pocket," reported James Hancox. Indeed, this discriminatory harassment is something black men and women have come to expect in cities across the nation (Moss and Tilly 2001).

There is other evidence that supports the existence of lingering discrimination. When Josh Cowan was walking home from work from the nearby predominantly white city of Collinsville, the police followed him three blocks. Then they stopped their vehicle, pushed him down, and then pinned him to the ground with their heels. They handcuffed him while they frisked him and "checked out" his identification. At the time, Josh was certain they intended to kill him. However, they eventually uncuffed him and told him to head home; apparently they had the wrong suspect. Carlos, Josh, James, and others said that such an event was a common circumstance. In fact, at least once annually there is a local, state, or national report on a black man whose death by a police officer is under investigation.

Men here feel it is their responsibility to teach boys about these dangers. Many men explained how they talked with their sons about what to do when confronted by police. Josh Cowan recalled that he told his son to "not move unless the cop says to." He provided details:

> Do not reach for your wallet. Do not scratch your head. Do not move. Because the next thing you know, they'll be saying you were reaching for a weapon and BAM! That's it.

Others had similar directions for their boys:

> Never, if you can help it, be out by yourself in these small towns around here. The police will not hesitate to stop you; to take you in; to beat you. They will

not hesitate. Always have an ID or something with your name on it. Don't be alone. And always tell somebody where you gonna be.

I tell my son to stay away from white women. Stay away from white neighborhoods. Those people will set you up. If you work for them, they are going to blame you if something is missing. If you having sex with their daughter, then they going to say you raped her. There's many a time that things like that happened.

In this city, men have many worries regarding their sons—more than can be covered in this chapter. However, with regard to violence, they fret over potential personal hostilities. Fathers also take measures to keep their boys away from what they perceive are the wrong types of activities and youth. Yet these men are also quite apprehensive about the "run-ins" many predict all black men in the city will potentially have with area police. By far, their greatest concern is that their black boys, because they are black and male, will be victims of police homicides.

Developing an effective strategy to protect daughters and sons under these circumstances is difficult. Often work schedules and other responsibilities made them unavailable to supervise children as much as they would like. Moonie Johnson, a father of two grade school boys, juggled much of his time between three out-of-town part-time jobs. Romeo Weeks supervised his preteen daughter between long commutes to two different jobs. Carlos did not allow his friends to come into the house when he was not at home or after 8:00 P.M. when his daughter was likely to be in her nightgown. He tried to make certain that she came home directly after school. He tried to keep track of her friendship network and her school grades. Like many single parenting fathers in this city, he lived with his mother and solicited her assistance with his children. She helped monitor the girl's activities and telephone conversations. Despite these constraints, many of these fathers felt that heavy supervision was the primary means of protecting girls and boys from troubles.

Overall, the strategies that these men employed to mitigate personal violence toward their children supports previous research on the topic. They say that parents must provide constant supervision for children. However, their reports expand the definition of potential harms to boys and girls in this city. These reports specifically identify the police as a threat to physical and emotional well-being. Incidents of police abuses and killings, or legal homicides, are high in African American urban communities and it is no different here in the St. Louis metropolitan area.[1] Still, police abuse of power is not the only form of state-abetted violence.

Streets of Peril

There is a pocket of houses sandwiched in between the city's State Street, Interstate Highway 64, and just west of the Schnuck's supermarket. Old, leaf-laden trees pepper the lawns of both the abandoned and lived-in properties. Abandoned properties are easily distinguished by their dilapidated porches, boarded windows and doors, or the grass and weeds that seem to wave at passers-by on windy spring mornings. These were all once stately homes. Many are two story brick, with fireplaces and large front porches. Before African Americans became the dominant population, working-class and middle-income whites owned and lived in these properties. Homes here differ somewhat from those on the city's south end—they are generally more impressive, stately. But in East St. Louis no neighborhood, house, or family is spared from the dearth of services or the pollutants that hang over this metropolitan region. For fathers here, safety is an elusive concept.

Thirty-seven-year-old Arnie Millier, father of two children, knows this all too well. He and his children live with his mother in her home. The house is located on a small side street just off State Street. Few cars come this way; their house and the one next door are the only livable properties left on this road. Yet debris somehow finds its way to their block, creating hazards for those who venture out.

On a crisp school day morning last year, his son slipped in the grass of an empty lot and cut his hand on the jagged edge of a broken bottle that lay hidden beneath the beauty of red and yellow fall leaves. There was so much blood that a path of red trailed behind the boy as he rushed home to his father. Arnie was certain a "major artery had been cut."

> I didn't panic, you know, I got him to the emergency room as fast as I could . . . but you know it's those kind of times when you wonder what your life would be like if you lived somewhere else. 'Cause then, you know, he could've fallen but then the glass probably wouldn't have been there in a nicer neighborhood. Here they don't really clean the streets and people's always tossin' their trash. It's dangerous for little kids here. You think, what if some fiend leaves a used needle [hypodermic needle] on the playground. Or what if somebody tricks your kid into trying crack or something. Then you wonder if the doctors' gonna give him the kind of attention he deserves. See we on aid so that means that we can't just get the best doctor, we can't pay for that. We got to get what they give us. And frankly, sometimes I don't think the city, the doctors really care.

His mother too had experienced a severe trauma. She broke her hip in a fall on an ice-sheeted street. The city had not put salt on many side streets even after several days of harsh winter weather. Arnie blamed the city for the injury. From his perspective, "they should've threw salt on the street so old people don't fall and get hurt." A year after his son's accident the scar from the cut and four stitches was barely visible. Still, it was an aching reminder to Arnie. "You just feel vulnerable."

Vulnerable indeed. Litter on the streets of East St. Louis is a common sight. A scavenger will likely find old tires, broken refrigerators, milk cartons filled with used automobile oil, ragged clothing, battered bicycles, and other trash in just about any empty lot. But pollution takes on various forms in this city. The air, water, and soils here have been pummeled with harsh toxins for decades. The small city has 153 hazardous waste handlers. Twenty-six East St. Louis businesses have reported toxic releases; many of these are aerial. Typical contaminants in and around East St. Louis include arsenic compounds, lead, carbon monoxide, nitrogen dioxide, and various other compounds, many of which are known to cause cancer. Such an environment is a health hazard to the lives of all residents. Yet it is a particular threat to young children, who experience unusually high rates of asthma and lead poisoning. Adult men and women suffer high rates of psychosis, cancer, nervous disorders, and intestinal disorders (Illinois Department of Public Health 1998, 2003a,b).

But this is not the only issue. Men voice concern (publicly and privately) over reports of lead poisoning, hazardous neighborhood dumpsites, and the danger of abandoned buildings. With 40 percent of housing built prior to 1950 and 13 percent of all housing vacant, fathers and their families seek quality housing amid a shortage of adequate living quarters. The city is peppered with vacant lots and fire-gutted buildings. Moreover, almost 50 percent of families pay rent to absentee landlords who provide insufficient maintenance to the existing structures, many of which have high levels of lead. Adult men have been raised and now bring up their own children on dirty streets amid the haze of pollutants.

Breathing the Air

Six months prior to our first meeting, Brian Jennings's oldest daughter, Trelise, was rushed to the hospital suffering from a severe asthma attack. Two years prior, her Auntie Mary, Brian's sister, had died of the malady. Brian recalled the incident with sadness. "She was just sitting at home and then she couldn't breathe. She didn't have any medicine so we called the ambulance but it was like, there wasn't anything they could do at that point." Sixteen percent of poor children suffer from asthma (Centers for Disease Control 2004). The family was devastated, and when Trelise was diagnosed with the same ailment, Brian was wrought with concern. He thought perhaps it was something in her diet. He had heard that people can get it from eating too much fried foods. But Trelise's doctors informed him otherwise.

He began to read about the illness and learned that it disproportionately targeted black children, even here in East St. Louis. He learned that relative to other children, black children were more likely to die from asthma. He developed a four-pronged strategy that he hoped would prevent her from having a fatal attack. First, he keeps their house spotless and as dust free as possible. This means that he gets up early every morning to dust the furniture, wipe the cabinets, and sweep the linoleum floors throughout the house. Second, he does not allow anyone, not even his mother, to smoke in the house or around Trelise.

His mother resented this at first and thought that Brian blamed her for causing asthma to develop in both his sister and his daughter. With time, though, Brian convinced her that smoking was an irritant to asthma patients and contributed to their ill health. Third, he made certain that he always had her medicine on hand and that she knew how to use it in his absence. Finally, he simply watched over his daughter and worried. "I don't like for her to be bouncing on the bed or running outside. I just worry. I think, 'If I'm not watching her all the time then the time when I'm not there, that's when it's [a deadly asthma attack] gonna happen." So he watches her and feels guilty when he must go to work or run errands. But from his perspective, he can't "change the whole environment" and his is the only solution.

In terms of strategies of care and protection, fathers here often placed their children's needs above their own. Brian himself rarely visited a physician. Among other things, a lack of health insurance and busy work schedules discouraged working fathers from seeking health care. Additionally, many fathers just did not accept that doctors could "fix" most of their ailments. According to one father, "If I'm tired, and believe me I'm always tired, that just mean I need more sleep. If I'm losing weight, like I did last year, then that just mean I need to eat more, take better care of myself. This stuff is common sense."

Most fathers expressed similar sentiments. On the other hand, they wanted the best medical care for their children. Nonetheless, fathers here say they are not quite sure how to treat the diagnosis or the consequences of some illnesses. This was especially true when children were diagnosed with lead poisoning and other harms that were linked to the environment. In 2002 approximately 10 percent of the 4,000 children age six and under tested for lead poisoning had hazardous levels (Illinois Department of Public Health 2002). According to one father,

> I'm not sure that there's anything wrong with her. They got to show exactly what's wrong cause I just don't see it.
>   She [his son's teacher] told me I need to move to another house because of the lead thing . . . but I told her, I can't do it. Then what? I don't love my son?

I love my son but I don't know what to do. Where do you move in East St. Louis that ain't just like the place you just moved from?

Another father was also frustrated with his living arrangement:

> I wish I could just pack up, move my kids to another city, another state—but, and you know I'm embarrassed to say this, but I can barely pack a bag full of groceries at the supermarket. I don't know where I'm gonna get the money to move out.

Still others use haphazard means to protect their children from continued poisoning. In the case below, a father assumed his son had been poisoned by the many layers of old paint that were once peeling from his bedroom walls:

> I have him sleep in the same room as me, so he's not in his room where the problem is. That's where I think the problem is so I hope that this works. Then, when I can, I let him stay with his grandmamma.

If the culprit was the paint, the substance was never professionally removed and it was likely still present throughout other parts of the house. Many fathers were not quite sure of how or why children contracted specific cases of lead poisoning. Still, they felt that their watchful eyes could help to prevent the illness. According to the father below,

> I just watch him so that he don't get into anything that may make him sick.

Landlords in this city are notoriously absentee and slow to address issues of health and safety in the homes and apartments they rent. Many renters say nothing about concerns for fear that an actively voiced position may lead to their eviction. One father summarized the words of others:

> It just seems like we stuck sometime. Can't do right by our loved ones.

The environment in East St. Louis is hostile to the health of children. Many fathers have some understanding of the consequences toxins, pollutants, and diminished city services have on their children's welfare. Nevertheless, it seems that many must learn about dangers the hard way—that is after an injury or an illness has developed. Too, it also seems that fathers feel that they had insufficient resources to provide their children with a safe environment They reported feelings of inadequacy when it came to protecting their sons and daughters from health hazards. One father offered an analogy:

> It's like all I can do is put a band aid on his [son's] hurt. That takes care of the scar but there's a whole 'nother sickness inside that I can't see to do

nothin' about. You know . . . the Band-Aid just ain't enough but it's all I got to work with.

Housing

East St. Louis housing stock poses an additional threat to children's health and fathers' ability to manage safety. Much of it is old and deteriorating. Many fathers, like others in the city, reside in rental property. Among those I met, none owned their own homes, though a few lived in houses owned by their parents. Regardless, houses were always in need of repair. Fathers used a large part of their meager incomes toward rents and house repairs. Many found that they constantly had to "fix up" the rental property in which they and their families resided so that it remained livable. In nearby predominantly white towns like Edwardsville and Glen Carbon, families generally pay for major repairs and remodeling by using special insurance, remodeling loans, credit lines, or cash. But few men here are able to access such financial services. Nor do they have a substantial savings account from which they can draw. In fact, of the twenty-nine fathers mentioned in this chapter, only three had bank accounts. Others stored their money "around the house," in their "back pockets," or spent it immediately on bills, food, other essentials and minor wants.

Troy Penelton, father of eight-year-old Justin, was standing next to a stack of mismatched roofing tiles when we first met. He planned to replace the roof on the home he and his sister had rented for the past three years. The roof was aged and long overdue for repair. On rainy days the floors of the house were scattered with pails and buckets. This was the family's attempt to catch the drips of water that splattered through the brown-stained ceiling. The landlord of the property was rarely available by phone and seldom visited his many properties in the area. This is not unusual here. Many residents have similar complaints about property owners—many of whom do not live in the city. They earn substantial earnings from property because they accept Section 8 renters, who live below poverty level and receive housing assistance from the federal government, but also because they choose not to keep up the property. Thus the money earned from rents goes into their bank accounts and only a minimal amount is used to maintain the houses and apartments. Renters often have to fix broken pipes, furnaces, and toilets themselves.

Still, for Troy Penelton, at least his was a landlord who did not complain when the costs of minor repairs were taken out of the monthly rent checks. Many tenants in this city found this compromise a workable solution for small projects such as a leaky toilet or sink. But it was hardly acceptable for more costly repairs such as a broken furnace, a decayed roof, or broken water pipes. Sometimes, these expensive projects required more imaginative solutions.

Part of Troy's collection of roofing supplies and materials were gifts from neighbors. However, some were plundered from active construction sites located in the St. Louis metropolitan area. This is how he replaced broken cabinets and pipes. When he wanted his son to be able to go outside and play in the yard, this is the method he used to acquire wire fencing and posts. This strategy of maintaining a livable space was potentially a costly one. If he had been caught stealing the items it would not have been his first arrest. Six years ago he was arrested for lifting three furnaces from a newly built apartment community near Edwardsville, Illinois. He found this trade helpful in terms of his own rental situation, but it was also lucrative given the many East St. Louis residents who were met by similar housing circumstances. Not only could he supply materials and appliances, he could also install them for a relatively low price. This was a business that kept "change" in his pocket. Unfortunately, it was also a business that kept him at constant risk of arrest.

Admittedly, this was not the best way to make a living, especially since he was the primary caretaker of his son, a father figure to his sister's children, and contributed income to the household. "I would hate to go to the pen because of what I do," he offered, "but there really . . . if you got people to look after then sometimes you got to sacrifice yourself for them; . . . you just hope that they understand if something happens."

Other fathers here agreed, and several had purchased appliances and other materials from Troy. Manny Paul explained,

> Well, if you wait for the landlord to come around then you may as well forget that. You S.O.L. You better figure outta way to fix that roof yourself or your children are just gonna get wet. You better figure out a way to do it yourself 'cause your rent check don't buy nothin' from the landlord. That's just a fact.

Cleaning up the Neighborhood

Galen, a father of three, decided to do something about the empty house next door to the home he shared with his Aunt Merle. The house had stood abandoned for years and phone calls to the city and the county failed to raze it. A couple of winters ago, a pack of dogs had taken to the spot. They went in and out through the missing front door and nibbled on the bits of food they scavenged from the garbage dumped on the property lawn. These dogs terrified neighborhood children and adults. Not long ago, across the river in St. Louis, Missouri's "black side" of town, a black child was torn to death by loose hounds such as these (Jonsson 2001).

Local East St. Louis officials listened to residents' complaints, but ownerless dogs were a common problem throughout the city. Catching them was a costly service this abandoned city did not have the funds to begin in earnest. In St. Louis, it was the public killing of a child by wild dogs and the subsequent media attention that moved the county and city to seriously confront the menace—at least these are the thoughts of many residents. Men in East St. Louis thought that a similar scenario would need to occur in this city before the problem could be adequately addressed.

Consequently Galen, like so many parents, was left on his own to determine a solution to the situation. He was one of two adult men who lived on his street and sometimes the older women around here looked to him for protection. Early one Saturday morning, he arose from bed, grabbed his handgun and some ammunition, and headed toward the old house. He took aim through a busted front window and shot the dogs while they slept. At least two escaped. If this were not enough, the dogs did not live alone. Mice scurried about the tall grass and the bags of trash as he made his way into the house to assess his work. He told his young children to stay home and play until he could make sure that these dogs were no longer a worry.

More recently, Auntie, who always had her eyes to the window, noticed teenagers heading into the dilapidated structure. She was sure that this was the beginning of a crack house and asked her nephew to investigate. What he found instead was what appeared to be a space where young people sat, smoked, drank, and had sex. Empty cans of beer, wine bottles and an old, brown-stained mattress lay on the floor of the former dining area. Galen and his Auntie surmised that this rendezvous was simply a prelude to collective drug use and dealings. Galen contacted the city, hoping that the owner of the property could be forced to clean it up.

He posted Keep Out signs on the windows and with the help of a neighbor, boarded up the doors. His next step was to tear the structure down himself, board by board. He explained,

> I think this is the difference between living here and living somewhere else like where white people live. You got to worry about the bad element. Your children count on you to protect them from this shit. If you don't watch for it, it'll be in your backyard.

Some residents here participate in organized neighborhood cleanups and beautification projects that temporarily improve the lawns and streets for children's play. Some arrange work schedules so that they can walk their children to and from school. Mostly, though, men in this city say that they generally act alone to protect their families. According to Mark Neil,

> You can't really count on no one really . . . least not the city. They can't protect you from some of the things that's out here. You just got to do it yourself.

Others voiced a similar attitude. Robert Mooney summarized the thoughts of many others:

> If you want something done around here, you got to do it yourself. Don't wait around for nobody. A man can't wait for somebody else to protect his kids and his family, he got to move on that his own self.

FATHERS, ABANDONED CITIES, AND FUTURE RESEARCH

In the larger project of which this chapter is a part, I argue that poor people are increasingly residing in places where processes of development and investment are not made in the interests of citizenry. Abandoned cities are devastated on multiple levels. Many fathers here have inadequate incomes and low levels of education. Rather than building human capital directly, state, regional, and federal solutions tend to center on the development of business and financial capital. In the early 1990s the city was declared an enterprise zone. As such, businesses receive tax credits for investing in the city and employers receive tax credits for hiring dislocated and poor workers. Business in these areas may also receive exemptions from utility taxes and sales taxes as well as building fee waivers. In addition to being an enterprise zone, St. Louis, Missouri, and East St. Louis, Illinois, together were selected as one of sixteen national Brownfield showcase communities. The designation is intended to spur the regional cleanup of industrial and commercial properties so expansion and redevelopment are not complicated by issues of contamination. While there has been some business development in this city, the few minimum wage jobs they offer do little to improve the lives of most people here. Further, this policy encourages the development of vice-related enterprises such as casinos, taverns, liquor stores, and strip clubs. These perpetuate negative images of the city and contribute to the personal violence from which fathers guard children.

Research on fathers, concentrated poverty, and the effect on children's outcomes could continue to develop theoretical and empirical examinations of the consequences of growing up poor and the strategies parents develop to mitigate negative outcomes. Certainly, we still know very little about how African American fathers think about their father roles in these environments. How does their participation in illegal activities (e.g., drugs, burglary, etc.) contribute to the dangers affecting their children? How do they protect their children when they live in separate households or when they are in and out of jail? What specific paternal behaviors directly influence children's well being? The answers to these pressing questions would contribute to policies and programs that focus on individuals and family systems. Findings in this chapter provide support consistent with earlier studies (Anderson 1990; DeSena 1990; Edin and Lein 1997; Puntenney 1997). Fathers in this city work with neighbors to enhance community property. They protect daughters from noxious friends and other men who may blur the lines of child–adult relationships. They call on their mothers and sisters to help monitor their children in their absence. However, findings from studies in this tradition will do little to advance the quality of life for children in abandoned cities. From my view, meaningful social science research on poor populations is that which intends to improve their lives. Enterprise zones, Brownfield showcase, and smaller-scale projects miss the essence of the problem that confronts urban poverty: it is not accidental. Rather, it is the effect of decisions made by corporate and state leaders to disinvest in workers and families for profit and capital.

Future research should examine how fathers understand the structural elements that sustain the toxic environments in which they rear their children. How do they perceive the connections between local governments, regional politics, and national trends as it relates to their neighborhoods and communities? How do they work individually and collectively to affect the decisions of local and state leadership? How do they account for the decisions made by state and corporate leaders? Do they link the multiple hazards in poor areas to issues of race and relationships of political, social, and economic power? Will a poor person's folk sociology of the causes of social abandonment and disinvestment be sufficient to empower poor mothers and fathers to come together to demand the kinds of creative, progressive, reconstructive urban policies that center on the lives of the people—the men, women, and children—who live there?

Current urban-centered policies benefit only those who do not live in these dangerous, soul-searing, impoverished places. A change in policy will only occur when poor fathers, mothers, and families demand that their children and place not be abandoned. The task of the social scientists is to explain the processes of inequity that sustain abandoned communities.

NOTE

1. Ismael Lateef Ahmad, "Demotion urged in Sgt. Moran beating case," *St. Louis American,* September 24–30 1998, 1; Tim O'Neil, "Missouri study on traffic stops mirros others," *St. Louis Post-Dispatch,* June 3, 2001, 1; Valerie Scremp and Denise Hollinshed, "Police killings of 2 aim scrutiny at deadly force," *St. Louis Post-Dispatch,* June 18 2000, 1; Tim Bryant, "Suspect's family sues acquitted city officer," *St. Louis Post-Dispatch,* March 17, 2001, 3; Melinda Roth, "On the hot seat," *Riverfront Times,* July 7–13 1999, 10–14.

REFERENCES

Amato, P., and Gilbreth, J. (1999). Nonresident fathers and children's well-being: A meta-analysis. *Journal of Marriage and the Family, 61,* 557–73.

Anderson, E. (1990). *Streetwise: Race, class, and change in an urban community.* Chicago: University of Chicago Press.

Blankenhorn, D. (1995). *Fatherless America: Confronting our most urgent social problem.* New York: Basic.

Bluestone, B., and Harrison, B. (1982). *The deindustrialization of America: Plant closings, community abandonment, and the dismantling of basic industry.* New York: Basic.

Brodsky, A. (1996). Resilient single mothers in risky neighborhoods: Negative psychological sense of community. *Journal of Community Psychology, 24,* 347–63.

Burton, L. (1995). Family structure and nonmarital fertility: Perspectives from ethnographic research. Report to congress on out-of-wedlock childbearing (PHS 95-1257; pp. 147–65). Washington, DC: Department of Health and Human Services.

Carlson, M., and McLanahan, S. (2002). Father involvement in fragile families. In C. Tamis-LeMonda and N. Cabrera (Eds.) *Handbook of father involvement: Multidisciplinary perspectives* (pp. 461–88). New York: Erlbaum.

Centers for Disease Control. (2004). Summary health statistics for U.S. children: National health interview survey. U.S. Department of Health and Human Services, Series 10, 221. Washington, DC.

Coles, R. (2002). Black single father: Choosing to parent full-time. *Journal of Contemporary Ethnography, 31* (4), 411–39.

Coley, R., and Chase-Lansdale, P. (1999). Stability and change in paternal involvement among urban African American fathers. *Journal of Family Psychology, 13,* 416–35.

DeSena, J. (1990). *Protecting one's turf: Social strategies for maintaining urban neighborhoods.* New York: University of America Press.

Duncan, D. E. (1996). Growing up under the gun: Children and adolescents coping with violent neighborhoods. *Journal of Primary Prevention, 16,* 343–56.

Edin, K., and Lein, L. (1997). *Making ends meet: How single mothers survive welfare and low-wage work.* New York: Russell Sage Foundation.

Edin, K., and Nelson, T. (2001). Working steady: Race, low-income work, and family involvement among noncustodial fathers in Philadelphia. In E. Anderson and D. Massey (Eds.), *Problem of the century: Racial stratification in the United States* (pp. 374–404). New York: Russell Sage Foundation.

Fordham, S. (1996). *Blacked out: Dilemmas of race, identity, and success at Capital High.* Chicago: University of Chicago Press.

Furstenberg, F. (1993). How families manage risk and opportunity in dangerous neighborhoods. In W. J. Wilson (Ed.), *Sociology and public agenda* (pp. 231–58). Newbury Park, CA: Sage.

Furstenberg, F. (1995). Parenting in the inner city: Paternal participation and public policy. In W. Marsiglio (Ed.), *Fatherhood: Contemporary theory, research, and social policy.* (pp. 119–47). Thousand Oaks, CA: Sage.

Hamer, J. (2001). *What it means to be daddy: Fatherhood for black men living away from their children.* New York: Columbia University Press.

Hamer, J., and Marchioro, K. (2002). Becoming custodial dads: Exploring parenting among low-income African American fathers. *Journal of Marriage and the Family, 64* (1), 116–30.

Illinois Department of Public Health. (2002). *Health statistics.* Springfield, IL.

Illinois Department of Public Health. (2003a). *Childhood lead poisoning surveillance report.*

Illinois Department of Public Health. (2003b). *Illinois county cancer statistics review incidence 1996–2000.* Division of Epidemiologic Studies.

Illinois Department of Public Health. (April 3, 1998). *Health consultation.* Certain-Teed Corporation, East St. Louis, St. Clair county. CERCLIS NO. ILD984903153.

Jarrett, R. (1997). African American family and parenting strategies in impoverished neighborhoods. *Qualitative Sociology, 20,* 275–88.

Jarrett, R., Roy, K., and Burton, L. (2002). Fathers in the hood: Qualitative research on low-income African-American men. In C. S. Tamis-LeMonda and N. Cabrera (Eds.), *Handbook of father involvement: Multidisciplinary perspectives* (pp. 211–48). Mahwah, NJ: Erlbaum.

Johnson, W. (2001). The determinants of paternal involvement among unwed fathers. *Children and Youth Services Review, 23,* 513–36.

Jonsson, G. (2001). Mother of boy killed by dogs will go to son's funeral: Authorities give her permission to travel. *St. Louis Post-Dispatch*, March 15, p. B2.

Kozol, J. (1992). *Savage inequalities.* New York: HarperCollins.

Lerman, R., and Sorensen, E. (2000). Father involvement with their nonmarital children: Patterns, determinants, and effects on their earnings. *Marriage and Family Review, 29,* 75–95.

Letiecq, B., and Koblinsky, S. (2004). Parenting in violent neighborhoods: African American fathers share strategies for keeping children safe. *Journal of Family Issues, 26* (6), 715–34.

Lewis, O. (1975, reprint). *Five families: Mexican case studies in the culture of poverty.* New York: HarperCollins.

Litt, J. (1999). Managing the street, isolating the household: African American mothers respond to neighborhood deterioration. *Race, Gender and Class, 6* (3), 90–101.

McLanahan, S., Garfinkel, I., and Mincy, R. (2001). Fragile families, welfare reform, and marriage. *Policy Brief,* no. 10. Washington, DC: Brookings Institution.

Mohr, W., Fantuzzo, J., and Abdul-Kabir, S. (2001). Safeguarding themselves and their children: Mothers share their strategies. *Journal of Family Violence, 16,* 75–92.

Moss, P., and Tilly, C. (2001). *Stories employers tell: Race, skill, and hiring in America.* New York: Russell Sage Foundation.

News and Views. (2004). Leaving half a generation behind: Only a slim majority of young blacks ever finish high school. *Journal of Blacks in Higher Education.* April 30, 43, p. 52.

Puntenney, D. (1997). The impact of gang violence on the decision of everyday life: Disjunctions between policy assumptions and community conditions. *Journal of Urban Affairs, 19,* 143–61.

Roy, K. (2004). Three block fathers: Spatial perceptions and kin-work in low-income neighborhoods. *Social Problems, 51,* 528–48.

Theising, A. (1997). *East St. Louis: Made in the U.S.A.* Dissertation. University of Missouri-St. Louis.

U.S. Bureau of the Census. (2001). *Supplementary survey profile.* St. Clair County.

USA Today (1999). Crossing racial lines, coalition reaches to fathers. Thursday, June 17, 10D.

Wacquant, L. (2002). Scrutinizing the street: Poverty, morality, and the pitfalls of urban ethnography. *American Journal of Sociology, 107* (6), 1468–1574.

Wilson, W. J. (1989). *The truly disadvantaged: The inner-city, the underclass, and public policy.* Chicago: University of Chicago Press.

13

Mexican American Fathering
in Neighborhood Context

Scott Coltrane, Scott A. Melzer, Eric J. Vega, and Ross D. Parke

Many fathers support their children and shape their development in profound ways. Although social science research has documented a variety of fathering practices in the past few decades, studies have typically focused on white, middle-class fathers. This has led to calls for more research on ethnic minority fathers, and for research that places fathering in its neighborhood, economic, and cultural contexts (Buriel and DeMent 1997; Cabrera and Garcia-Coll 2004; Cabrera, Tamis-LeMonda, Bradley, Hofferth, and Lamb 2000).

Using an ongoing longitudinal study of Mexican American families in southern California (See Parke et al. 2004), we examine the situational context of Mexican American fathering, in part through comparisons to fathering among non-Latino whites (European Americans). We focus on how neighborhood problems and support influence paternal monitoring and interaction with children. Before turning to the current research, we briefly summarize past scholarship on levels and impacts of father involvement, ideals and practices in Latino families, the theoretical relationship between social class and parenting, and neighborhood influences on father involvement.

WHY FOCUS ON MEXICAN AMERICAN FATHERS?

The Latino population is growing rapidly. Latinos (Hispanics) are projected to comprise nearly one-quarter of the U.S. population by the year 2050, and Mexican Americans constitute two-thirds of the total Latino population. Latinos tend to be employed in the service sector and occupy jobs with low pay, limited benefits, few opportunities for advancement, and periodic instability. Because of low wages received by their parents, over a third of Latino children under eighteen live in poverty, more than three times the rate for non-Latinos (U.S. Census 2003). These patterns, coupled with the fact that Latinos have more children and larger households than non-Latinos, demonstrate that a disproportionate number of Latino children are reared in situations with severely limited financial resources (Cauce and Rodriguez 2002). Research shows that living on a limited income is associated with a host of risk factors for families and children, including the stress of living in high crime neighborhoods (Rank 2004).

Latino families are of particular interest because of their traditional strengths, their high fertility rates, and their emphases on child rearing and extended family bonds. Latinos typically have higher levels of extended "familism" when compared with other ethnic groups of various class levels (Vélez-Ibáñez 1996). Familism is a central value reflecting strong family cohesion, with emphasis on the group over the individual and requirements for respect and obedience toward parents and other elders (Vega, Kolody, Valle, and Weir 1991). An extended family network that lives in close proximity can provide social, emotional, and instrumental support as family members share responsibilities, especially those related to child care. This system of social support increases resources available and has been described as essential for healthy adjustment in Latino families, especially for children (Gonzales, Knight, Morgan-Lopez, Saenz, and Sirolli 2002; Vega et al. 1991).

Although most Latinos live in urban and suburban neighborhoods, stereotypes about Latino families have often been based on rural families from earlier historical time periods and on assumptions about uniformly shared values (Halgunseth 2004; McLoyd, Cauce, Takeuchi, and Wilson 2000). The image of Latino families in popular culture and scholarly research has been fairly homogeneous (and typically pejorative; see Buriel and De Ment 1997; Mirandé 1997), but contemporary Latino families are quite diverse in terms of generational status, acculturation, economic conditions, and family practices (Buriel and De Ment 1997; Cabrera and Garcia-Coll 2004; Leyendecker and Lamb 1999). To overcome such stereotypes, recent research has focused on Mexican American families, often demystifying stereotypes of either disengaged or rigid and controlling fathers preoccupied with defending their masculinity (Zinn and Wells 2000).

Our focus on Latino fathers and families reflects their numerical ascendance, but also stems from a concern about future generations. Latino youth have the highest levels of drug and alcohol use, and the highest high school dropout levels of all ethnic groups (Therrien and Ramirez 2000). Latino youth rank second only to African American populations in prevalence of risky sexual activity, teen pregnancy, and gang-related behavior (U.S. Department of Education 1995; National Center for Health Statistics 2000). These youth and their behaviors are often treated as deviant; however, few studies have focused on how

fathers contribute to or ameliorate potential youth problems in the rough neighborhoods where many of these children grow up (Phares and Compas 1992).

SOCIAL AND ECONOMIC CONTEXTS OF MEN'S PARENTING

The relation between socioeconomic status and father involvement is complex, but most sociologists start with the observation that individuals in different social locations are socialized differently. In general, different forms
and levels of education, skills, and knowledge (e.g., "cultural capital") both
reflect and reproduce class relations within a society (e.g., Bourdieu 1977).
Kohn (1977) and others suggest that the type of work that adults perform in
their everyday lives shapes the values they hold about children's behavior and
the techniques they use to raise their children. Thus, although all parents want
the best for their children and subscribe to broadly similar ideals drawn from
popular culture (Hays 1996), some research suggests that working-class parents are more likely to value children's outward appearance, conformity, and
obedience to authority, whereas middle-class parents are more likely to value
autonomy, expressiveness, exploration, and intentions. Parenting values and
practices are thus seen as shaping personalities and preparing the next generation to occupy certain types of jobs in a class-stratified society.

Although differences in parenting ideals and practices seem to be narrowing
in American society, various aspects of parenting continue to differ by social
class. Recent studies show that class position influences critical aspects of family life, including time use, language use, and kin ties. In a study of African
American and white families, Lareau (2003) showed how class-based "cultural
logics" of child rearing tend to correspond to, or conflict with, institutional standards, thus shaping the life chances of working- and middle-class children in different ways. Regardless of race, middle-class parents engage in practices of
"concerted cultivation" by fostering and assessing their children's talents, opinions, and skills. They schedule their children for a myriad of activities, reason
with them, hover over them, intervene on their behalf outside the home, and
make deliberate and sustained efforts to stimulate their cognitive and social skills
(2003, 238). Poor and working-class parents, in contrast, face tremendous economic constraints, frequently talk about money, and tend to view their children's
development as unfolding spontaneously. They focus on providing for their children by giving them comfort, food, and shelter. She labels this working-class
style of child rearing "the accomplishment of natural growth" and shows how it
deviates from the concerted cultivation of middle-class child rearing (2003,
239). Although an individual family may move up or down the economic ladder
because of job or family changes, these researchers remind us that class-linked

"cultural logics" of child rearing help reproduce the class structure. They do not explain in detail, however, how specific neighborhood and cultural contexts interact with family traditions and wealth accumulation to produce different parenting styles.

NEIGHBORHOOD AND COMMUNITY INFLUENCES ON FATHERING

Sociologists often invoke the term "social capital" to reference the actual or potential resources linked to possession of a durable network of more or less institutionalized social relationships (Bourdieu 1985; Coleman 1988). Concerning fatherhood, social capital includes reference to men's connections with individuals and organizations in the larger community, particularly the school and neighborhood. Marsiglio and Cohan (2000, 85) note that "fathers may maintain contacts with adults in the community who either interact with their children (e.g., teachers, coaches, employers, ministers, neighbors) or could provide them with resources and opportunities if called upon." Although social capital is thus typically conceptualized as an asset, some researchers also note that at an individual level, it can have either positive or negative consequences. Social ties can promote control over deviant behavior and allow access to resources, but they can also restrict individual freedoms and prohibit outsiders from gaining access to resources through particularistic preferences (Portes 1998).

Although many researchers have begun to pay attention to the ways that family structure and involved fathering might increase children's social capital, most of this research has focused on white middle-class families (Amato 1998; Cabrera and Garcia-Coll 2004). Other researchers note that the concept of social capital is inherently variable, contextual, and conditional, suggesting that social relations leading to constructive outcomes for one group may not lead to constructive outcomes for another group (Bankston and Zhou 2002). To understand how social capital is linked to fatherhood in different contexts, it is important to compare how ethnic minority and majority fathers interact with neighbors, utilize friendships, and interact with community institutions on behalf of their children. This line of research opens the door to a focus on the positive aspects of social support in ethnic minority neighborhoods, and to a focus on the differential use of social capital by Mexican American fathers when compared to European American fathers.

Research on ethnic minority families remains rare, and studies considering neighborhood influence still tend to focus on poor single mothers. Until recently, much of this research assumed that fathers contributed little to the everyday aspects of parenting in poor ethnic neighborhoods, and that this limited father involvement contributed to a culture of poverty. Countering the stereotypes promoted by this research, but acknowledging the importance of unemployment on family formation, a recent comprehensive review found that both African American and Latino fathers reported higher levels of monitoring and supervising of their children than European American fathers (McLoyd et al. 2000). Such findings raise the possibility that poor men of color are responding to the threats that their neighborhoods pose to their children, albeit in authoritarian ways that diverge from white middle-class norms valuing children's emotional expression (Chao 1994; Mirandé 1997).

Vélez-Ibáñez (1996) shows how various social and economic pressures have historically compressed Mexican Americans into culturally and politically subordinated populations. In response, Mexican American neighborhoods have developed systems of reciprocity and exchange that rely on frequent visiting and mutual aid. Using concepts like "clustering" and "funds of knowledge," Vélez-Ibáñez (1996) shows how information is utilized for family subsistence and raising children. He describes how multiple households provide an opportunity for children to be part of a zone of comfort that is familiar yet experimental. Thus parents who restrict neighborhood play may not necessarily be exerting themselves in a domineering, authoritarian fashion. Rather, child supervision may be accomplished by establishing play zones based on the parent's knowledge of neighborhood threat. According to Vélez-Ibáñez, parental establishment of safe zones in collaboration with nearby kin allows Mexican immigrant children in poor neighborhoods to experiment and grow without fear of dangerous consequences.

Such research begins to show how neighborhoods (particularly poor urban areas) can directly affect childhood outcomes and indirectly impact children through situated parenting styles (O'Neil, Parke, and McDowell 2001). Jarrett (1997, 49) notes that "several explanations—including neighborhood resource, collective socialization, contagion, competition, and relative deprivation theories—have been proposed to identify the mechanisms by which neighborhoods impair cognitive, economic, and social outcomes." Dohan (2003) observes that most such studies are predicated on the image of the low-income community as an unwitting victim of crime in the same way that a sick person is the unwitting host of a disease: "Scholars draw on the language of infection when they use epidemiological models to help describe the spread of social problems from one neighborhood to another" (2003, 150). Other scholars speak of criminal infection metaphorically, suggesting, for example, that gangs are invading organisms that prey on a community by recruiting youth to participate in illicit activities. Although this research is still in its infancy, researchers have found only modest neighborhood effects on child outcomes after controlling for other effects (O'Neil et al. 2001). Most research continues to ignore the potential positive influence of social support in poor ethnic neighborhoods and ignores the observation that crime may be the only way to make ends meet in economically marginalized communities or groups (Dohan 2003; Edin and Lein 1997).

Though researchers have attempted to isolate how fathering is influenced by broad socioeconomic conditions distinct from other neighborhood conditions, it is virtually impossible to separate them. A typical model describes exogenous forces (e.g., housing discrimination, racism, labor-market conditions, migration, etc.) producing "neighborhoods of concentrated disadvantage" (Gephart and Brooks-Gunn 1997, xvii). Neighborhoods then vary by formal opportunities and constraints, dangers, networks, and ethnic composition, with all of these heavily influenced by the extent of poverty. In turn, fathers and their families respond to these neighborhood conditions in various ways, based in part on individual and family characteristics, as well as cultural and economic factors. Finally, children's developmental outcomes result from the complex interplay of these processes.

ASSESSING FATHER INVOLVEMENT IN SITUATED CONTEXTS

As demonstrated in comprehensive reviews (Marsiglio, Amato, Day, and Lamb 2000; Pleck 1997; Pleck and Masciadrelli 2003), father involvement is influenced by various factors, with no single factor responsible for different types of involvement. Studies report contradictory findings for factors like income, education, age, family size, and birth timing, and few consider the role of neighborhood conditions. Research on fathering in two-parent households shows that men have increased their parenting involvement in the past few decades, both in absolute terms and in relation to mothers. Simultaneously, however, average levels of fathers' interaction with, availability to, and responsibility for children lag well behind those of mothers (Coltrane 2004; Pleck and Masciadrelli 2003). According to most researchers (see Baumrind 1978), an authoritative style of parenting (including fathering) that combines warmth and control creates the best environment for child development, though there are debates about whether this style applies equally to all ethnic groups and whether more authoritarian styles (less warmth, more control) can be equally or more effective for some subgroups (e.g., Asian Americans, African Americans, and Latinos; see Chao 1994; Garcia-Coll et al. 1996).

In chapter 1 of this volume, Marsiglio, Roy, and Fox note, "Individuals 'do family' in specific places and structured settings" (p. 3). These authors identify five primary and interrelated properties associated with fathering sites, three of which we incorporate in our analysis. Building on the model described above, *social structural conditions*, such as institutional inequality along ethnic lines, leave fathers with varying levels of power and access to valued resources. Instigating a renewed focus on neighborhoods, Wilson (1987) argues that neighborhoods impoverished by the decline of manufacturing and middle-class flight have disproportionately impacted poor urban people of color. Also, *physical conditions* in neighborhoods may, for example, lead fathers to alter their parenting strategies based on the degree of threat to their children or the extent of support they receive from neighbors. As noted above, neighborhood problems are a result of social structural conditions, whereby ethnic families are concentrated in poorer areas that are more racially segregated. Residents in turn may pursue forms of social support or isolation in response to various threats. Finally, *symbolic/perceptual* properties are uniquely important to the current research, as fathers report on perceived characteristics of their neighborhoods. Much of the research on neighborhoods uses "objective" measures compiled at an aggregate level. For example, researchers obtain data on employment rates, racial and ethnic composition, mean household size, and so forth. O'Neil and colleagues (2001) argue that subjective measures are also needed because individuals' perceptions are important determinants of behavior. Thus fathers in the same neighborhood may perceive different degrees of threat to their children's well-being, and therefore monitor them differently.

The editors of this volume also offer a number of secondary properties associated with fathering sites, two of which are uniquely important to our research. First, *institutional and cultural conditions* such as norms regarding family (e.g., increased familism) are important components of fathering (Coltrane, Parke, and Adams 2004). As well, "structural inequalities embedded in race/ethnicity, class, and sexual orientation distinctions also prominently shape the contexts of fatherhood experiences" (Marsiglio et al., chapter 1, p. 11). We highlight structural inequalities and cultural conditions while examining specific neighborhood conditions and fathering. Neighborhood contexts influence parenting because fathers' sense of *personal power and control* may vary with their perceived sense of safety in their communities. Fathers living in dangerous neighborhoods may adopt different parenting practices than those in safer suburban neighborhoods because of their perceived power (or lack of power). In the past, fathering practices have been assumed to stem from cultural differences, differential social class location, or different family structures. Here we entertain the possibility that neighborhood factors can become primary determinants of fathering practices, especially for families of color.

LINKING NEIGHBORHOODS WITH
CLASS, CULTURE, AND FATHERING

Recently Hofferth (2003) used a nationally representative sample to isolate the significance of various contexts on father involvement in two-parent families. She found that Latino fathers (mostly Mexican American) were more permissive than other fathers, exhibiting less control and greater responsibility for child care than European American fathers. Countering popular stereotypes, Hofferth found that both black and Latino fathers exercised more responsibility for children than white fathers. Even though both African American and Latino families lived in less desirable neighborhoods, only the African American fathers showed higher levels of monitoring (Hofferth 2003). Hofferth suggested that because many Latinos live in majority Latino neighborhoods where collective monitoring is more common, there could be reduced demand for fathers' individual monitoring. Further, this same research found that Latino fathers exhibited less control over their children than European American fathers, while African American fathers demonstrated greater control.

A key caveat throughout the literature on how neighborhood conditions are related to fathering is that, though these relationships are generally significant, they are usually neither strong nor the primary factor in determining child outcomes. Fathering, for example, may be adjusted in response to children's behavior, which in turn is partly the result of neighborhood characteristics. However, several studies have identified specific parental strategies in response to dangerous neighborhoods, including increased monitoring, chaperoning or having older kin accompany younger children, spending more time (sometimes forced) at home with family members, and working with neighbors to monitor and protect these areas (Burton and Jarrett 2000; Vigil 1997). Several researchers argue that neighborhood effects on parenting, though important, are smaller than those related to personal characteristics, family structure, and socioeconomic indicators (Burton and Jarrett 2000; Lehman and Smeeding 1997).

DATA AND METHODS

We rely on initial data from a longitudinal study in progress examining how economic stress affects Southern California Mexican American and European American families. With the help of public elementary schools, we recruited 278 families (167 Mexican American, 111 European American) with at least one child in the fifth grade (Coltrane et al. 2004; Parke et al. 2004). The site of the study is referred to as the "Inland Empire," and is situated to the east of Los Angeles, northeast of Anaheim, and north of San Diego. The Riverside/San Bernardino metropolitan area is a working-class region with a Latino population of over 1 million that ranked 250th out of the nation's 311 metropolitan statistical areas in per capita income during the 1990s. Data were collected via separate face-to-face interviews with mothers, fathers, and children lasting two to four hours.

CHARACTERISTICS OF MEXICAN AMERICAN FAMILIES

Three-fourths of the Mexican American fathers in the study were born in Mexico and came to the United States after age fifteen, making them first-generation immigrants, and rendering their children part of the second generation. Following sampling criteria designed to focus on children who had completed all their schooling in the United States, all families had been living in the United States for at least five years. More than eight of ten children were born in the United States. To avoid creating problems for the families, we did not ask about citizenship or residency status, but the vast majority identified as Mexican American (rather than Mexicano). Seventy-one percent of the Mexican American parents elected to be interviewed in Spanish (rather than English). In contrast, over 80 percent of the Mexican American children chose to be interviewed in English. This signals that these families were undergoing acculturative processes across generations that put special strains on parenting and family relations. Using the Acculturative Rating Scale for Mexican Americans (Cuellar, Arnold, and Maldonaldo 1995), we found that 57 percent of parents scored in the Mexican-oriented range, 32 percent scored in the bicultural range, and 11 percent scored in the Anglo-oriented range.

To better understand the social location of Mexican American families in the region, it is helpful to compare them to their European American counterparts who live in the same communities. Because we drew our Mexican American and European American samples from the same public schools, the families live in proximity. A preponderance of cities and unincorporated communities in the Riverside/San Bernardino region have no single racial/ethnic group constituting a majority of the population. Even greater levels of ethnic diversity are found in public school enrollments, with non-Latino whites constituting a minority of students in most of the schools in the larger unified districts of the region. Although most neighborhoods in the region also include different races and ethnicities, many poorer neighborhoods have high concentrations of Mexican Americans and many wealthier neighborhoods have high concentrations of European Americans because of income and wealth differences.

Table 13.1 shows that the Mexican American families in the study, like those in the larger population, had much lower incomes, on average, than their European American counterparts. Total household income for the Mexican American families ranged from $2,900 to over $200,000 per year, with only 2 percent of families earning more that $100,000. Mean annual household income for the Mexican Americans was $35,769, with 30 percent earning at least $40,000 per year and 33 percent earning $20,000 or less. In contrast, household income for the European American families ranged from $5,000 to over $500,000 per year, with 19 percent of families earning over $100,000 per year, 79 percent of families earning at least $40,000, and only 5 percent earning $20,000 per year or less. Educational differences between the two ethnic groups were similarly large, with the Mexican American men attending just over nine years of schooling (equivalent to less than a high school diploma) and the European American men averaging fourteen years of schooling— equivalent to two years of college or trade school after high school.

Although the European American families enjoyed incomes that were on average twice as high as those of the Mexican American families, they were only moderately more likely to be homeowners than the Mexican Americans. Table 13.1 shows that 76 percent of the European American families were homeowners, and that the mean value of the houses they occupied in 1998 was over $187,000. In contrast, 64 percent of the Mexican American families were homeowners, with their houses worth an average of $90,505. The relatively high rate of homeownership among moderate-income Mexican Americans was facilitated by several local real estate market shifts resulting in low prices (by California standards) for modest, older single-family homes in the 1980s and 1990s.

Table 13.1. Family Characteristics by Ethnicity

Family Demographics	Mexican American	European American
Annual household income (mean)	$35,769	$81,759***
Proportion owning/buying their home	64%	76%*
House value (mean for homeowners)	$90,505	$187,189***
Father's age (mean)	38.9	42.4***
Father's years of education (mean)	9.3	14.2***
Number of children (mean)	3.3	2.7***
Proportion of households containing other adults	32%	23%*
Proportion interviewed in Spanish	71%	0%***
Proportion of mothers employed	47%	65%**
N	167	111

*p < .05   **p < .01   ***p < .001

Although the Mexican American fathers in the study were about three years younger than their European American counterparts (39 vs. 42 years), they were likely to have more children living in the home (3.3 vs. 2.7). They were also more likely to have other adults living in the home (32 vs. 23 percent). The presence of more adults and children, coupled with the fact that they were living in smaller houses in older neighborhoods, contributed to more crowded living conditions among the Mexican Americans. Whereas 47 percent of mothers in the Mexican American families were employed outside the home, 65 percent of European American mothers held jobs outside the home.

FINDINGS

Table 13.2 presents data on the father's perception of problems in the neighborhood. For every issue listed, the Mexican American fathers were significantly more likely than the European Americans to say that it was a problem. Concerning poverty, 67 percent of Mexican American fathers said that unemployment and homelessness were problems in their neighborhood, compared to less than a quarter of European American fathers. Delinquency was similarly much more common for Mexican Americans, with 62–70 percent of the Mexican American fathers reporting that delinquent gangs, drug use or dealing, or groups of teenagers hanging out created a nuisance in their neighborhoods. Property crimes were common in the neighborhoods where Mexican American families lived, with over 70 percent of Mexican American fathers reporting that vandalism and the stealing of toys, bikes, and other property was a problem, compared to about 40 percent of European Americans. The largest contrast between ethnic groups was for violent crimes. Approximately two out of three Mexican American fathers reported that assaults, muggings, and shootings were a problem in their neighborhoods, whereas only about one in six European American fathers made the same observation. In summary, our data confirm what others have reported: Mexican Americans are much more likely to live in threatening neighborhoods than their European American counterparts.

Turning to the child's perceptions of neighborhood problems, a slightly different pattern emerges. We asked children to indicate the extent to which various problems limited their activities. Although we found some differences by ethnicity, they were generally smaller than the ones we found for fathers' reporting about neighborhood problems. For example, half of both Mexican American and European American children reported that their activities were limited by gangs of teens hanging out, whereas Mexican American fathers

Table 13.2. Neighborhood Problems and Paternal Monitoring by Ethnicity

Neighborhood Problems	Mexican American	European American
Percentage of fathers saying it is a problem in neighborhood		
Unemployment	67%***	22%
Homelessness	67%***	16%
Drug use or dealing in the open	62%***	18%
Delinquent gangs	69%***	24%
Groups of teenagers hanging out creating a nuisance	70%***	32%
Toys, bikes, other property gets stolen	71%***	43%
Vandalism	71%***	39%
Assaults and muggings	65%***	17%
Shootings	69%***	17%
Percentage of children saying problem limits their activities		
Activities limited by gangs of teens hanging out	50%	50%
Activities limited by toys, bikes, property being stolen	51%	44%
Activities limited by tagging and graffiti (vandalism)	40%**	23%
Activities limited by beatings (assaults and muggings)	38%*	26%
Activities limited by shootings	41%**	23%
Paternal Monitoring		
Percentage of fathers who allow their child to play in front of their home without adult supervision (some, a lot)	24%***	64%
Percentage of fathers strongly agreeing: My children can spend as much of his/her free time as s/he wants in the afternoon with friends.	22%***	49%
I make sure I know where my child is and what s/he is doing.	74%**	60%
Father and child go for a walk together:		
Father report (often, very often)	33%*	20%
Child report (often, very often)	33%**	15%
Father and child go shopping together:		
Father report (often, very often)	68%***	41%
Child report (often, very often)	40%**	24%

*p < .05   **p < .01   ***p < .001

were more than twice as likely as European fathers to report gangs as a problem. Similarly, although more Mexican American than European American children said that their activities were limited by toys, bikes, and property being stolen, the difference between ethnic groups was not statistically significant. For the other five items asked of children, Mexican Americans were significantly more likely to report that the neighborhood problem limited their activities. About 40 percent of Mexican American children said that they were limited by tagging and graffiti, beatings, or shootings. Meanwhile, only about 25 percent of European Americans reported the same tendency.

Fifth grade children appear to see less neighborhood danger than their fathers. This sets up a situation in which fathers feel a need to regulate children's activities in the neighborhood. Because they are more likely to live in dangerous neighborhoods, Mexican American fathers are more likely to monitor their children's outside activities than are European American fathers. As shown in table 13.2, only 24 percent of Mexican American fathers reported that they allow their children to play in front of their home without adult supervision, compared to 64 percent of European American fathers. Similarly, only about 22 percent of Mexican American fathers strongly agreed with the statement, "My children can spend as much of his/her free time as s/he wants in the afternoon with friends." In contrast, 49 percent of the European American fathers strongly agreed with this statement. Finally, 74 percent of Mexican American fathers strongly agreed that they "make sure they know where their children are and what they are doing," significantly more than the 60 percent of European Americans who concurred.

Mexican American fathers are also more likely than European American fathers to walk with their children in the neighborhood. According to both fathers' reports and children's reports, 33 percent of Mexican American fathers and children often took walks together, a proportion that is significantly higher than European fathers' (20 percent) and children's (15 percent) reports. Similarly, Mexican American fathers were much more likely than their European American counterparts to report that they went shopping with their children. In addition to responding to neighborhood threat, these patterns of fathers interacting with children in public areas were shaped by greater availability of neighborhood grocery stores in European fathers' neighborhoods and Mexican Americans' lower levels of car ownership.

Although most studies of low-income neighborhoods focus on how families are neglected by banks and businesses, infected by drug use, and exploited by violent gangs, there is another reality to life in such environments. The Mexican American fathers in our study shared a sense of isolation from the dominant culture at the same time that they were attempting to share in its economic benefits. Thirty-two percent of the fathers reported that they had been treated rudely or badly because of their ethnicity, and almost as many agreed that it was difficult to get a job or a promotion because of their ethnicity (results not shown in tables). Seventy percent of Mexican American fathers considered racial conflicts in their neighborhoods to be a problem, a perception that was more than three times higher than among European American fathers. The sense of isolation in some Mexican American neighborhoods stems from the perception that the dominant culture and its institutions do not care about the residents who live there. Sixty-five percent of Mexican American fathers agreed that police do not respect people of Mexican descent, and 72 percent agreed that police did not care about their problems. As noted above, because of racism and economic marginalization, many low-income communities do not simply oppose crime, but rather engage it dynamically in various and contradictory ways (Dohan 2003). More than one in ten of the Mexican American families we studied reported that they had a family member who was picked up by the police or arrested. The double burden of fearing gang violence and fearing the police who were supposed to stop it has been suggested as a source of alienation among Mexican American immigrants (Portes and Rumbaut 2001).

In a major comparative study of immigrant populations in the United States, Portes and Rumbaut (2001, 278) describe Mexican immigrants as living in the weakest communities and experiencing the lowest levels of coethnic support observed among the many ethnic groups that they studied. In contrast, we found levels of support among our Mexican American sample to be remarkably high, especially in light of the comparatively short time they had lived in their neighborhoods and the many overt dangers they faced.

Table 13.3 shows that the Mexican American families in our study had lived in their current neighborhood for an average of five or six years, whereas their European American counterparts had lived in their neighborhoods for an average of between eight and nine years. Despite this shorter residency, a greater proportion of Mexican American families reported that they had other family members living in their neighborhoods. Mexican American fathers were also more likely to report that they had someone over to their house to socialize than the European American fathers. In contrast, the European American fathers reported that they were more likely to stop on the street and chat with someone from their neighborhood. These patterns reflect greater possibilities for informal public social contact in safer neighborhoods, and the pressure to socialize within the confines of one's own home in more impoverished or dangerous neighborhoods.

Seventy-four percent of Mexican American fathers reported that they were part of a close-knit neighborhood where people are friendly and help each other out, a proportion significantly higher than reported by European American fathers. Because Mexican American families live in neighborhoods that

Table 13.3. **Neighborhood Contact and Support by Ethnicity**

	Mexican American	European American
Length of time lived in neighborhood (mean no. years)	5.7	8.7***
Proportion with family living in the neighborhood	32%*	22%
Neighborhood Social Contact		
Percentage with some activity in past month, fathers' report:		
Asked someone from your neighborhood over to your house or went over to their house for a meal, to play cards, watch TV, etc.	46%*	34%
Stopped to chat with someone from your neighborhood on the street	70%**	84%
Neighborhood Support		
Percentage of fathers agreeing:		
I am part of a close-knit neighborhood where people are friendly and help each other out.	74%*	61%
I can call on my neighbors to lend me a hand without feeling that I am imposing on them.	78%	71%
My neighbors help me out by looking after my children if I want to run a brief errand.	57%	57%
Older children in the neighborhood keep an eye on the younger ones when they're all playing outside.	49%	53%
Percentage of children (frequently or very frequently):		
Ask a person in the neighborhood for help (like carrying packages, fixing a broken toy or bike)	15%*	6%
Give help to a person in the neighborhood (carrying packages, gardening, watching another child, etc.)	25%	21%

*p < .05   **p < .01   ***p < .001

have more crime and violence, it is remarkable that they reported levels of social support that rivaled those of European Americans. Nevertheless, Mexican Americans and European Americans reported roughly similar levels of neighborly support from adults and children. And children's reports confirmed the same pattern, with Mexican American children significantly more likely to report that they asked someone from the neighborhood for support and slightly more likely to report that they gave help to someone in the neighborhood.

The influence of neighborhood context was significant in both ethnic groups for the important parental dimension of emotional warmth. Mexican American and European American fathers who lived in more supportive neighborhoods were more likely to show affection to their children, nurture them, accept them, respect their ideas and opinions, and promote their creative growth (results not shown in tables). Most of the research on ethnic minority fathers has heretofore focused on the constraining influence of low-income neighborhoods rather than on variation in the supportiveness of those neighborhoods. This analysis suggests that, at least for Mexican American families, scholars should pay as much attention to the potential positive influence of neighborhood support as they do to the potential negative influence of neighborhood crime, threat, and decay.

DISCUSSION

One key element in the social cohesion of these neighborhoods was the sense of belonging that the Mexican American families forged. Although these neighborhoods were plagued by violence and gangs, they also provided support to their residents. We suggest that their sense of belonging was enhanced by a preponderance of homeownership in the neighborhood, and also by the presence of kin. Although ethnic minority populations are typically described as deficient in social capital, these Mexican American immigrant families were developing social bonds by forging relations with kin and neighbors. In the process, they were buffering their children from hardship and protecting them from neighborhood threats.

Countering unidirectional theories of poverty, neighborhood decline, and family disorganization, we observed the simultaneous occurrence of threat and support in these neighborhoods. Rather than conceptualizing neighborhood decline and neighborhood support as separate and competing trajectories, we see them as working relatively independently. In some cases, neighborhood decline can undermine all forms of familial and extrafamilial support, but in others it can work to bolster the resolve of families and encourage them to monitor their children in ways that can buffer them from possible future risky behaviors.

One key finding from our study concerns the links between fathers' perceptions of neighborhood and fathering behavior. Mexican American fathers, in contrast to European Americans, perceived greater threats and danger in their neighborhoods; in turn, they were more restrictive and protective of their children as evidenced by higher levels of monitoring and supervision. Rather than viewing Mexican American fathers as simply restrictive, we can view them as protective and acting responsibly in response to the perceived level of neighborhood threat. Thus parenting strategies may develop as an adaptive response to unsafe and unpredictable environments. This evidence for Mexican American fathers is consistent with earlier work with African American families (Brody et al. 2001; Furstenberg, Cook, Eccles, Elder, and Sameroff 1999). Based on studies focusing primarily on mothers, African American parents residing in unsafe neighborhoods tended to use more authoritarian (i.e., restrictive and controlling) parenting strategies to protect their children. Moreover, children in these contexts benefited from these authoritarian parenting practices in terms of their adjustment (Brody et al. 2001), while majority children are often harmed by the use of these authoritarian practices (Baumrind 1978).

There are several reasons for the positive links between restrictive parenting and better child adjustment. First, greater control in harsh environments may, in fact, protect children from potentially harmful threats (e.g., deviant peers, gangs, guns). Second, children in racial/ethnic minority groups may interpret parental behavior differently than majority white children. The use of authoritarian tactics is generally more normative and viewed as an acceptable child rearing style in ethnic neighborhoods (Corral-Verdugo, Frias-Armenta, Romero, and Munoz 1995; Sonnek 1999; for a similar argument about Asian Americans, see Chao 1994). Third, the context in which parental restrictiveness occurs is critical to understanding its impact on children. For example, the link between harsh parenting and child outcomes may depend on whether parental disciplinary actions are carried out in the context of a warm, supportive family environment. To the extent that there is a supportive parent–child relationship and marital harmony, the effects of restrictive practices are likely to be more beneficial. Only when there is a hostile parent–child relationship will there be negative outcomes associated with the use of these practices.

Turning to our own findings, it is likely that the relatively authoritarian practices we observed in response to neighborhood threat will have minimal detrimental impacts on the children since these same Mexican American fathers reported more involvement with their children (e.g., walk and shop together). In other analyses from our project, we discovered that less acculturated Mexican American fathers with traditional views about gender were highly involved with their children (Coltrane et al. 2003). We also discovered that overt conflict in Mexican American marriages was a better predictor of child emotional problems than hostile parenting (Parke et al. 2004) and that father's use of physical punishment was associated with more behavior problems in children only when there was a hostile family climate. If there was a warm and supportive family atmosphere, the link between harsh fathering and child adjustment was not evident (Schofield 2004). Hence it is important to consider both the restrictiveness and the emotional warmth of the father–child relationship to understand how paternal practices affect child development.

Our findings suggest a complex profile of Mexican American fathers as restrictive, protective, and loving at the same time. As normative definitions of fathering continue to change, it is important to recognize that fathering practices continue to vary according to the presence of neighborhood threat and neighborhood support. We should also remember that such variations also carry different meanings according to ethnic, cultural, and family traditions. We could better understand the influence of fathers on children if we attended to such differences and analyzed them in their situated contexts.

FUTURE RESEARCH

Our findings suggest a variety of ways that future research might contribute to a better understanding of situated fathering. To begin, fatherhood studies should routinely include ethnic minority families so that comparative analyses and within-group analyses can be performed. Studies should also strive to collect more information about neighborhoods and economic contexts, because both of these factors tend to be salient for fathering. We found that family size and house size shaped opportunities for individual privacy or group interaction, and that home ownership played an important role in how family members felt about their neighborhoods. These are important variables to include in future studies of fathers and families.

Economic and neighborhood factors influence mothering as well as fathering, but men's conventional roles as breadwinner and protector may be especially affected by variations in the earning power of fathers or their ability to keep their children safe. Although we did not report on data for mothers, we also advocate the collection of identical information from mothers and fathers, so that assessments of the joint and net influences of mothering and fathering might be isolated. Similarly, data from the children's perspective is potentially useful in developing a more complete understanding of family dynamics and isolating the reasons that some parental actions carry grave consequences whereas others seem to matter very little.

A key insight from our analysis is that neighborhood support can be just as important as neighborhood danger in shaping parenting practices and presumably child outcomes. This suggests that future research should focus on the ways that all ethnic groups forge ties with other adults and children, share resources and support, and negotiate living in hostile environments. Of particular note in our study was the impact of the presence of extended kin. Although kin networks may be particularly important to Mexican American families, we would like to see more studies comparing the kin networks of various ethnic groups. Finally, the neighborhood data we collected were extremely reliable and related to many individual and family process variables. We encourage other family and child researchers to include such measures in their studies so that we can develop more ecologically sensitive models of family and human development. Although most sociologists use aggregate data (e.g., census) to explore neighborhood effects, our emergent findings suggest that parents' perceptions of neighborhood threats and supports may be better predictors, especially for family process and child outcome variables. Whenever possible, we encourage researchers to include comparable subjective measures of neighborhood quality in future family studies.

Future research on Mexican American fathers ought to pay close attention to the role of social class, familism, and masculinity in shaping fatherhood ideals and fathering practices. To what extent are these issues related to the sorts of neighborhoods and jobs that are available to Mexican American men and their families? How do they shape men's expectations for themselves, their wives, and their children? These and other important questions might be answered if future research paid more attention to the situated character of fathering practices.

REFERENCES

This research was supported in part by grants from the National Institute of Mental Health (MH54154); the College of Humanities, Arts, and Social Sciences, University of California, Riverside; and the Center for Rural Mental Health, Iowa State University. Correspondence regarding this chapter should be addressed to Scott Coltrane, University of California, Riverside, Department of Sociology, Riverside, CA 92521.

Amato, P. (1998). More than money? Men's contributions to their children's lives. In A. Booth and A. Crouter (Eds.), *Men in families* (pp. 241–78). Mahwah, NJ: Erlbaum.

Bankston, C. L., and Zhou, M. (2002). Social capital as process: The meanings and problems of a theoretical metaphor. *Sociological Inquiry, 72* (2), 285–317.

Baumrind, D. (1978). Parental disciplinary patterns and social competence in children. *Youth and Society, 9,* 239–76.

Bourdieu, P. (1977). *Outline of the theory of practice.* Cambridge: Cambridge University Press.

Bourdieu, P. (1985). The forms of capital. In J. G. Richardson (Ed.), *Handbook of theory and research for the sociology of education* (pp. 241–58). New York: Greenwood.

Brody, G. H., Ge, X., Conger, R., Gibbons, F. X., Murry, V. M., Gerrard, M., and Simons, R. L. (2001). The influence of neighborhood disadvantage, collective socialization, and parenting on African American children's affiliation with deviant peers. *Child Development, 72,* 1231–46.

Buriel, R., and De Ment, T. (1997). Immigration and sociocultural changes in Mexican, Chinese, and Vietnamese American families. In A. Booth, A. C. Crouter and N. Landale (Eds.), *Immigration and the family* (pp. 165–200). Mahwah, NJ: Erlbaum.

Burton, L. M., and Jarrett, R. L. (2000). In the mix, yet on the margins: The place of families in urban neighborhood and child development research. *Journal of Marriage and the Family, 62,* 444–65.

Cabrera, N., and Garcia-Coll, C. (2004). Latino fathers. In M. E. Lamb (Ed.), *The role of the father in child development* (4th ed., pp. 98–120). New York: Wiley.

Cabrera, N., Tamis-LeMonda, C. S., Bradley, B., Hofferth, S., and Lamb, M. E. (2000). Fatherhood in the 21st century. *Child Development, Millennium Issue, 71,* 127–36.

Cauce, A. M., and Rodriguez, M. D. (2002). Latino families: Myths and realities. In J. M. Contreras, K. A. Kerns, and A. M. Neal-Bernett (Eds.), *Latino children and families in the United States* (pp. 3–25). New York: Praeger.

Chao, R. (1994). Beyond parental control and authoritarian parenting style. *Child Development, 65,* 1111–19.

Coleman, J. S. (1988). Social capital in the creation of human capital. *American Journal of Sociology, 94,* 95–121.

Coltrane, S. (2003). Fathering: Paradoxes, contradictions, and dilemmas. In M. Coleman and L. Ganong (Eds.), *Handbook of contemporary families* (pp. 224–43). Thousand Oaks, CA: Sage.

Coltrane, S., Parke, R. D., and Adams, M. (2004). Complexity of father involvement in low-income Mexican American families. *Family Relations, 53,* 179–89.

Corral-Verdugo, V., Frias-Armenta, M., Romero, M., and Munoz, A. (1995). Validity of a scale of beliefs regarding the "positive" effects of punishing children: A study of Mexican mothers. *Child Abuse and Neglect, 19,* 669–79.

Cuellar, I., Arnold, B., and Maldonado, R. (1995). Acculturation rating scale for Mexican Americans II. *Hispanic Journal of Behavioral Sciences, 17,* 275–304.

Dohan, D. (2003). *The price of poverty: Money, work, and culture in the Mexican American barrio.* Berkeley: University of California Press.

Edin, K., and Lein, L. (1997). *Making ends meet.* New York: Russell Sage Foundation.

Furstenberg, F. F., Cook, T., Eccles, J., Elder, G., and Sameroff, A. (1999). *Managing to make it.* Chicago: University of Chicago Press.

Garcia-Coll, C., Lamberty, G., Jenkins, R., McAdoo, H. P., Crnic, K., Wasik, B. H., and Vasquez-Garcia, H. (1996). An integrative model for the study of developmental competencies in minority children. *Child Development, 67,* 1891–1914.

Gephart, M. A., and Brooks-Gunn, J. (1997). Introduction. In J. Brooks-Gunn, G. J. Duncan, and J. L. Aber (Eds.), *Neighborhood poverty: Vol. 1. Context and consequences for children* (pp. xiii–xxii). New York: Russell Sage Foundation.

Gonzales, N. A., Knight, G. P., Morgan-Lopez, A., Saenz, D. S., and Sirolli, A. (2002). Acculturation, enculturation, and the mental health of Latino youths: An integration and critique of the literature. In J. M. Contreras, K. A. Kerns, and A. M. Neal-Barnett (Eds.), *Latino children and families in the United States* (pp. 45–74). New York: Praeger.

Halgunseth, L. C. (2004). Continuing research on Latino families: El pasado y el futuro. In M. Coleman and L. Ganong (Eds.), *Handbook of contemporary families* (pp. 333–51). London: Sage.

Hays, S. (1996). *The cultural contradictions of motherhood.* New Haven, CT: Yale University Press.

Hofferth, S. L. (2003). Race/ethnic differences in father involvement in two-parent families: Culture, context, or economy? *Journal of Family Issues, 24,* 185–216.

Jarrett, R. L. (1997). Bringing families back in: Neighborhood effects on child development. In J. Brooks-Gunn, G. J. Duncan, and J. Aber (Eds.), *Neighborhood poverty: Vol. 2* (pp. 48–64). New York: Russell Sage Foundation.

Kohn, M. (1977). *Class and conformity.* Chicago: University of Chicago Press.

Lamb, M. E. (2003). *The role of the father in child development.* Hoboken, NJ: Wiley.

Lareau, A. (2003). *Unequal childhoods.* Berkeley: University of California Press.

Lehman, J. S., and Smeeding, T. M. (1997). Neighborhood effects and federal policy. In J. Brooks-Gunn, G. J. Duncan, and J. L. Aber (Eds.), *Neighborhood poverty: Vol. 1* (pp. 251–78). New York: Russell Sage Foundation.

Leyendecker, B., and Lamb, M. E. (1999). Latino families. In M. E. Lamb (Ed.), *Parenting and child development in "nontraditional" families* (pp. 247–62). Mahwah, NJ: Erlbaum.

Marsiglio, W., Amato, P., Day, R. D, and Lamb, M. E. (2000). Scholarship on fatherhood in the 1990s and beyond. *Journal of Marriage and the Family, 62,* 1173–91.

Marsiglio, W., and Cohan, M. (2000). Contextualizing father involvement and paternal influence: Sociological and qualitative themes. *Marriage and Family Review, 29,* 75–95.

Marsiglio, W., Roy, K., and Fox, G. L. (2005). Situated fathering: A spatially sensitive and social approach. In W. Marsiglio, K. Roy and G. L. Fox (Eds.), *Situated fathering: A focus on physical and social spaces.* Lanham, MD: Rowman & Littlefield.

McLoyd, V. C, Cauce, A. M., Takeuchi, D., and Wilson, L. (2000). Marital processes and parental socialization in families of color: A decade review of research. *Journal of Marriage and the Family, 62,* 1070–93.

Mirandé, A. (1997). *Hombres y Machos.* Boulder: Westview.

National Center for Health Statistics. (2000). Retrieved January 2004, from http://www.cdc.gov/nchs/

O'Neil, R., Parke, R. D., and McDowell, D. J. (2001). Objective and subjective features of children's neighborhoods. *Applied Developmental Psychology, 22,* 135–55.

Parke, R. D. (1996). *Fatherhood.* Cambridge, MA: Harvard University Press.

Parke, R. D., Coltrane, S., Duffy, S., Buriel, R., Dennis, J., Powers, J., French, S., and Widaman, K. W. (2004). Economic stress, parenting, and child adjustment in Mexican American and European American families. *Child Development, 75,* 1632–56.

Phares, V., and Compas, B. E. (1992). The role of fathers in child and adolescent psychopathology: Make room for Daddy. *Psychological Bulletin, 111,* 387–412.

Pleck, J. H. (1997). Paternal involvement. In M. E. Lamb (Ed.), *The role of the father in child development* (3rd ed., pp. 66–103). New York: Wiley.

Pleck, J. H., and Masciadrelli, B. P. (2003). Paternal involvement: Levels, sources, and consequences. In M. E. Lamb (Ed.), *The role of the father in child development* (4th ed., pp. 222–71). New York: Wiley.

Portes, A. (1998). *Economic sociology of immigration.* New York: Russell Sage Foundation.

Portes, A., and Rumbaut, R. G. (2001). *Legacies: The story of the immigrant second generation.* Berkeley: University of California Press.

Rank, M. R. (2004). The disturbing paradox of poverty in American families. In M. Coleman and L. Ganong (Eds.), *Handbook of contemporary families* (pp. 469–89). London: Sage.

Schofield, T. J. (2004). Parenting, marital quality, and child outcomes. Unpublished master's thesis, University of California, Riverside.

Sonnek, S. M. (1999). Perception and parenting style: The influence of culture (Hispanic American, Euro American). Doctoral dissertation, University of Wyoming 2001. *Dissertation Abstracts International, 60,* 6B.

Therrien, M., and Ramirez, R. R. (2000). The Hispanic population in the United States: March 2000. *Current Population Reports* (pp. 20–535). Washington, DC: U.S. Government Printing Office.

U.S. Department of Education. National Center for Education Statistics. (1995). *The condition of education.* Washington, DC: U.S. Government Printing Office.

U.S. Census Bureau. (2003). The Hispanic population in the United States: March 2002. *Current Population Reports* (pp. 20–545). Washington, DC: U.S. Government Printing Office.

Vega, W. A., Kolody, B., Valle, R., and Weir, J. (1991). Social networks, social support and their relationship to depression among immigrant Mexican Women. *Human Organization, 50,* 154–62.

Vélez-Ibáñez, C. (1996). *Border visions.* Tucson: University of Arizona Press.

Vigil, J. D. (1997). *Personas Mexicanas: Chicano high schoolers in a changing Los Angeles.* Fort Worth, TX: Harcourt Brace College.

Wilson, W. J. (1987). *The truly disadvantaged: The inner city, the underclass, and public policy.* Chicago: University of Chicago Press.

Zinn, M. B., and Wells, B. (2000). Diversity within Latino families: New lessons for family social science. In D. H. Demo, K. R. Allen, and M. A. Fine (Eds.), *Handbook of family diversity* (pp. 252–73). New York: Oxford University Press.

14

Devoted Dads: Religion, Class, and Fatherhood

W. Bradford Wilcox and John P. Bartkowski

The new millennium has witnessed an outpouring of scholarly interest in religion and fatherhood (Bartkowski and Xu 2000; Bartkowski 2004a,b; Dollahite 2003; King 2003; Marks and Dollahite 2001; Palkovitz 2002; Wilcox 2002, 2004). This research builds on and enriches a large literature on the causes and consequences of father involvement (Coltrane 1996; Doherty, Kouneski, and Erickson 1998; Marsiglio 1991; Lamb 1997). Father involvement is important for a range of reasons—from its contributions to gender equity to the positive effects such involvement has on child well-being (Amato 1998; Coltrane 1996). Not surprisingly, given the long-standing ties between religion and child rearing in the United States (Christiano 2000), recent research on religion and fatherhood indicates that religiosity is linked to the extent and style of contemporary fathering.

In studies relying on nationally representative samples, religious attendance is tied to a neotraditional model of fatherhood that incorporates high levels of involvement, emotional support, and a strict approach to discipline (Bartkowski and Xu 2000; King 2003; Wilcox 2002, 2004). This model falls between "authoritative" and "authoritarian" styles of parenting, though closer to the authoritative style of parenting described in Diana Baumrind's (1971) classic study of parenting styles (see also Wilcox 1998). Religiously observant fathers might be described as authoritative insofar as they are more involved with their children, are more likely to report praising and hugging their children, are less likely to yell at their children, and are more likely to monitor their children's activities outside the home, compared to fathers who do not regularly attend religious services (Bartkowski and Xu 2000; Wilcox 2004). Religious fathers might be described as authoritarian insofar as they are more likely to resort to corporal punishment than fathers who are less religious (Wilcox 2004).

But recent research on religion and fatherhood has yet to examine how the relationship between religion and father involvement (level and style) may vary by class. Given class variations in gender norms, stress, institutional environments, and social capital (Kohn 1977; Lareau 2003)—not to mention parenting norms and behaviors (Lareau 2003)—religiosity's influence may be moderated by a father's socioeconomic status. Moreover, religious congregations play a unique role in low-income communities as institutional anchors of moral convention and virtuous behavior (Anderson 1999). Focusing on resident fathers, we explore the connections between religion, income, and father involvement using survey data from the National Survey of Families and Households (NSFH) and qualitative data from an ethnographic study of fatherhood programs targeted at economically disadvantaged men. Our analyses suggest that religion exerts a particularly powerful influence on lower-class fathers. We also speculate on how the links between religion, class, and fatherhood are mediated by spatial factors.

RELIGION, CLASS, AND FATHERHOOD: SURVEYING THE LITERATURE

Two central questions motivate this analysis: (1) Why is religious involvement associated with the extent and style of father involvement among residential fathers? (2) How does the influence of religion on fatherhood vary by class (measured here by income)? We focus on five religious factors, four of which we theorize vary by class.

Familism

Religious institutions typically lend religious and moral legitimacy to the ideology of familism (Christiano 2000; Wilcox 2004). Familism is the idea that the family is a paramount source of emotional meaning and moral order in society, and individuals should accord family roles and responsibilities the utmost respect. Familism encompasses, for instance, dedication to the marital vow, opposition to divorce, and the belief that adult children should be the primary caregivers of infirm, elderly parents (Wilcox 2004).

Religious institutions are one of the few social sites where fathers encounter a familistic ideology, and its attendant discourse, rituals, and norms. By teaching that the family has been ordained by God, by endowing family roles—including fathering—with transcendent significance in rituals such as infant baptism, and by stressing the divine origin of family-related moral norms, religious institutions foster and reinforce fathers' commitment to familism (Bartkowski and Xu 2000; Wilcox 2002, 2004). From Promise Keepers rallies, where fathers promise to love, protect, and live out biblical values in service of their families, to synagogue services where fathers recite an *aliyah* (blessing) for their newborn son or daughter, religious institutions serve as social sites that reinforce men's commitment to fathering by supplying them with a range of rituals and discourses that cast fatherhood in a supernatural light. Consequently religious organizations create a unique cultural environment in which men can publicly proclaim their devotion to other members of their family, and can be held accountable by significant others for honoring these commitments (Bartkowski 2004a,b).

Previous research indicates that married resident fathers who attend religious services frequently (several times a month or more) are significantly more likely to endorse familistic attitudes, compared to fathers who attend religious services infrequently or not at all (Wilcox 2004). Familism, in turn, is associated with significantly higher reports of paternal affection among fathers of school-age children (Bartkowski and Xu 2000; Wilcox 2004). Thus one reason religious attendance may be linked to a more affectionate style of parenting among fathers is that men encounter familistic discourse and rituals in religious congregations and religious locales. However, familism does not vary by class among married fathers—at least when class is measured in terms of income (Wilcox 2004). Accordingly, we do not think that class-based variations in how religiosity affects fathers can be traced to class-based differences in fathers' familism.

Masculinity

Many of the social institutions that fathers encounter in their daily lives foster gender norms and practices that are not conducive to fathering. In particular, three of the institutions that play a central role in fathers' lives—work, leisure (e.g., drinking with friends and coworkers at a bar), and entertainment (e.g., watching Monday Night Football)—often impinge on their willingness and ability to devote time and emotional energy to family life. Specifically, these institutions and activities often require and reward time spent away from family life, as with businesses that encourage workers to put in "face time" outside normal working hours. These institutions and activities also can foster a style of masculinity marked by toughness, individual accomplishment, risk taking, and emotional reticence, all of which can stand in tension with the practical and emotional tasks of family life (Coltrane 1989; Kimmel and Messner 2003; Messner 1992).

For instance, fathers highly devoted to sports may come to understand masculine identity principally in terms of toughness and aggression while exhibiting a willingness to trade family time for weekends away "with the guys" or weekends spent watching sports on television. Although athletics is often viewed as a venue for father–son bonding, empirical research reveals that sports-minded fathers' emotional attachment to their sons is often predicated on the extent to which sons compete successfully (e.g., Messner 1992, 27–30). Likewise, sports-minded fathers who have daughters who do not share their passion for sports may be less inclined to spend time with them. This is not to say that sport uniformly exerts a poisonous influence on men's character (e.g., Bartkowski 2004a; Wacquant 2004). Nonetheless, much of the culture of sport cultivates some of the pernicious aspects of masculinity (Messner 2002) and, by extension, may detract from men's prioritization of family relationships.

By contrast, religious institutions offer a family-centered ethos to fathers where masculinity is closely linked to familial involvement. Religious institutions provide a wide range of opportunities for fathers to spend time with their children. Religious fathers attend weekly worship services with their family, teach Sunday school classes to youth and other families, participate in youth mission trips and summer camps, and supervise Boy Scout troops that are sponsored by their local congregations (Wilcox 2004). Congregations also valorize father involvement by formally celebrating Father's Day, organizing scripture study groups for fathers, and offering community picnics and breakfasts where fathers are encouraged to form relationships across generational lines (Bartkowski 2004a,b). In these ways, religious organizations create a unique space, in both physical and cultural terms, for constructively linking fathers to their families (Bartkowski 2004a). Thus religious institutions are one of the few settings in the social world in which men have opportunities to invest time and earn status by tending to their families.

Indeed, religious institutions may be particularly important in fostering a family-oriented masculinity among lower-class men. With poor and working-class men's access to conventional avenues for masculine achievement curtailed (e.g., higher education, professions), such men are more likely to live, play, and work in social environments governed by a hypermasculine ethos and street culture that encourages risk taking (e.g., Anderson 1999; Wacquant 2004). Men in such communities avoid the "stigma" of feminization by holding misogynistic gender norms, adopting more predatory sexual strategies, being less involved with their families, and showing less affection toward their children (Arrighi and Maume 2000; Lareau 2003; Wilcox 2002).

By contrast, religious institutions in such communities offer lower-class fathers an environment where familial involvement can safely be linked to their masculinity. This is especially true of conservative Protestant churches, which tend to have higher numbers of poor and working-class fathers, as well as pastoral leadership teams that are composed of strong male role models who stress the importance of male familial involvement (Bartkowski 2001; Edgell 2005; Wilcox 2004). In these churches, men's domestic involvement is often promoted by patriarchal authority structures in the congregation that seek to draw clear boundaries against antifamily behavior (Bartkowski 2001). Overseen by male pastors, conservative Protestant congregations masculinize religious involvement, making the cultivation of spirituality and moral virtue legitimate "manly" pursuits. Pastors in such churches commonly remind their male congregants that their most important "job" is not that for which they are paid, but that of a family man.

Stress

Stress often leads parents, including fathers, to resort to a more authoritarian or neglectful approach to parenting (Elder, Nguyen, and Caspi 1985; McLeod, Kruttschnitt, and Dornfield 1994; McLeod and Shanahan 1993). Fathers confront a variety of stresses in their lives—from medical illness to a death in the family to unemployment or underemployment. This stress, in turn, can harm fathers' interaction with their children. Fathers who are stressed tend to be more impatient, more prone to lash out at their children with yelling and spanking episodes, and more neglectful of their children.

Religious institutions can buffer against life stresses that would otherwise harm father–child interactions. Religion tends to cast a "sacred canopy" of meaning and social support over individuals' lives in ways that make them more resilient to stress in at least three ways (Berger 1967). First, religious teachings can endow suffering and misfortune with meaning that makes stressful events easier to handle for fathers. Second, religious practices such as prayer or meditation can help fathers make sense of stressful events, cast these events from their consciousness, and be reflective about how stress is affecting their parent–child relationship. Finally, the social and emotional support afforded by fellow believers can also help fathers deal with the stresses they encounter in their lives (Ellison 1994; Durkheim 1951).

Religious participation should be particularly valuable in helping lower-class fathers deal with stress. Compared to upper-income fathers, lower-income fathers typically face more life stresses. They are more likely to experience financial pressures, poor working conditions, disordered neighborhoods, racial or ethnic discrimination, and difficulties in their interaction with a range of public institutions (e.g., local law enforcement) (Lareau 2003; Wilson 1996). The cumulative weight of these stresses is one central reason that lower-income fathers tend to be less involved and affectionate with their children, and more prone to authoritarian behavior, than their up-per-income counterparts (Kruttschnitt, McLeod, and Dornfield 1994; McLeod et al. 1994; Wilcox 2004). Consequently religious participation's ability to mitigate the social and emotional consequences of stressful events should be particularly important in making lower-income fathers resilient in the face of misfortune.

Public Institutions

Religious institutions provide fathers with a set of social skills and experi-ences that may make them more skilled and confident fathers. Specifically, in venues ranging from church finance committees to men's groups, religious congregations offer fathers opportunities to cultivate their leadership, speak-ing, and social skills (Verba, Schlozman, and Brady 1995). As they participate in religious, social, and civic activities sponsored by their local congrega-tions, fathers also have the opportunity to develop their sense of agency, effi-cacy, and even autonomy in the social world. Finally, religious institutions also stress the divinely ordained dignity of individuals in ways that may bol-ster fathers' sense of self-confidence. Thus fathers who are active in their lo-cal congregations may adapt a more active and affectionate style of relating to their children that they have learned, in part, from their experiences as an active congregant (Wilcox 2002).

Of course, fathers spend much of their time in the public worlds of market, state, and civil society. These public institutions also shape their parenting dispositions and behaviors (Kohn 1977; Lareau 2003). The work environ-ments that poor and working-class fathers encounter often are marked by rou-tinization, dependence on authority, and a lack of efficacy and agency (Kalle-berg, Reskin, and Hudson 2000; Kohn 1977; Wilson 1996). These work environments do not provide lower-class fathers with the opportunities to cul-tivate the social skills and sense of self-confidence that are associated with an active and engaged approach to family life (Arrighi and Maume 2000). More-over, due in part to their lack of education, their comparatively fewer social skills, and their lower levels of efficacy, poor and working-class fathers are less likely to be civically and politically engaged; they are also more likely to have negative experiences with civic and public institutions (Lareau 2003; Verba et al. 1995; Wuthnow 2002). Consequently lower-class fathers' inter-actions with state and civic institutions are not likely to offset their work ex-periences in ways that would make them more active and emotionally en-gaged fathers.

Another reason that religious participation may be more valuable to lower-income fathers than to higher-income fathers is that lower-income fathers are particularly likely to benefit from the skills and confidence they acquire in and through religious participation (Verba et al. 1996). Because higher-income fathers experience more flexible, complex, and autonomous work environments, and benefit from their comparatively higher social status in their interactions with public and civic institutions, they may acquire authoritative parenting dispositions and skills from a range of nonreligious sources. Accordingly, religious participation may not have a marked affect on their approach to parenting. By contrast, poor and working-class fathers may depend more on religious participation to acquire the social skills and self-confidence associated with an authoritative parenting style.

Networks and Norms

For a range of religious and familial reasons, religious institutions tend to attract a disproportionate number of families with children (Ammerman 1997; Stolzenberg, Blair-Loy, and Waite 1995; Wilcox, forthcoming). In turn, these family-centered social networks foster an intensive parenting ethic and a range of parenting norms in the service of this ethic. Fathers are encouraged by other parents in these networks to spend substantial amounts of time with their children, to foster faith and character in their children, and to treat their children with respect (Wilcox 1998, 2002). These family-centered, religion-based social networks foster these norms by providing formal and informal venues for parenting advice, formal and informal symbolic rewards for involved and effective parenting, and informal sanctions for neglectful or abusive parenting. So, for instance, a father who works voluntarily on Saturdays might be encouraged by another father in his church to leave work behind one weekend and instead join his teenage son on a weekend campout for the church youth group. Thus the family-centered networks and norms found in religious congregations should foster higher levels of father involvement and affection among fathers who are religiously active.

These family-centered networks and norms should be particularly important in cultivating an active and expressive style of fathering among poor and working-class fathers. Compared to fathers whose household income falls above the median, lower-income fathers are less likely to devote lots of time to one-on-one interaction and youth activities, they are less affectionate with their children, and they are more likely to use a strict style of discipline (Lareau 2003; Wilcox 2004). The networks and norms they confront in their social environment are less child-centered and more authoritarian, compared to the networks and norms that dominate middle- and upper-class social environments (Lareau 2003). The parenting norms that lower-income fathers encounter are, of course, linked to the structural factors—deadening work, limited economic resources, and negative experiences with public institutions—they encounter in their social environments (Lareau 2003; Wilson 1996).

Hence, in all probability, the gap between religious parenting norms and secular parenting norms is probably larger for lower-income fathers than higher-income fathers. For instance, the ethnographic research of Anderson (1999) suggests that religion plays a central role in the lives of good fathers—"decent daddies"—in inner-city Philadelphia. According to Anderson, the decent father is a pillar of his community who "stands for propriety, righteousness, religion, and manhood" and "tries to supply [his family] not only with food, clothing, shelter, and other material things but with spiritual nurturance as well" (1999, 189). The decent father fosters respect for authority, hard work, self-reliance, and God in his children through an intensive, strict parenting style. And decent fathers "derive great support from their faith and church communit[ies]" (Anderson 1999, 38). Thus we predict that religious participation is more consequential in fostering authoritative parenting behaviors among lower-income than higher-income fathers, in part because lower-income fathers benefit more from the family-oriented social networks and norms they encounter in religious congregations.

But Anderson's ethnographic work, as well as the extant research on religion and parenting, suggests that there is one way in which religious participation reinforces rather than works against lower-class parenting norms (Lareau 2003). Religious institutions, especially the conservative Protestant ones that dominate the religious landscape of black and white lower-class America, stress the importance of paternal authority (Anderson 1999; Bartkowski and Wilcox 2000). The father represents divine justice and is expected to provide admonishment and correction when his children are disobedient or misbehaving. Specifically, fathers are encouraged to spank their children when they misbehave and to monitor their activities both inside and outside the home. But they are also discouraged from yelling at their children, which is interpreted as a sign that the father has lost his sense of self-control. Any loss of parental self-control reflects poorly on the father, who is supposed to model the sovereignty of God to his children (Bartkowski and Wilcox 2000; Wilcox 2004). Accordingly, we would expect that the religious endorsement of corporal punishment and parental authority makes churchgoing poor and working-class fathers especially likely to use corporal punishment and monitor their children, insofar as religious participation adds additional legitimacy to a strict disciplinary style that is seen as appropriate in poor and working-class communities (Lareau 2003). But we would also expect such fathers to be less likely to yell at their children because yelling is not sanctioned in their religious congregations.

Hypotheses

This review of the literature leads us to offer two hypotheses about the links between religious participation, class, and the extent and style of father involvement: *Hypothesis 1:* Fathers who attend religious services weekly or more are more likely to adapt an authoritative approach to ordinary interaction with their children that encompasses high levels of involvement and an affectionate approach to parenting, and lower-income fathers will be most affected by such weekly religious attendance. *Hypothesis 2:* Fathers who attend religious services weekly or more are more likely to adapt an authoritarian approach to discipline that encompasses high levels of corporal punishment and monitoring but low levels of yelling, and lower-income fathers will be most affected by such weekly religious attendance.

DATA AND METHODS

In our quantitative empirical analysis, we focus on a subset of the 1987–1988 National Survey of Families and Households (NSFH), 2,548 respondents who were married residential fathers of school-age children (ages five to eighteen) at the time of the survey (Sweet, Bumpass, and Call 1988). The statistics and analyses used in this study are based on weighted data, adjusted for over-samples of racial and ethnic minorities, and families with stepchildren.

For our dependent variables, we focus on respondent reports of activity in six different domains of father involvement in NSFH: one-on-one interaction, youth-related activities, affection, corporal punishment, yelling, and monitoring one's children. To measure *one-on-one interaction*, we relied on respondents' reports of involvement in four activities. Each father reported how often he spent "time with the children . . . in leisure activities away from home (picnics, movies, sports, etc.)? . . . at home working on a project or playing together? . . . having private talks? . . . helping with reading or homework?" Responses ranging from 1 (never or rarely) to 6 (almost every day) were summed to create a scale based on the mean response to each of the items. Fathers were also asked how many hours per week they devoted to the following *youth-related activities*: school activities, community youth groups (e.g., Scouts), sports activities, and religious youth groups. Fathers were asked how often they praised their children and how often they hugged their children. Fathers who indicated that they praised and hugged their children very often were coded as *very affectionate*.

We also explored three variables that tapped their approach to disciplining and monitoring their children. Fathers were asked how often they spanked or slapped their children, from 1 (never) to 4 (very often). This was our measure of *spanking*. They were also asked how often they *yelled* at their children, from 1 (never) to 4 (very often). Finally, fathers were asked if their children were supposed to tell them their whereabouts when they were away from home. Fathers who indicated that their children were expected to tell them (or their wife) of their whereabouts at all times were coded as *highly monitoring*.

For our primary independent variables of interest, we rely on respondent reports of religious attendance in NSFH. Fathers who attended religious services once a week or more were coded as *weekly attendees*. We also controlled for a range of sociodemographic factors, known to be associated with father involvement, that might otherwise confound any relationships between religion and father involvement. (Details on control variables are available from the authors upon request.)

For each of our dependent variables, we estimated two ordinary least squares (OLS) regression models for continuous outcomes and two logistic regression models for binary outcomes. These models focused on two subsets of approximately 1,275 fathers to examine whether the relationship between religious involvement and fathers' behavior varied by income: the first focuses on a subsample of fathers with household incomes below the median of $33,860 in 1987–1988; the second focuses on a subsample of fathers with household incomes above the median of $33,860. (For missing data on household income, we relied on fathers' educational attainment to impute household income.) The results we report in tables 14.1 and 14.2 are net of the sociodemographic control variables we included in our models.

As an additional source of data, we draw on qualitative research Bartkowski conducted on four faith-based fatherhood programs in rural Mississippi. Families and children in Mississippi face an array of social disadvantages, including higher incidences of poverty, inadequate education, food insecurity, family dissolution, and teen pregnancy than is found in many other states (e.g., Annie E. Casey Foundation 2004; Bartkowski and Regis 2003; Cashwell, Bartkowski, Duffy, and Molnar, forthcoming). The methodology for studying these fatherhood programs, which were designed principally to reach economically disadvantaged men in rural Mississippi, has been explicated elsewhere (Bartkowski 2004b). Qualitative interviews were conducted with executive directors of faith-based organizations, program managers (fatherhood educators), and a sample of male participants in various Mississippi communities. Participants interviewed were African American men situated in small economically impoverished towns. Research instruments examined program dynamics and objectives from the standpoint of agency directors, fatherhood educators, and program participants, while focusing pointedly on the influences of program participation in the lives of men who completed them.

RESULTS

The Broad View: What the Survey Tells Us

Table 14.1 indicates that religious participation is associated with higher levels of father involvement among lower-income fathers but not higher-income fathers. Specifically, lower-income fathers who are weekly attenders spend significantly more time with their children in one-on-one activities such as reading to their children, compared to lower-income fathers who attend religious services infrequently or not at all. Furthermore, on average, lower-income fathers who attend weekly spend significantly more time—1.15 hours—in youth activities such as the Boy Scouts, compared to lower-income fathers who are not weekly attenders. But weekly attendance is not associated with higher levels of involvement among fathers whose incomes fall above the median. Thus religion appears to be particularly important in fostering father involvement among poor and working-class fathers.

Table 14.1 also indicates that religious participation is more likely to be associated with an affectionate parenting style among lower-income fathers than higher-income fathers. Here, however, religious participation boosts the odds that fathers are very affectionate with their children among both lower-income and higher-income fathers. Lower-income fathers who attend church weekly are 57 percent more likely to hug and praise their children very often, compared to lower-income fathers who do not attend church weekly. Likewise, higher-income fathers who attend church weekly are 31 percent more likely to hug and praise their children very often, compared to higher-income fathers who do not

Table 14.1. The Association between Weekly Religious Attendance and Father Involvement and Affection

Outcomes	Lower-Income Fathers	Upper-Income Fathers
One-on-one involvement	0.126 *[a]	0.039[a]
Youth activities	1.152***[a]	0.555[a]
Very affectionate	1.571**[b]	1.308*[b]

*< .05,   **< .01,   ***< .001
[a]OLS coefficients
[b]Odds ratios

attend church weekly. Overall, then, religious participation appears to foster a more authoritative approach to parenting on the part of fathers, but the effect of religion is markedly more powerful and consistent for lower-income fathers. Thus table 14.1 is consistent with the predictions made in hypothesis 1, such that religion functions as a cultural compensator for less privileged fathers.

What about discipline? Table 14.2 indicates that weekly attendance is generally associated with a more authoritarian approach to discipline among lower-income fathers but not higher-income fathers. Specifically, this table shows that lower-income fathers who attend weekly are significantly more likely to spank their children, compared to lower-income fathers who do not attend weekly. But there is no association between attendance and corporal punishment among higher-income fathers. We see a similar pattern when it comes to knowing the whereabouts of one's child. Lower-income fathers who attend weekly are 114 percent more likely to report knowing the whereabouts of their child, compared to lower-income fathers who do not attend weekly. But higher-income fathers who attend weekly are not more likely to report monitoring their children in this way. Thus table 14.2 generally suggests that religious attendance is associated with a more authoritarian approach to parenting among lower-income but not higher-income fathers.

In the population at large, an authoritarian parenting style is also linked to higher levels of yelling (Bartkowski and Wilcox 2000). Table 14.2 indicates, by contrast, that weekly religious attendance is associated with lower rates of yelling among both lower-income and higher-income fathers. But on this outcome, the effect size is markedly larger among higher-income fathers. This is the only outcome in this study where religious attendance is more consequential for higher-income fathers. We are not entirely sure why religious participation is a stronger predictor for higher-income fathers' behavior in this domain than in other domains. Interestingly, religious participation does not always have a stronger relationship with paternal behavior for lower-income fathers, compared to upper-income fathers.[1]

Table 14.2.   The Association between Weekly Religious Attendance and Father Discipline and Monitoring

Outcomes	Lower-Income Fathers	Upper-Income Fathers
Spanking	0.171***[a]	0.071[a]
Highly monitoring	2.141*[bc]	1.168[bc]
Yelling	−0.096*[ac]	−0.226***[ac]

*< .05,   **< .01,   ***< .001
[a]OLS coefficients
[b]Odds ratios
[c]Slope coefficients are significantly different by income at the p < .05 level

The Ethnographic Portrait: Religion as a
Cultural Resource in Fatherhood Education

We have demonstrated that religion does influence fathers, especially lower-income fathers. But how precisely does religion influence fathers, and how exactly do fathers rely on religion to invest their roles with purpose and meaning? To address these questions, we turn to qualitative data collected from lower-income men who completed faith-based fatherhood programs utilizing a curriculum, "The 7 Secrets of Effective Fathers." The seminar workbook defines the program's goal: "To encourage and challenge you to become the father God designed you to be" (National Center for Fathering [hereafter NCF] 2001, 4). The program describes fathers as "a steward of God's most prized resource, children" (p. 2) and the workbook encourages participants to begin by "asking the Father of all fathers for His insight and power to become obvious to us today. May He open our hearts and ears to His heart as it related to being a Dad" (p. 4).

These programs relied on an evangelical ideological framework that seeks to situate key family roles in a biblically based interpretative framework, thereby sacralizing these roles. Each of the "seven secrets" for effective fathering is supported by a biblical reference or series of scriptural verses, such as the reference to paternal protection and provision for the family found in 1 Timothy 5:8. Such is the case with secret 6, active listening, supported by the biblical verse James 1:19 ("Everyone should be quick to listen, slow to speak, and slow to become angry"). In this course, there is even a section on "touchstone passages" in the Bible that address fathering. These include a reference in Malachi 4:5–6 to God's ability to turn the hearts of fathers toward their children, and other verses that underscore the importance of children honoring their fathers and mothers (Exodus 20:12; Ephesians 6:2–3). A special section in this curriculum called "Notes on a Theology of Fathering" lists dozens of biblical verses related to fathering while explaining that the Bible contains nearly 1,200 references to the words father, fathered, forefathers, fatherless, and related terms. Beyond such theological edicts, these programs regularly provided men with a forum for practical social interaction with their children and children without involved fathers in the community. These programs fostered actual father–child interaction by sponsoring community service activities, picnics, cookouts, and collective participation in recreational activities such as attendance at local sporting events.

Men who were interviewed after completing these fatherhood education programs spoke about their experiences in ways that suggested these programs enabled them to revise their vision of fatherhood, to alter the ways they allocated their time, and to spread a sacred canopy of meaning and purpose over their lives, with clear implications for their sense of confidence and efficacy as fathers (see Bartkowski 2004b). One man who was expecting his first child soon commented, "I learned how to be a more effective father. Now that I am fixing to have a child, I know that I have to spend time with the child. . . . Money doesn't mean anything to a child. It's all spending time with that child." He also mentioned how much he "liked the spiritual part of the program. I am a child of God. I was born again. . . . Without God, you can't get nowhere." Another client in a different program said, "Spirituality is the key to success in the program. The Bible is a powerful book. . . . When you get saved, you have a new walk and a new talk."

When asked about what being a good father meant to them, men in these programs seized on the language of faith, spirituality, and religion to discuss the moral obligations that parents have to their children. This point is an important one. Religious rationales for parenting had been made available to men during the programs, and they had learned them well. As one graduate of a fatherhood program put it,

> There is a difference between what the world says a good father is and the biblical principles of being a good father, according to God's standard. The world might say that as long as you bring home the paycheck, are paying the bills, are doing forty hours, and your kids are not going hungry and have got shoes on their feet, you're being a good father, a good parent. But that's [not] necessarily true, because kids need attention. They need time. They need somebody to listen to them. They may have problems. They need to have confidence that they can talk to you about anything. School problems, peer pressure, whatever.

Another father in a different program, Kendall, commented, "We need to reconnect with our children. Children are gifts. They are gifts from God, and we need to treat them as such." Robert, in the same program as Kendall, added that men's participation in such programs and in religious groups is essential: "If we're not going to reconnect, we're going to lose our children. You can see it in the school system. If you have meetings, most of the mothers show up. Not the fathers. Even in churches and Sunday schools. I am a Sunday school leader, and we just have the females there. So we need more fathers involved."

Fathers who completed these programs talked poignantly about changes in their values brought about through program participation. In this sense, faith-based fatherhood programs offered a holistic approach to parenting, one that aimed to educate the "whole person." This holistic, value-oriented approach became apparent when participants were asked how the program had helped them. Cecil described how he learned to express feelings and experiences that he hadn't previously shared with anyone given the newfound relationships of trust with other men:

There were some things that I talked to them about that I couldn't talk to no one else about. . . . [The teacher said that what we discussed] was confidential and that it wouldn't go nowhere else, that it couldn't go nowhere else. So I talked about it and got it off my chest. It felt a whole lot better. . . . Before I got into this program, I couldn't [pause]. I really wasn't the type of guy [who got personal]. But after I learned and prayed [pause]. They prayed with me. And I become a better person because I could feel it in myself.

For Robert, "sharing" was also the key. But, for him, such sharing took the form of learning how to share himself and his time with other family members since he completed the fatherhood program. Here again, family relationships are endowed with a moral significance that is often missing in secular domains of social life:

One thing I have become more aware of [is] sharing [time with my family]. There are times when you think that it's going to be okay—that the kids can take care of themselves. But I have begun to share more as a result of the program. You don't know if you're going to be here tomorrow.

Dave offered this perspective, suggesting how his overall values and demeanor as a man have changed as a result of the program. His faith encourages him to do what is needed to connect with youngsters, regardless of stigma that paints child care as "unmanly."

[The program] has caused me to think about things that I probably would not have focused on. . . . One thing I picked up indirectly is that, as men, we've got to be willing to change. There are a lot of things that go on out there that we might not do because they are not manly or because they might make us look soft or whatever. . . . When asked [to do something] by my daughter, I might have said, "Well, that's something your momma would do." We have got to be willing to change and accept change. . . . Men—they can be hard and tight. But you just have to have fun and stuff [with your children]. So I picked that up.

When asked about his goals for the future and how the program might have influenced them, Dave confessed that he had not been the most involved father to this point in his life. And with the imminent arrival of his first grandchild, he vowed to change. Words that he had spoken to his wife in the past—"that's your baby"—was something he would never consider where grandparenting was concerned.

Although the portraits rendered here are not intended to be exhaustive, they do underscore the value of faith as a familistic resource, as a generator of positive masculinity, as a bulwark of psychological well-being, and as a source of strong social networks. Religious edicts (scriptural passages, theological teachings) define fatherhood as a moral obligation while underscoring men's distinctive and critical role in the realm of family life. This emphasis on a father's roles in the home runs contrary to mainstream cultural notions that, despite the ideological popularity of gender equality, still leave parenthood defined largely as a maternal responsibility in everyday practice. Moreover, these comments highlight the crucial role that religious networks and the trust forged through such relationships play in the lives of fathers. When men are linked to a religious community, fatherhood moves from the statements of abstract "new man" ideology ("dads should be involved with their kids") to questions about daily practice ("What have you done today to remain involved in the lives of your children?"). These networks encourage men to become actively involved in their children's lives by prioritizing family relationships above masculine forms of achievement championed in the secular world. These social networks also form relationships of accountability in which men's familial involvement will be consistently held to a higher standard—a subcultural standard defined in many traditions with reference to God as the "ultimate father"—when compared with the lip service paid to father involvement in the secular realm.

CONCLUSION

Taken together, our survey and qualitative data provide strong evidence that religious involvement is an important influence on paternal behavior, especially among lower-income fathers. Consistent with the larger literature on religion and parenting, involvement in religious organizations is strongly associated with higher levels of paternal affection and lower levels of paternal yelling for fathers across the economic spectrum. Moreover, this is the first study to examine whether the relationship between religion and father involvement varies by fathers' social class.

Religious involvement appears to matter more for lower-income resident fathers than for higher-income resident fathers. In contrast to middle- and higher-income fathers who often benefit from advantaged work environments and high levels of education, lower-income fathers often lack the cultural, financial, and institutional resources that other fathers can draw on as they interact with their children. Among fathers whose access to conventional avenues of success is curtailed, religion becomes an especially critical cultural resource. By providing social sites that offer opportunities for social participation and leadership, a religious message that makes sense of everyday life, and a strong commitment to a moral code of decent, family-centered living, religious institutions help lower-income fathers make up for these deficits.

The role of these religious institutions is particularly valuable in poor communities because so many of the social and civic institutions that poor and working-class men confront in their social world do not foster an active, engaged style of fathering. Our findings are consistent with recent research on educational achievement and crime, which finds that religious effects are uniquely beneficial for members of poor communities (Regnerus and Elder 2003). In other words, religious institutions offer crucial moral, social, and spiritual support for decent dads striving to do right by their children in low-income communities.

FUTURE RESEARCH

This study suggests that recent scholarly attention to the ties between religion and fatherhood should extend beyond religion's generic influence on fatherhood to focus more specifically on the ways in which religion's impact varies by social context. In this case, it seems that the types of norms, skills, experiences, and networks associated with religious institutions are particularly important in influencing the parenting behaviors of lower-income fathers. Specifically, religious participation is associated with a neotraditional style of fathering among lower-income fathers that encompasses comparatively high levels of involvement and affection, corporal punishment and monitoring, and comparatively low levels of yelling. This neotraditional style of fathering would seem to fall somewhere between the authoritative and authoritarian styles of parenting described in the literature on parenting (Wilcox 1998; Baumrind 1971).

We identified at least four potential mechanisms of religious influence: religious influences on men's orientation toward masculinity and family, the ways in which religious participation buffers against stress, the social skills and self-confidence afforded by the institutional environment found in religious congregations, and the family-oriented networks and norms associated with religious participation. Future research will have to determine the precise mechanisms through which religious involvement fosters higher levels of familial investments among lower-income men.

In particular, future research should explore how the physical and spatial characteristics of religious institutions do or do not reinforce familism, link masculinity to a strong family orientation, buffer against stress, and foster the skills and self-confidence that make for good fathering. An approach that is sensitive to the physical and spatial dimensions of the religion-fatherhood nexis would seek to answer questions such as the following: Is religious attendance as a family, for instance, more important in fostering dads' familism than a father's attendance apart from his family? Do religious icons and statues in the home allow men to integrate faith and fathering in unique ways? Are congregations that offer sex-segregated parenting classes more effective in motivating men to invest in parenting than congregations that offer parenting classes for both men and women? Beyond these concerns, ethnographic investigations of congregational and family life should examine the contexts in which men use religion as a cultural resource in the practice of fatherhood, and how the utilization of this resource shapes the everyday experiences of fathers and their families. Such research is uniquely suited to explore faith and fatherhood as a practical "accomplishment," thereby examining both success and struggle in relation to the goal of becoming a "decent dad." In such work, care should be taken to generate portraits of fatherhood from the perspective of multiple stakeholders—fathers themselves, as well as their children, wives, pastors, and male friends—coupled with detailed renderings of father–child events sponsored by religious organizations (e.g., campouts, cookouts, retreats). Such research could also detail the integration of fathers into family and religious life through such daily practices as family prayer and household rituals (e.g., family devotionals, scripture study), as well as events that give rise to the mutual constitution of faith, family life, and fatherhood (e.g., holding church-sponsored Boy Scouts activities in congregants' homes). Thus attention should be given to the wide variety of social encounters and cultural spaces that religious communities provide for father–child interaction, and the consequent sacralization of fatherhood through everyday practices in the home.

With only a few exceptions (e.g., Ammerman 1987; Bartkowski 2001, 2004a), the ethnographic study of religion, gender, and family life has still principally entailed focusing on women's experiences as wives and mothers (see Bartkowski 2001 for review). Often erroneously viewed as the arbiters and beneficiaries of religious patriarchy, men's involvement in congregational and family life has been left largely unexplored. Given the rich renderings of men's experiences that have flourished among qualitative researchers of gender and family life during the past two decades, the time seems ripe to "bring men back in" to the ethnographic study of religion and family life with a special focus on the practice and negotiation of "faithful fathering."

In sum, this chapter indicates that religious institutions are playing an important role in buffering against many of the social structural and cultural factors that push poor and lower-class fathers away from their families. We argue that four mechanisms—from the protective effects of religiosity on stress to the family-oriented networks associated with religious institutions—help explain the link between religiosity and a neotraditional style of fathering among lower-income fathers. Future research will have to confirm or disconfirm whether the mechanisms outlined in this chapter actually explain the relationships we have documented here. Researchers should also think seriously about how characteristics of physical contexts may help explain how these mechanisms link religious practice to an active, affectionate, but strict approach to fathering among men.

NOTE

This research was supported in part by the Lilly Endowment, grant 2002 2301-000. The qualitative study on fatherhood programs featured in this chapter was supported by the Rockefeller Institute of Government at SUNY-Albany.

1. Note that statistical tests of differences in slope coefficients indicated that the slope differences between lower-income and upper-income fathers were only significant for our last two outcomes (table 14.2). However, with the exception of our measure of affection, all of the other slope differences approached statistical significance at $p < .20$.

REFERENCES

Amato, P. R. (1998). More than money? Men's contributions to their children's lives. In A. Booth and A. C. Crouter (Eds.), *Men in Families: When do they get involved? what difference does it make?* (pp. 241–78). Mahwah, NJ: Erlbaum.

Ammerman, N. T. (1987). *Bible believers: Fundamentalists in the modern world.* New Brunswick, NJ: Rutgers University Press.

Ammerman, N. T. (1997). Golden rule Christianity: Lived religion in the American mainstream. In D. Hall (Ed.), *Lived religion in America: Toward a history of practice* (pp. 196–216). Princeton, NJ: Princeton University Press.

Anderson, E. (1999). *Code of the Street.* New York: Norton.

Arrighi, B. A., and Maume, D. J. (2000). Workplace subordination and men's avoidance of housework. *Journal of Family Issues, 21,* 464–87.

Bartkowski, J. P. (2001). *Remaking the godly marriage: Gender negotiation in evangelical families.* New Brunswick, NJ: Rutgers University Press.

Bartkowski, J. P. (2004a). *The Promise Keepers: Servants, soldiers, and godly men.* New Brunswick, NJ: Rutgers University Press.

Bartkowski, J. P. (2004b). Faith-based and secular parenting programs in rural Mississippi: A comparative case study. Roundtable on Religion and Social Welfare (Rockefeller Institute of Government at SUNY-Albany). www.religionand socialpolicy.org

Bartkowski, J. P., and Regis, H. A. 2003. *Charitable choices: Religion, race, and poverty in the post-welfare era.* New York: New York University Press.

Bartkowski, J. P. and Wilcox, W. B. (2000). Conservative Protestant child discipline: The case of parental yelling. *Social Forces, 79,* 265–90.

Bartkowski, J. P. and Xu, X. (2000). Distant patriarchs or expressive dads? The discourse and practice of fathering in conservative Protestant families. *Sociological Quarterly, 41,* 465–85.

Baumrind, D. (1971). Current patterns of parental authority. *Development Psychology Monograph, 4,* 1–103.

Berger, P. (1967). Religious institutions. In N. J. Smelser (Ed.), *Sociology: An introduction* (pp. 329–79). New York: Wiley.

Annie E. Casey Foundation. (2004). Kids count 2004 data book online. http://www .aecf.org/kidscount/databook/

Cashwell, S. T., Bartkowski, J. P., Duffy, P. A. and Molnar, J. J. (Forthcoming). What do private food agency directors know about charitable choice? *Sociology and Social Welfare.*

Christiano, K. J. (2000). Religion and the family in modern american culture. In S. K. Houseknecht and J. G. Pankhurst (Eds.), *Family, religion, and social change in diverse societies* (pp. 43–78). Oxford: Oxford University Press.

Coltrane, S. (1989). Household labor and the routine production of gender. *Social Problems, 36,* 473–90.

Coltrane, S. (1996). *Family man.* New York: Oxford University Press.

Doherty, W. J., Kouneski E. F., and Erickson, M. F. (1998). Responsible fathering: An overview and conceptual framework. *Journal of Marriage and the Family, 60,* 277–92.

Dollahite, D. C. (2003). Fathering for eternity: Generative spirituality in Latter-day Saint fathers of children with special needs. *Review of Religious Research, 44,* 339–51.

Dollahite, D. C., and Hawkins, A. J. (1998). A conceptual ethic of generative fathering. *Journal of Men's Studies, 7,* 109–32.

Durkheim, E. [1897] (1951). *Suicide.* New York: Free Press.

Edgell, P. (2005). *Religion and family: Understanding the transformation of linked institutions.* Princeton, NJ: Princeton University Press.

Elder, G., Nguyen, T. V., and Caspi, A. (1985). Linking family hardship in children's lives. *Child Development, 56,* 361–75.

Ellison, C. G. (1994). Religion, the life stress paradigm, and the study of depression. In J. S. Levin (Ed.), *Religion in aging and health: Theoretical foundations and methodological frontiers* (pp. 78–121). Newbury Park, CA: Sage.

Kalleberg, A. L., Reskin, B. F., and Hudson, K. (2000). Bad jobs in America: Standard and nonstandard employment relations and job quality in the United States. *American Sociological Review, 65,* 256–78.

Kimmel, M., and Messner, M. A. (2003). *Men's Lives.* New York: Pearson Allyn & Bacon.

King, V. (2003). The influence of religion on fathers' relationships with their children. *Journal of Marriage and Family, 65,* 382–95.

Kohn, M. L. (1977). *Class and conformity: A study in values.* Chicago: University of Chicago Press.

Kruttschnitt, C., McLeod, J. D., and Dornfield, M. (1994). The economic environment of child abuse. *Social Problems, 41,* 299–315.

Lamb, M. E. (1997). *The role of the father in child development.* New York: Wiley.

Lareau, A. (2003). *Unequal childhoods: Class, race, and family life.* Berkeley: University of California Press.

Marks, L. D., and Dollahite, D. C. (2001). Religion, relationships, and responsible fathering in Latter-day Saint families of children with special needs. *Journal of Social and Personal* Relationships, *18,* 625–50.

Marsiglio, W. (1991). Paternal engagement activities with minor children. *Journal of Marriage and the Family, 53,* 973–86.

Marsiglio, W. (1995). *Fatherhood: Contemporary theory, research, and social policy.* Thousand Oaks, CA: Sage.

McLeod, J. D., Kruttschnitt, C., and Dornfield, M. (1994). Does parenting explain the effects of structural conditions on children's antisocial behavior? A comparison of blacks and whites. *Social Forces, 73,* 575–604.

McLeod, J. D., and Shanahan, M. J. (1993). Poverty, parenting, and children's mental health. *American Sociological Review, 58,* 351–66.

Messner, M. A. (1992). *Power at play: Sports and the problem of masculinity.* Boston: Beacon.

Messner, M. A. (2002). *Taking the field: Women, men, and sports.* Minneapolis: University of Minnesota Press.

National Center for Fathering. (2001). *The 7 secrets of effective fathers.* Shawnee Mission, KS: National Center for Fathering.

Palkovitz, R. (2002). *Involved fathering and men's adult development: Provisional balances.* Mahwah, NJ: Erlbaum.

Regnerus, M. D., and Elder, G. H. (2003). Staying on track in school: Religious influences in high- and low-risk settings. *Journal for the Scientific Study of Religion, 42,* 633–50.

Stolzenberg, R. M., Blair-Loy, M., and Waite, L. J. (1995). Religious participation in early adulthood: Age and family life cycle effects on church membership. *American Sociological Review, 60,* 84–103.

Sweet, J. A., Bumpass, L. L., and Call, V. (1988). The design and content of the national survey of families and households. NSFH Working Paper no. 1, Center for Demography and Ecology, University of Wisconsin-Madison.

Verba, S., Scholzman, K. L., and Brady, H. E. (1995). *Voice and equality: Civic voluntarism in American politics.* Cambridge, MA: Harvard University Press.

Wacquant, L. (2004). *Body and soul: Notebooks of an apprentice boxer.* New York: Oxford University Press.

Wilcox, W. B. (1998). Conservative Protestant childrearing: Authoritarian or authoritative? *American Sociological Review, 63,* 796–809.

Wilcox, W. B. (2002). Religion, convention, and paternal involvement. *Journal of Marriage and Family, 64,* 780–92.

Wilcox, W. B. (2004). *Soft patriarchs, new men: How Christianity shapes fathers and husbands.* Chicago: University of Chicago Press.

Wilcox, W. B. (Forthcoming). Together bound: Church, sect, and family. In H. R. Ebaugh, *Handbook of religion and social institutions*. New York: Kluwer/Plenum.

Wilson, W. J. (1996). *When work disappears: The world of the new urban poor*. New York: Knopf.

Wuthnow, R. (2002). The United States: Bridging the privileged and the marginalized? In R. Putnam (Ed.), *Democracies in flux: The evolution of social capital in contemporary society*. New York: Oxford University Press.

Index

African American low-income fathers: abandoned communities, context of, 15, 255–56, 264–65, 271–72; "absent father" stereotype, 12, 187–88, 203; African American mothers and, 256, 257; children, involvement with, 256, 259, 261, 266, 281; children's health issues and, 265–66; child support, 187–88; environmental hazards, concern over, 15, 265, 266–67, 272; future research on, 271–72; housing, provision of, 268–69; identity work, 203; medical care provision, 267–68; methodology for study of, 257–59; neighborhood support, 257, 270; police, relations with, 262–63; as protectors, 15, 255, 257, 259–62, 265, 269–71, 272; as providers, 259, 268–69; single parenthood, 256, 263; studies of, 188, 257. *See also* Responsible Fatherhood (RF) programs

Asian American fathers, 19, 20, 22

baseball: ballparks, 36; catch, game of, ix, 8, 17, 141, 143–57 passim; father involvement and, ix, 141, 142–44, 147, 148, 152, 154–55; *Field of Dreams* (film), 154; gender and, 153, 158n10; historical development, 142–45; Little League, 144, 148, 151, 153, 154, 155; major league, 142, 145, 157; mothers and, ix, 152, 153, 158n6; sacralization of, 149, 154, 155, 158n8; suburbanization and, 147–48, 155; time and duration of, 148–50. *See also* sports; yards

blue-collar fathers. *See* working-class fathers

Boy Scouts of America, 309, 316

Canadian fathers: children, involvement with, 54, 55, 58–59, 62, 65, 66, 68; home improvement, 59–60, 65, 67, 68; identity work, 54, 62; methodologies for studies of, 50, 51–53; as protectors, 55–56, 57–58, 65, 68; as providers, 62; work, primacy of, 52, 60, 65, 66. *See also* mothers

century farms, 239, 241

consumption, 22–23

deployed military fathers: as authority figures, 221, 223, 227; boundary ambiguity, 227; children, involvement

meanings attached to, 193, 197–98; temporal dynamics, 193, 195–96, 204; work opportunities, 199
Roy, Kevin, vii, xi–xii, 216, 217, 282
rural sociology, 235–36, 237–38, 242–43. *See also* farm fathers

self-employed fathers, xiii, 12
situated fathering: cognitive dimension of, 6; fatherhood discourses, 14, 15, 19, 203; future research on, 19–24; gendered attributes, 13–14, 15, 18, 203; institutional and cultural conditions, 4, 11–12, 15, 18, 203, 211, 283; personal power and control, 4, 13, 15, 16–17, 18, 203, 283; physical conditions, 4, 7–8, 15, 18, 188, 193, 210, 211, 283; public/private spheres, 4, 10–11, 15, 193, 200; social structural conditions, 10, 15, 18, 24, 193, 283; symbolic/perceptual properties, 9–10, 15, 188, 189, 193, 283; symposium on, vii, viii; temporal dynamics, 4, 8–9, 15, 18, 193; theoretical framework of, viii, ix, 188, 210, 211; transitional elements, 12–13, 15, 18, 203. *See also* deployed military fathers; Responsible Fatherhood (RF) programs
social constructionism, 15, 164
space: class-based perceptions of, 44–45; definition of, 30–31; embeddedness of, 32, 33, 34; family life and, 3–4; future research on, 44–45, 64–68; gender and, 11, 45, 61, 62, 63, 249; horizontal organization of, 27, 28; identity and, 50; imagined place, 16, 27, 28, 41, 44; immediate place, 16, 17, 27, 28, 35–36, 37, 44; intermediate place, 16, 17, 27, 28, 38, 39–40, 44; moral hierarchy of, 34; moral leverage and, 28–29, 38; studies of, 50, 51–52; "tyranny of place," 44, 45; vertical

organization of, 16, 27, 28, 29, 34. *See also* home; middle-class fathers; situated fathering; time
sports: basketball, 5, 156; children, paternal involvement with, ix, 156–57; coaching, 21; football, ix, 156, 158n11; masculinity and, 21, 157n2, 301–2 one-on-one, 156–57; soccer, xi, 21, 80, 145, 156, 157, 158n5. *See also* baseball
St. Louis (Mo.), 31, 33, 38
stepfathers: biological fathers and, 10, 73, 76, 78, 79, 82–83, 94, 95; birth mothers and, 76, 79, 86, 89, 95; boundary work, 74–75, 79; extended families and, 79, 89–90, 94; family introductions, 86–87, 88; future research on, 92–95; home and, 13, 78–79, 80, 84–85, 93, 94; identity construction, 73, 74, 79, 84, 85, 86, 89, 91, 92, 93, 95; interracial families, 91–92; methodology for study of, 76–77; parents of, 89–90; public situations, 79, 83–84, 85, 87, 92, 94–95; spatial concerns, vii, 11, 12, 17; stepchildren, involvement with, 73, 74–76, 79, 80–84, 85, 89, 91, 92, 93
symbolic interactionism, 15, 74, 93, 100–101, 164

Thoreau, Henry David, 235, 237, 249
time: family and, 49, 51, 54–55, 58, 66; space and, viii, 24, 64–65; subjective experience of, 51; Uniform Time Act, 150, 155, 158n9. *See also* situated fathering; space
truck drivers. See OTR (over-the-road) fathers

United States: African American families, social contexts of, 187; children with parents in military, 209; divorce rate, 99; Latino population, 277; male workers

About the Contributors

Joyce Adkins, Ph.D., Colonel, USAF, currently serves as the director for clinical practices at the Department of Defense Deployment Health Clinical Center. She received a Ph.D. in psychology from Peabody College of Vanderbilt University and an M.P.H. from Harvard School of Public Health. Her research focus has been on occupational health and safety, preventive stress management, and organizational health issues.

Sarah M. Allen, Ph.D., part-time faculty member in the School of Family Life at Brigham Young University, received her Ph.D. in family relations from the University of Guelph in Ontario, Canada. She has published in the *Journal of Marriage and the Family* and the *Journal of Family Psychology*.

Elaine A. Anderson, Ph.D., professor of family studies, University of Maryland, focuses her research on family and health policy and service provision arenas, and low-income and ethnically diverse populations. She has conducted policy analysis/research for the U.S. Senate, the Connecticut and Minnesota state legislatures, and several presidential campaigns. She is past chair of the family policy section, past vice president for public policy, and past program chair for the National Council on Family Relations. She is codirector and founder of the Maryland Family Impact Seminar. She is also a fellow in the National Council on Family Relations. eanders@umd.edu

John P. Bartkowski, Ph.D., professor of sociology at Mississippi State University. His work examines the intersection of religion, gender, family, and social welfare. He has published several monographs, the latest of which is *The Promise Keepers: Servants, Soldiers, and Godly Men*. He is currently completing two books—one on the contours and effects of Latter-day Saint teen religiosity, and another on evangelical parenting.

Donna Bauer has farmed in southwest Iowa since 1977. She received her sociology degree, with an emphasis on environmental studies, in 1994, from Iowa State University. She is a longtime member and one-time board member of Practical Farmers of Iowa. She remains involved in many local rural-entrepreneurial projects.

Michael M. Bell, Ph.D., associate professor of rural sociology at the University of Wisconsin–Madison. Two central themes can be heard in all of his work: dialogics and the sociology of "nature," broadly conceived. He is the author, along with Gregory Peter, Susan Jarnagin, and Donna Bauer, of *Farming for Us All: Practical Agriculture and the Cultivation of Sustainability* and, with Michael Carolan, of *An Invitation to Environmental Sociology.* He is also the editor, along with Hugh Campbell and Margaret Finney, of the forthcoming *Country Boys: Masculinity and Rural Life.* michaelbell@wisc.edu

Beth S. Catlett, Ph.D., assistant professor in the Women's and Gender Studies Program at DePaul University. Her scholarship focuses on feminist approaches to studying families. She has been particularly interested in applying a feminist paradigm to understanding men's family relationships and male aggression. Her recent work has appeared in *Violence and Victims, Men and Masculinities,* and *Fathering.* bcatlett@depaul.edu

Scott Coltrane, Ph.D., professor of sociology, associate dean of the College of Humanities, Arts, and Social Sciences, and associate director of the Center for Family Studies at the University of California–Riverside. Coltrane is past president of the Pacific Sociological Association and the author of over fifty articles and chapters, as well as several books about families, including *Family Man, Gender and Families, Sociology of Marriage and the Family,* and *Families and Society.* His most recent NIH-funded research projects investigate the impact of economic stress and the meaning of fatherhood and stepfatherhood in Mexican American and European American families. Coltrane @ucr.edu

Kerry Daly, Ph.D., professor in the Department of Family Relations and Applied Nutrition, is one of the founding directors of the Centre for Families, Work, and Well-Being at the University of Guelph in Ontario, Canada. He received his Ph.D. in sociology from McMaster University, Hamilton, Ontario.

He is cochair of the Father Involvement Research Alliance, a Canadian national organization of researchers, practitioners, and policy makers. His current research interests focus on the way that families negotiate and navigate time pressures in their lives, the changing meaning of fatherhood, and the challenges families face in trying to harmonize their work and family life. He is editor of the recent book *Minding the Time in Family Experience: Emerging Issues and Perspectives* and author of *Families and Time: Keeping Pace in a Hurried Culture*. He is married and a father of two teenage children. kdaly@uoguelph.ca

Anthony Faber is a doctoral candidate in child development and family studies at Purdue University, specializing in marriage and family therapy. His research interests include developmental processes within stepfamilies, attachment and affect regulation, and transitional issues related to military families. He currently is a research assistant at the Military Family Research Institute at Purdue University.

Greer Litton Fox, Ph.D., Distinguished Service Professor at the University of Tennessee in the Department of Child and Family Studies. Her research on family violence has received support from the National Institute of Justice and the Centers for Disease Control. Her recent work has focused on father involvement, especially in working class families. glfox@utk.edu

Todd L. Goodsell, Ph.D., assistant professor of sociology in the Department of Sociology at Brigham Young University, received his doctoral degree from the University of Michigan, Ann Arbor, in 2004. His research is in the areas of culture, community, family, fatherhood, and qualitative methods. He has published in *Rural Sociology*.

Jennifer F. Hamer, Ph.D., associate professor of sociology in the African American Studies and Research Program at the University of Illinois at Urbana-Champaign. Her work focuses on the study of African American families and her books include *What It Means to Be Daddy: Black Men Who Live Away from Their Children* and *On Hope and a Prayer: Black Families in an Abandoned City*. jhamer@uiuc.edu

Susan K. Jarnagin, Ph.D., has a master's degree in agronomy and a Ph.D. in rural sociology from Iowa State University. She works in the Graduate College at Iowa State University, teaches English to immigrants, works on environmental protection and agricultural issues in Mexico, and tends her garden.

Ralph LaRossa, Ph.D., professor of sociology, Georgia State University, is the author of *Conflict and Power in Marriage: Expecting the First Child*; *Transition to Parenthood: How Infants Change Families* (with Maureen Mulligan LaRossa); *Becoming a Parent*; and *The Modernization of Fatherhood: A Social and Political History.* He also has written on the semiotics of Father's Day and Mother's Day, the history of childhood, the social construction of parenthood, and the nature and scope of qualitative research. His most recent work focuses on the impact of World War II on the culture of fatherhood in America. socrel@panther.gsu.edu

Bethany L. Letiecq, Ph.D., assistant professor of health and human development, Montana State University, conducts research on issues related to under-resourced families, alternative family formation and functioning, parenting, and family policy. She has published in such journals as *Family Relations*, *Journal of Family Issues*, *Personal Relationships*, and *Fathering*. With Elaine Anderson and Denise Skinner, she is coeditor of *Teaching Family Policy: A Handbook of Course Syllabi, Teaching Strategies and Resources.* bletiecq @montana.edu

Shelley MacDermid, Ph.D., professor in the Department of Child Development and Family Studies at Purdue University, where she also directs the Center for Families and codirects the Military Family Research Institute. Dr. MacDermid earned an M.B.A. in management and a Ph.D. in human development and family studies from the Pennsylvania State University. Her research focuses on relationships between job conditions and family life, with special interests in organizational size, adult development, and organizational policies. shelley@purdue.edu

William Marsiglio, Ph.D., professor of sociology, University of Florida. Marsiglio's writings focus on the social psychology of male sexuality, reproductive health, fertility, and fatherhood. In addition to his numerous articles on various aspects of men's reproductive and fathering experiences, Marsiglio's recent books on these topics include *Stepdads: Stories of Love, Hope, and Repair*; *Sex, Men, and Babies: Stories of Awareness and Responsibility*; and *Procreative Man.* His most recent writings on men and reproductive issues introduce a novel conceptual tool, the Procreative Identity Framework, for exploring how men become aware of their ability to procreate and its meaning for them over time. He lectures at national and international conferences on men's issues, and consults for national surveys about male sexuality and fatherhood in the United States and Canada. marsig@soc.ufl.edu

Patrick C. McKenry, Ph.D. (deceased), professor of human development and family science and African American and African studies, Ohio State University. Published numerous articles, book chapters, and books in the area of family stress and coping, with a focus on gender, race, and social class variations. He served as guest editor and was also a member of numerous editorial boards in these areas of scholarship.

Scott A. Melzer, Ph.D., assistant professor of sociology, Albion College, has published on men's responses to actual and perceived loss of power and status as individuals within families and as a group in the United States. Melzer's research examines the implications of threats to masculine identities and hegemony by identifying responses ranging from men's interpersonal violence against female partners to their engaging in conservative reactionary politics.

Matthew Mishkind, Ph.D., received his doctorate in psychology from the University of Vermont. He has done work in the areas of deployment health care and general health services, patient and consumer satisfaction, and survey research and methodology. He formerly held the position of medical informatics officer at the Deployment Health Clinical Center at Walter Reed Army Medical Center. He is currently a consultant with Hay Insight, the employee and customer survey division of the Hay Group, a global organizational and human resources consulting firm.

Rob Palkovitz, Ph.D., professor of individual and family studies at the University of Delaware. His research interests are in fathering and intergenerational relationships and development, with a particular emphasis on the relationships between patterns of father involvement and men's adult development. He is currently studying transitions within fathering, characteristics of resilient fathers in challenging circumstances, and fathers in the "launching" phases of fathering. Along with his family, he regularly does volunteer work with inner city foster and fatherless children. Palkovitz received his bachelor's degree in psychology from the University of Virginia, and his masters' and doctoral degrees in developmental psychology from Rutgers University. He and his wife Judy enjoy actively co-parenting their growing family. They have four sons and two daughters-in-law. robp@udel.edu

Ross D. Parke, Ph.D., Distinguished Professor of Psychology at the University of California-Riverside, and director of the UCR Center for Family Studies. Parke is the author of books and articles on fathers, families, and child development, with particular attention to the distinctive role of fathers in play patterns, the relationship between parent–child interaction and children's social competence, and the relations between children's social relationships and academic competence. Former president of the Society for Research on Child Development and editor of *Developmental Psychology* and *Journal of Family Psychology,* he has been PI or Co-PI on multiple federally funded studies of child care, children's social development, economic stress, and the meaning of fathering and stepfathering.

Gregory Peter, Ph.D., assistant professor of sociology at the University of Wisconsin–Fox Valley. He earned a B.A. in East Asian Studies with an environmental studies minor at UW–Madison, an M.S. in rural sociology, and Ph.D. in sociology at Iowa State University. He is the coauthor of *Farming for Us All: Practical Agriculture and the Cultivation of Sustainability*, a book chapter, several articles, and dozens of research presentations on rural sociology, sustainable agriculture, and the interface between the environment and society. He is also an applied sociologist conducting fieldwork and consulting for governmental and nongovernmental agencies. gpeter@uwc.edu

Kevin Roy, Ph.D., assistant professor of family studies, University of Maryland. Roy's research examines the life course of men on the margins of family and the work force. Through a mix of participant observation and life history interviews, he has explored the intersection of policy systems, such as welfare reform and incarceration, with parents' care giving and providing roles. His recent research focuses on the maintenance of intergenerational relationships, the emergence of men's generativity, and systems of social support among low-income and minority fathers. Roy has published in *Social Problems, Journal of Family Issues*, and *Family Relations*. kroy @umd.edu

Jeremy P. Sayers received B.A. degrees in philosophy and psychology from the University of New York at Buffalo and his M.S. in child and family studies at the University of Tennessee. He has had a long-term interest in trucker life. A master arborist, he is also the father of two children under five, Sophie and Sebastian.

Rona Schwarz, Ph.D., is currently a senior research associate for the Military Family Research Institute at Purdue University. She earned a Ph.D. in child development and family studies from Purdue University. Her research focuses on children's shyness and social anxiety, peer relationships in childhood and adolescence, family relationships, and social-emotional development.

Michelle L. Toews, Ph.D., assistant professor of family and consumer sciences at Texas State University–San Marcos, received her doctorate from Ohio State University. Her research interests include separation violence, conflict and coparenting after divorce, and fathering after divorce.

Eric J. Vega, M.A., Ph.D. candidate at the University of California–Riverside in the Department of Sociology. He is the coauthor of publications investigating the linkages between institutions of higher education and their emerging corporate online counterparts and on the effects of the perception of threat on grassroots mobilization. As a graduate researcher at the UCR Center for Family Studies, his current research centers on the interplay between family dynamics and the educational outcomes of family members.

Howard M. Weiss, Ph.D., professor and head of the Department of Psychological Sciences at Purdue University and codirector of the Military Family Research Institute at Purdue University. His research focuses on emotions in the workplace and particularly on the work and family consequences of emotional experiences. He is a fellow of the Society for Industrial and Organizational Psychology, the American Psychological Association, and the American Psychological Society.

W. Bradford Wilcox, Ph.D., assistant professor of sociology at the University of Virginia, studies religion, fatherhood, marriage, and parenting. He is the author of *Soft Patriarchs, New Men: How Christianity Shapes Fathers and Husbands*. Wilcox has also published in the *American Sociological Review*, *Social Forces*, and *The Responsive Community*. He has previously held research fellowships at the Brookings Institution, Princeton University, Yale University, and the University of Pennsylvania. Professor Wilcox's research on religion and the family has been featured in the *Los Angeles Times*, *Washington Post*, *Washington Times*, *USA Today*, and numerous NPR stations. wbw7q@virginia.edu